Advertising That Reminds:
Walldog Art and
Other Vintage Signs

Robert A. Olson

Whispering Oak Publishing
Orangevale, CA
roa1@comcast.net

ISBN: 978-1-7371663-2-0

Table of Contents

Introduction

This book is dedicated to walldogs everywhere, past and present.

Two earthquakes that rocked the Northern California city of Santa Rosa in 1969 required the demolition of a building that the jolts had rendered unsafe. Removal of that building revealed a hidden surprise: old but remarkably well-preserved advertising art that embellished the newly exposed wall of the adjoining building — the one shown on the cover of this book.

That revelation triggered my interest in learning more about this vintage art and its history, and set me off on a journey of discovery that has spanned many years since. During the course of my travels and ad hoc field research, I located an elderly man (Caleb Whitbeck) who had been a "walldog" artist — a sign painter. Noting that this bit of Americana had been overlooked as an art form, he introduced me to the fraternal society of "Walldoggers," *men* who painted ads on building walls to sell products and services of the day. This compilation is dedicated to those sign painters.

I say *men* because a one-cent 1898 envelope mailed to Emery Bonker in Andover, New Jersey, says "Do your own sign work or the new women will have your job." This is an early example of anti-women propaganda.

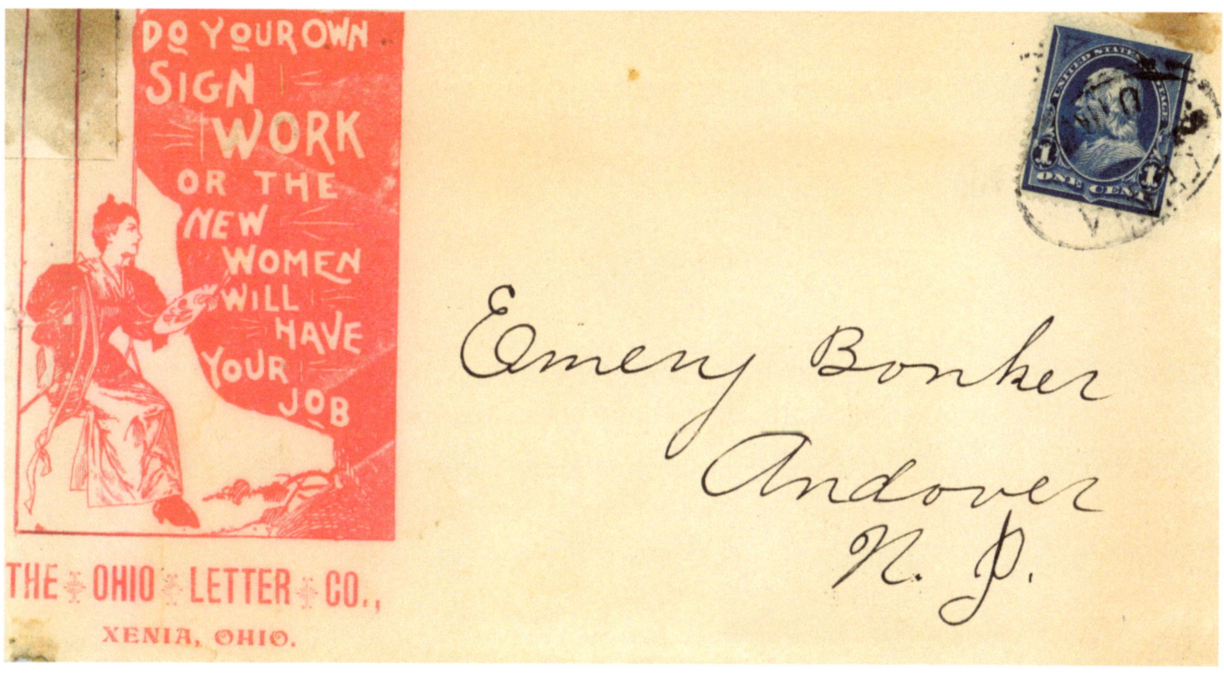

While many walldog art examples have been lost to demolitions, weather, concealment by adjoining buildings, and local laws requiring limitation of such advertising to the current uses of the stores, it endures through modern walldoggers, muralists, preservationists, and graffiti artists. I understand that their name comes from "working like dogs" on exterior building walls, probably using durable but dangerous lead-based paints, tall ladders, and suspended scaffolding.

An article titled "Walldogs and the Disappearing Art of Painting Signs on Buildings" (www.atlasobscura. com/articles) noted that "it was in the mid-1930s, and the Works Progress Administration was assembling a Historical Records Survey—personal accounts about different professions—as a kind of oral history of American workers. They sent writers out to scour the country, hoping to create a portrait of its workforce. They interviewed all kinds of people, including a few sign-painters like the man from Chicago. At the time, sign-painting was a fairly common job, and many sign painters did, indeed, get around. While most cities had their own sign shops, many smaller towns and rural areas depended on traveling artisans to do their sign-painting."

Appreciation of vintage wall advertising is sparking a renaissance of sorts.

The International Walldog Mural and Sign Art Museum in Pontiac, Illinois, dedicated to preserving this art form, declares that "The Walldogs are a group of highly skilled sign painters and mural artists from all over the globe. The Walldog Movement is quickly gaining popularity, and is a great way for small towns to boost their tourism. Imagine a 'pack' of talented artists descending upon your town to paint the most beautiful murals you can imagine. Every wall that a fellow Walldog touches springs to life with images of local places, people, and products that have historic significance to each town. There are a few ways to invite the Walldogs to your community. One way is to host a 'Walldog Festival' and the other way is to commission Walldog Artists to paint one or more murals." See www.thewalldogs. com to learn more.

Intended to show examples of walldog art, this book presents only about half of the photos from my collection. Pictures were often hard to get because of distance, narrow alleys, traffic, access difficulties, and limitations due to my camera and photographic skills.

I sprinkled this book with some non-walldog signs, such as early neon signs, because I found them interesting.

Thanks go to many friends and colleagues who, over many, many years, sent me photos, 35 mm slides, pictures, e-mails, and addresses that might be of interest to me. They include Joe Coates, Washington, D.C.; Bob Denton, Auburn Hills, Michigan; Claire Fisher, Fair Oaks, California; Gary and Gillian Carr, Winnipeg, Manitoba, Canada; Harry Lambright, Syracuse, New York; Terry Haney, Woodland Hills, California; and Marti Childs, Davis, California.

Special appreciation goes to my patient wife, Natalie, who majored in decorative art and art history. She trod streets and alleys with me in search of signs, tolerated my stopping the car suddenly when a painted barn side or other old sign appeared, and helped organize and select the contents of this book.

Robert A. Olson
Whispering Oak Publishing
8485 Whispering Oak Lane
Orangevale, CA 95662

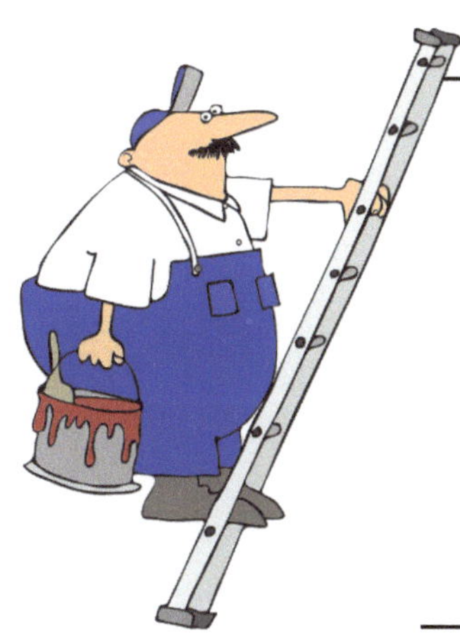

Household-related signs

Wedgewood Stoves were made from the 1930s to the 1950s. First opened in 1919, the company became renowned for their products' quality and durability. They are sold today as vintage stoves used by antique lovers and cooks.

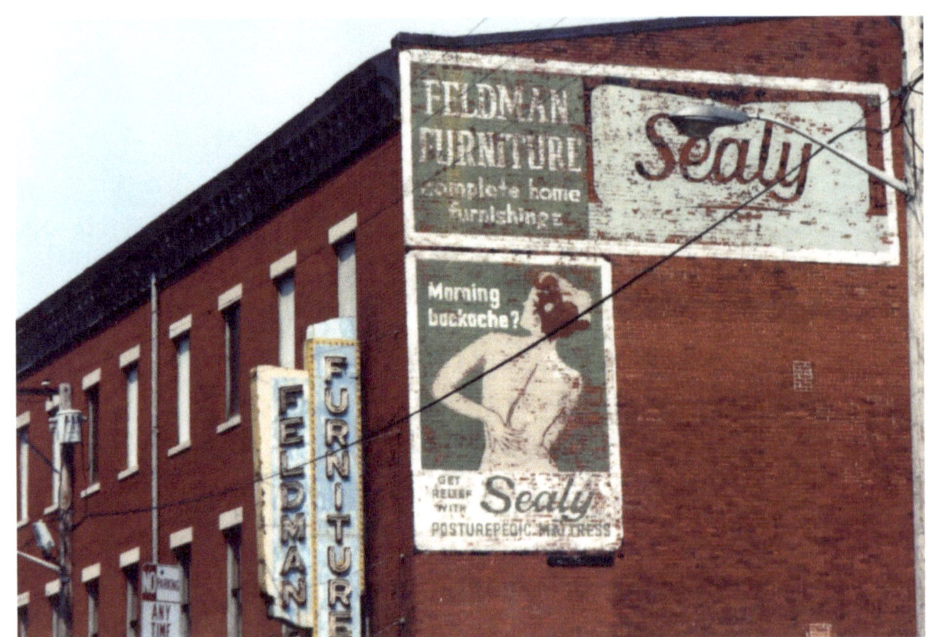

Cambridge, MA

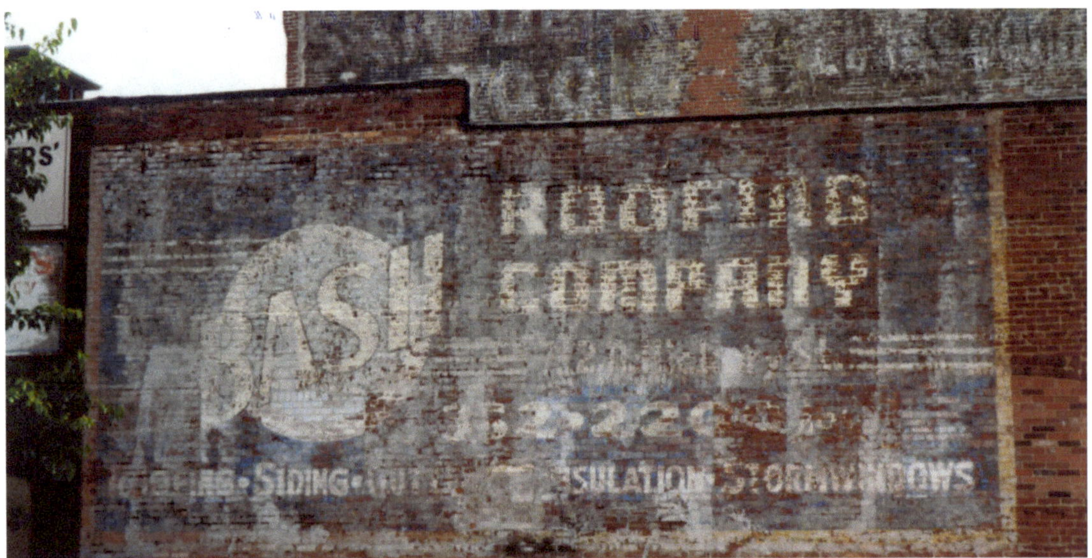

Urbana, IL

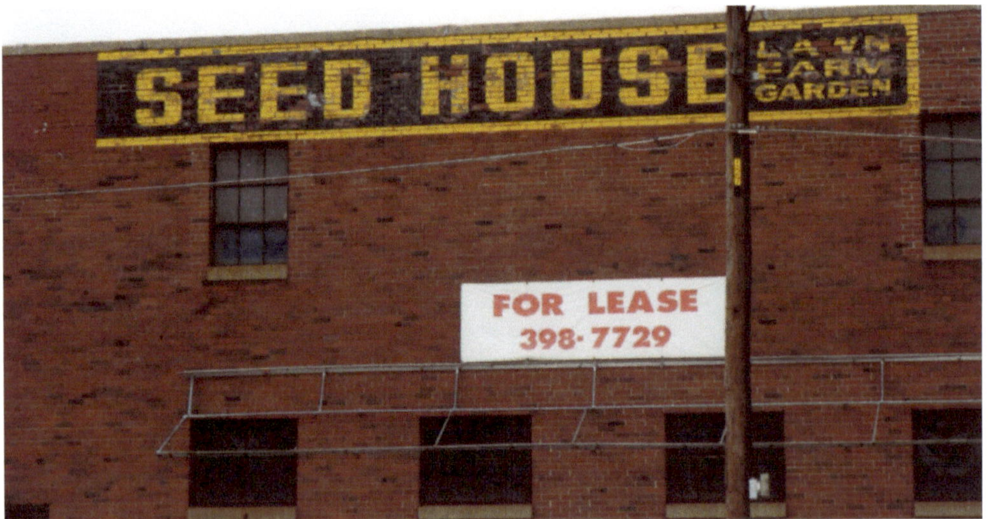

Urbana, IL

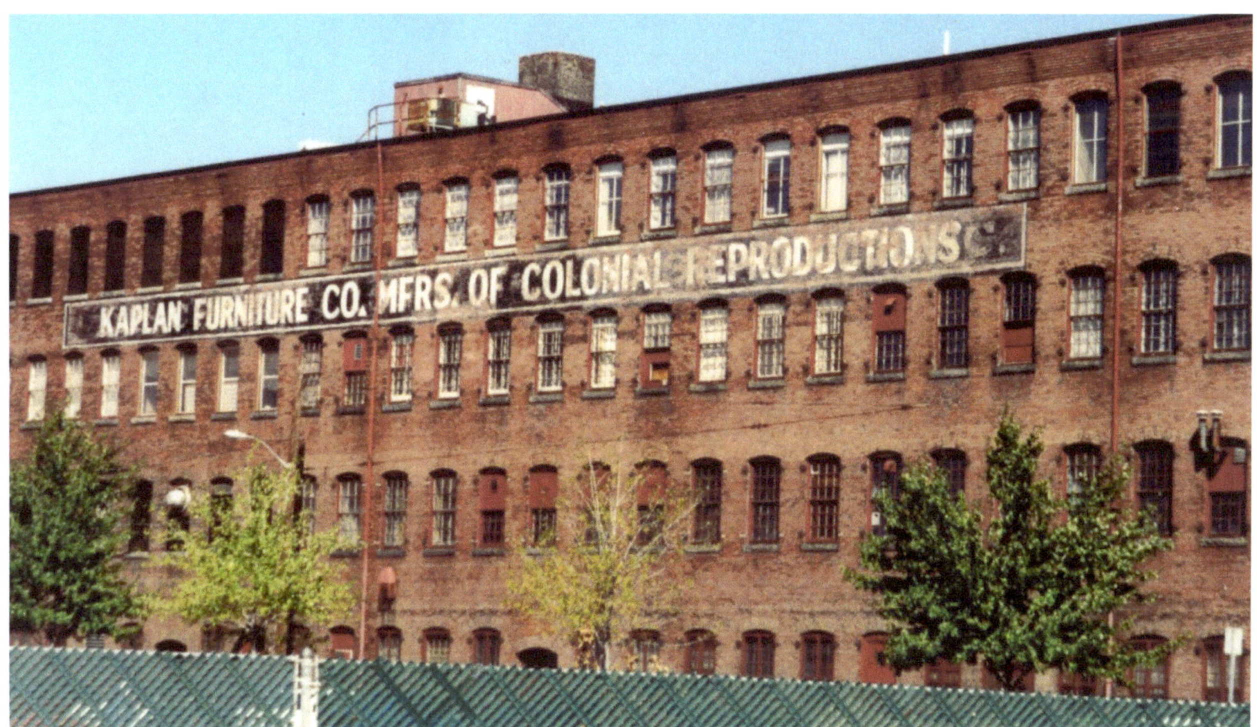

Cambridge, MA

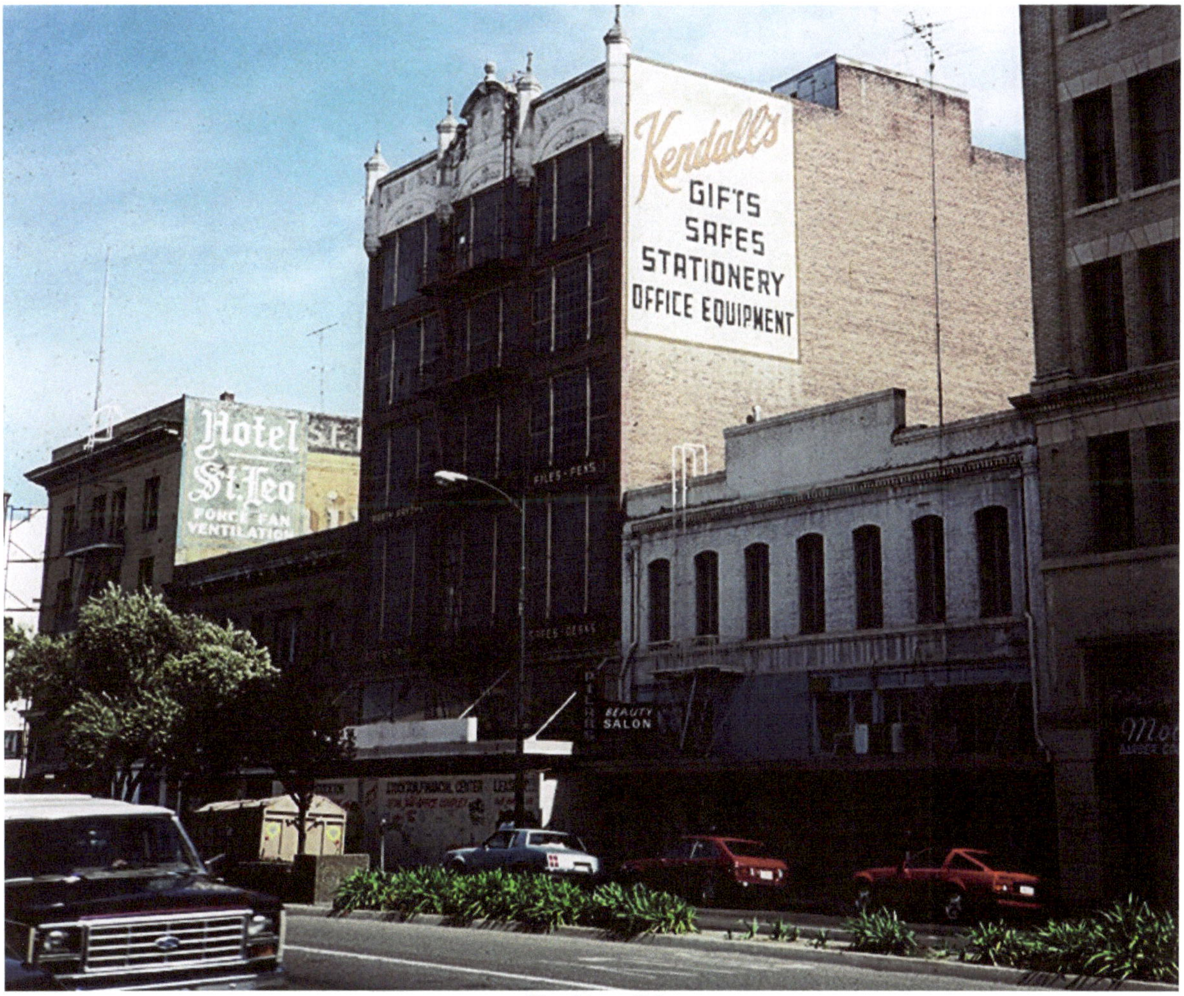

Stockton, CA

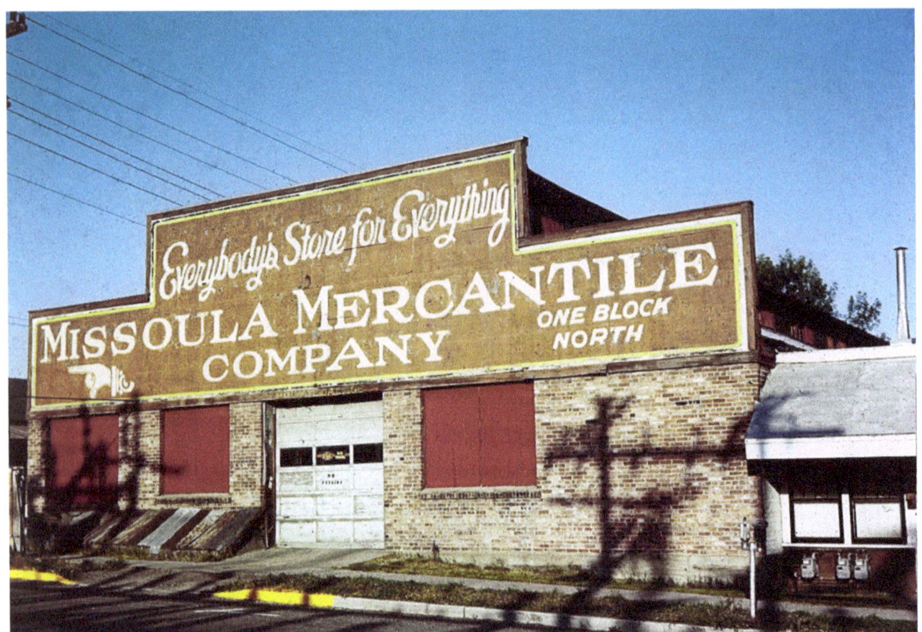

Missoula, MT

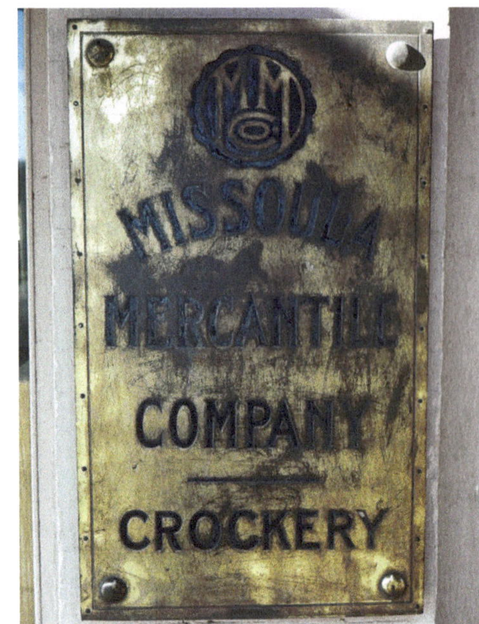

Missoula, MT

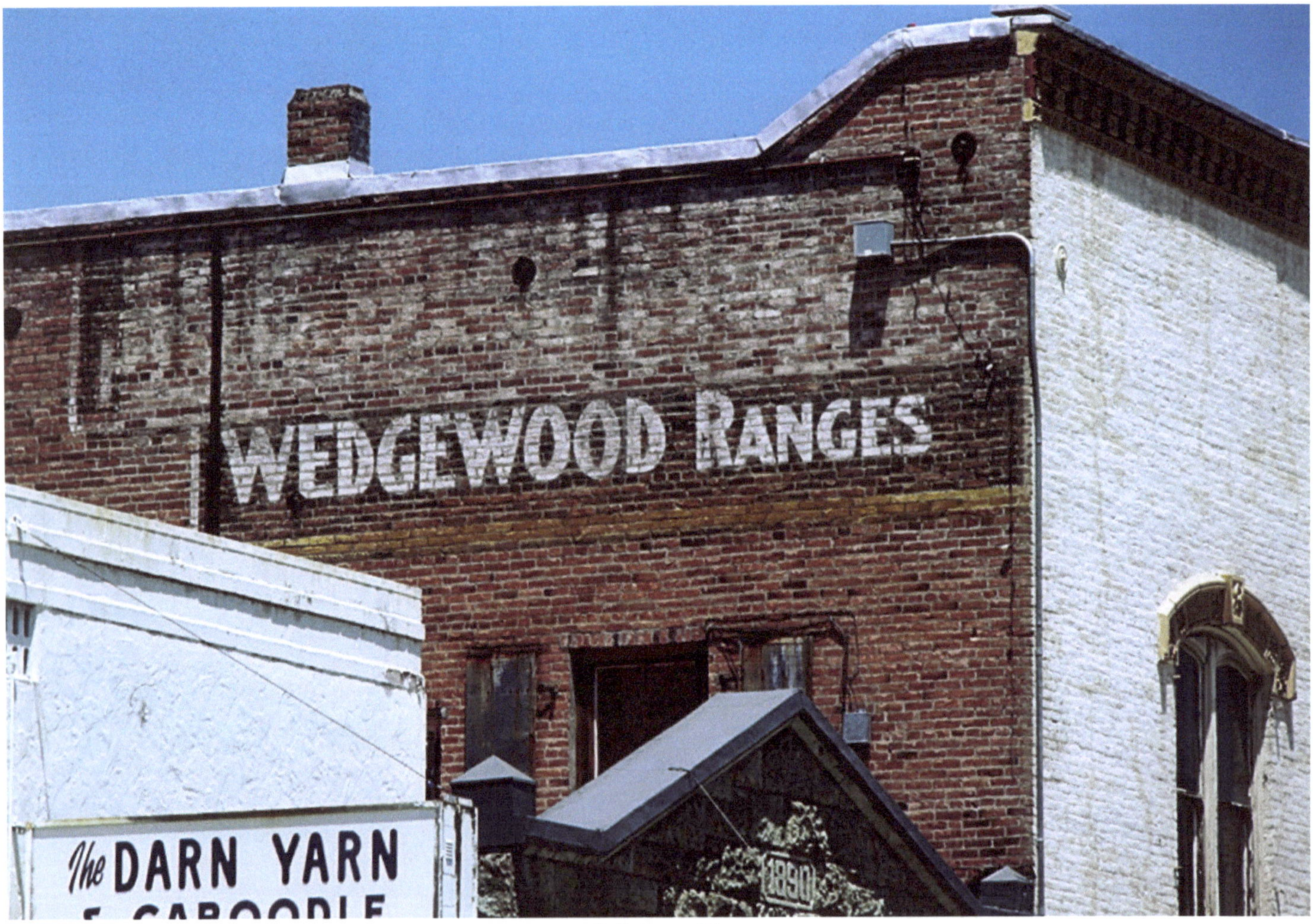

Calistoga, CA

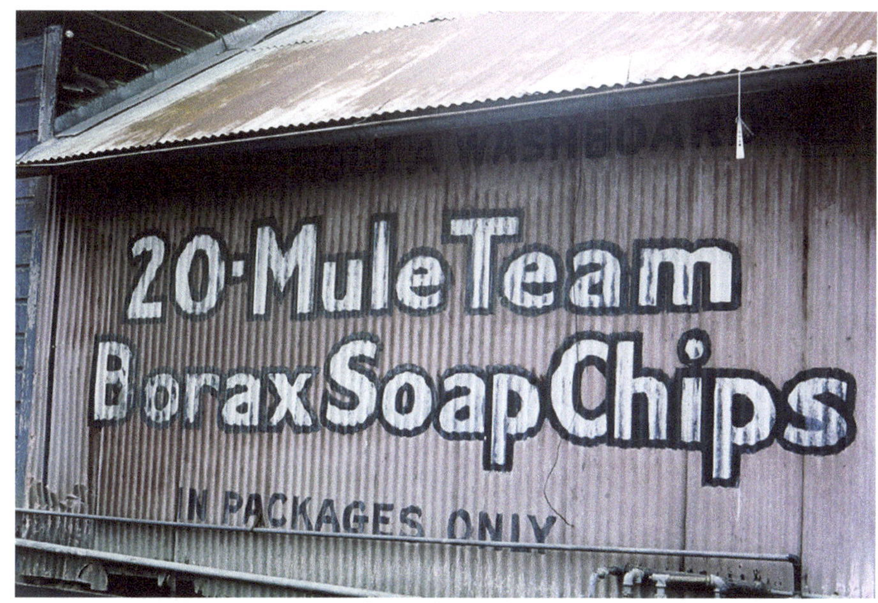

Santa Rosa, CA

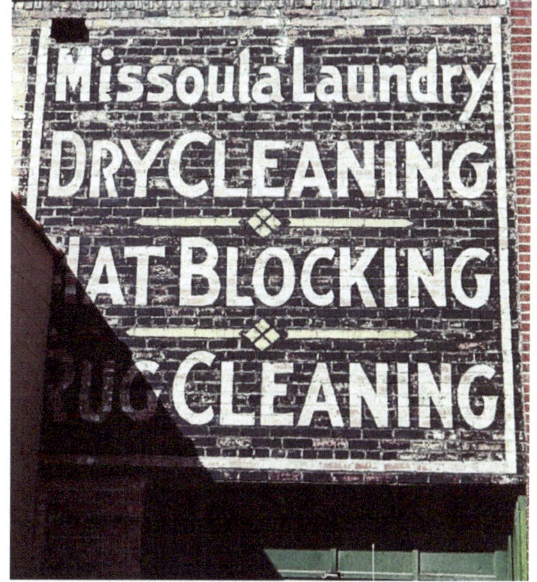

Missoula, MT

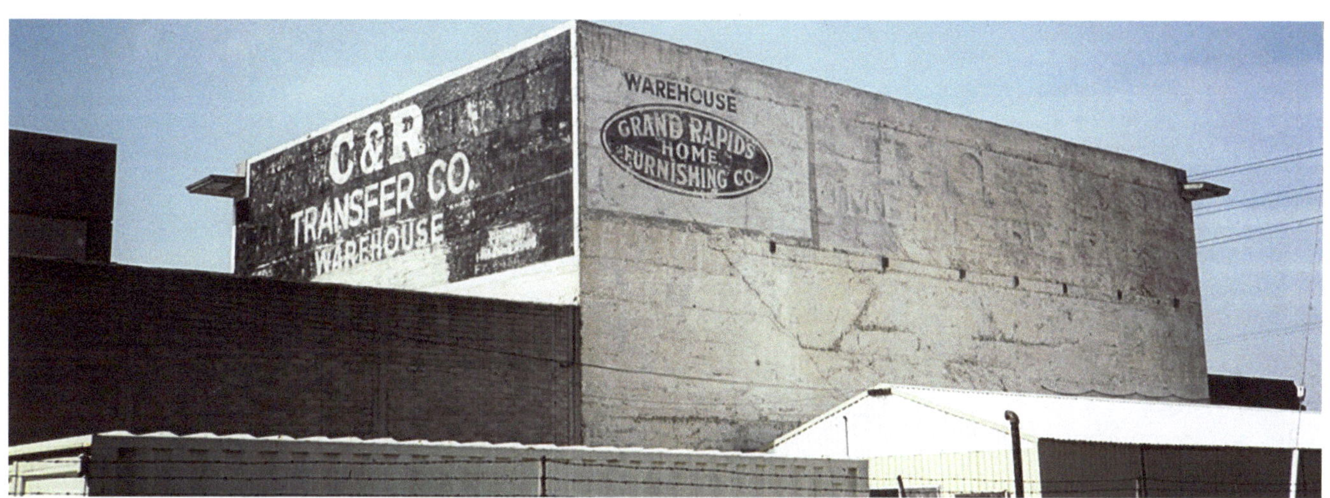

San Diego, CA

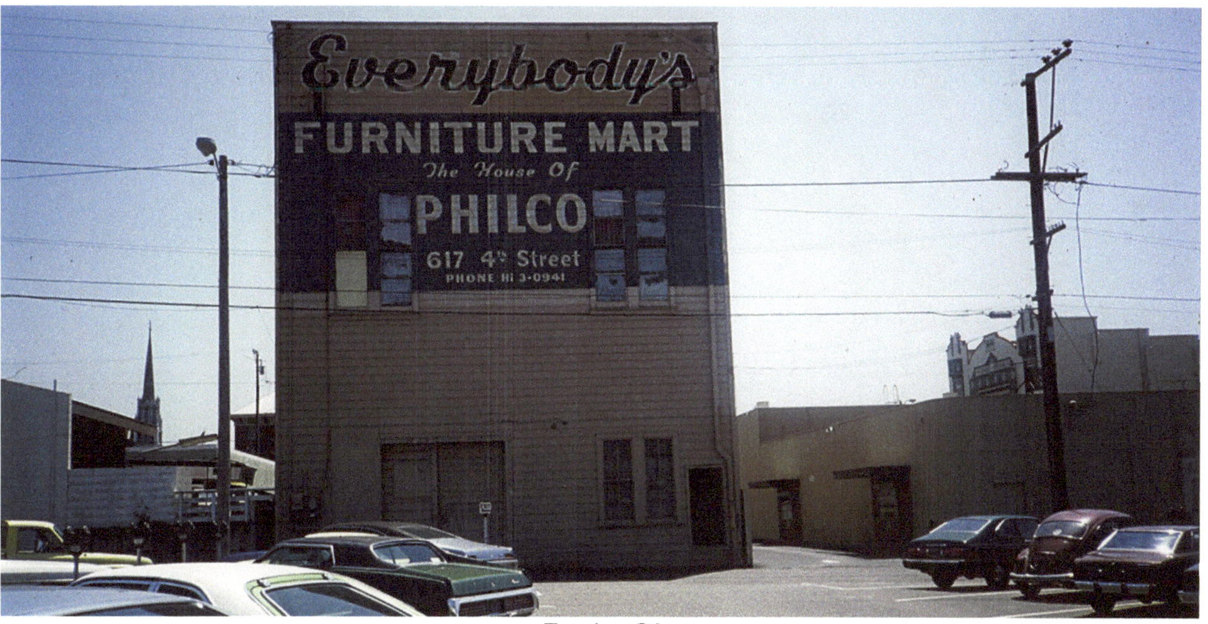

Eureka, CA

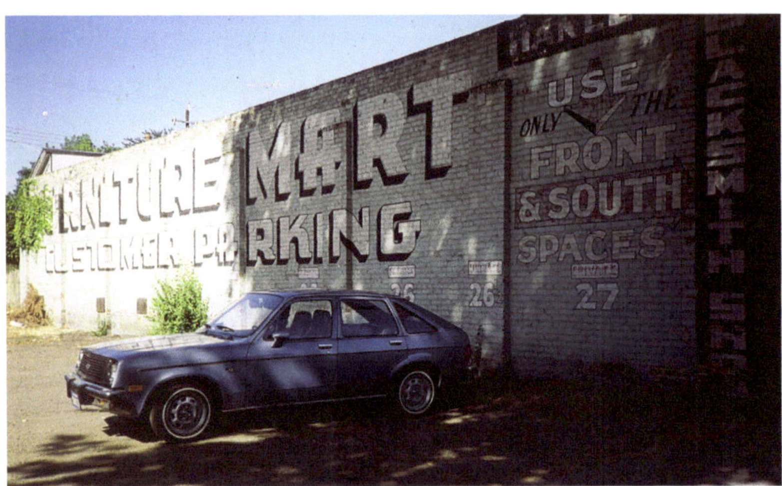

Sacramento, CA

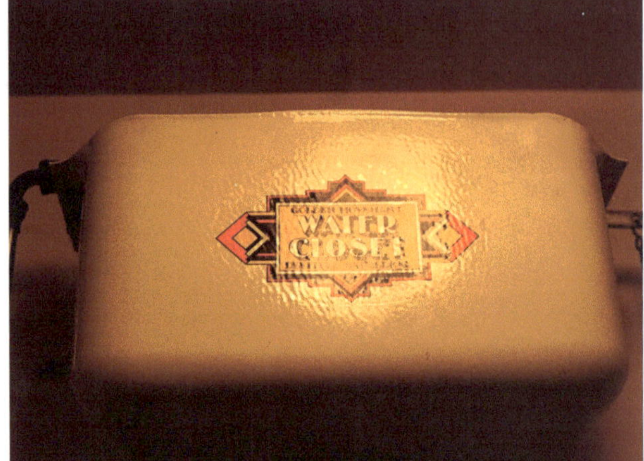

Fairfield, CA

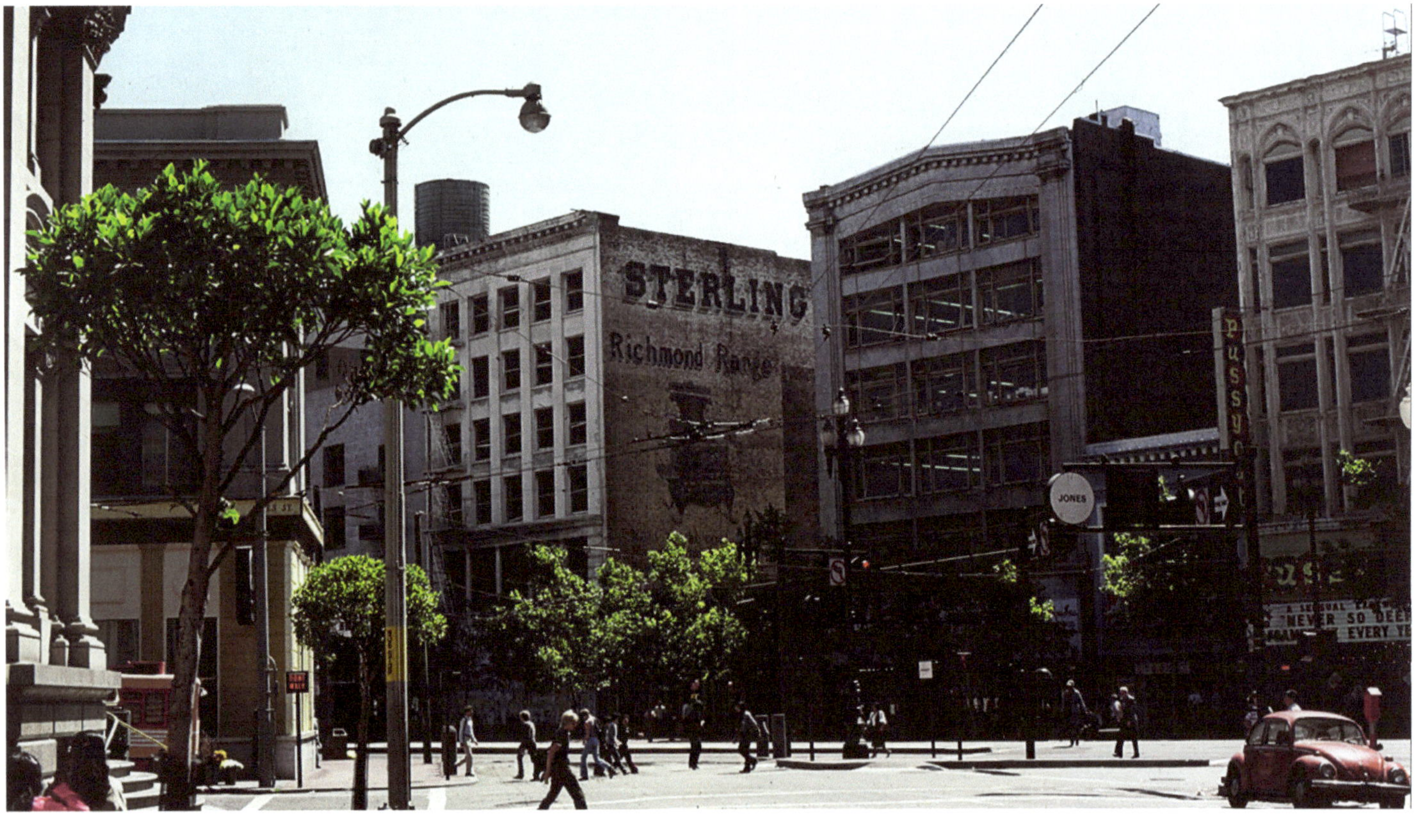

San Francisco, CA

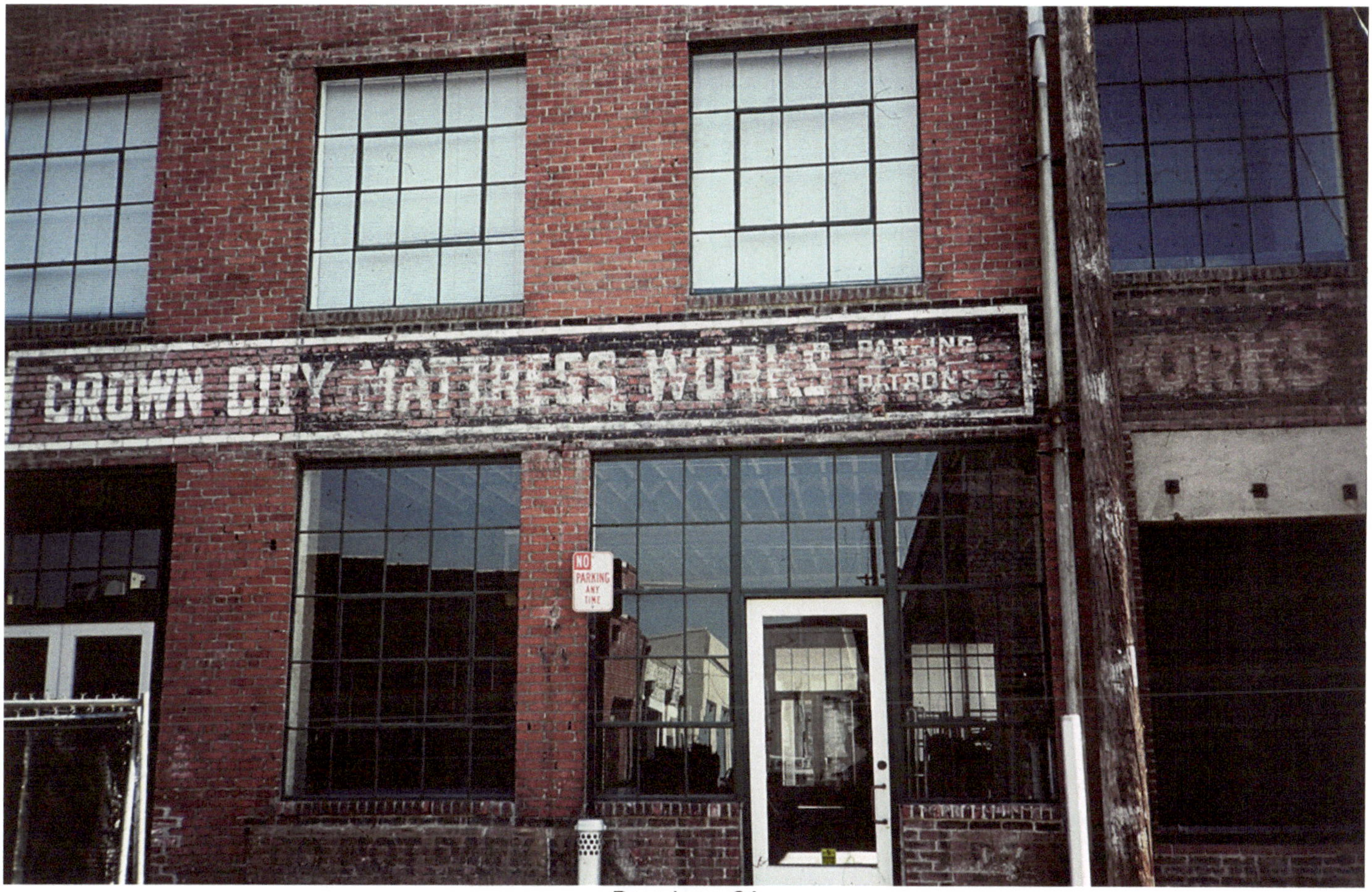

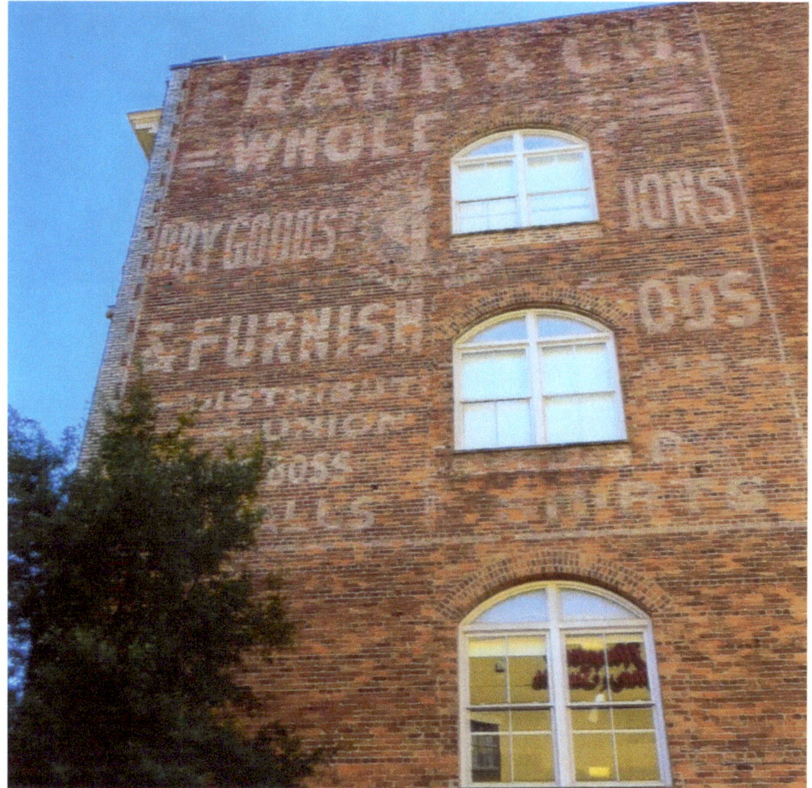

Pasadena, CA

Silverton, OR

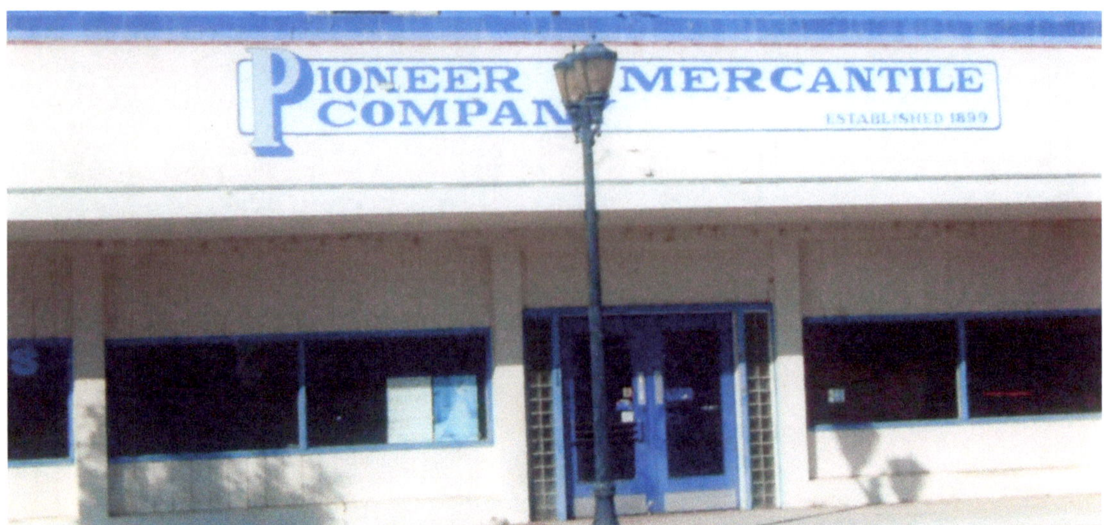

Bakersfield, CA

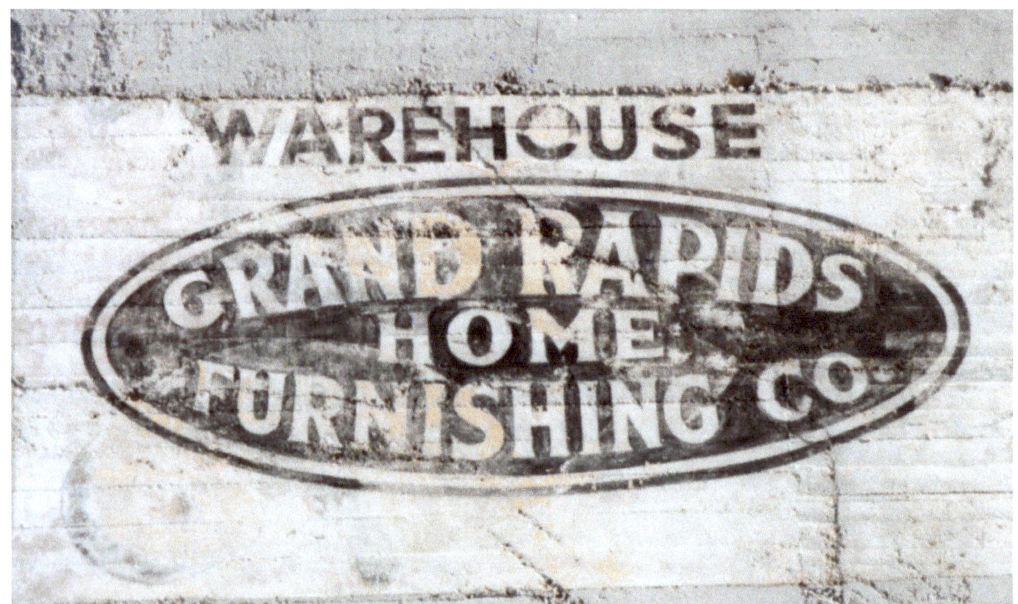

San Diego, CA

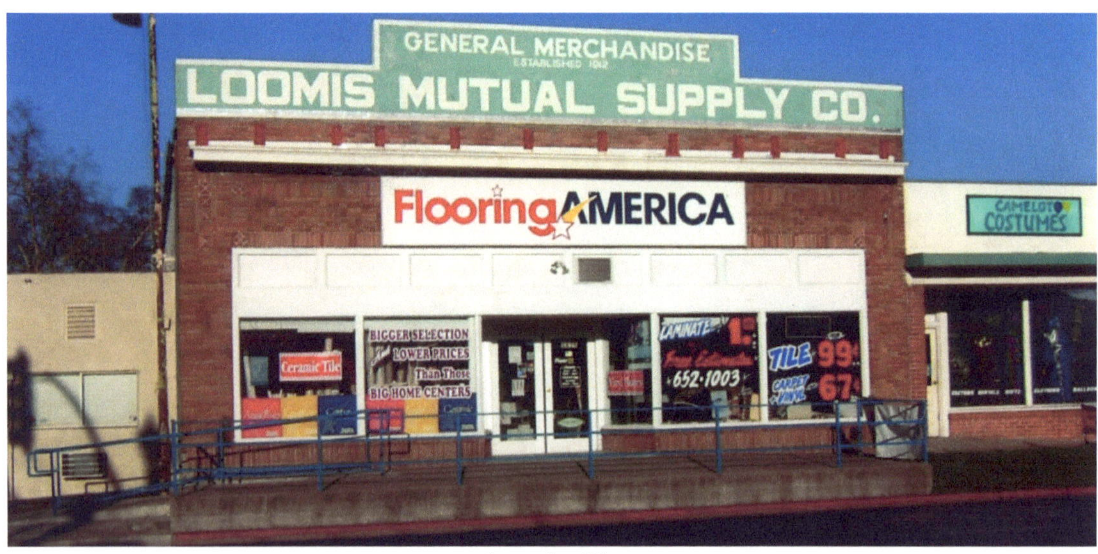

Loomis, CA

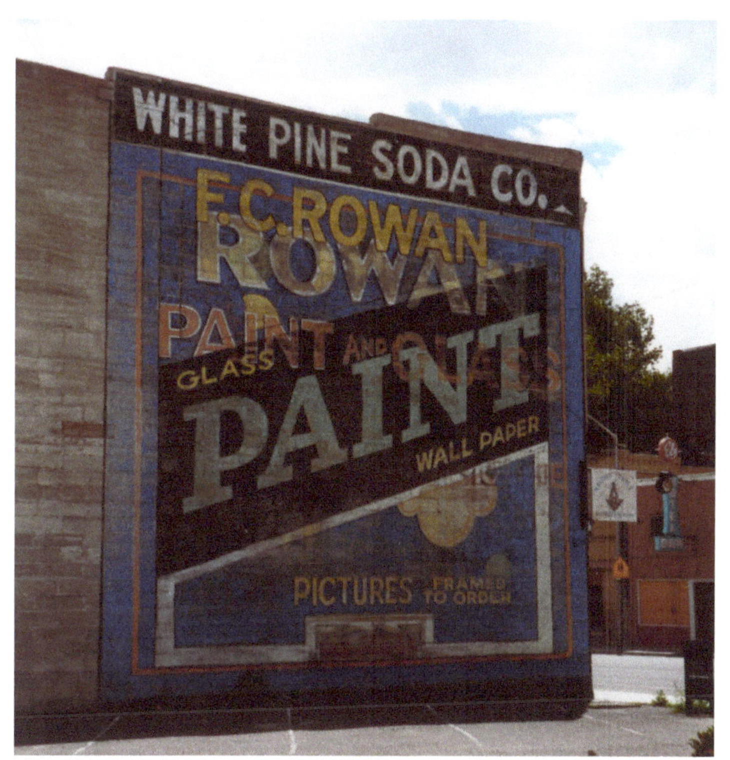

Ely, NV

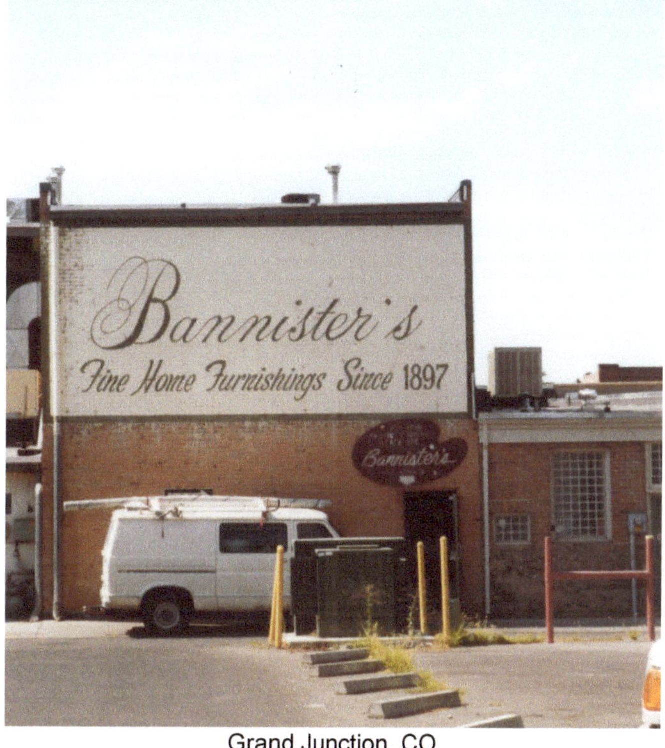

Grand Junction, CO

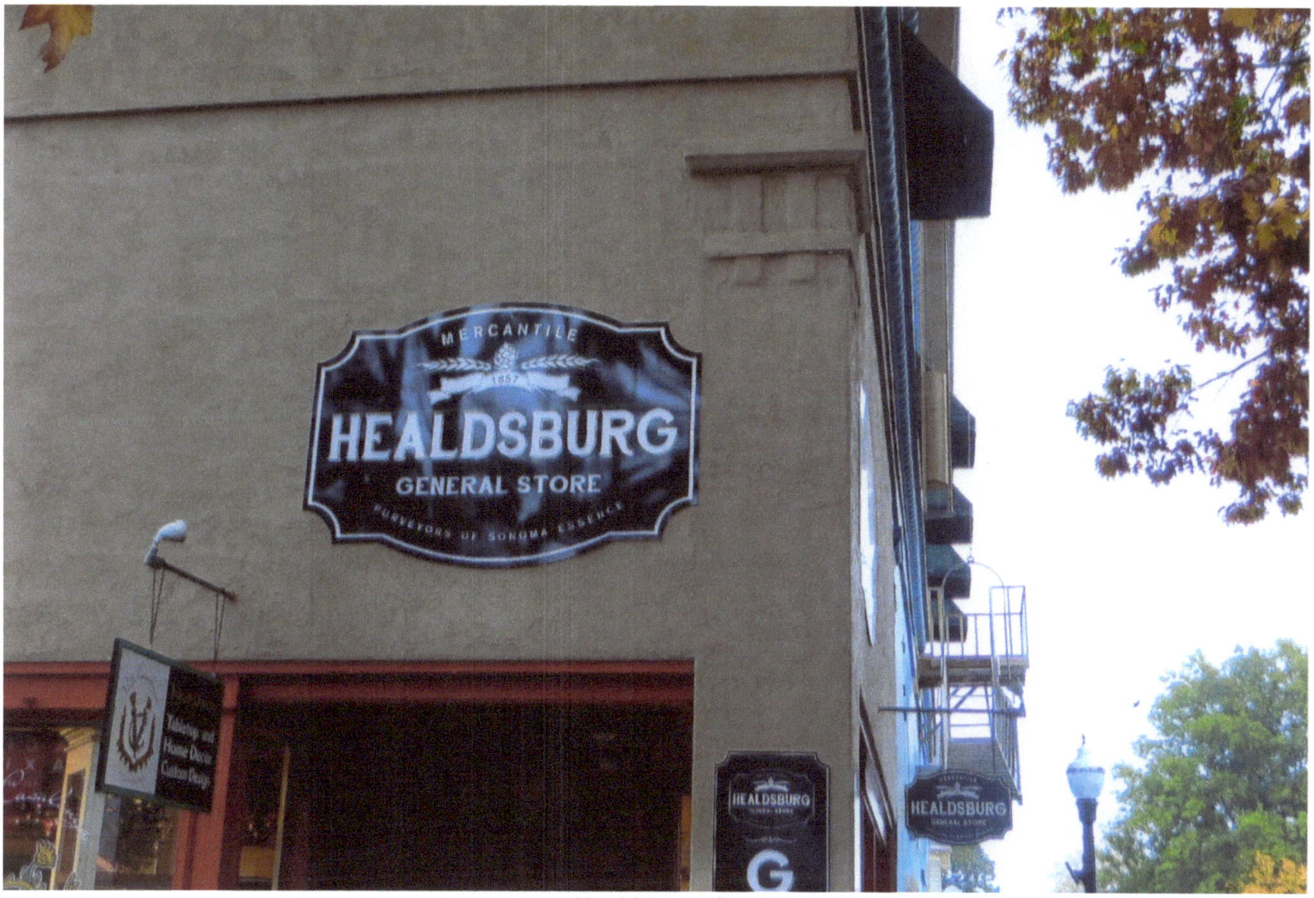

Healdsburg, CA

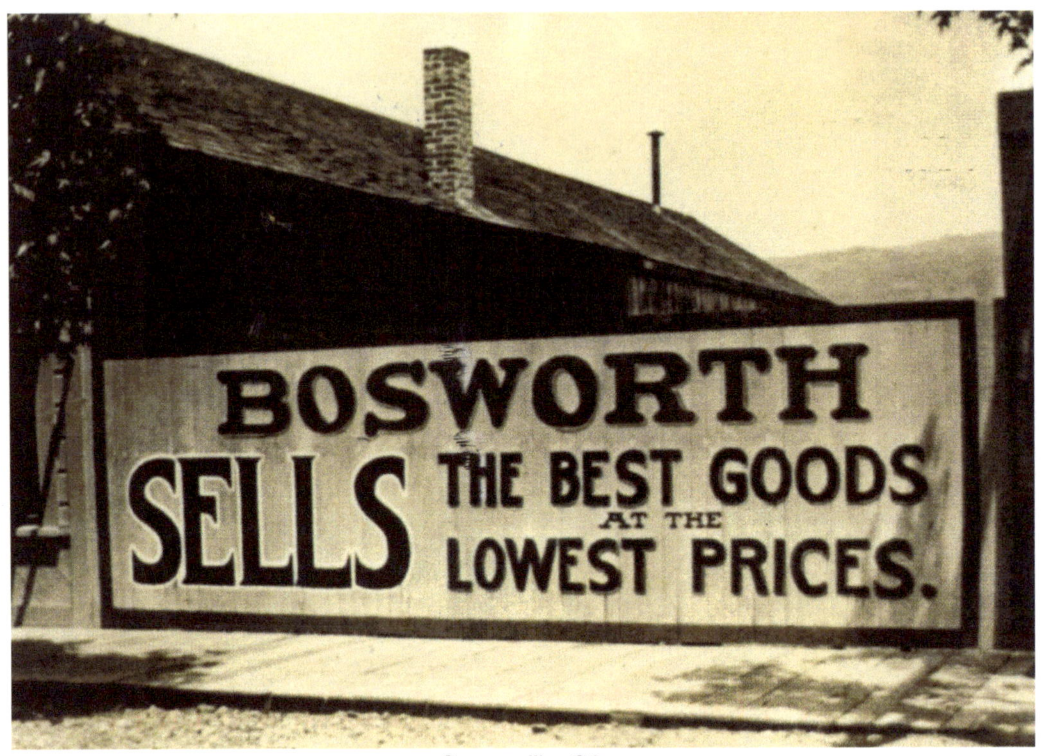

Geyserville, CA

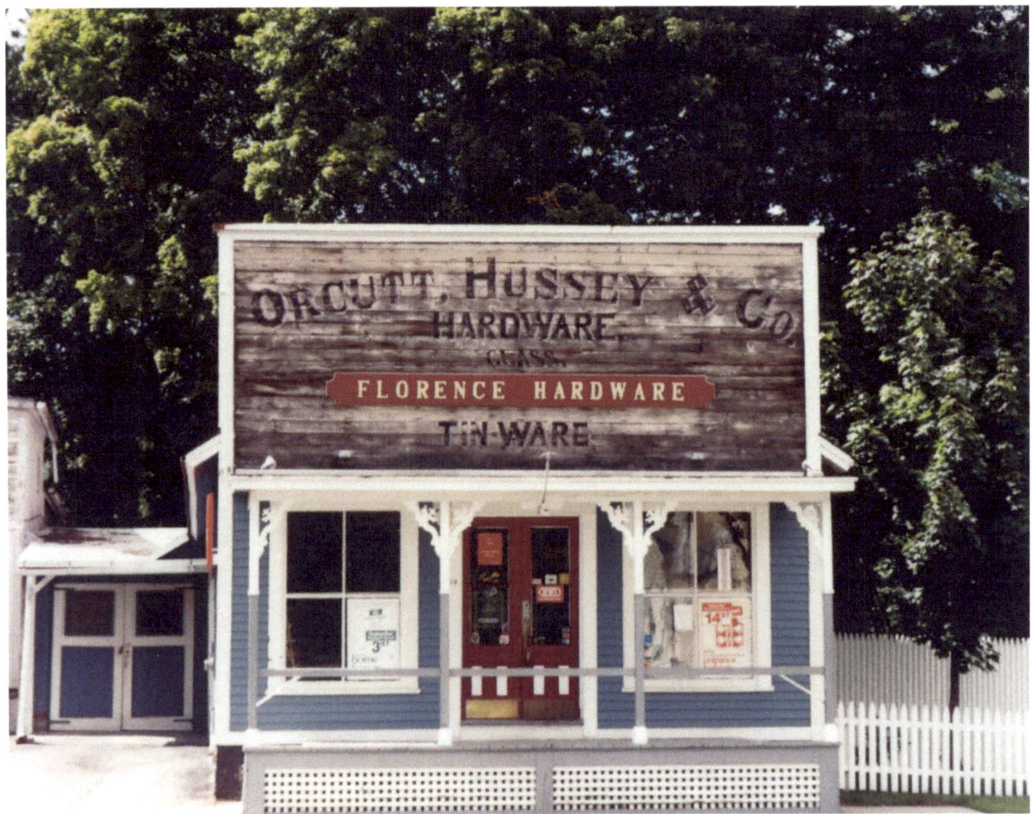

Florence, MA

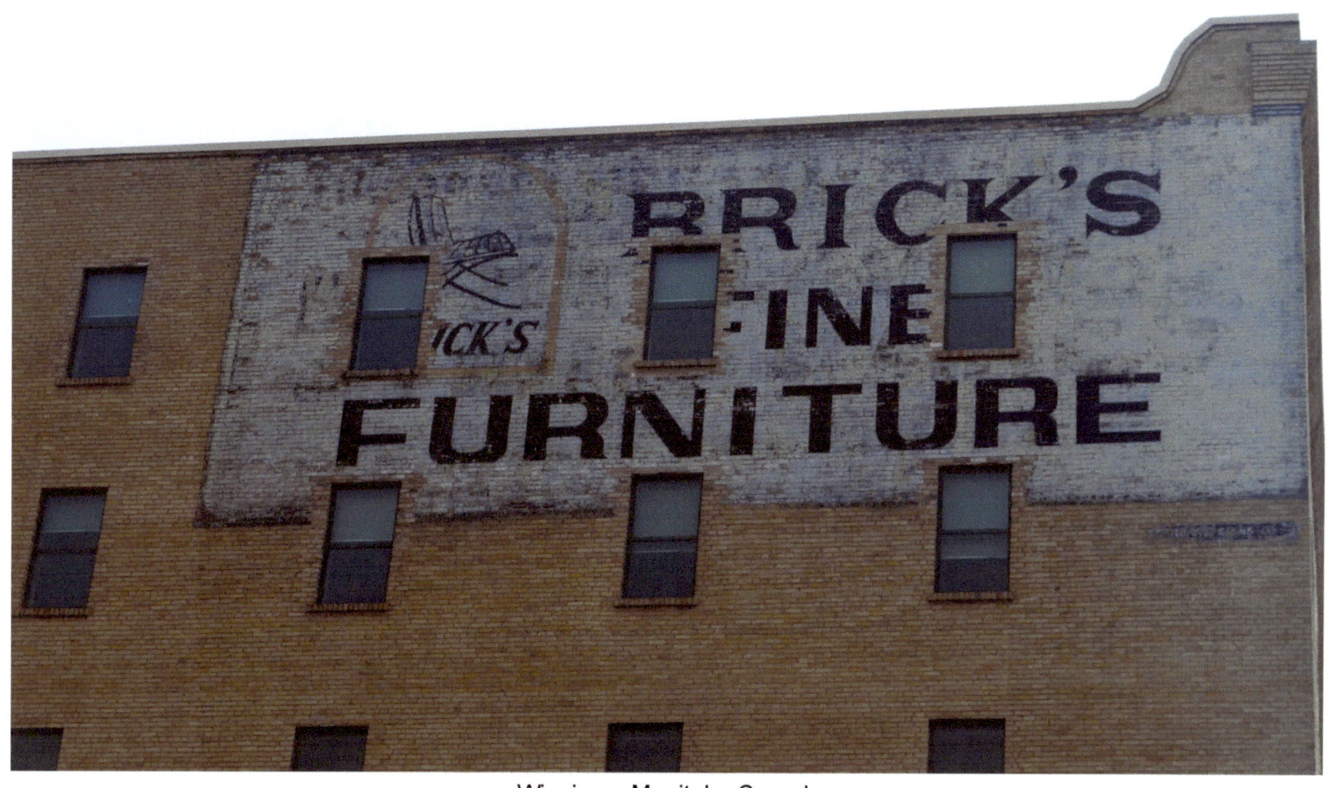

Winnipeg, Manitoba,Canada

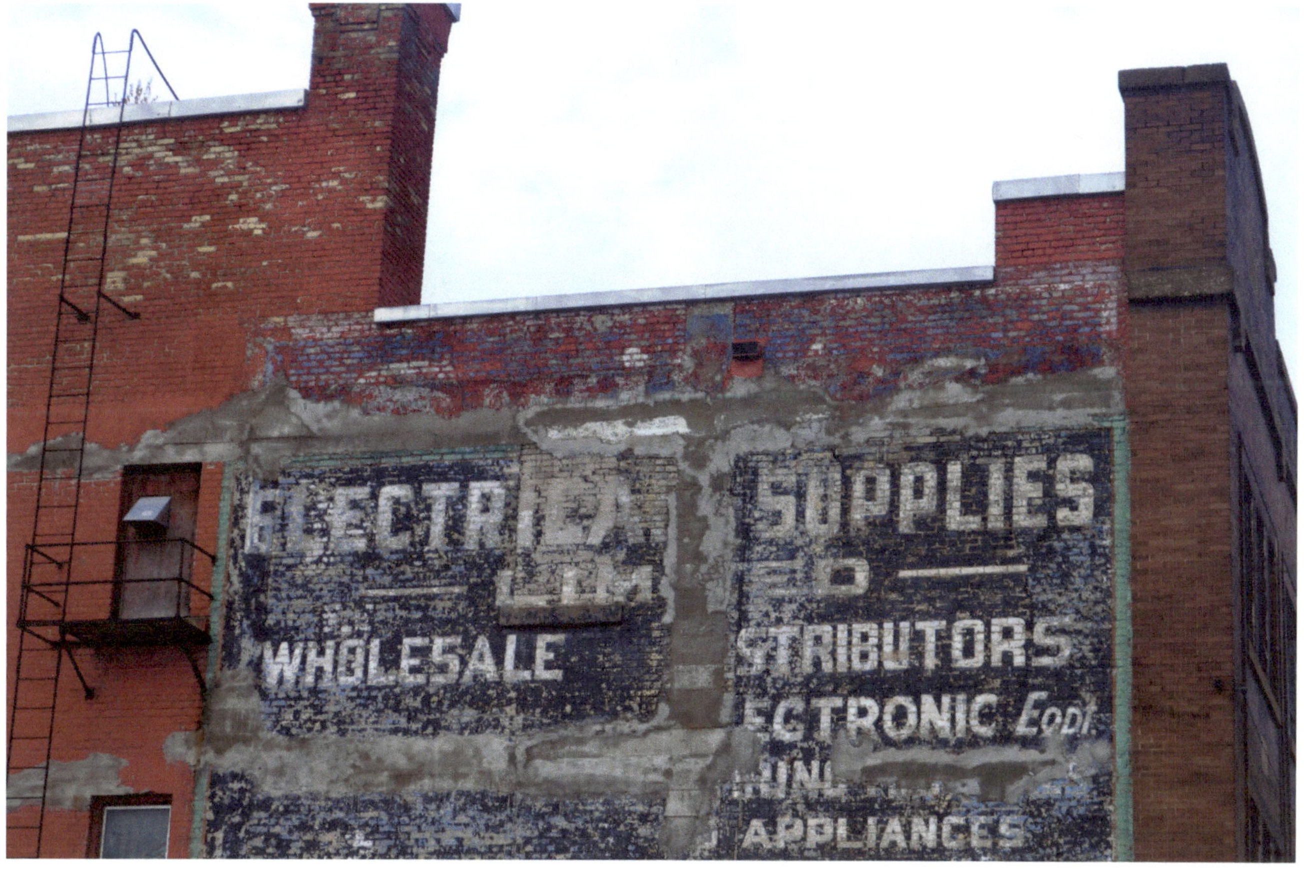

Winnipeg, Manitoba, Canada

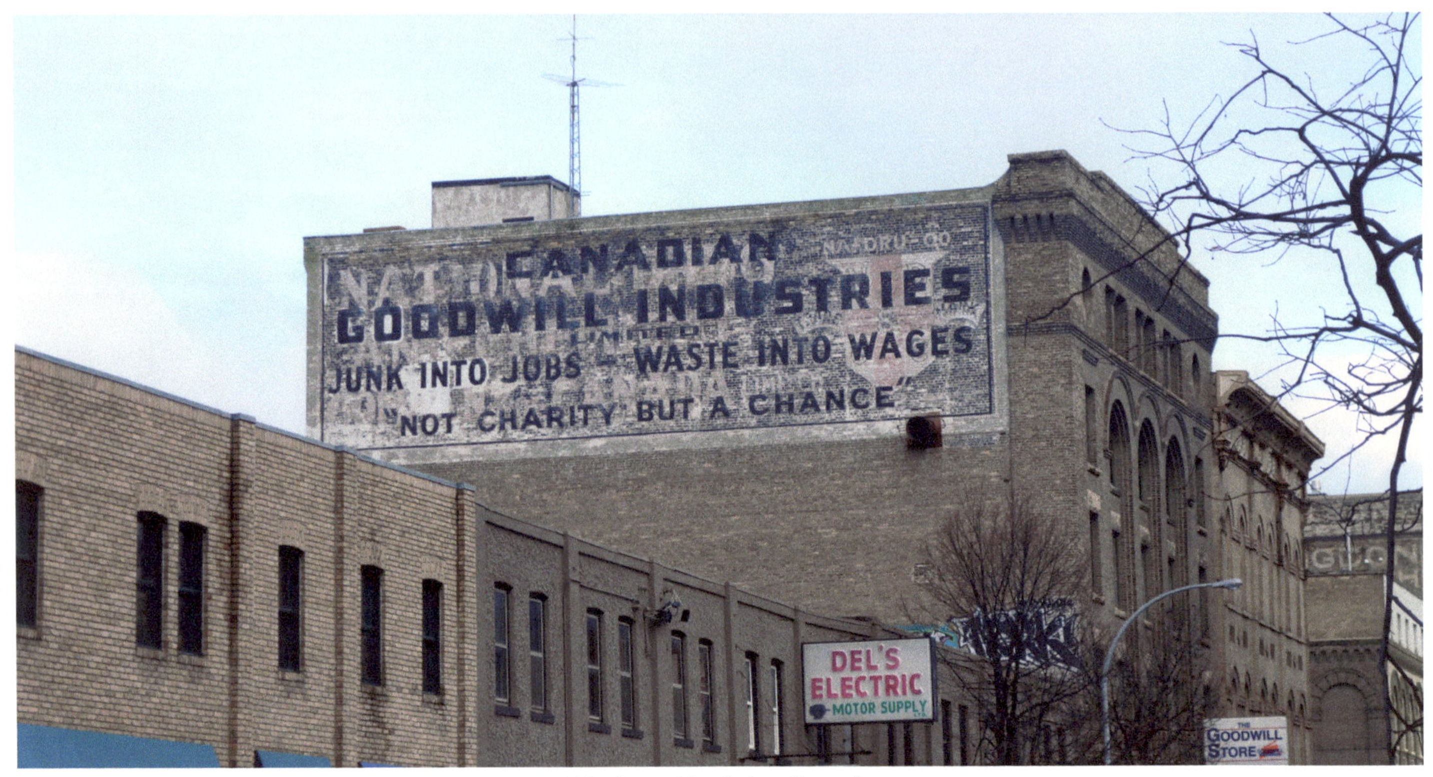

Winnipeg, Manitoba, Canada

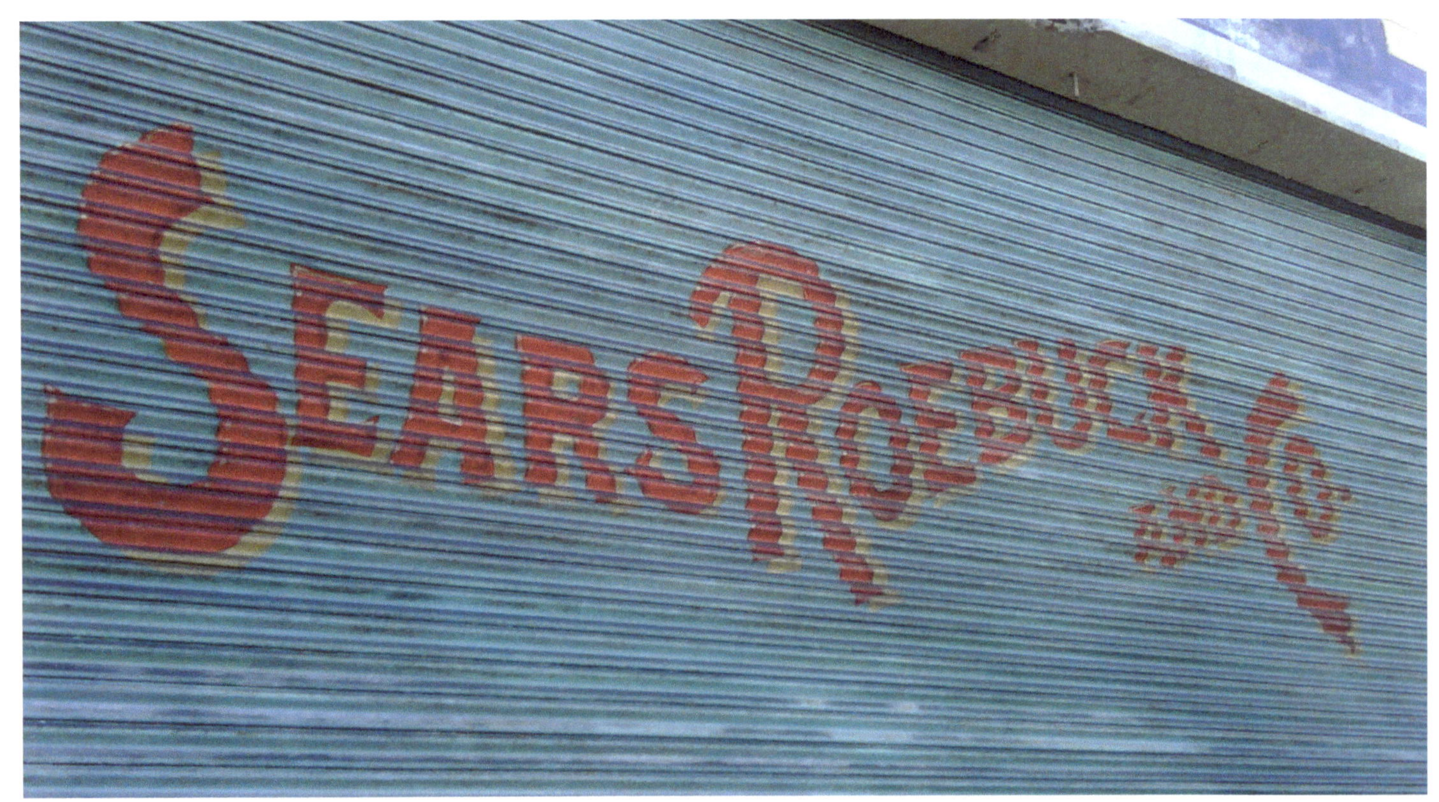

Astoria, OR

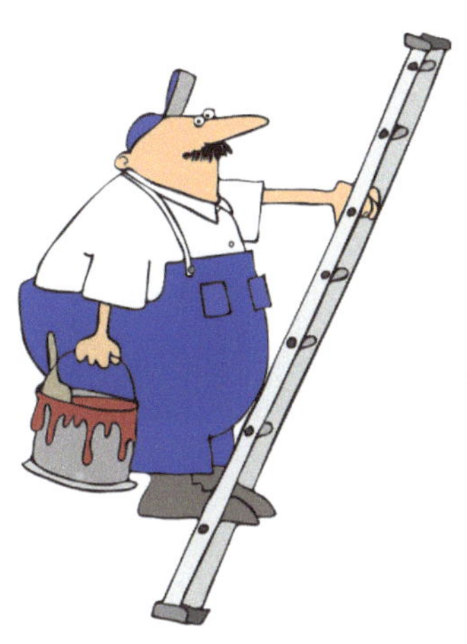

Clothing-related signs

Levi Strauss, known worldwide for its denim jeans, was founded in 1853 when Levi moved to San Francisco from Bavaria to open a west coast branch of his brother's New York dry goods business.

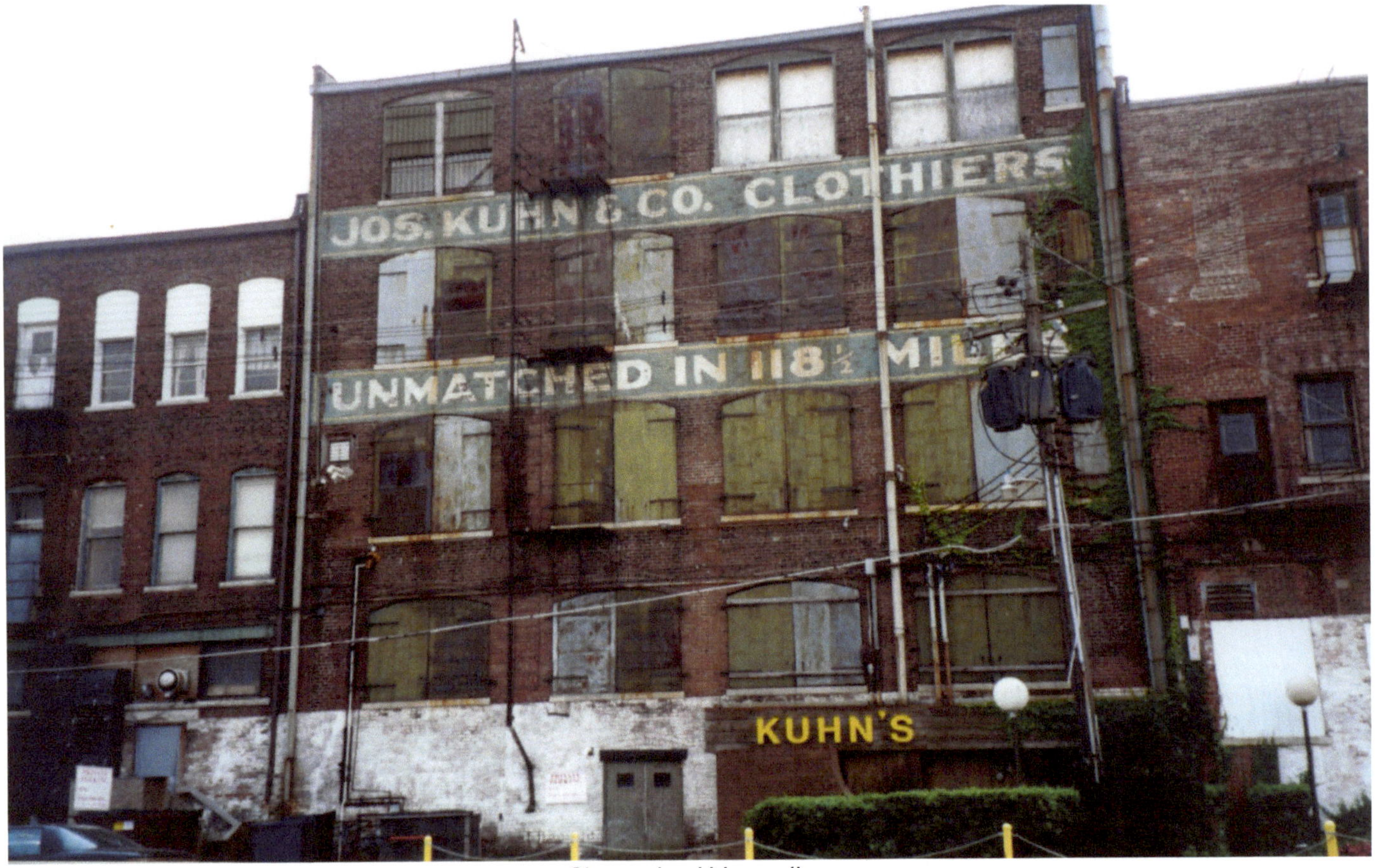

Champaign-Urbana, IL

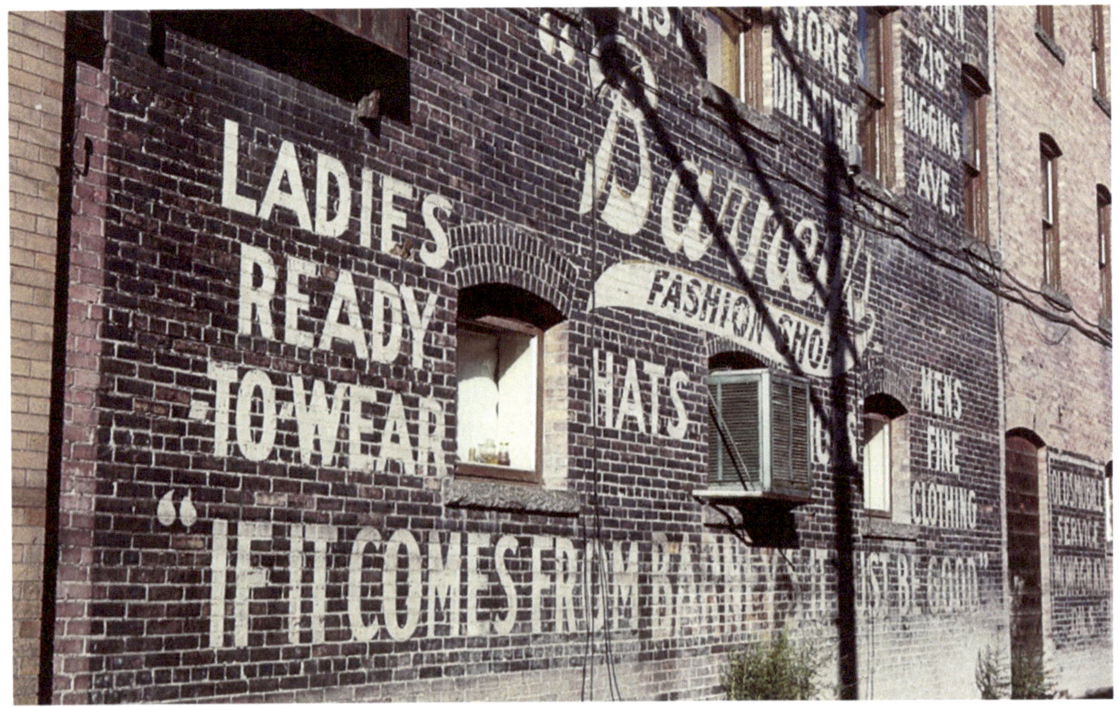

Missoula, MT

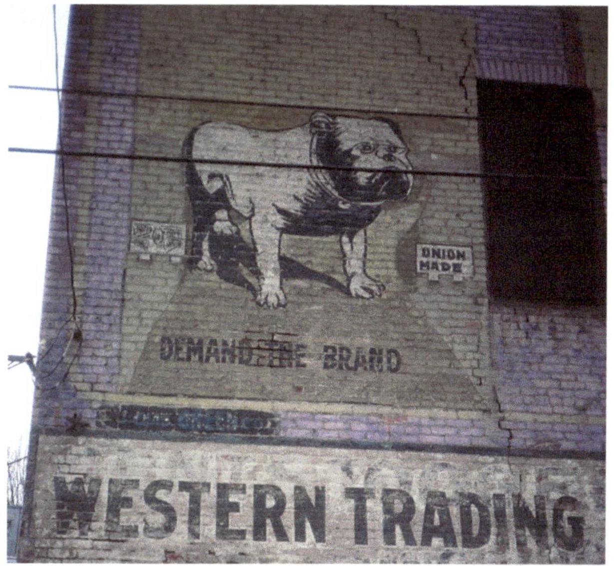

Colusa, CA

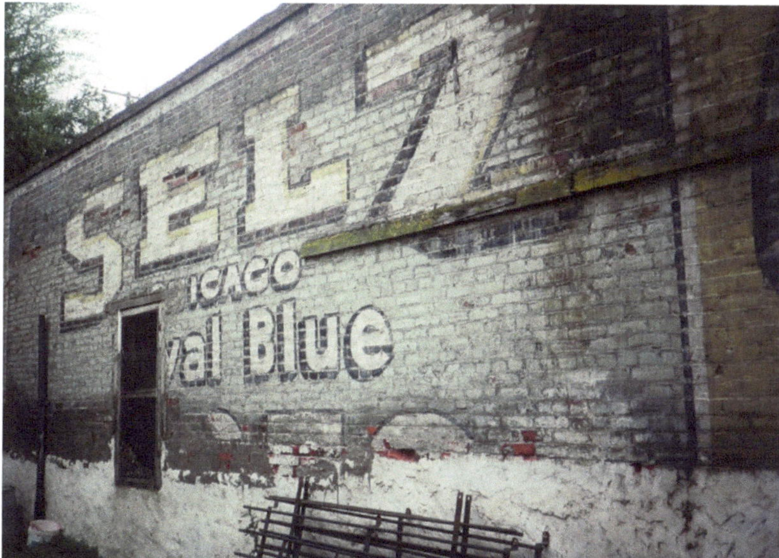

Colusa, CA

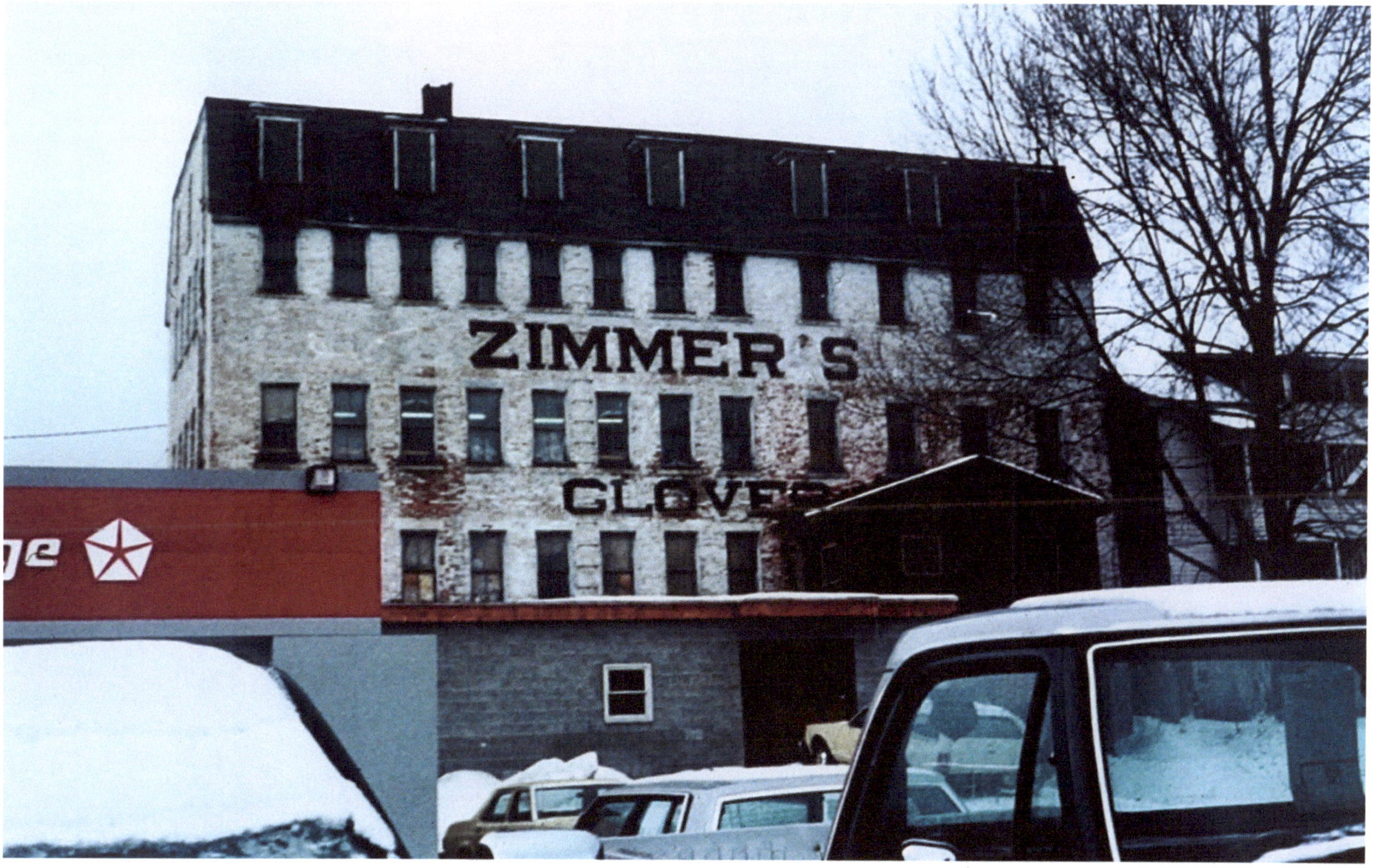

Gloversville, NY

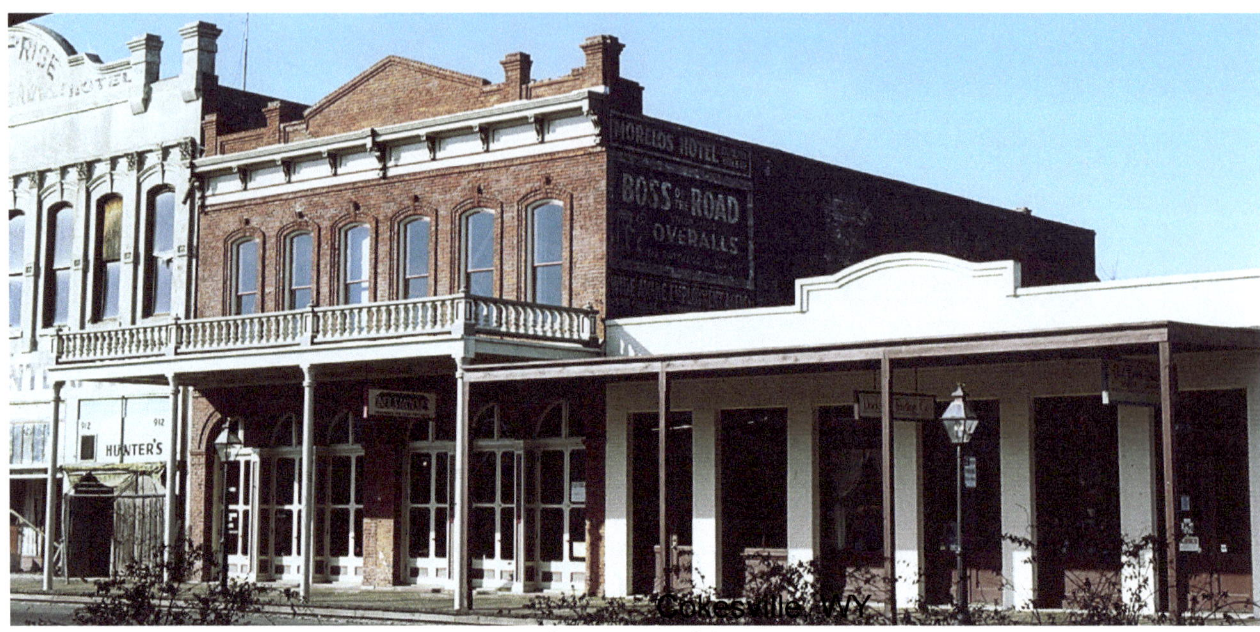

Sacramento, CA

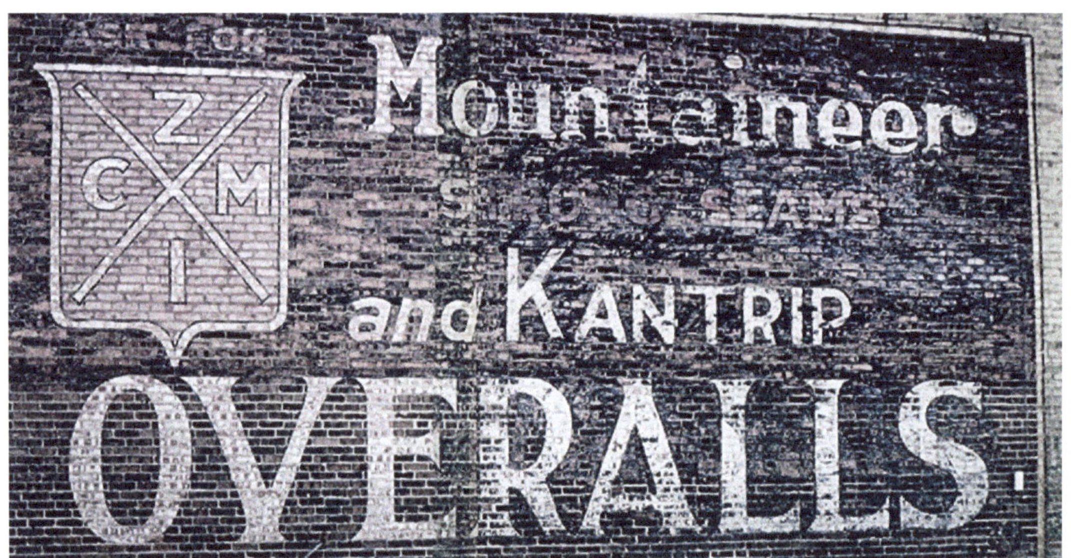

Cokesville, WY

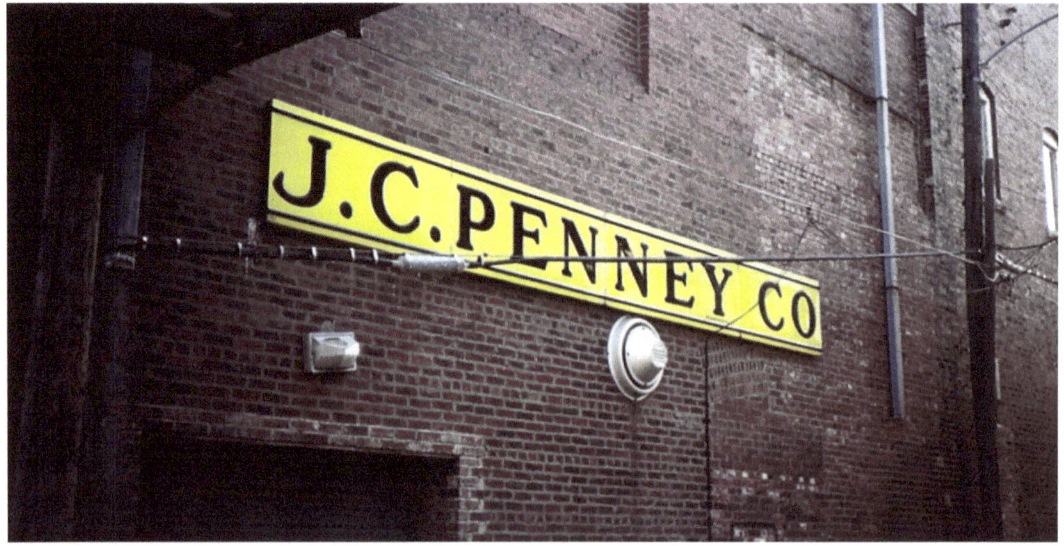

Manhattan, KS

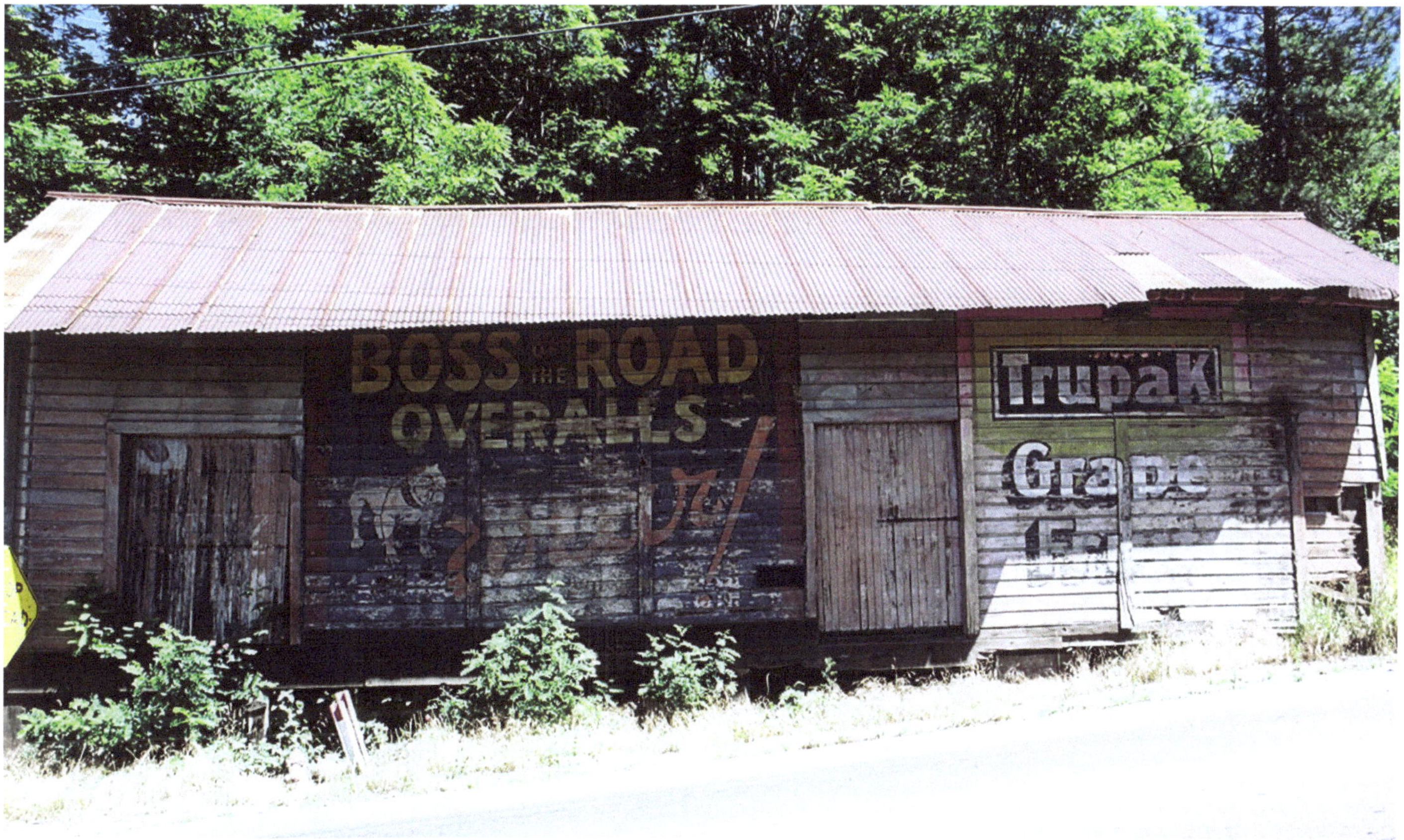

Nevada City, CA

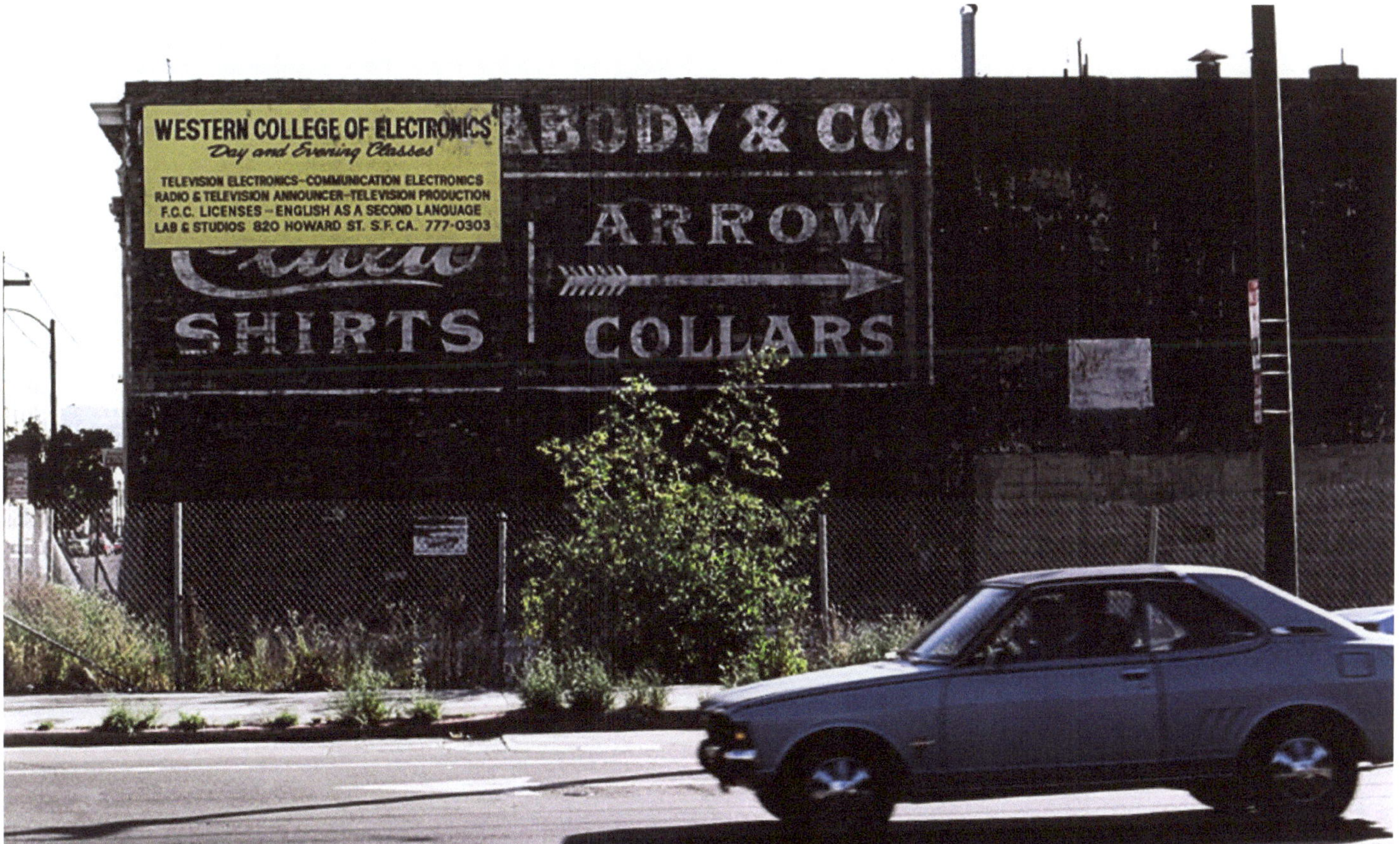

San Francisco, CA

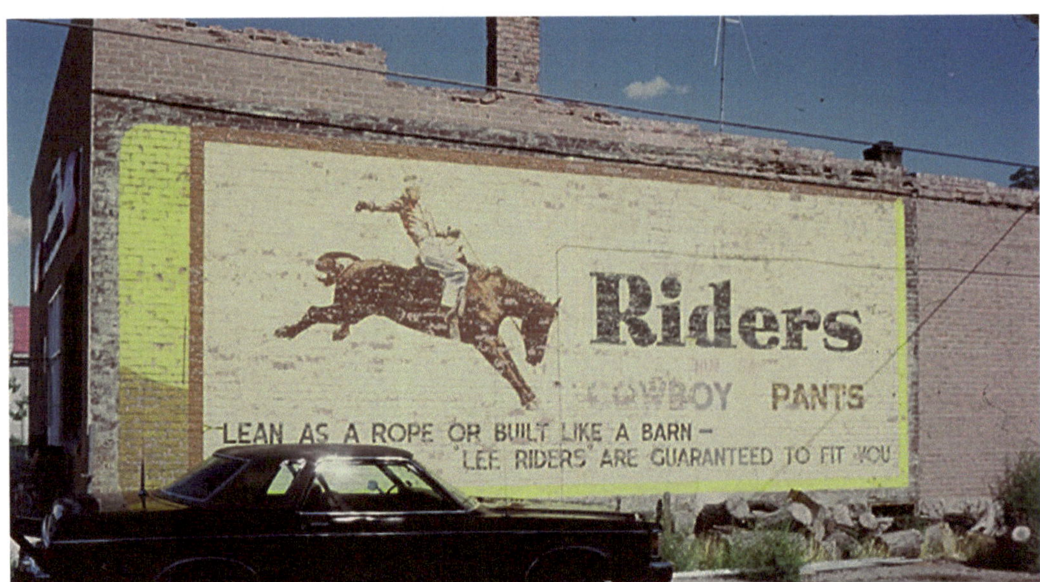

Minersville, UT

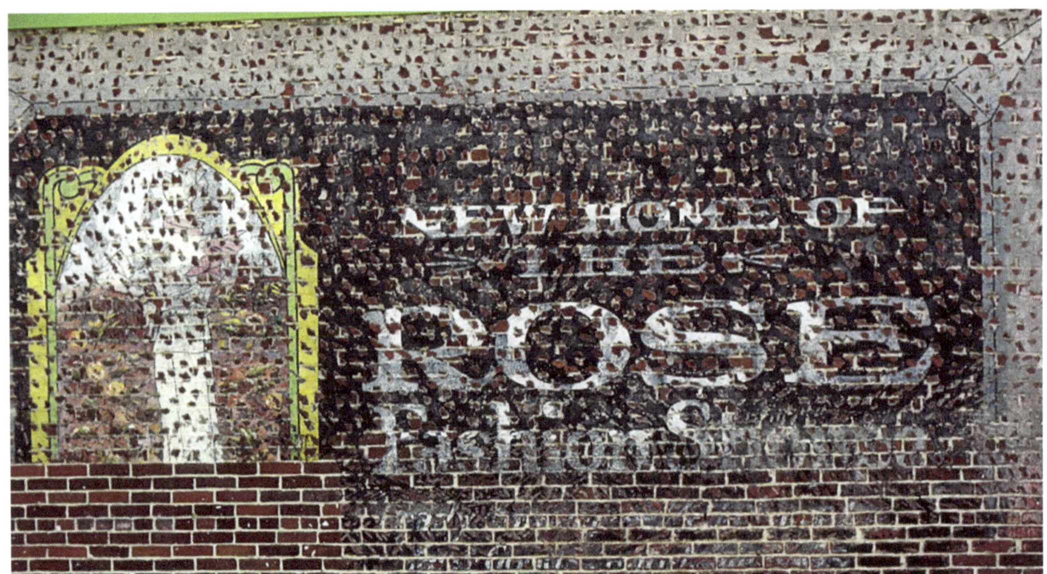

Nevada City, CA

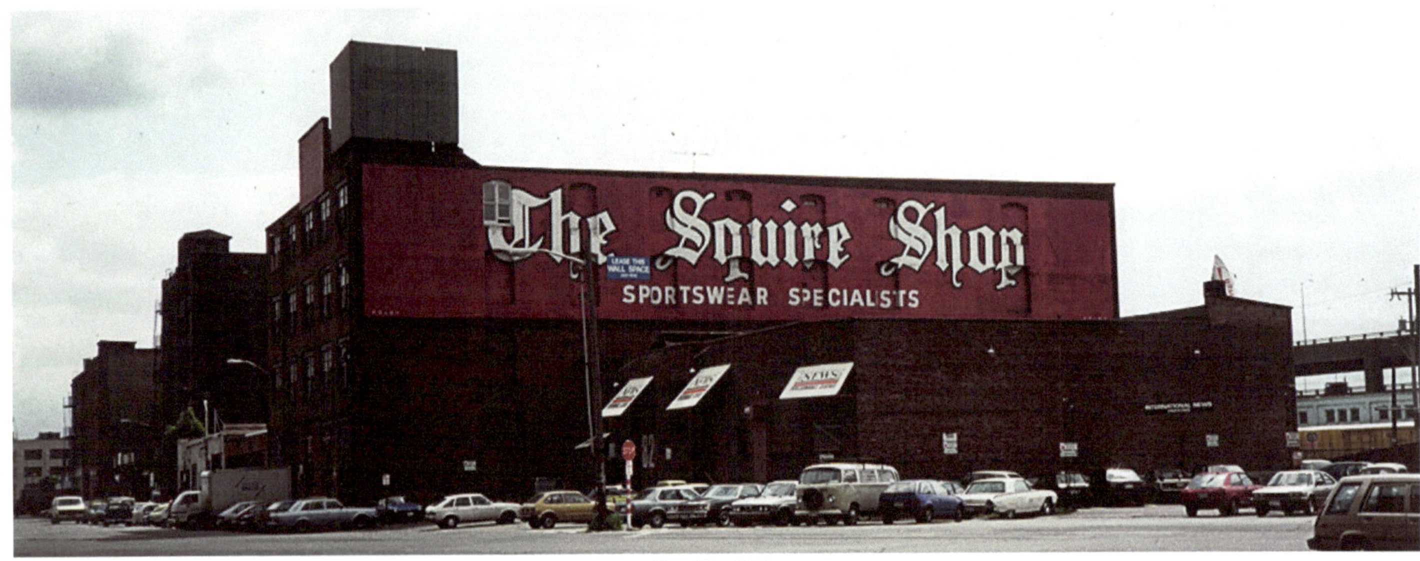

Seattle, WA

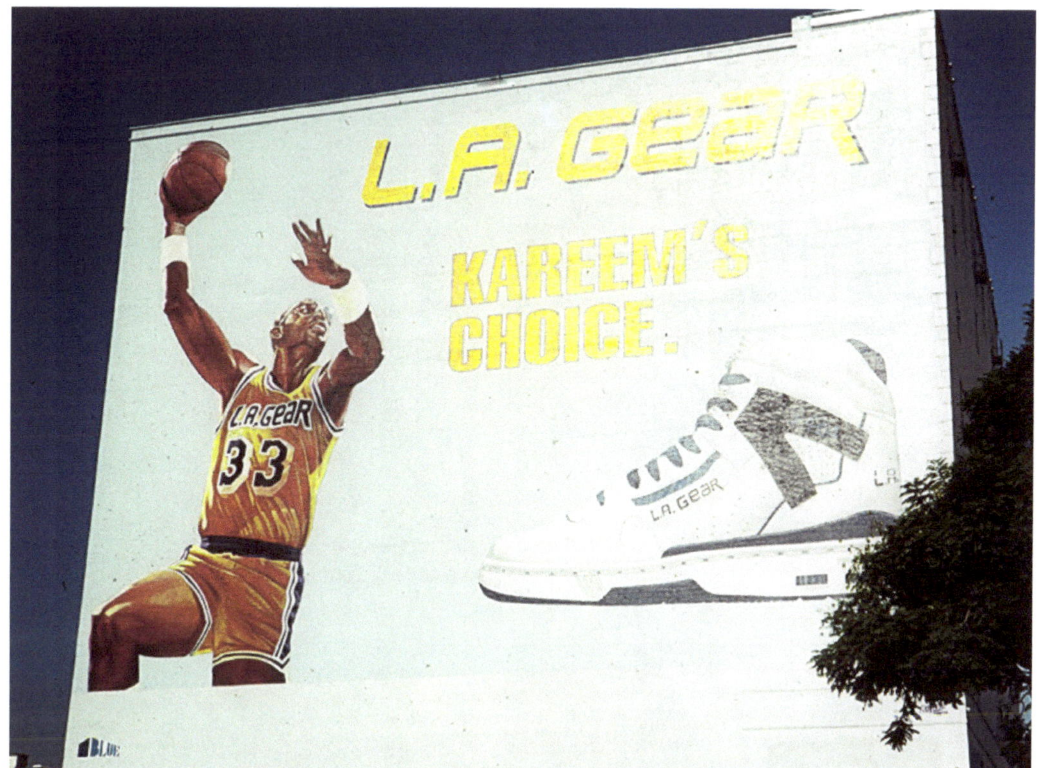

Los Angeles, CA

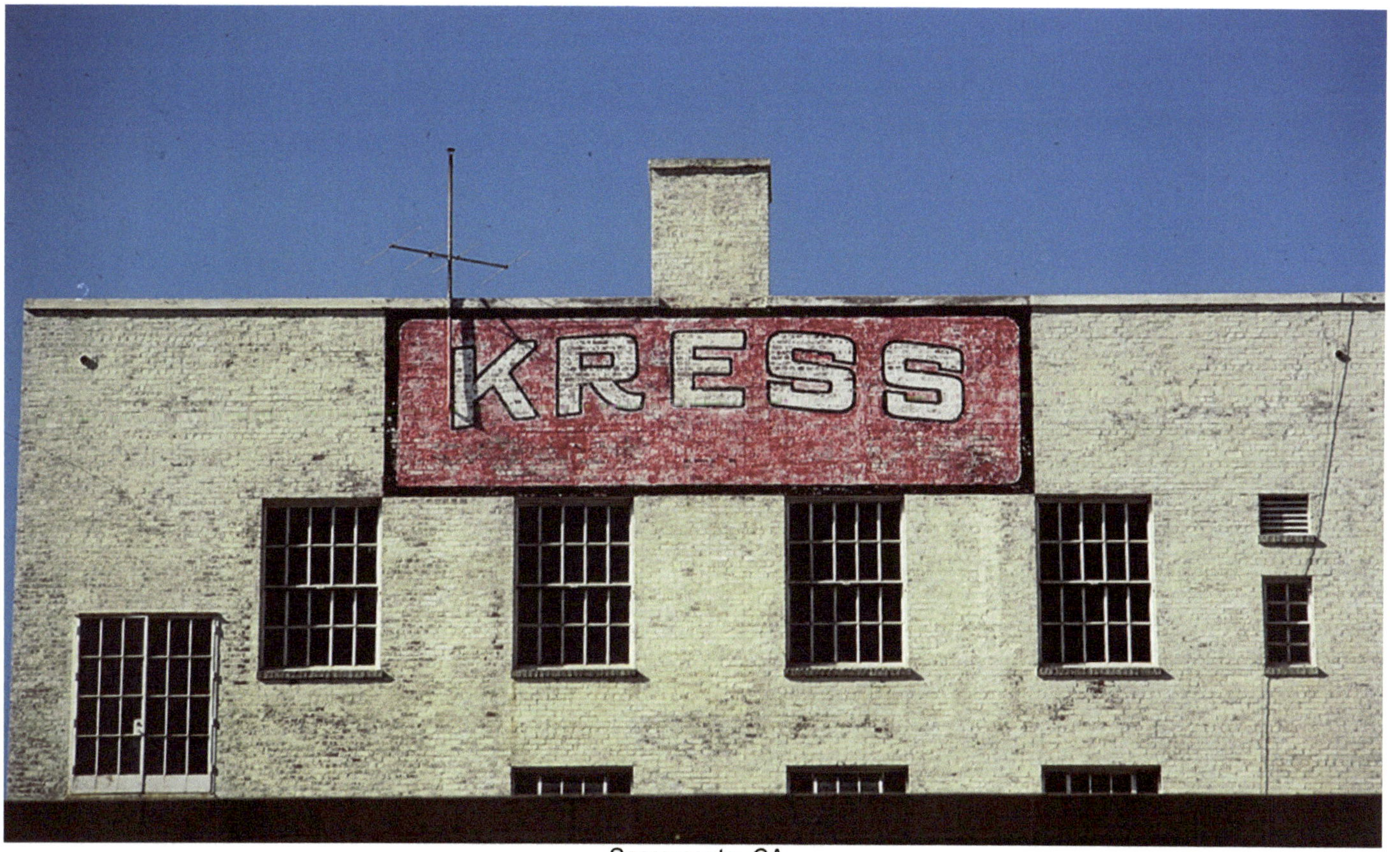

Sacramento, CA

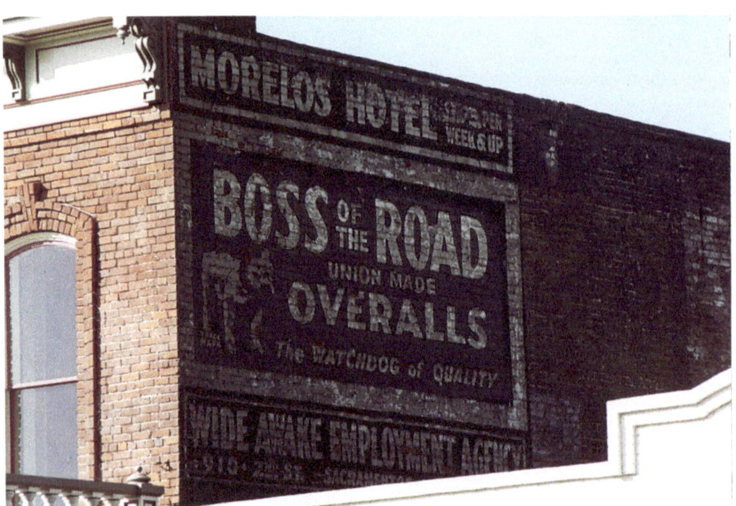

Sacramento, CA

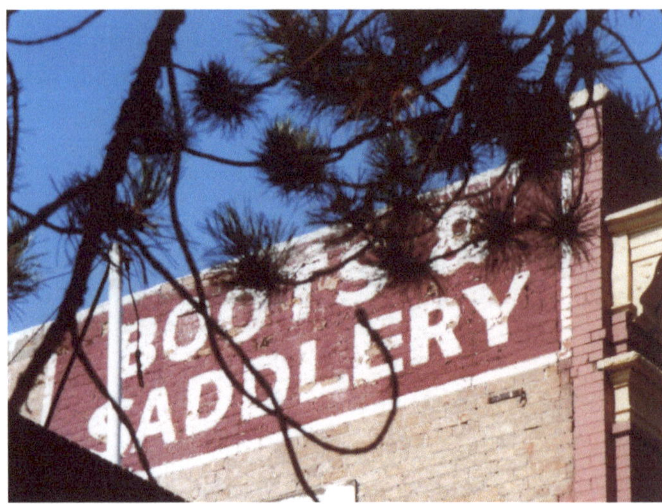

Grand Junction, CO

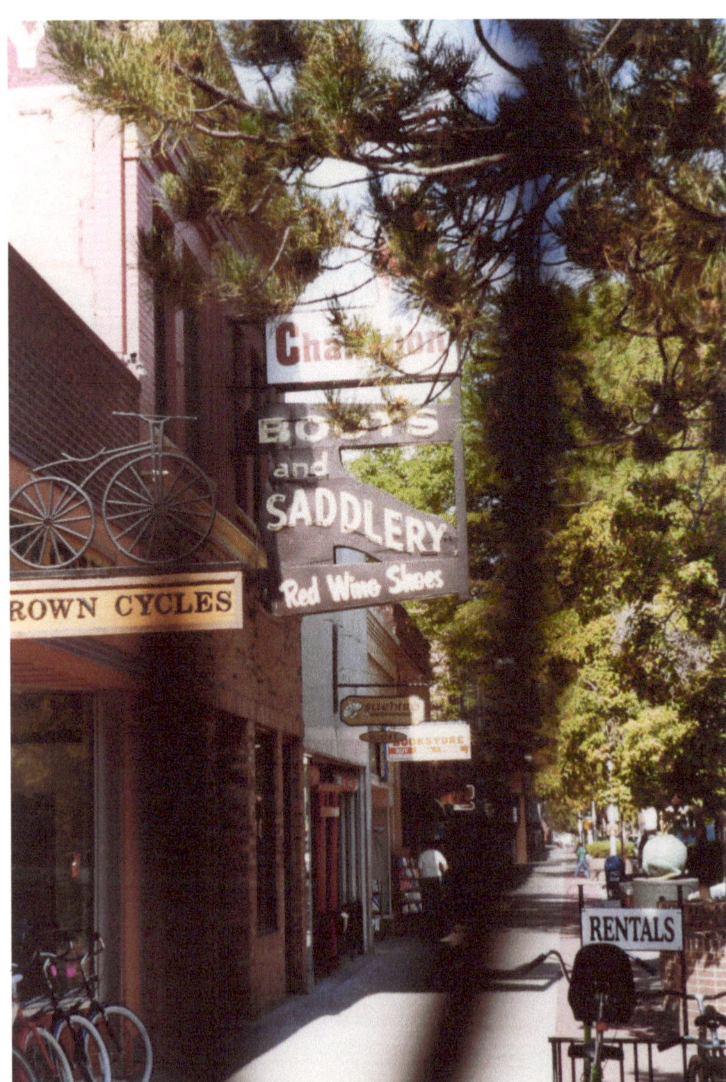

Grand Junction, CO

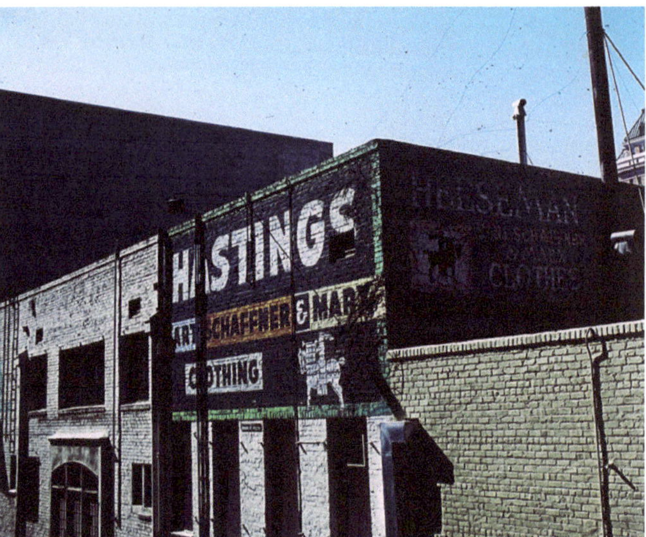

Sacramento, CA

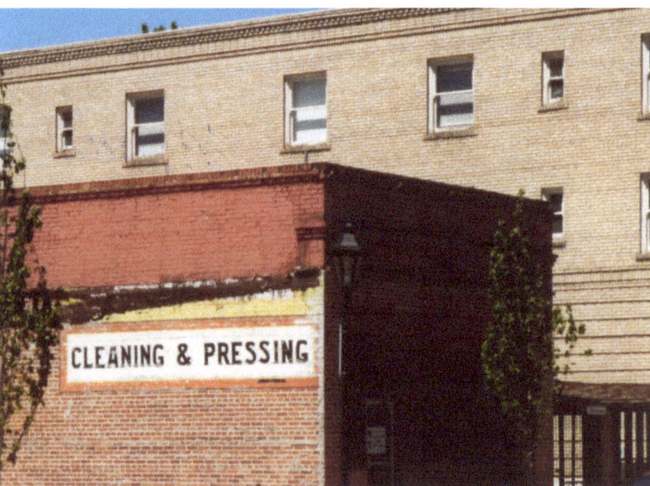

Minden, NV

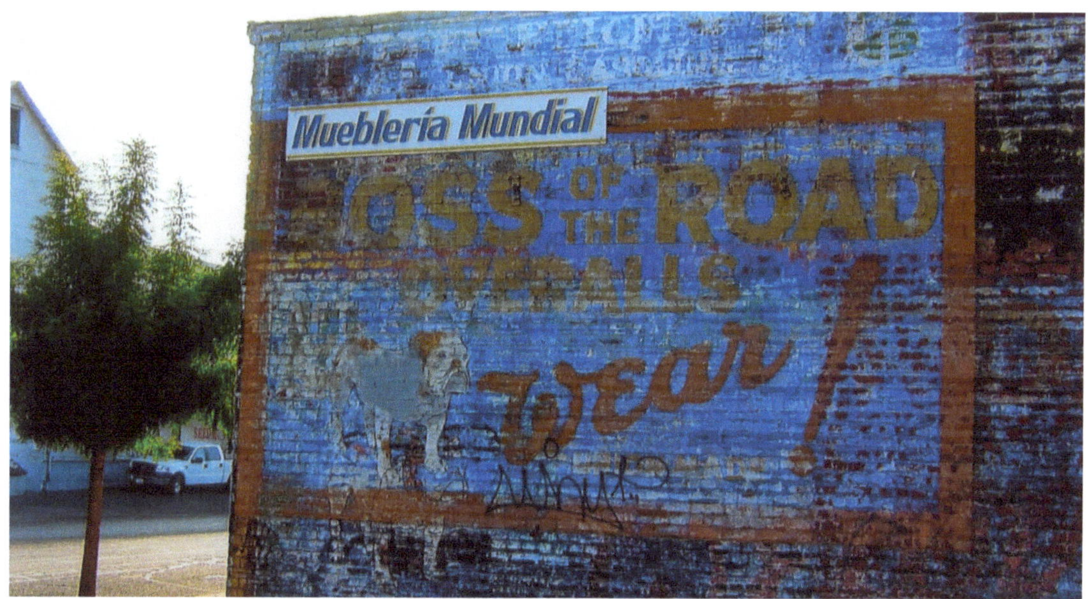

Unknown location

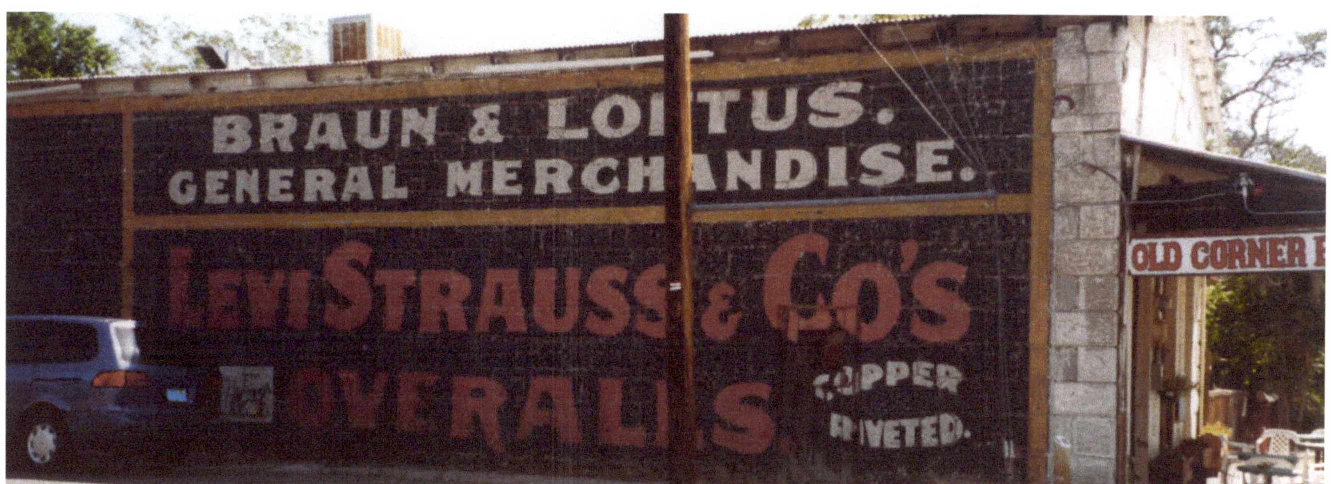

Dayton, NV

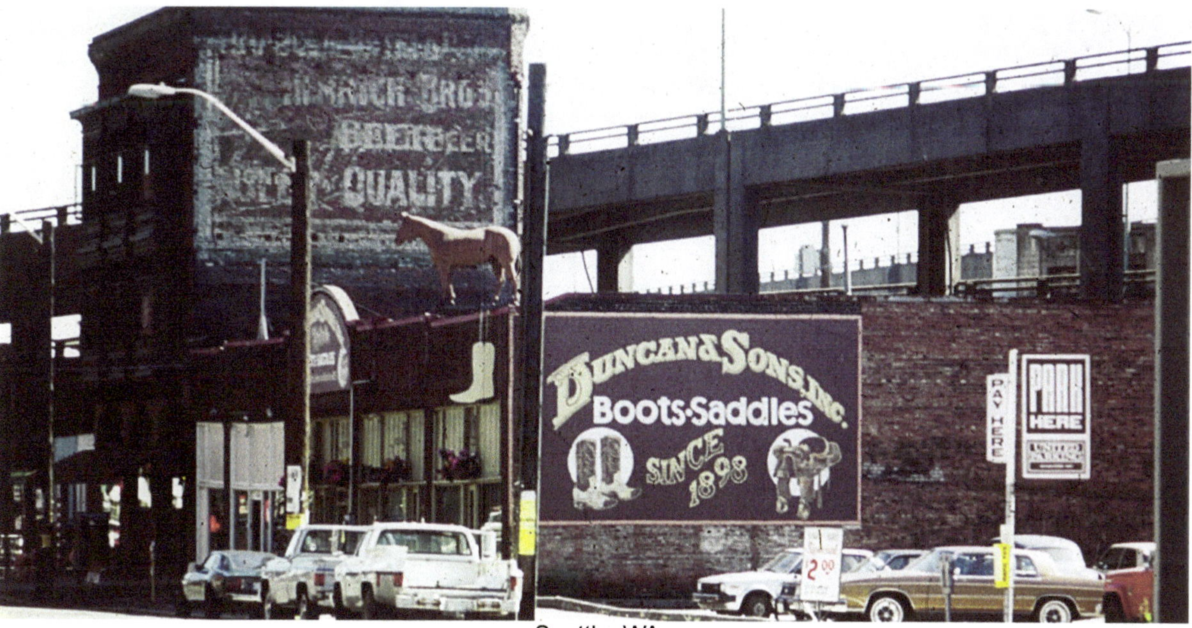

Seattle, WA

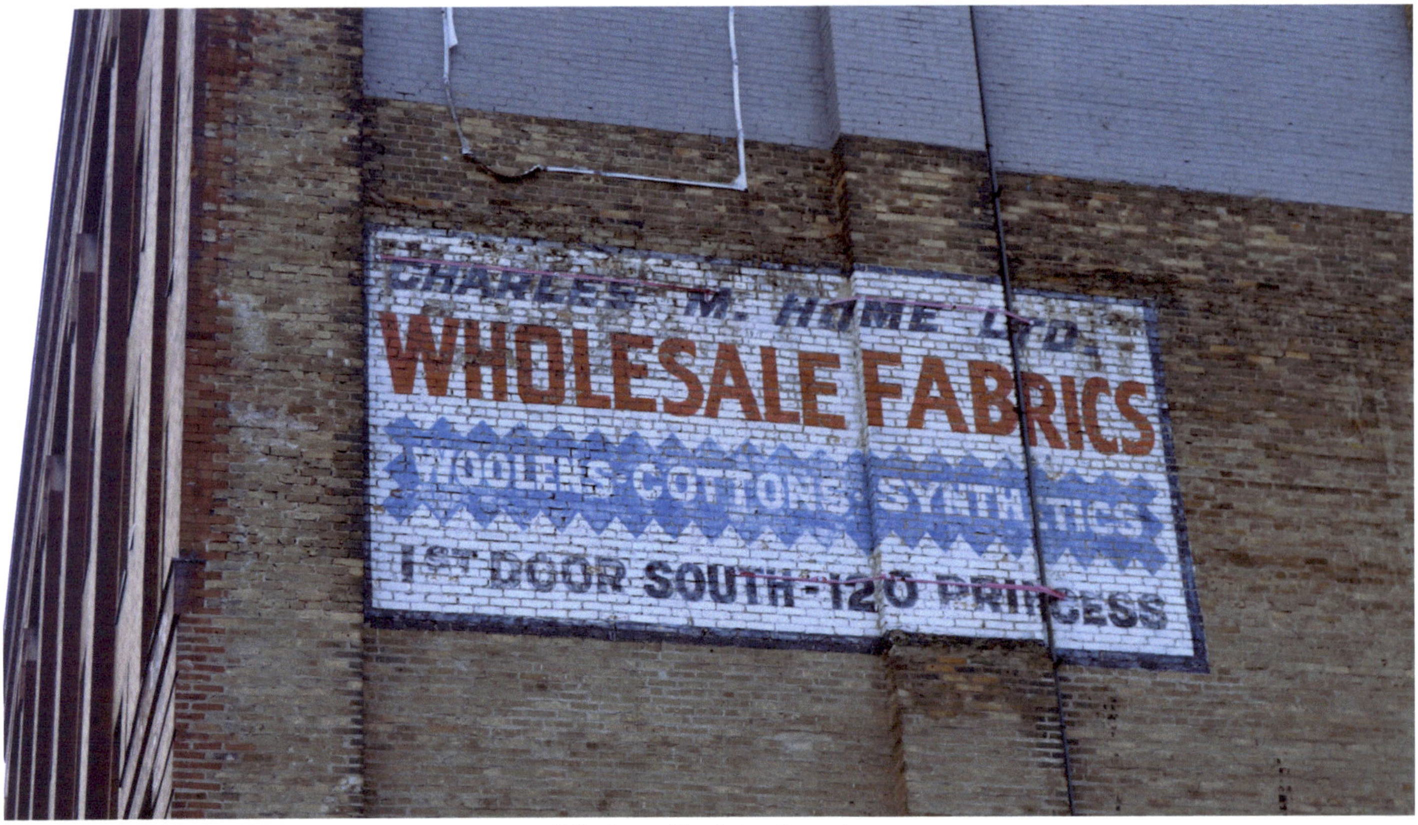

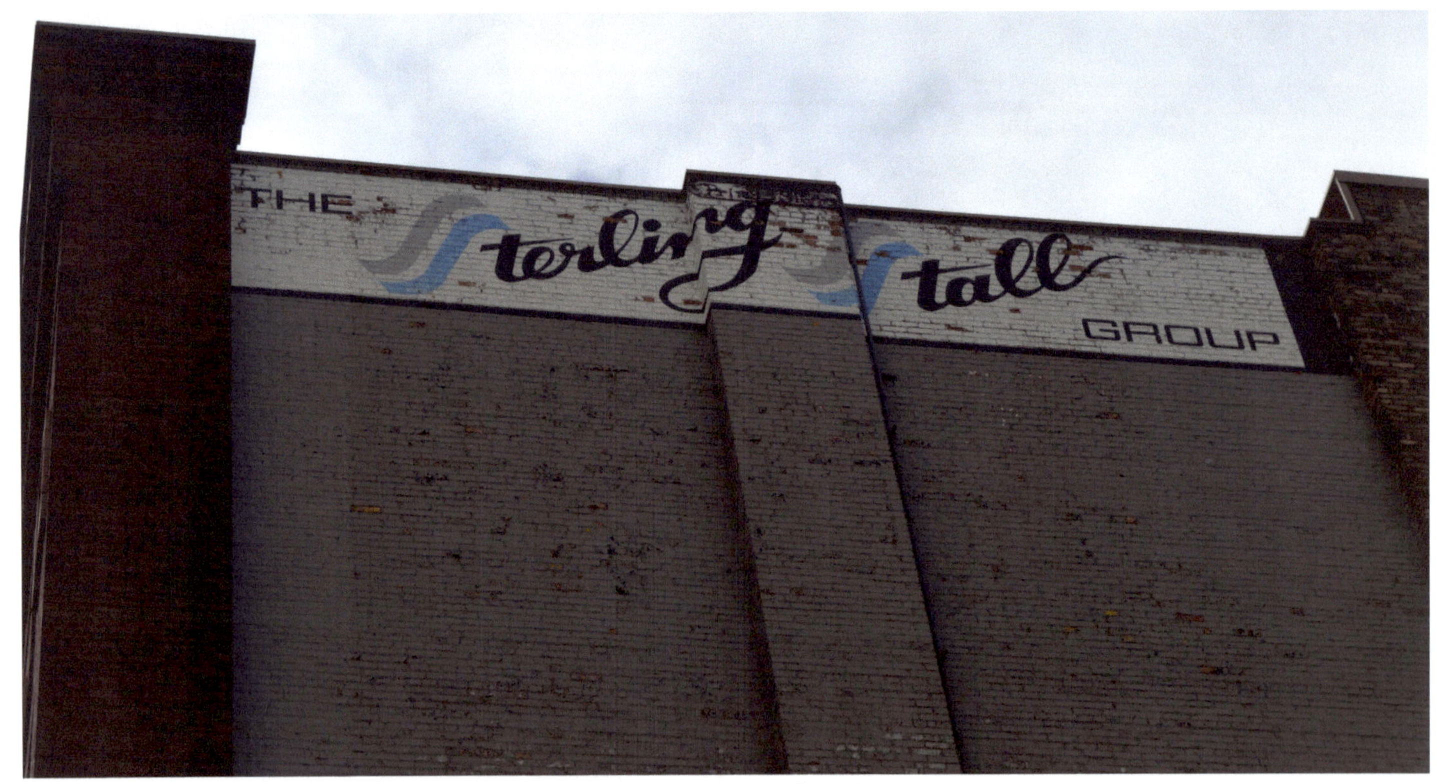

Winnipeg, Manitoba,Canada

Winnipeg, Manitoba, Canada

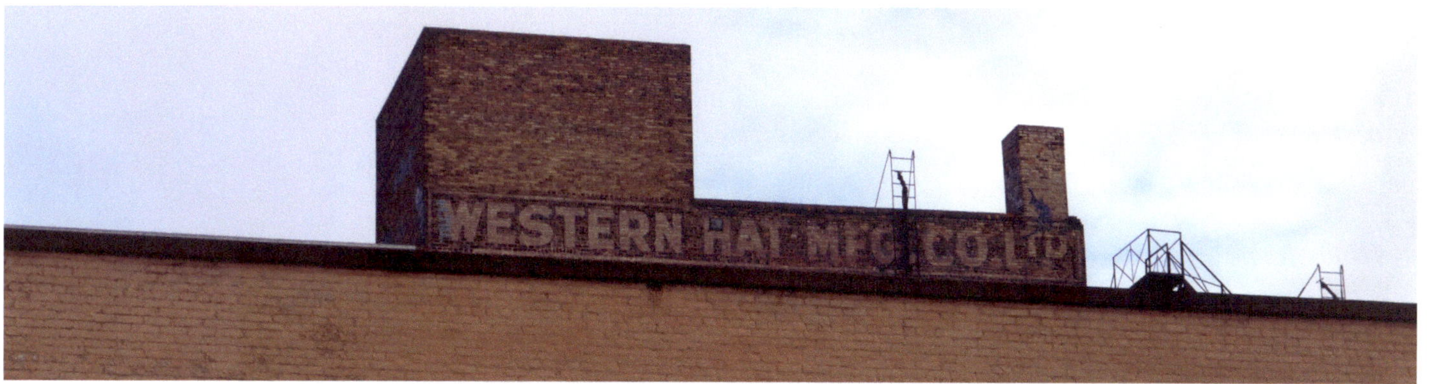

Winnipeg, Manitoba, Canada

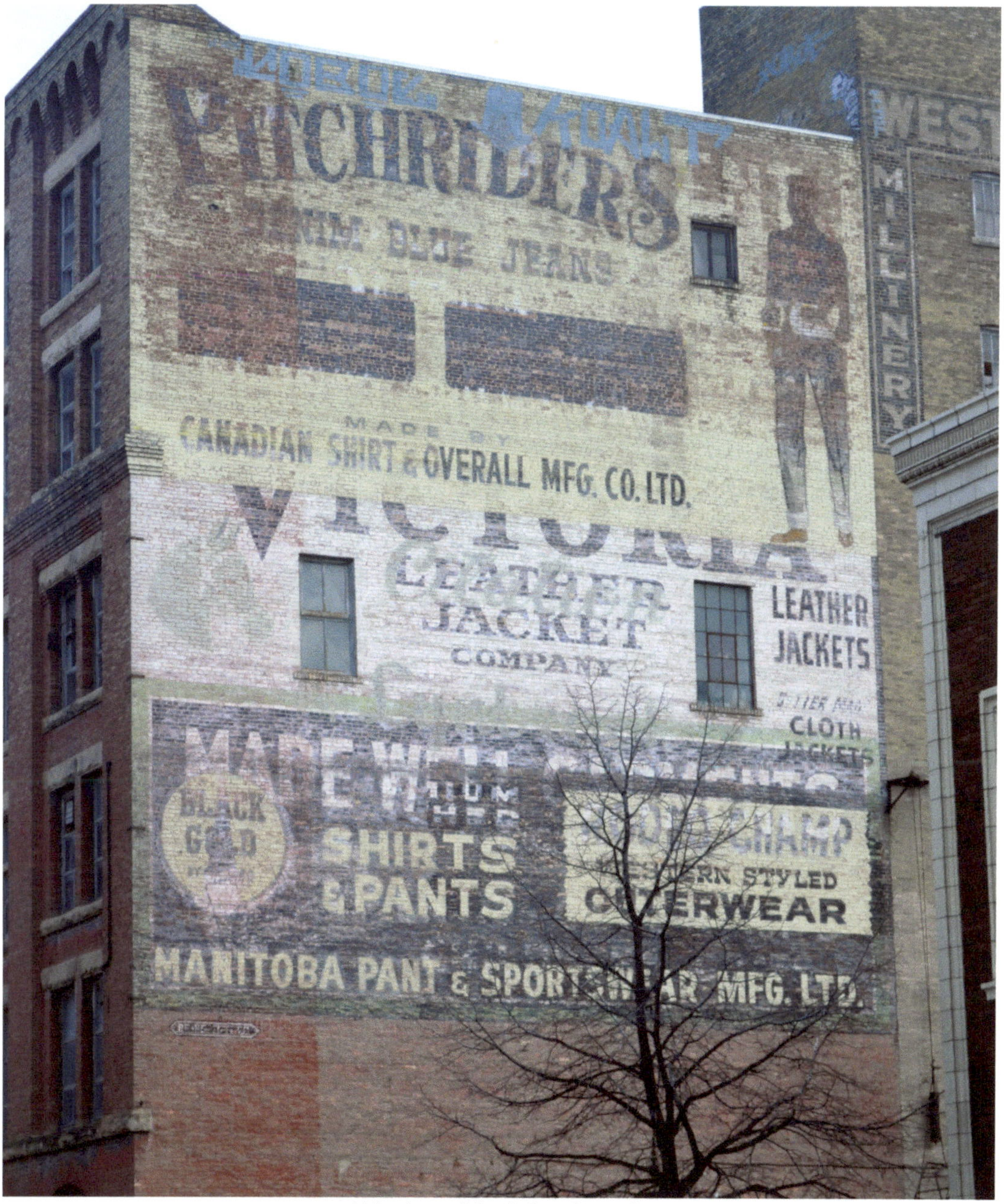

Winnipeg, Manitoba, Canada

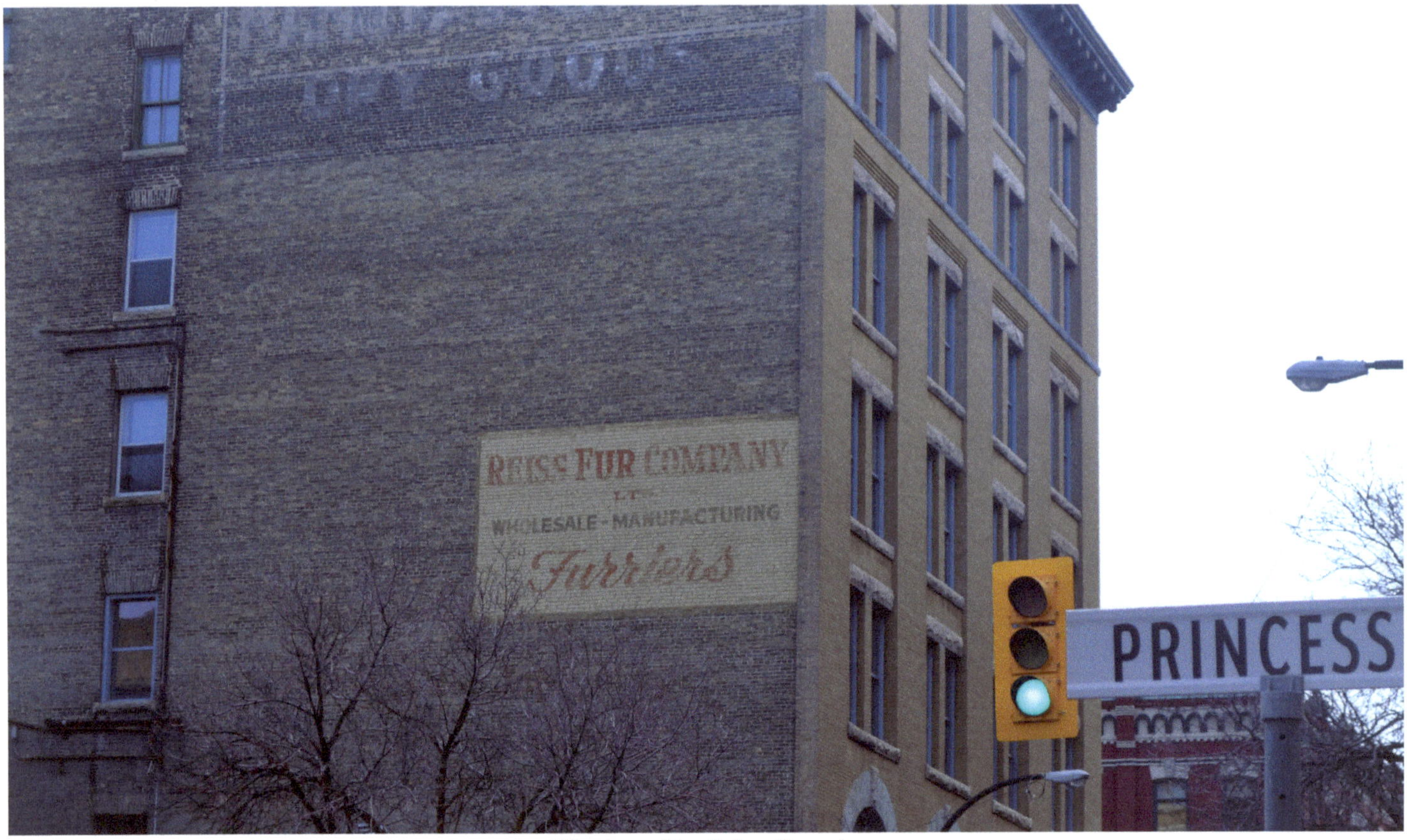

Winnipeg, Manitoba, Canada

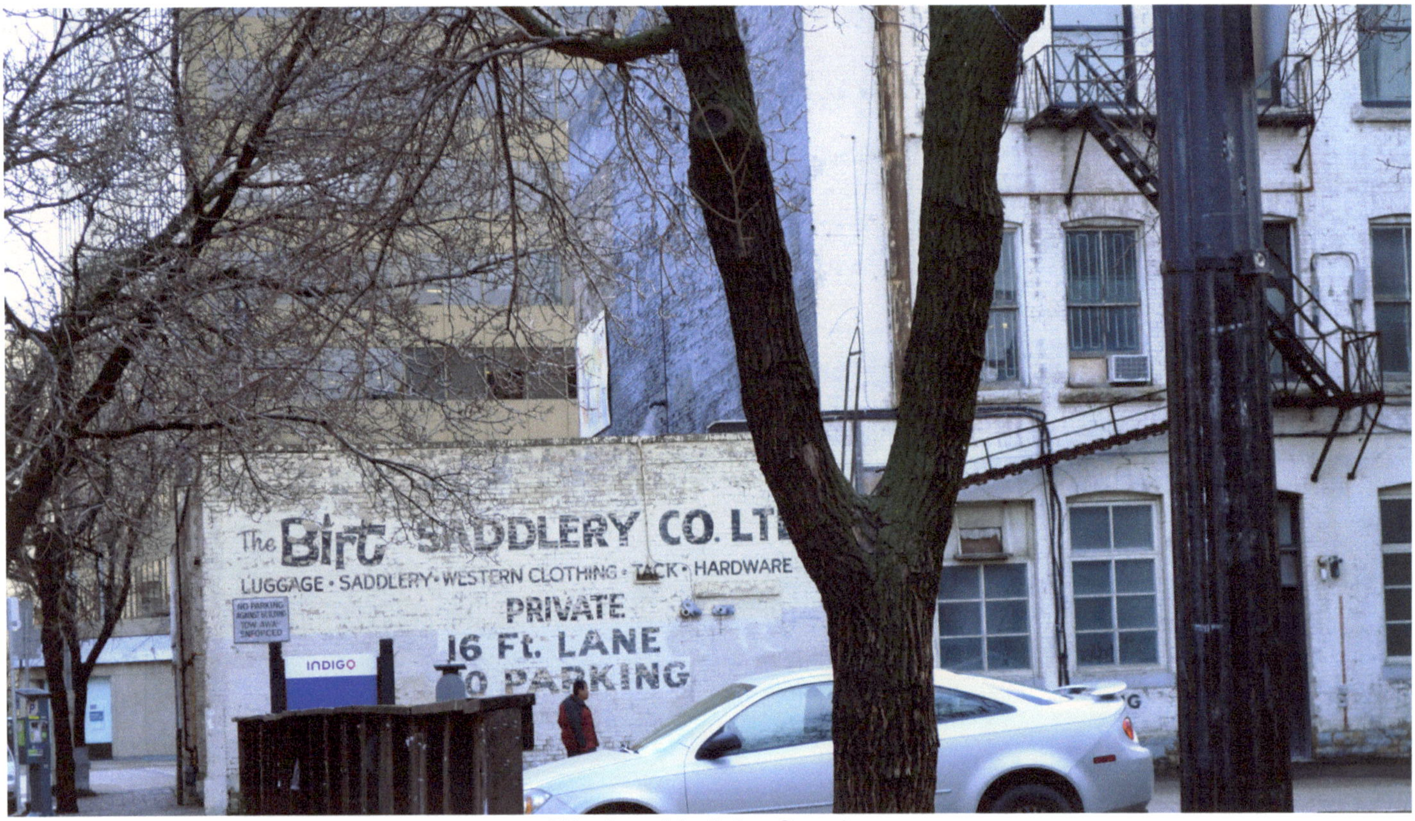

Winnipeg, Manitoba, Canada

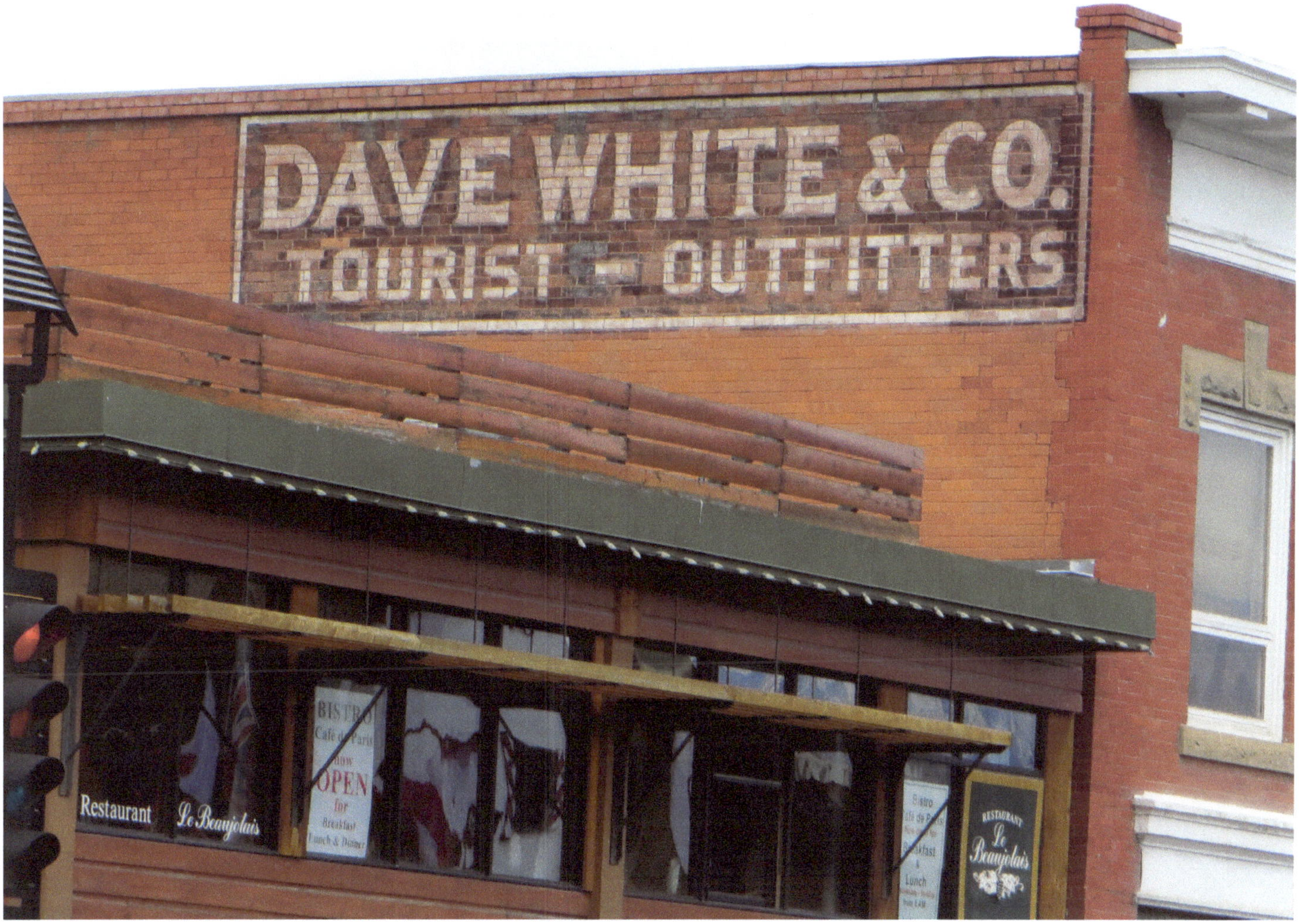

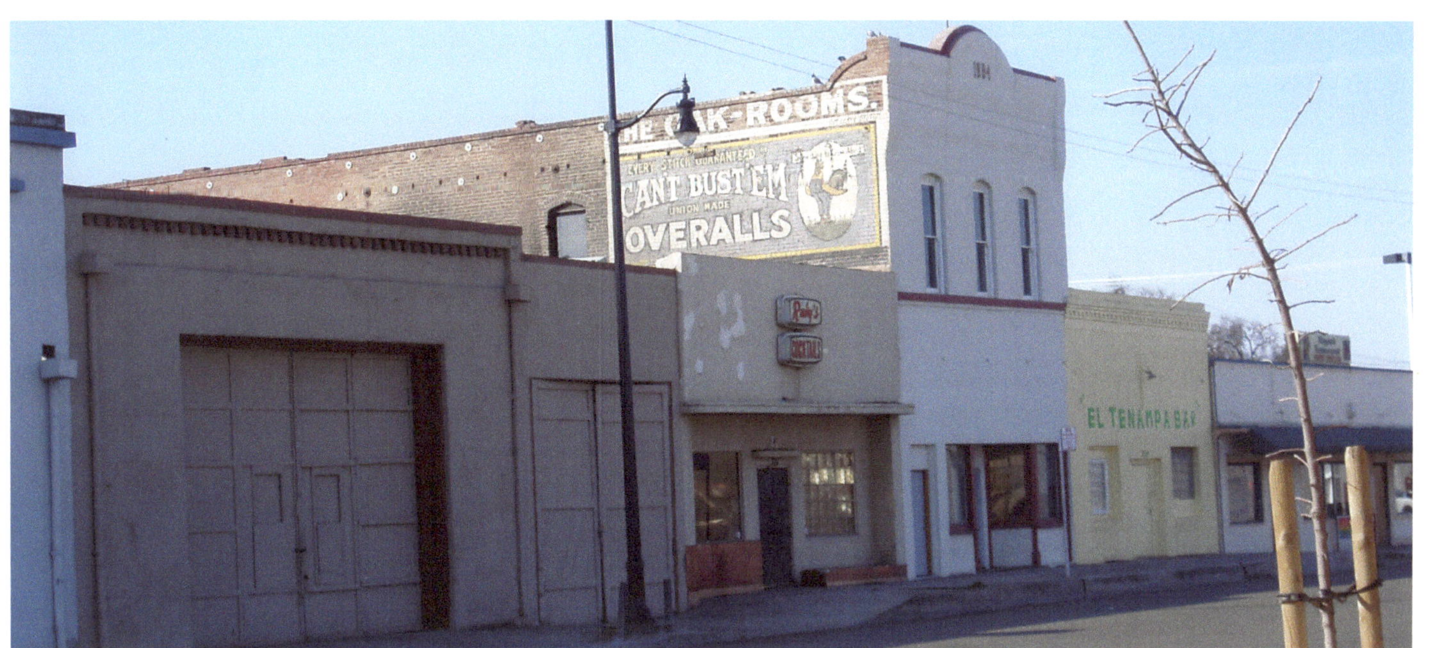

Banff, Alberta, Canada

Lemoore, CA

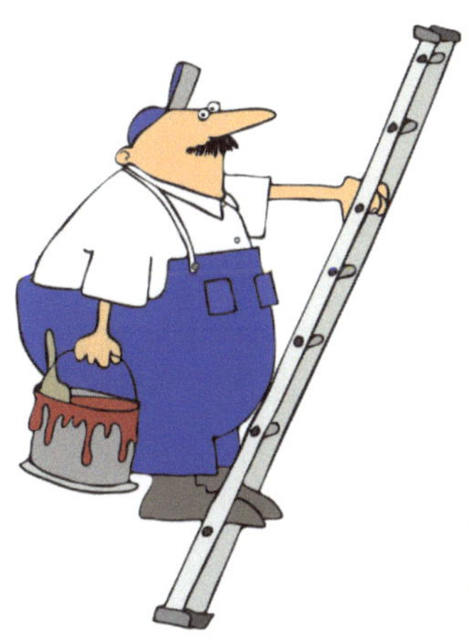

Food & Beverage-related signs

The story of Bisquick, "a new product which revolutionized American eating habits," originated on a Southern Pacific train connecting Portland with San Francisco.

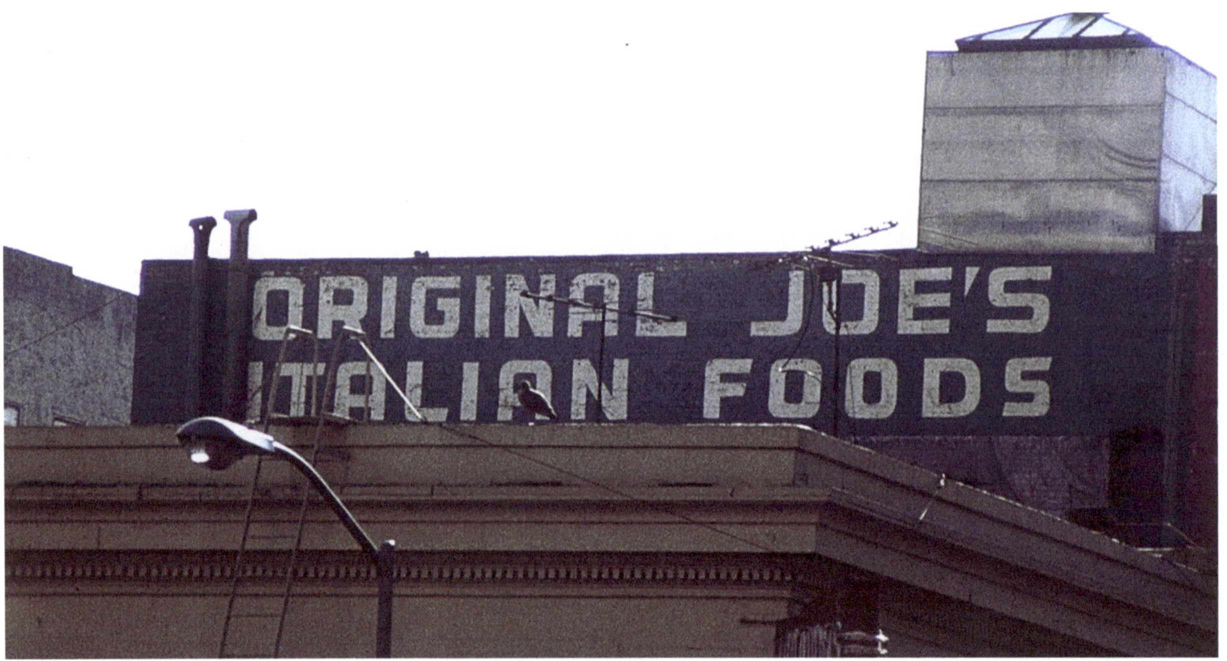

San Francisco, CA

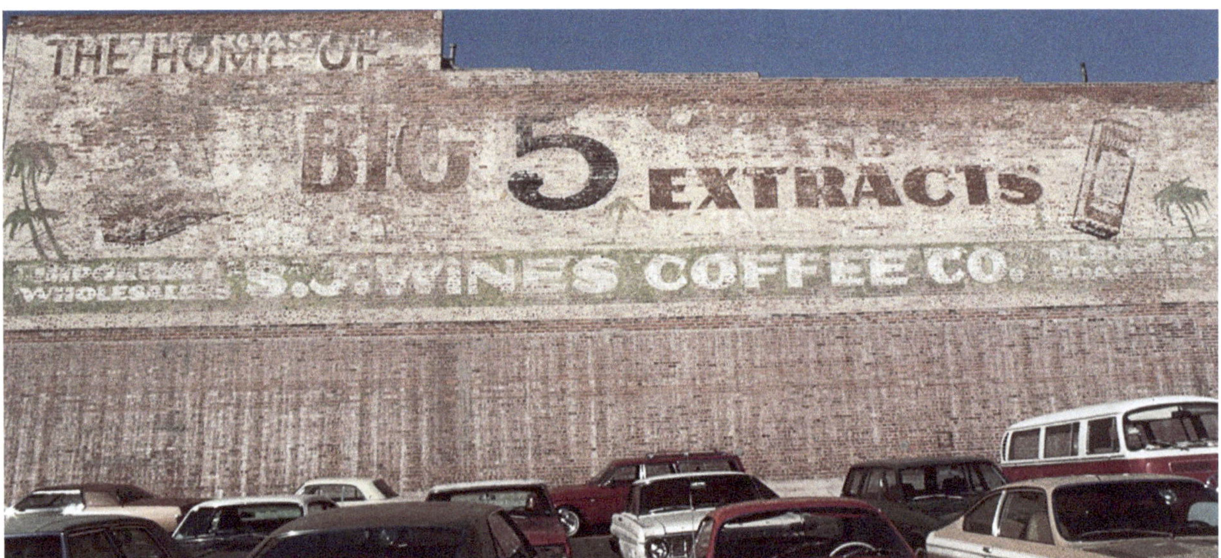

San Diego, CA

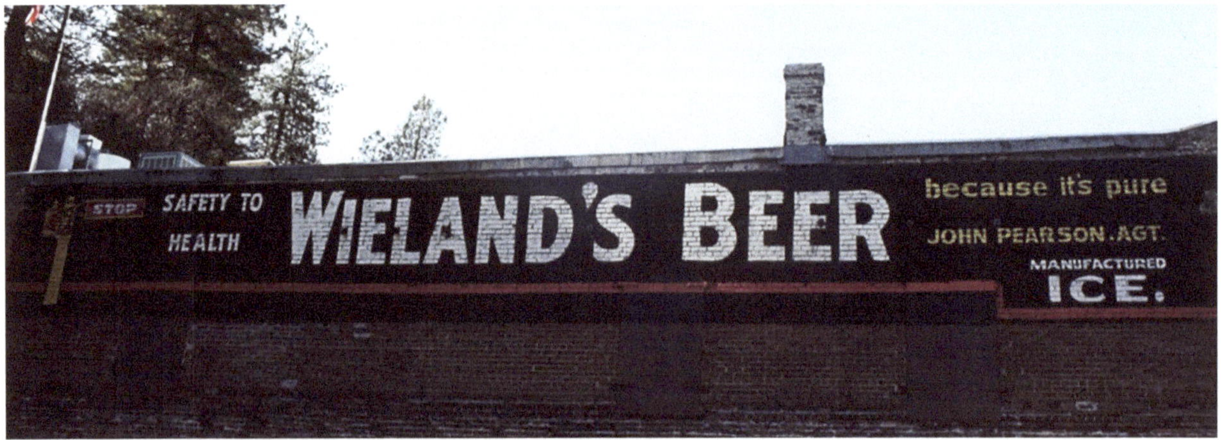

Placerville, CA

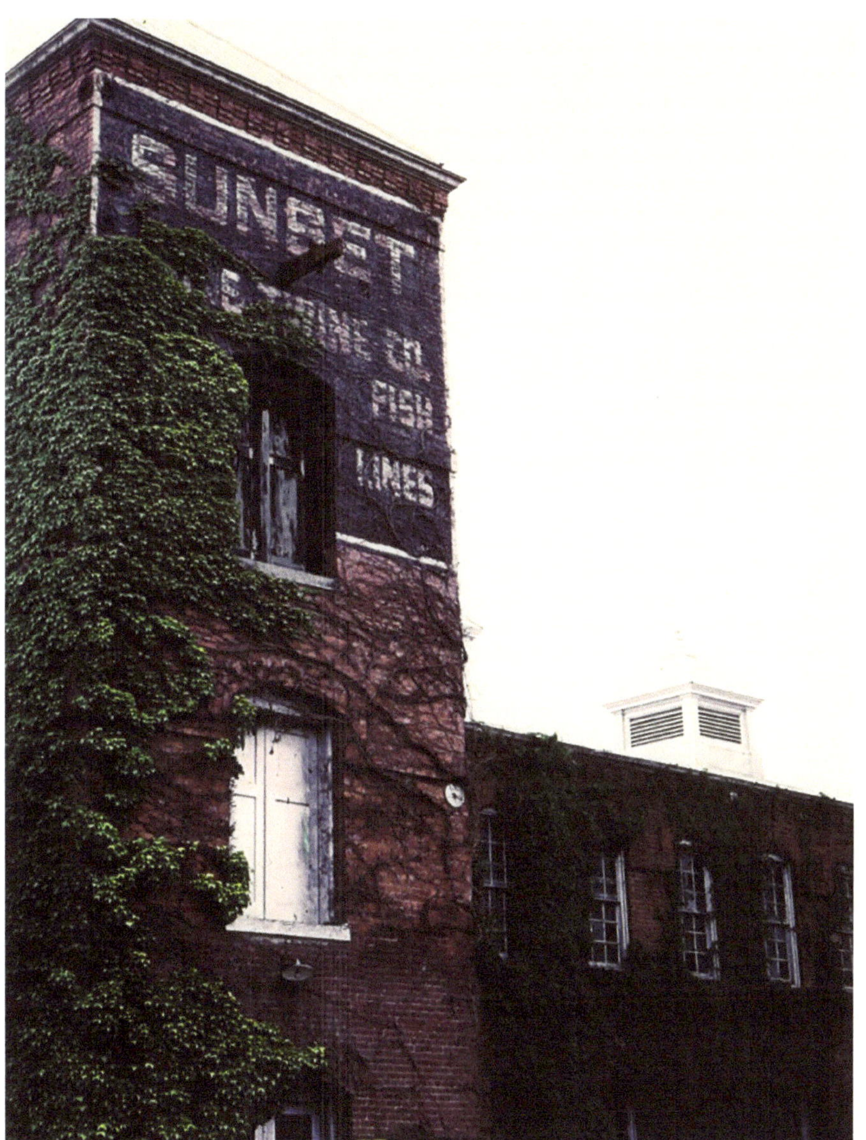

Petaluma, CA

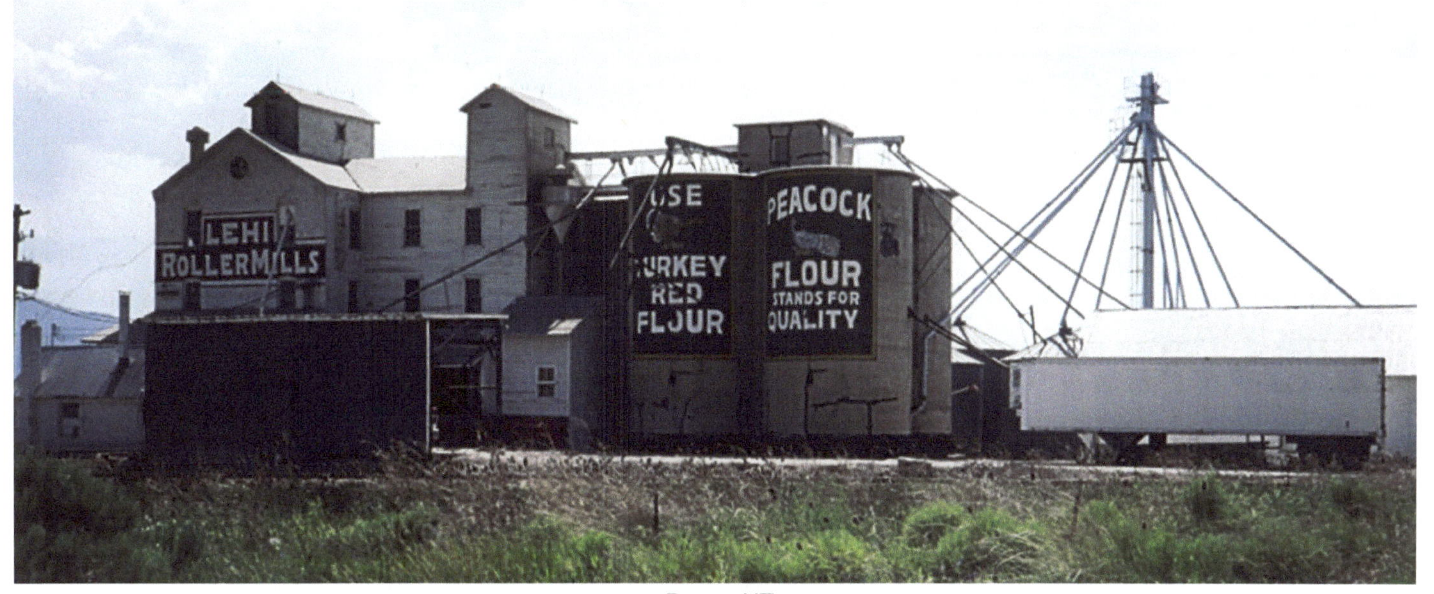

Provo, UT

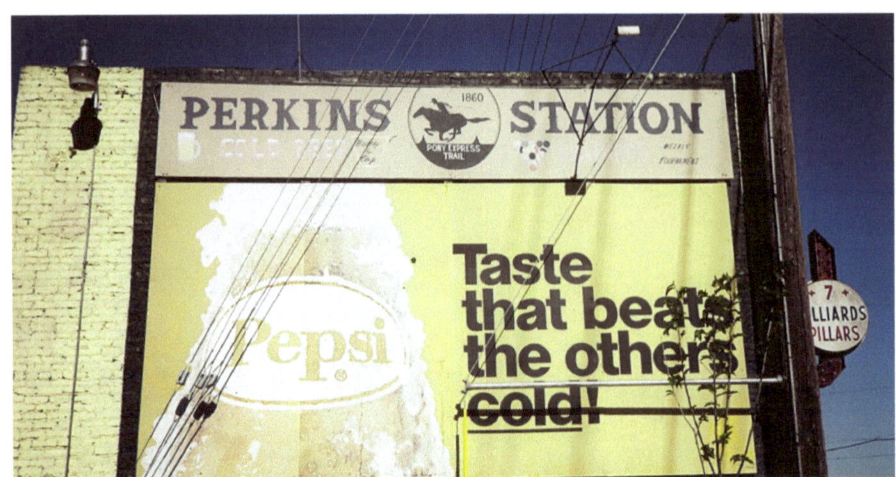

Sacramento, CA

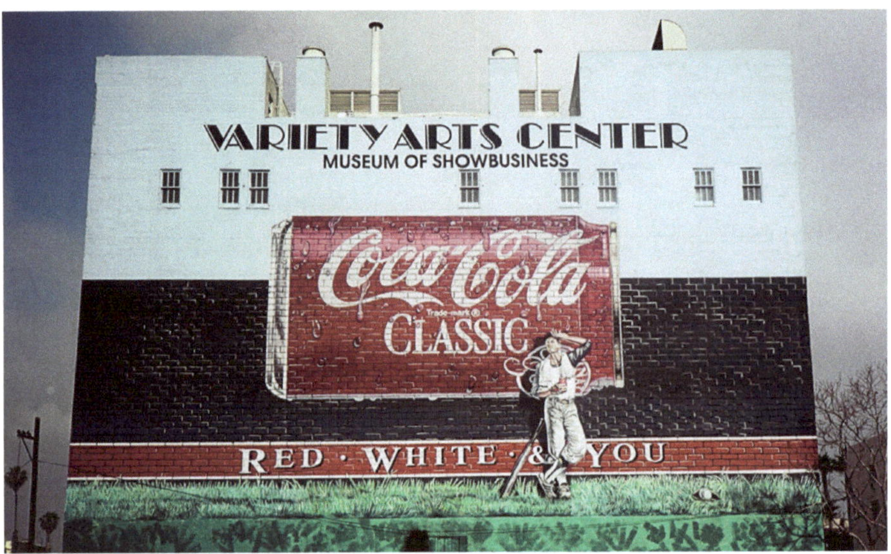

Los Angeles, CA

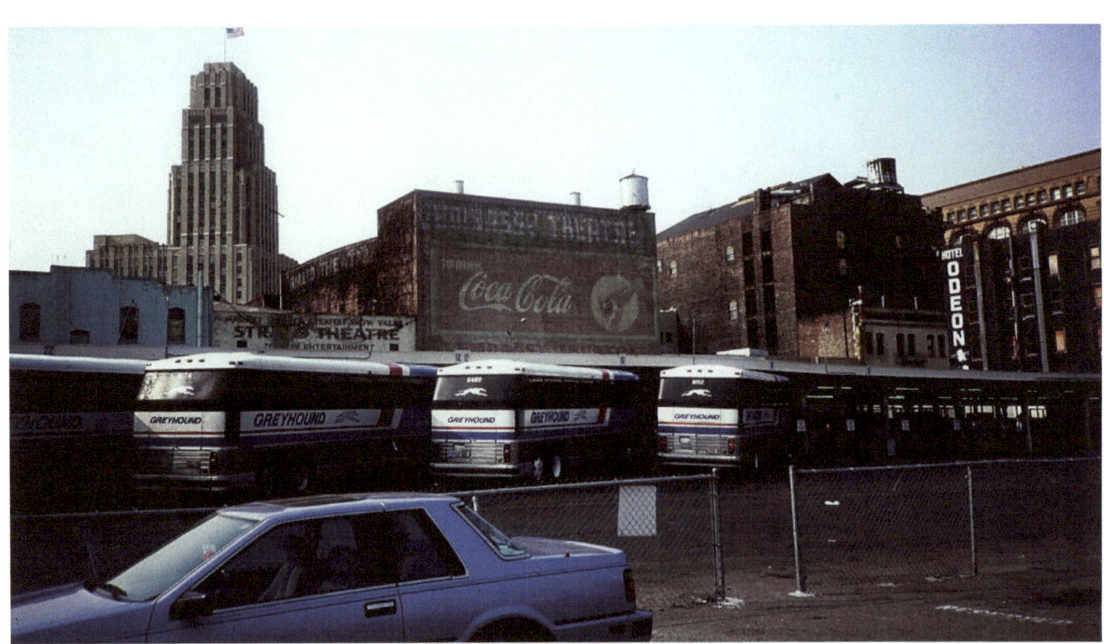

San Francisco, CA

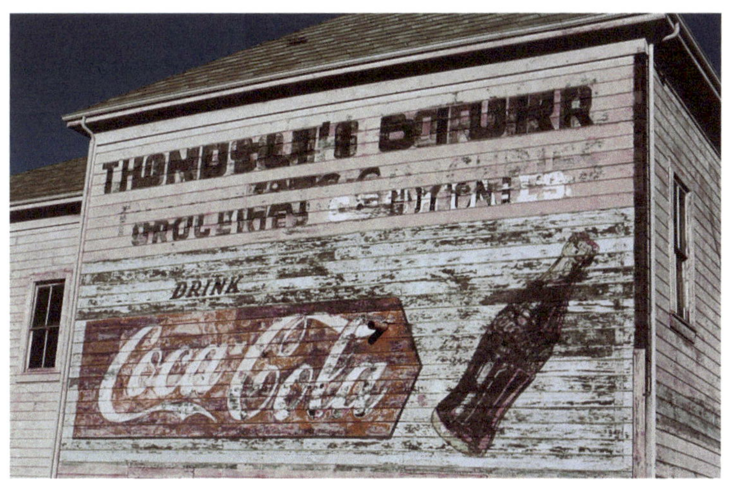

Cordelia, CA

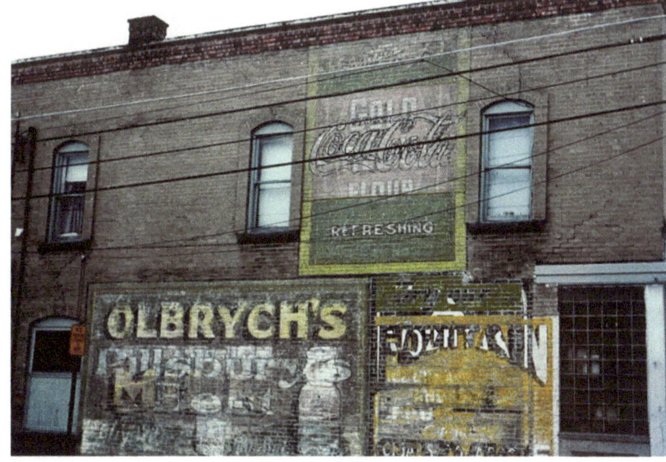

Gloversville, NY

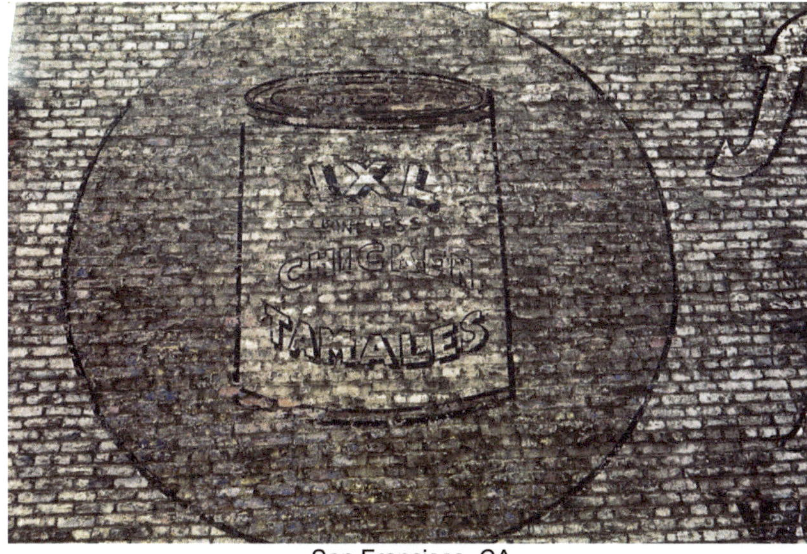

San Francisco, CA

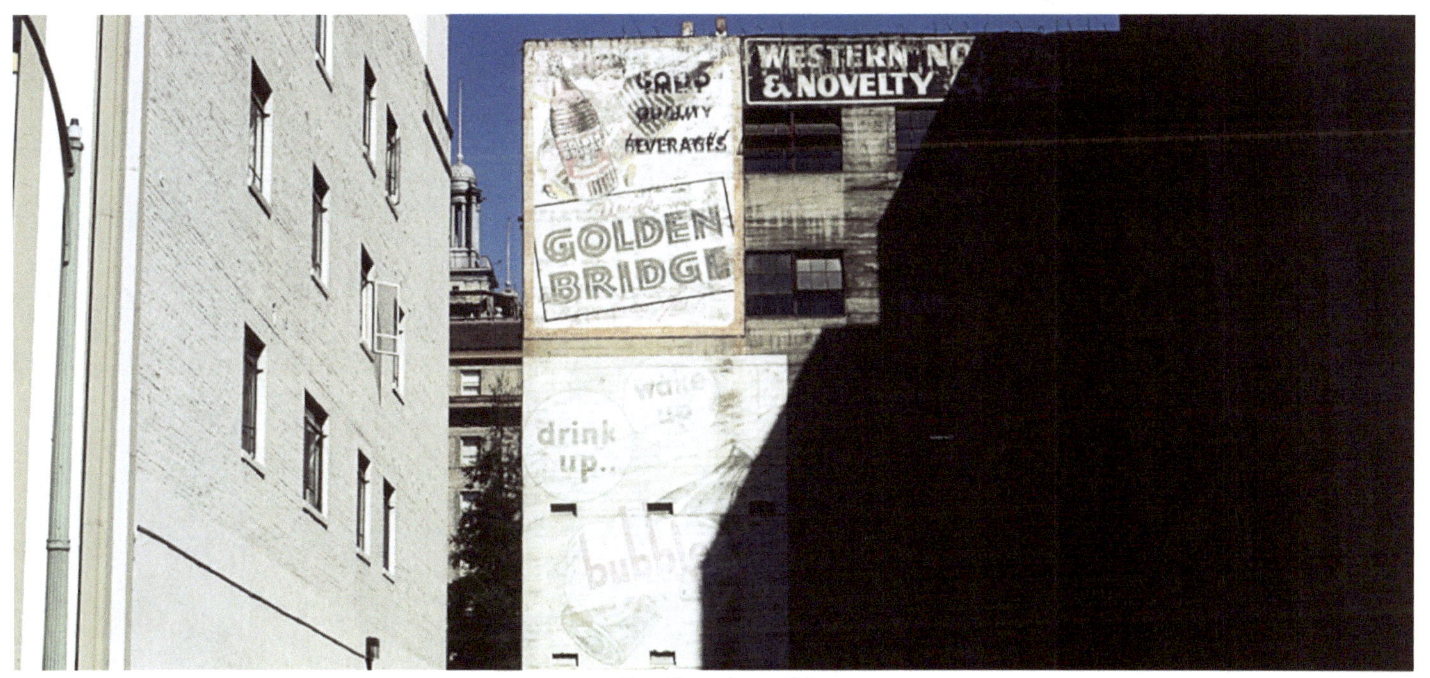

San Francisco, CA

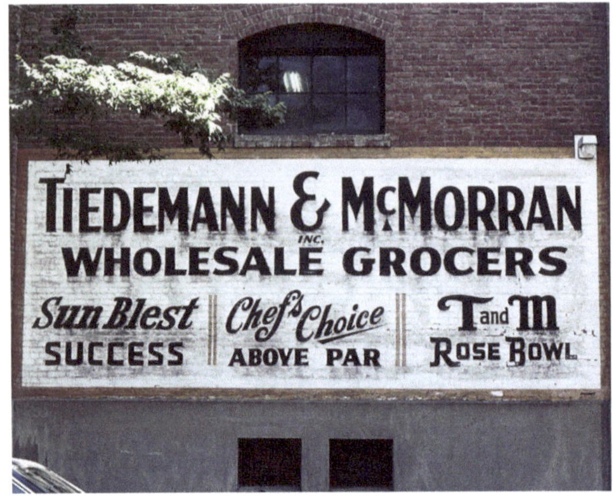

Sacramento, CA

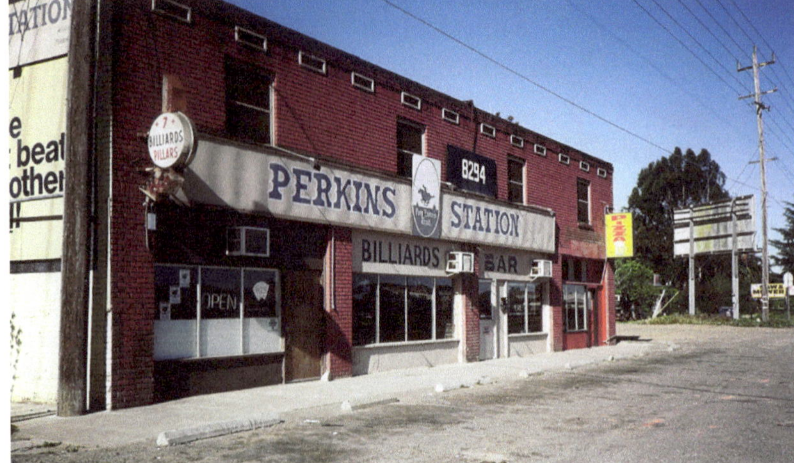

Sacramento, CA

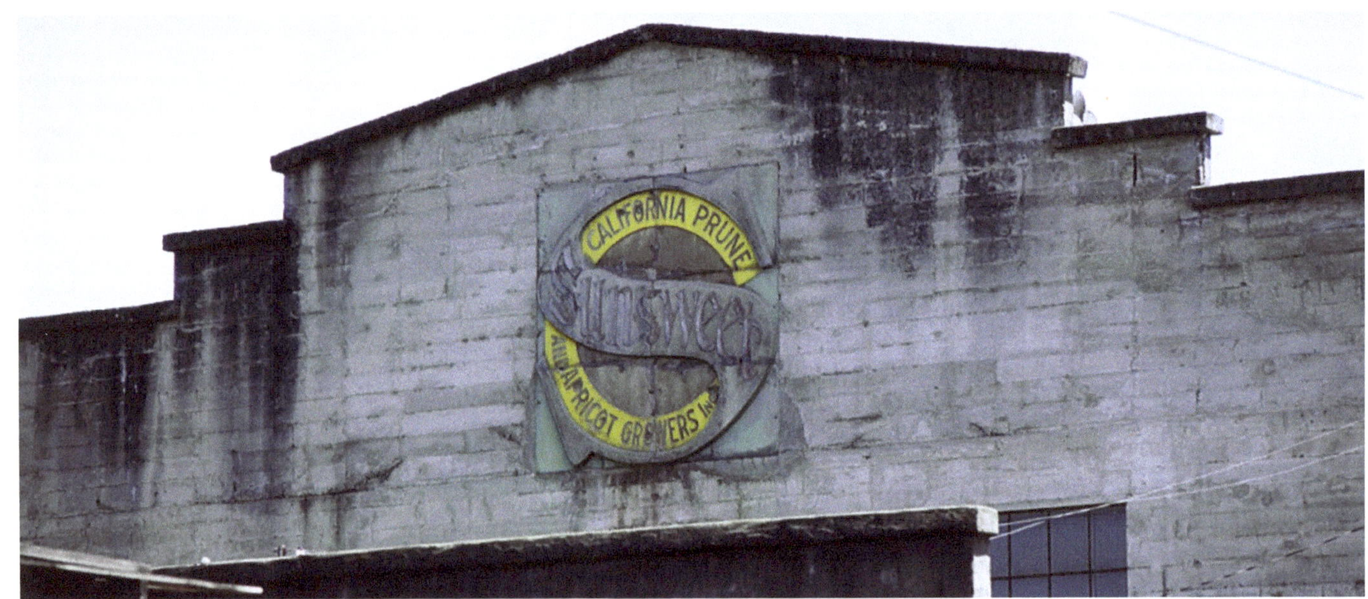

California

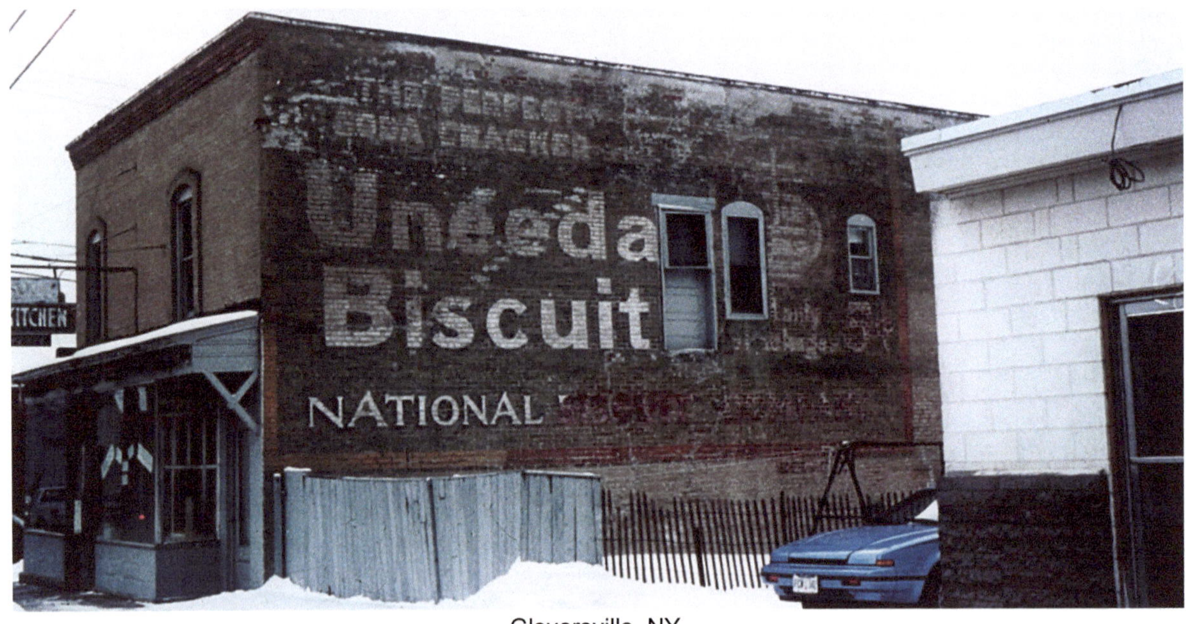

Gloversville, NY

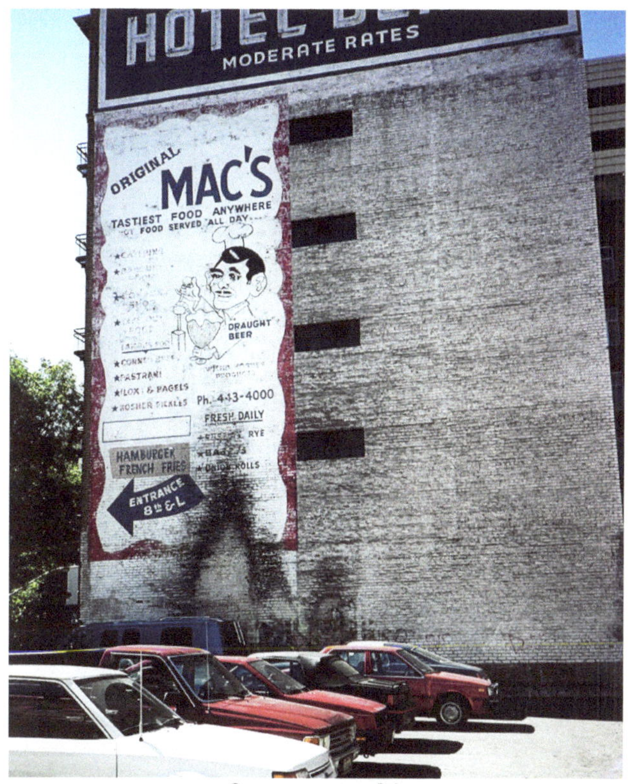

Sacramento, CA

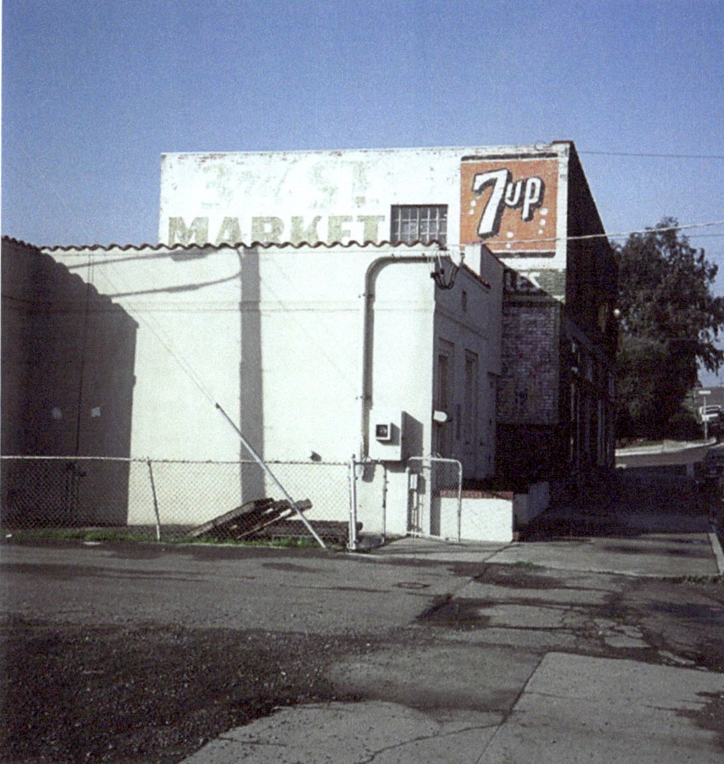

Rodeo, CA

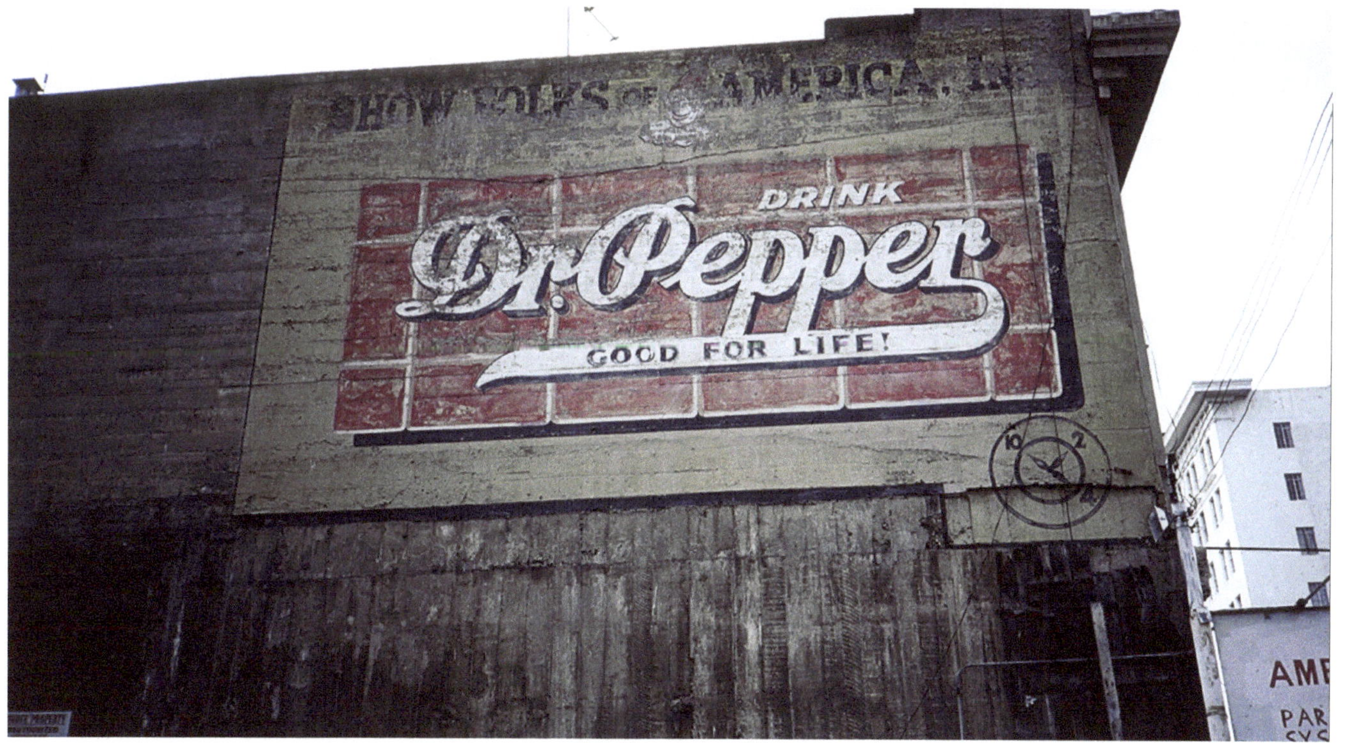

San Francisco, CA

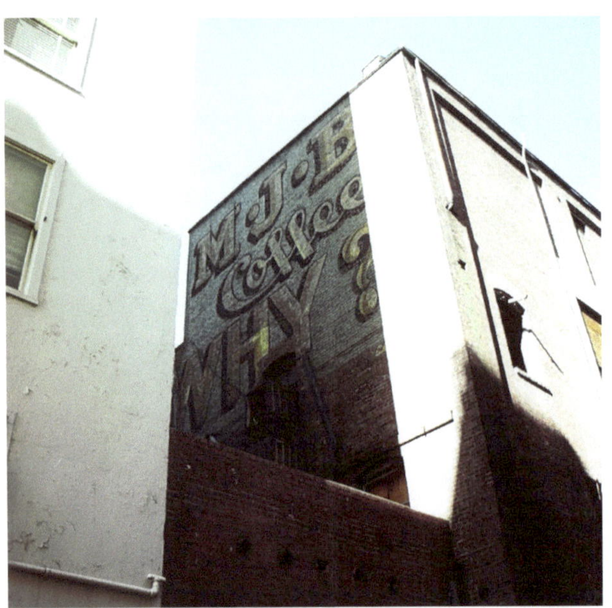

Sacramento, CA

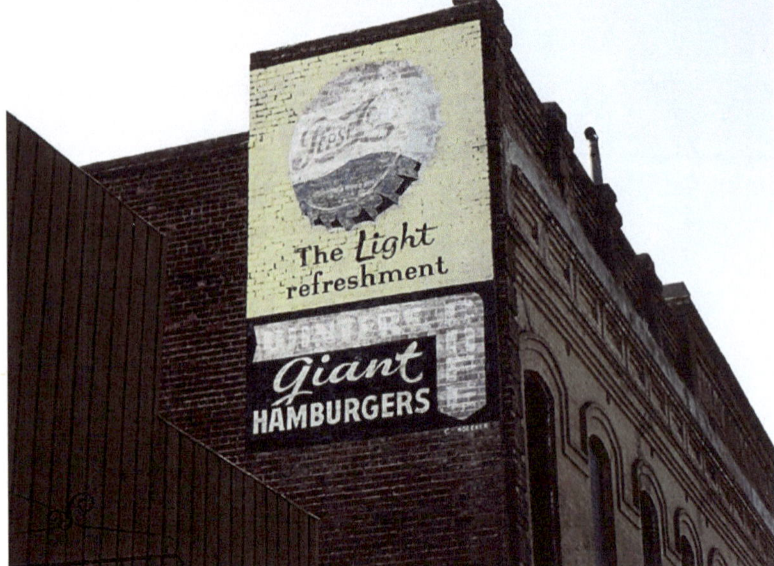

Winters, CA

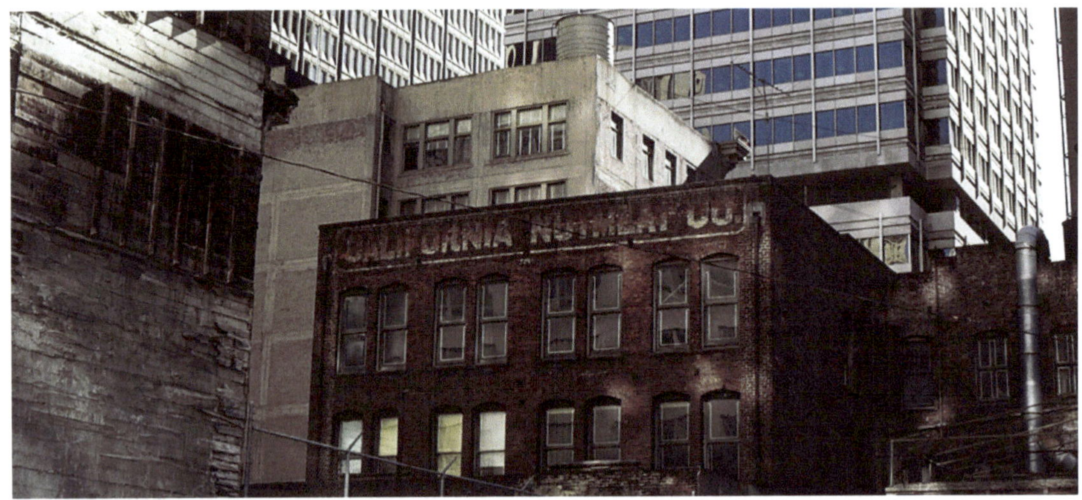

San Francisco, CA

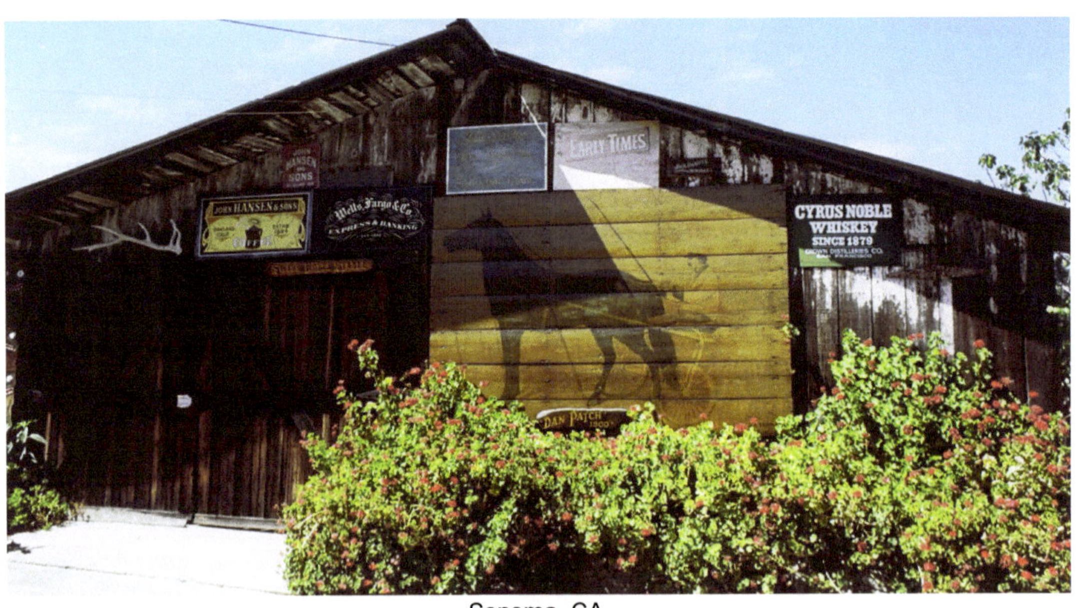

Sonoma, CA

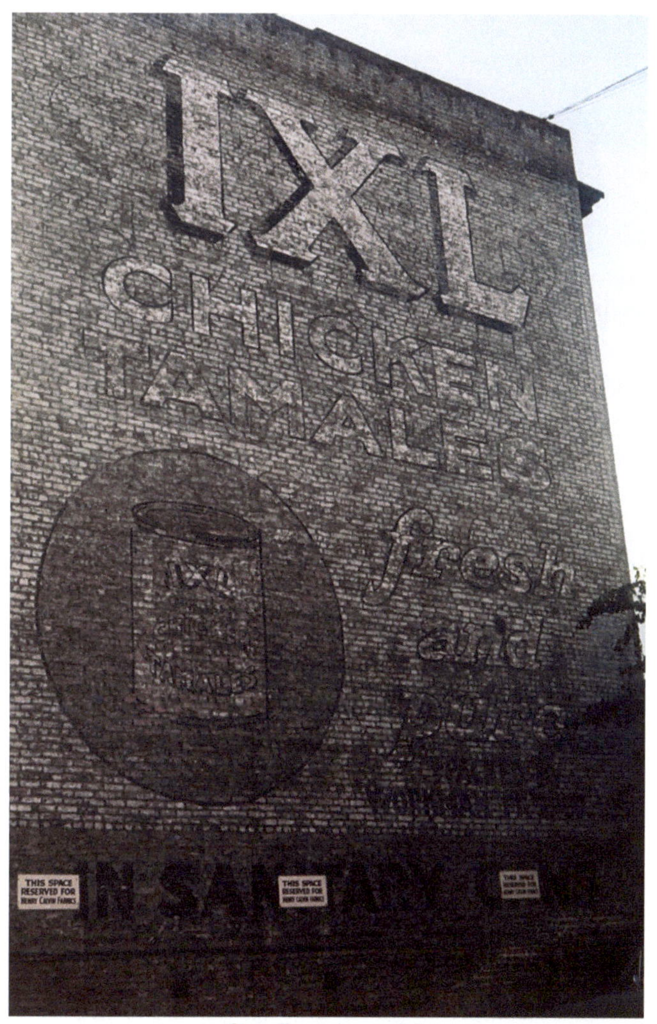

San Francisco, CA

San Francisco, CA

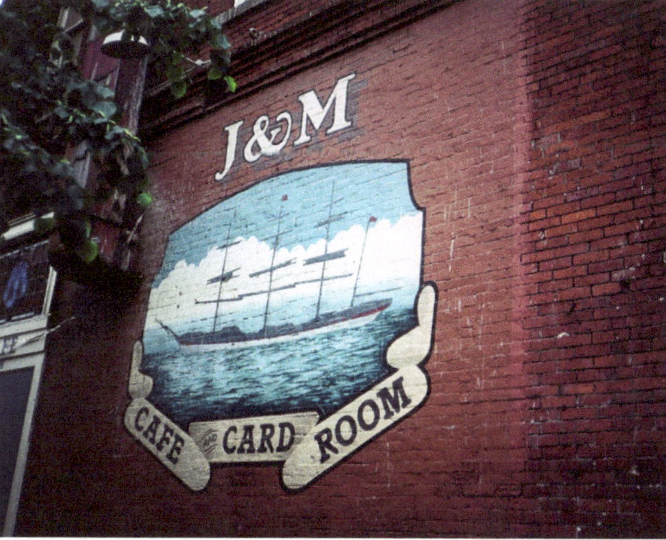

Seattle, WA

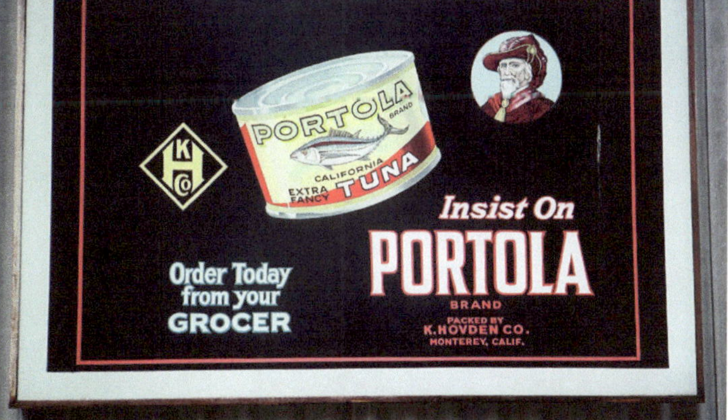

Monterey, CA

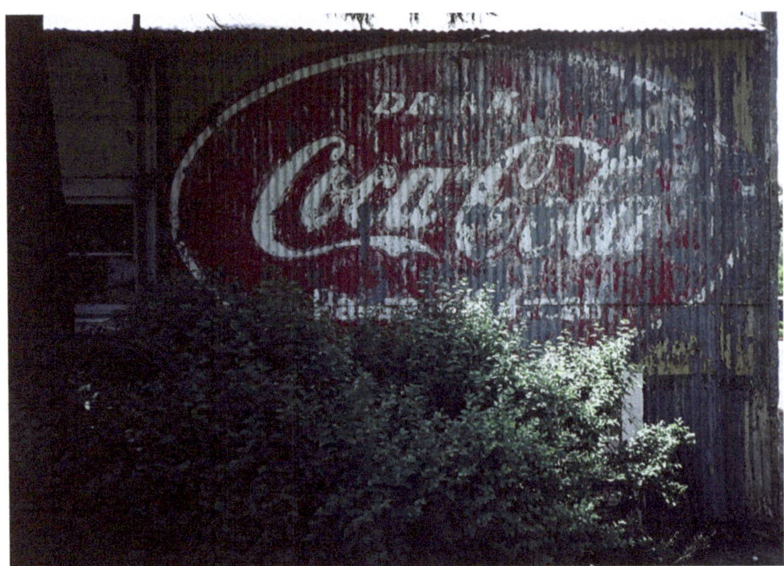

Livermore, CA

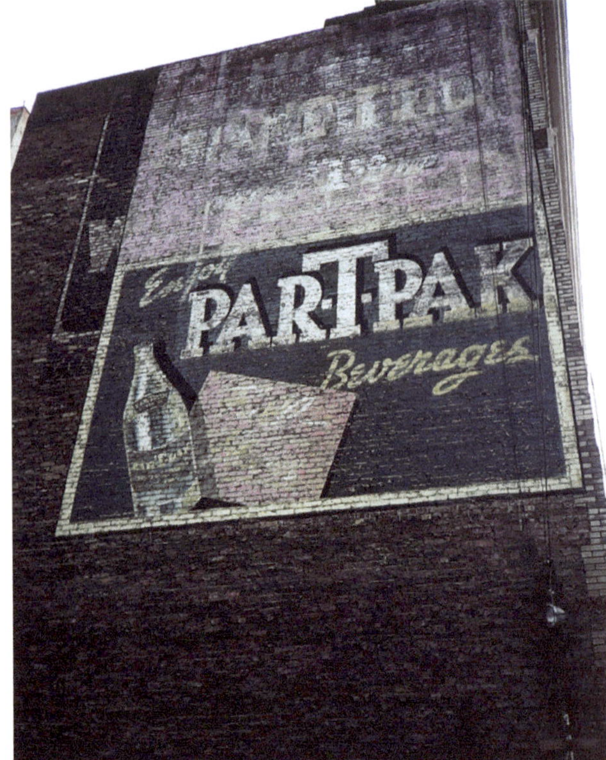

San Francisco, CA

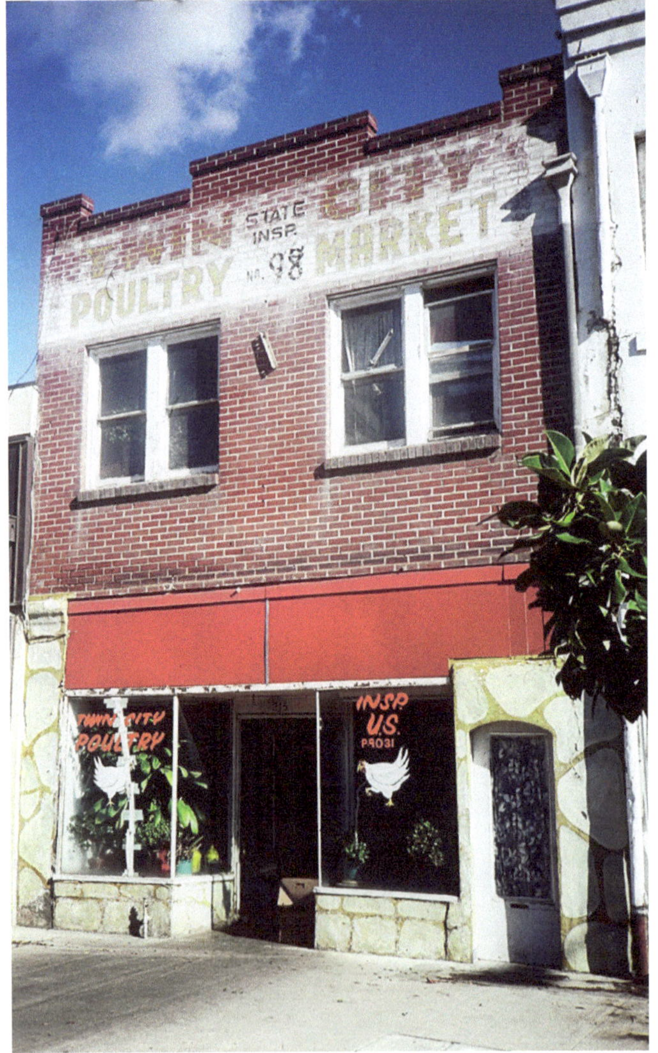

Marysville, CA

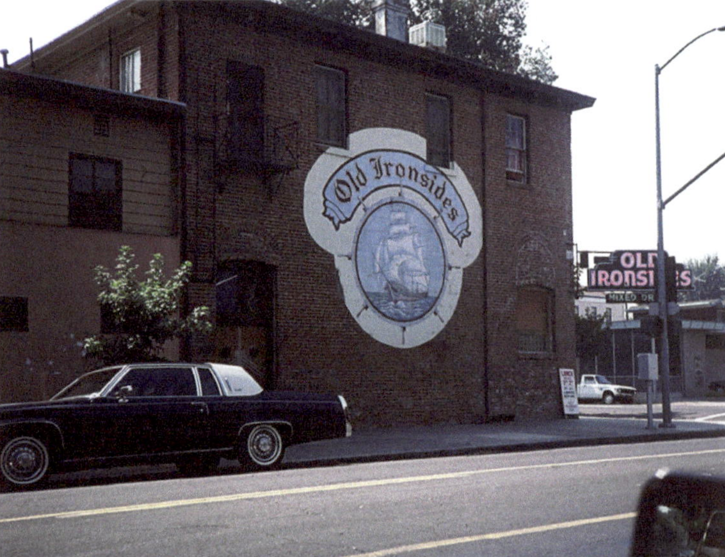

Sacramento, CA

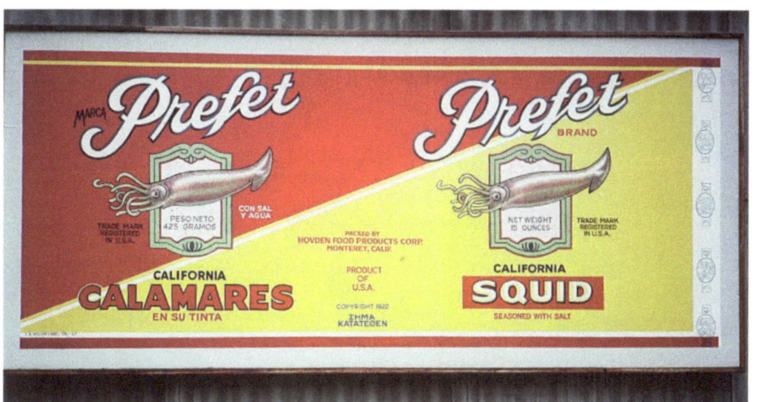

Monterey, CA

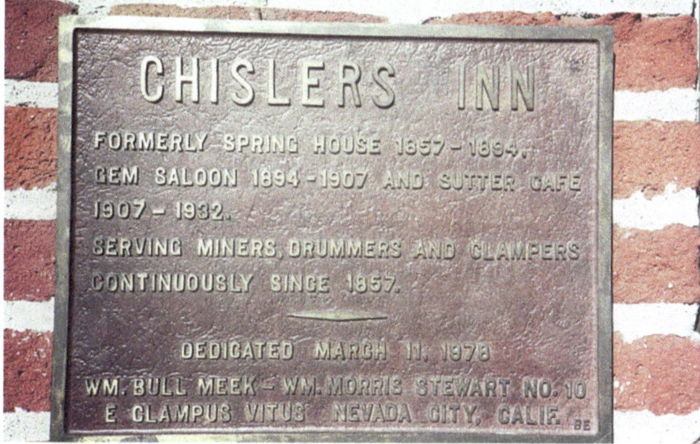

Nevada City, CA

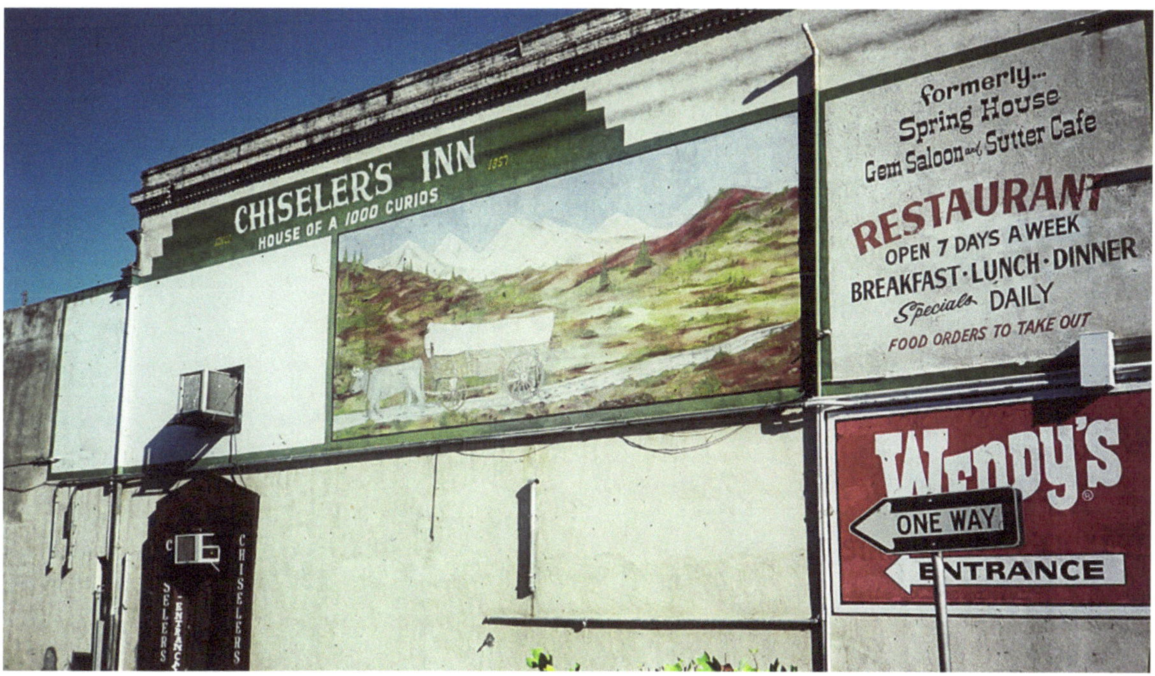

Nevada City, CA

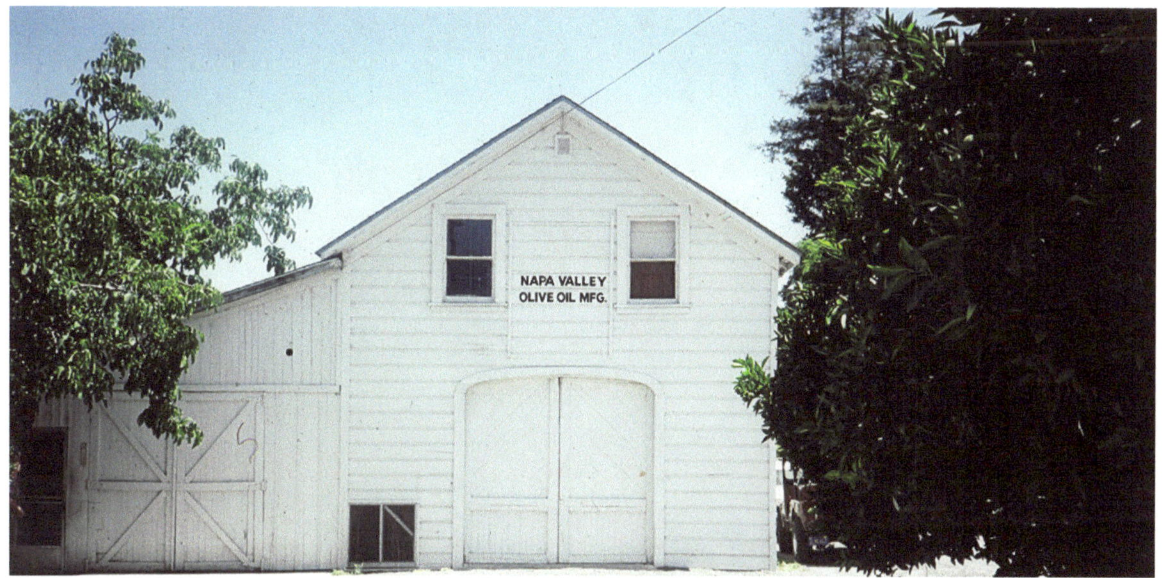

St. Helena, CA

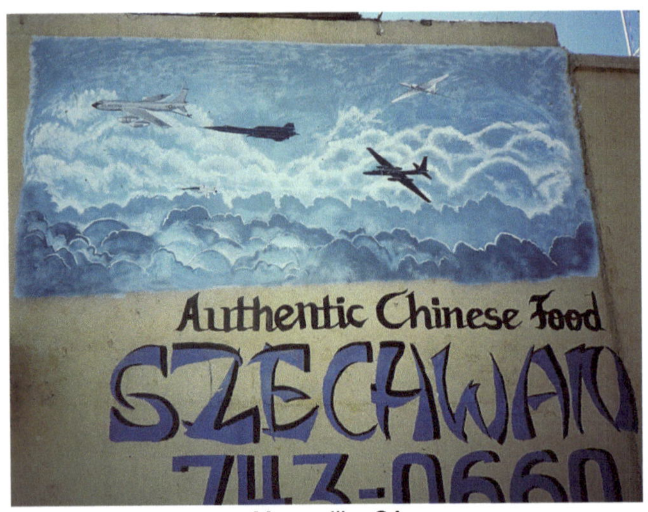

Marysville, CA

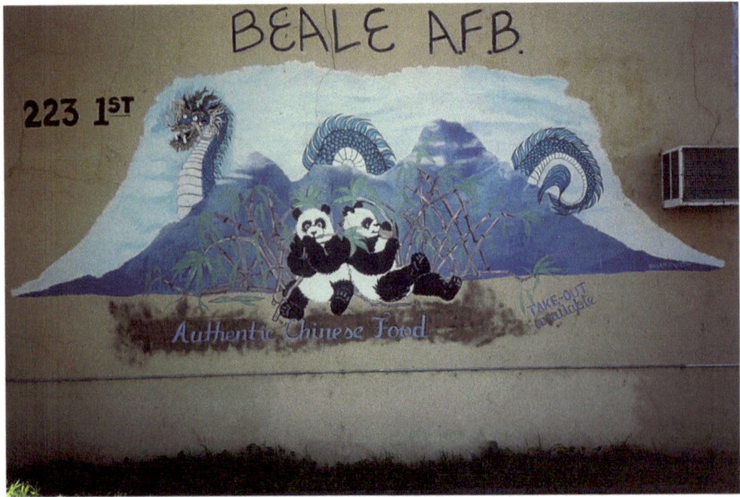

Marysville, CA

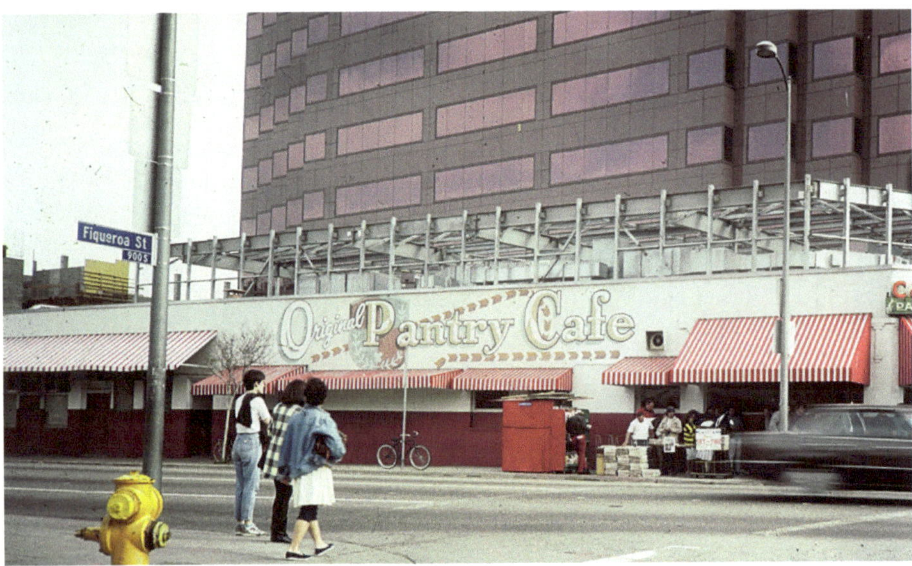

Los Angeles, CA

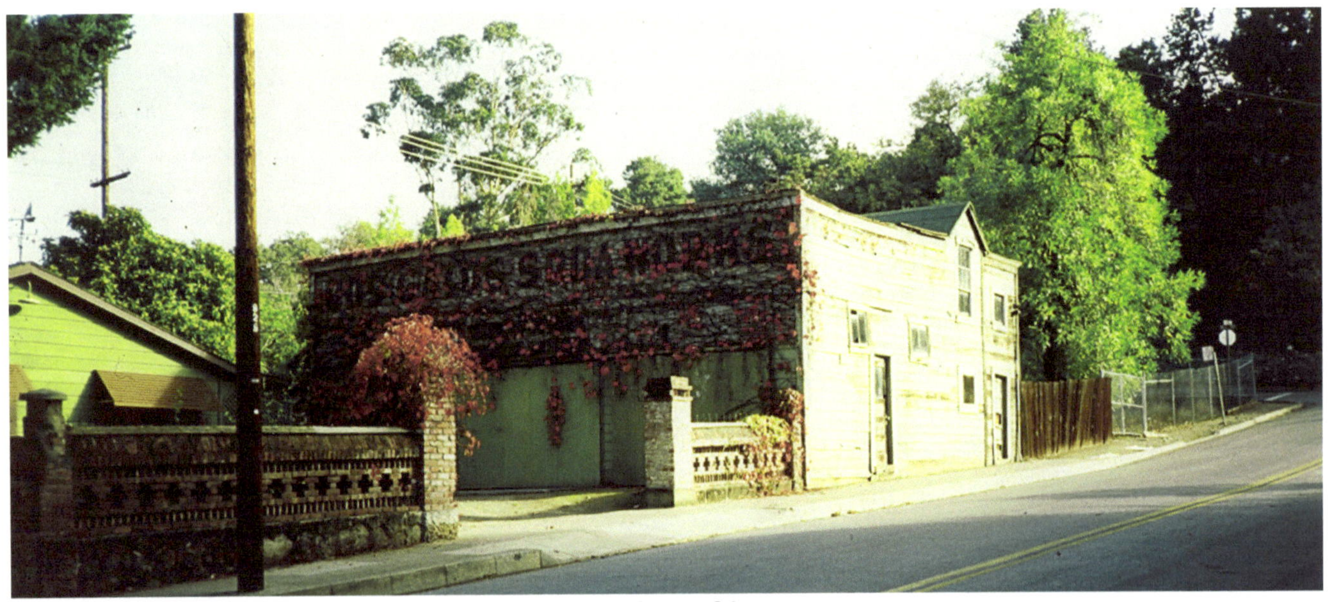

Los Gatos, CA

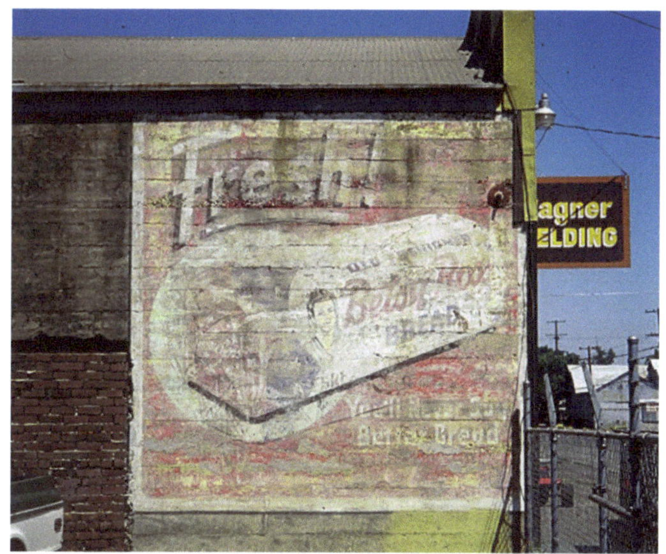

Sacramento, CA

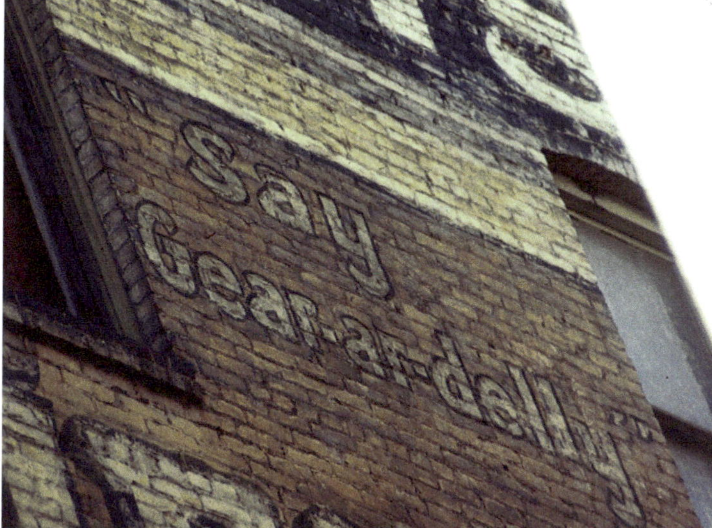

Sacramento, CA

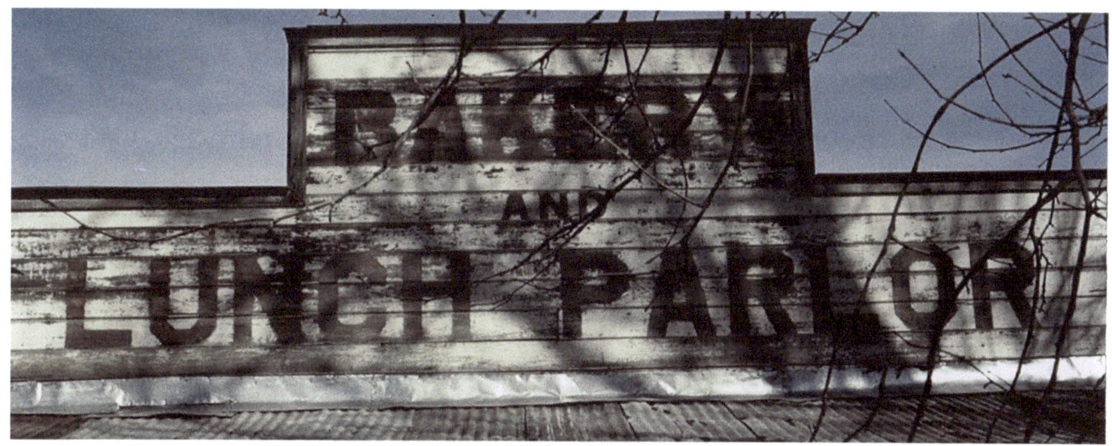

Locke, CA

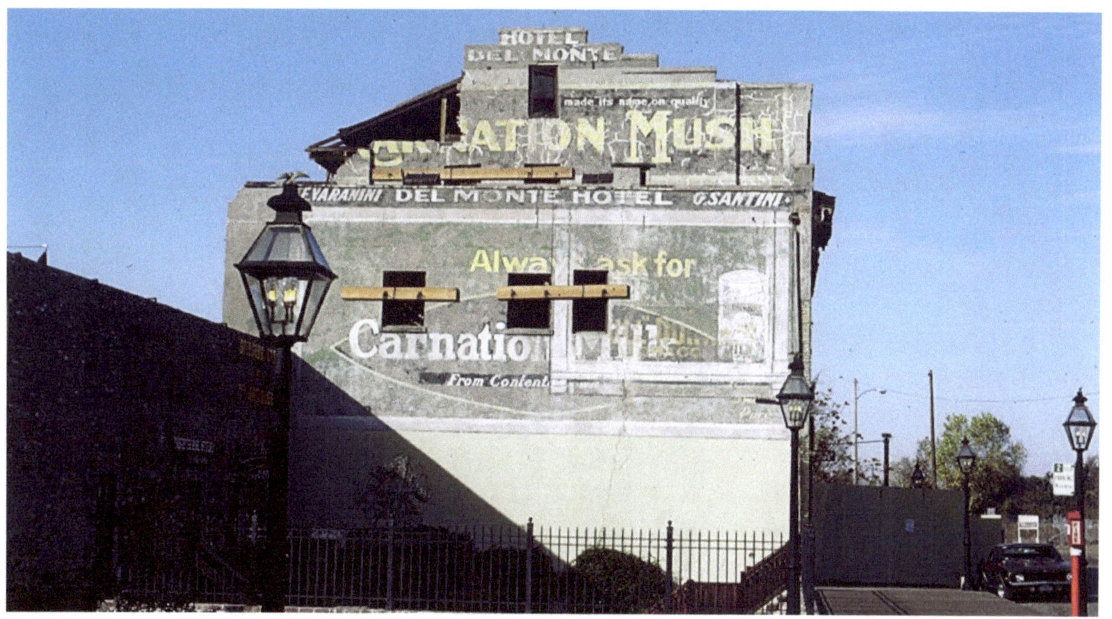

Sacramento, CA

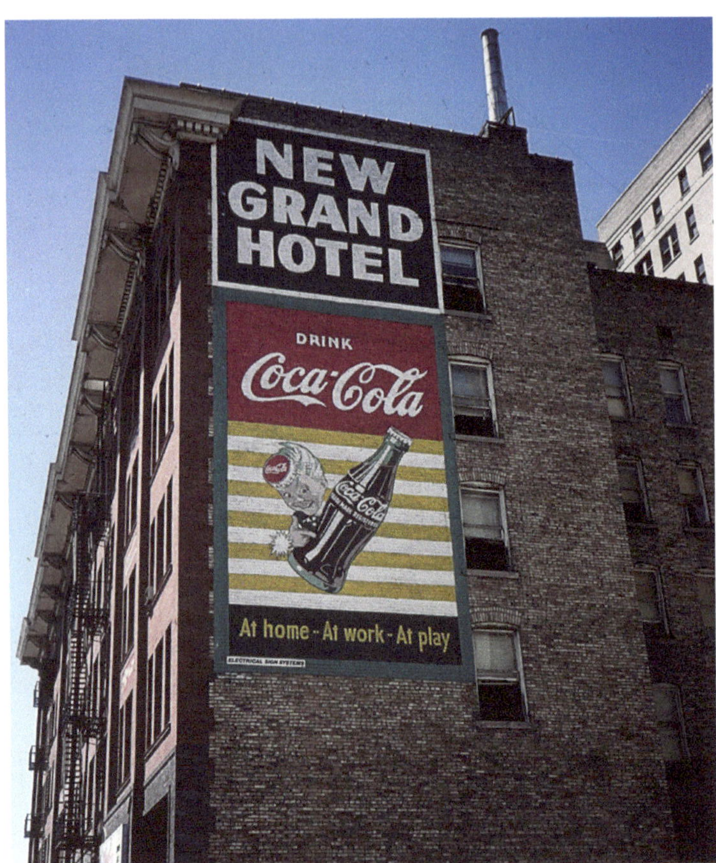

Salt Lake City, UT

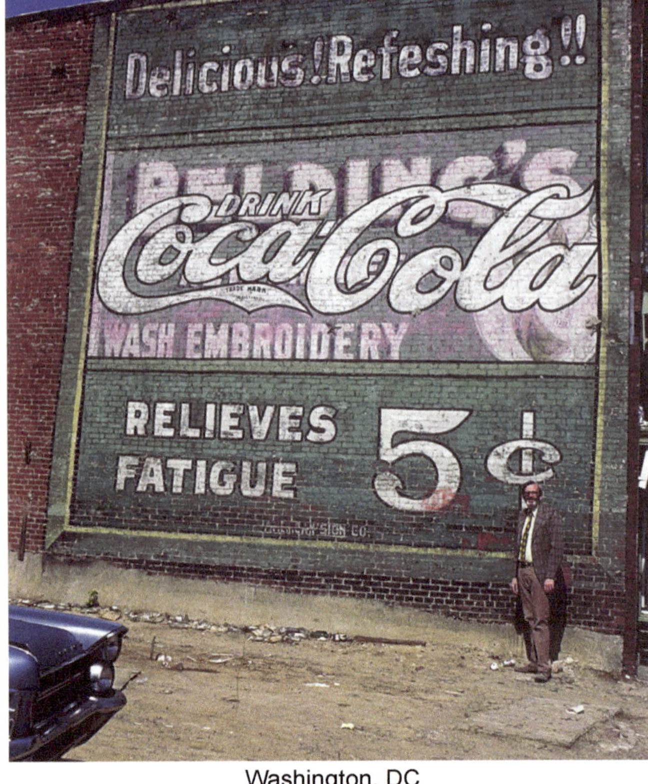

Washington, DC

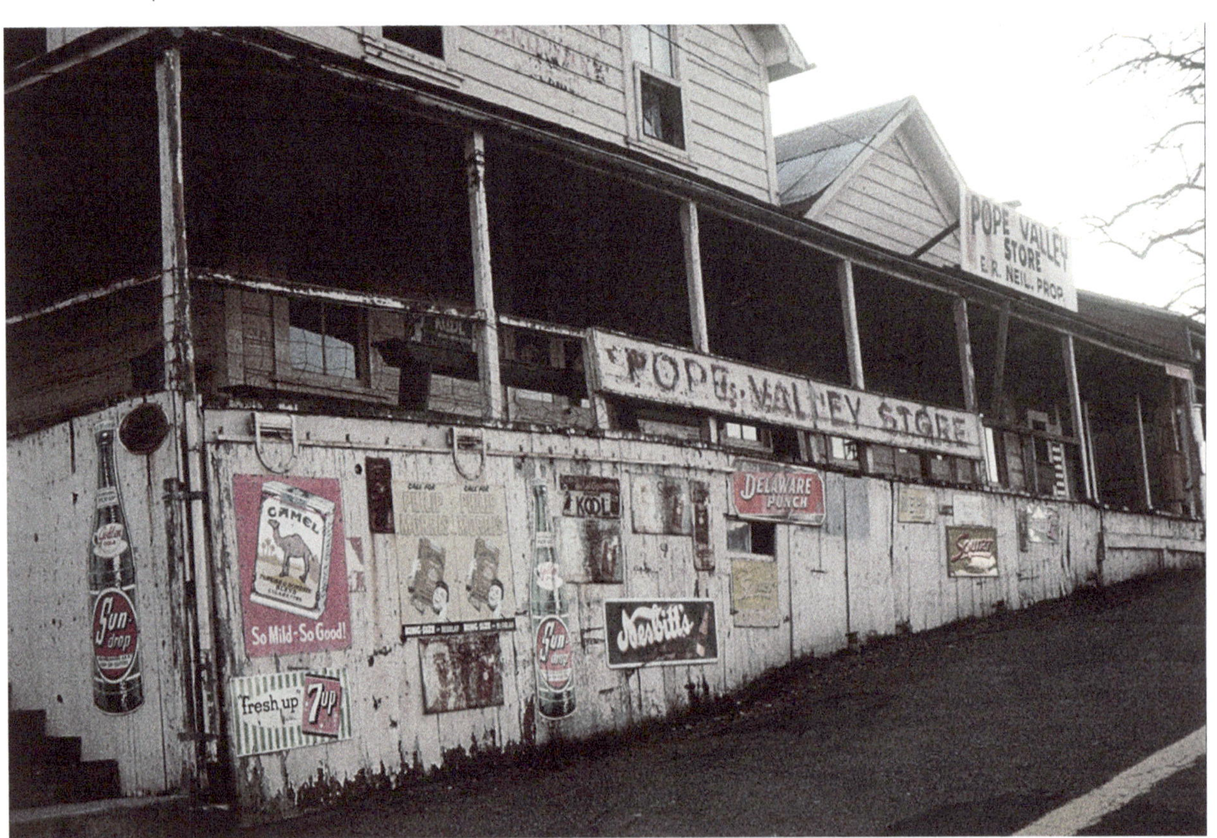

Pope Valley, CA

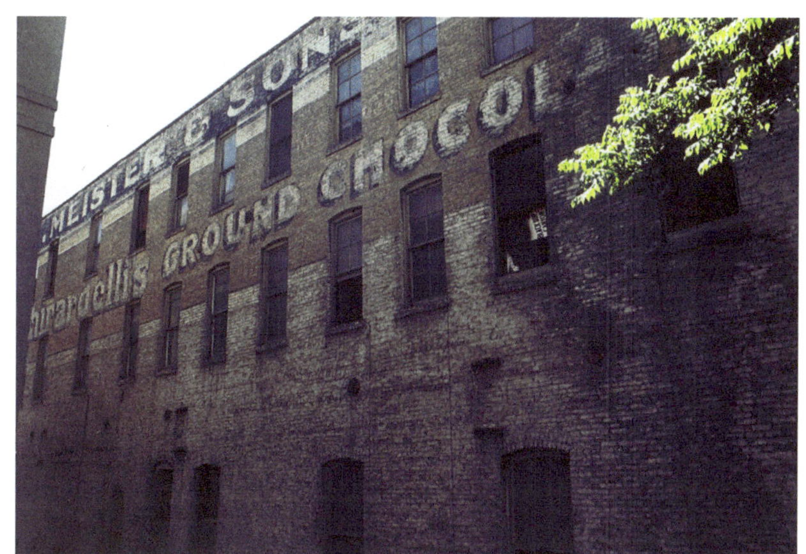

Sacramento, CA

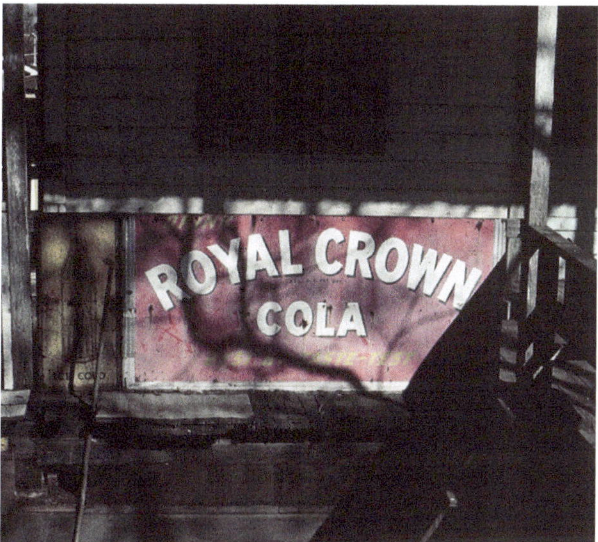

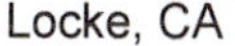

Locke, CA

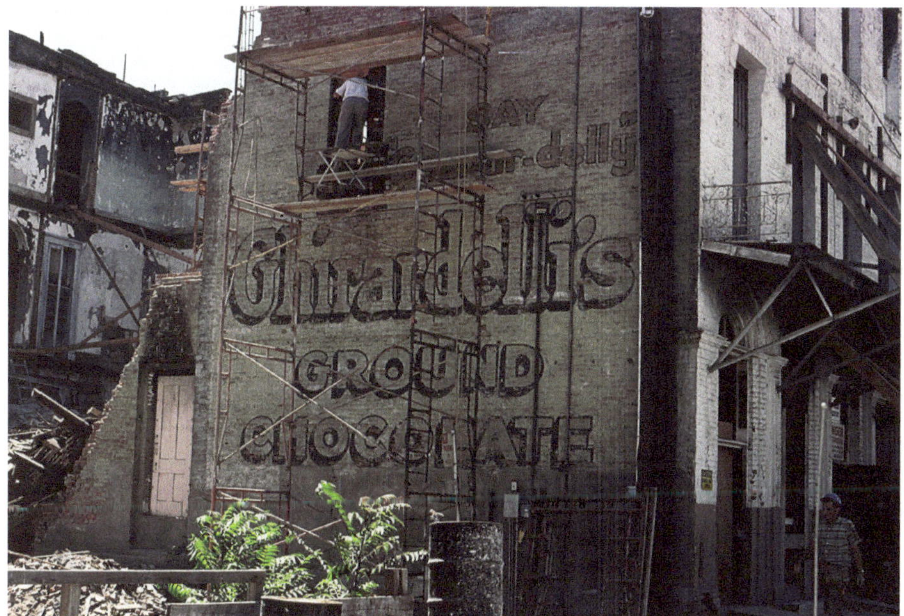

Sacramento, CA

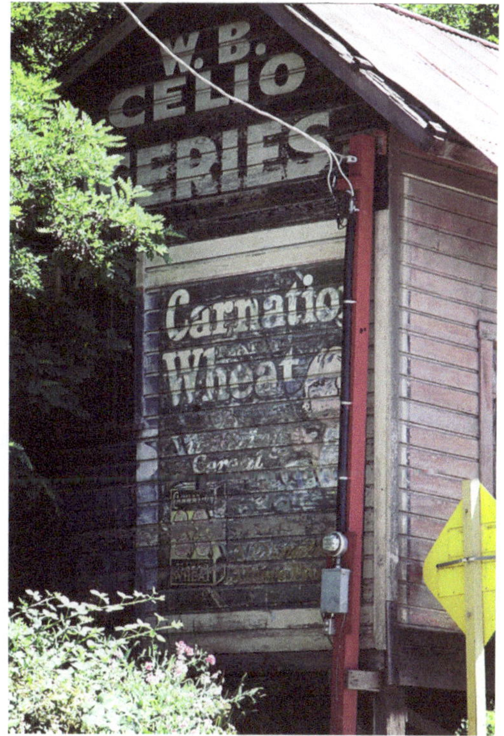

Nevada City, CA

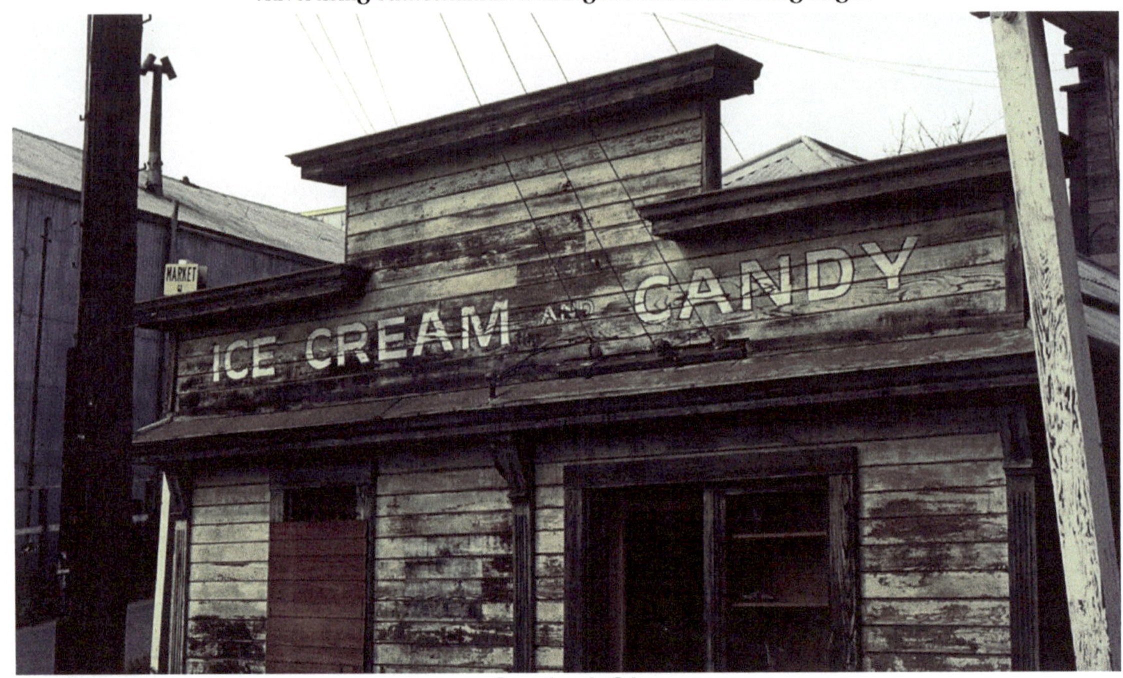

Courtland, CA

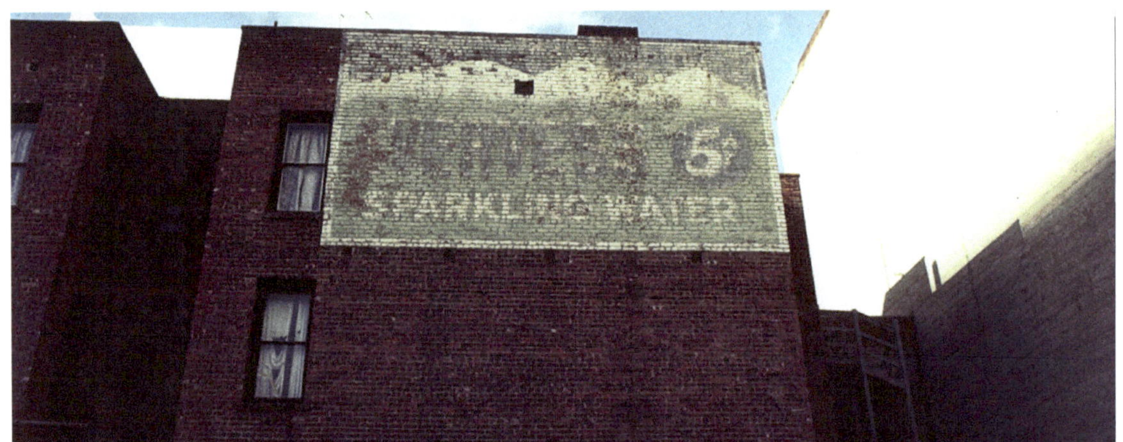

San Francisco, CA

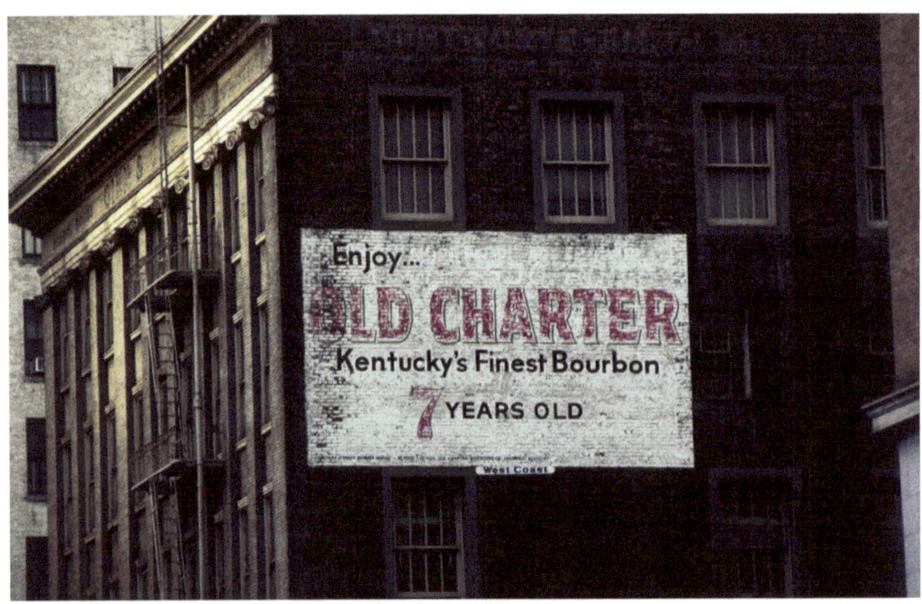

San Francisco, CA

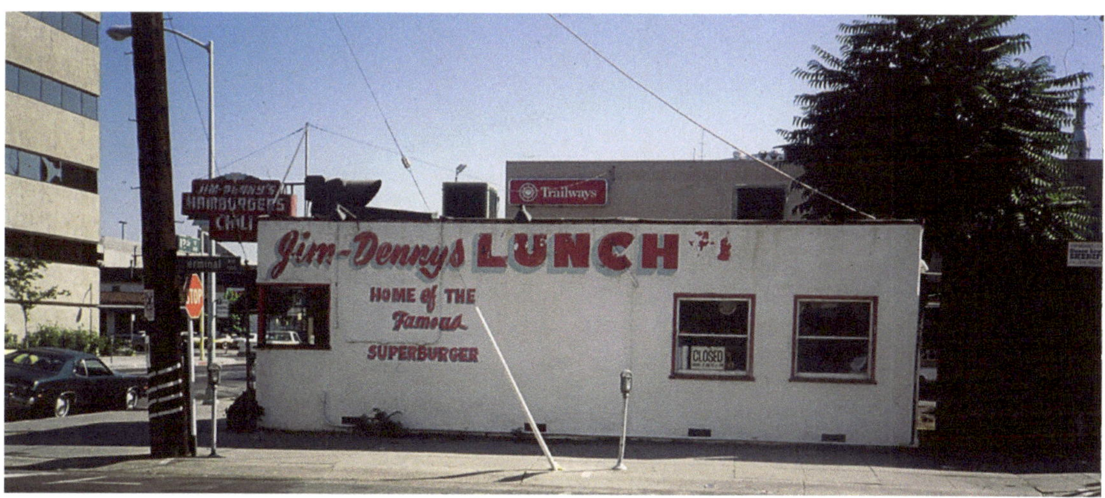

Sacramento, CA

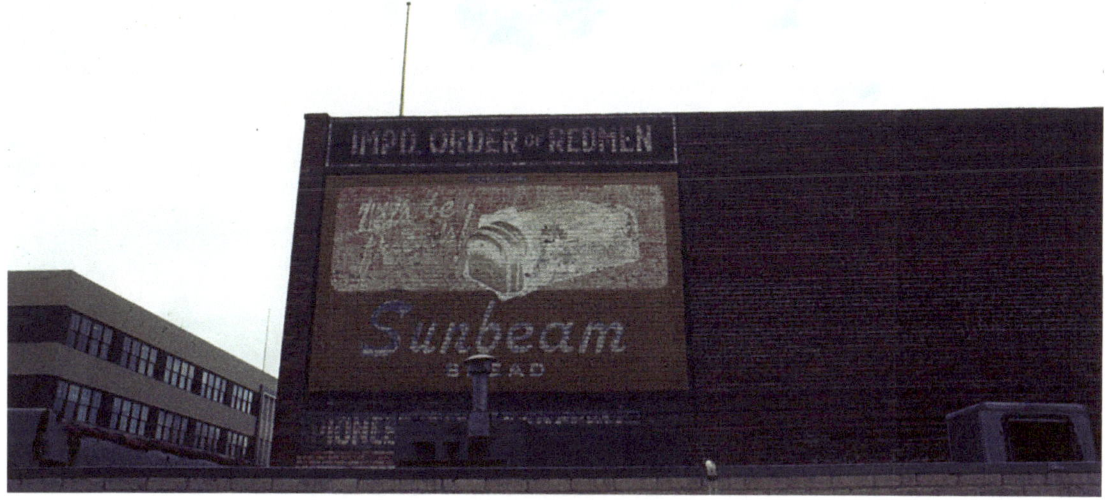

Sacramento, CA

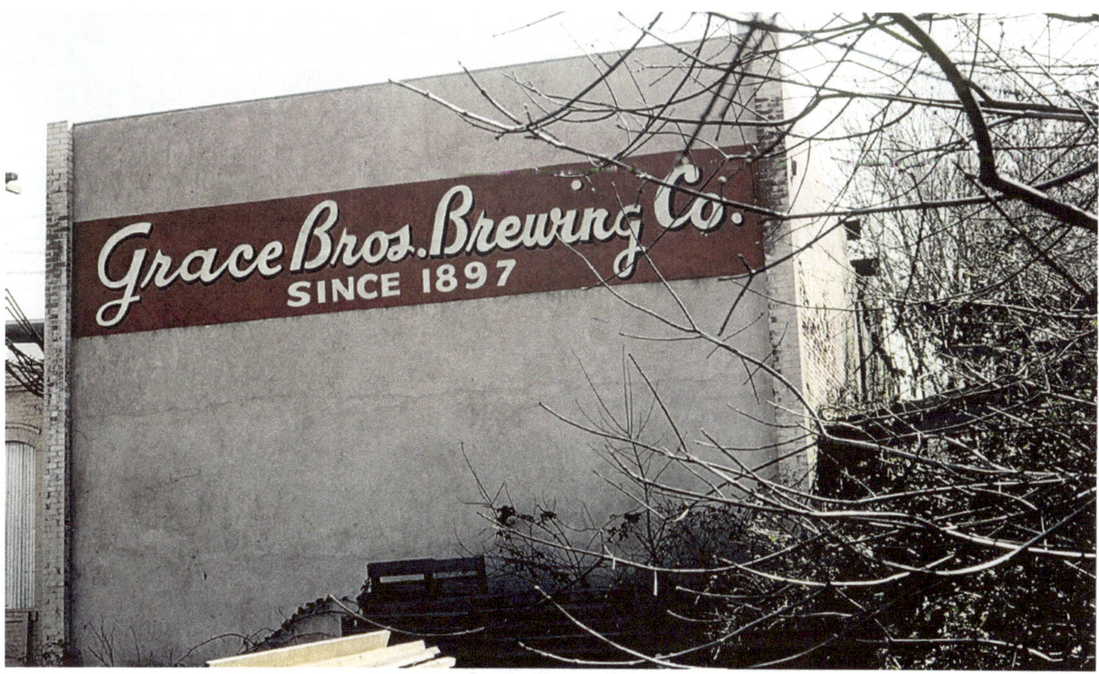

Santa Rosa, CA

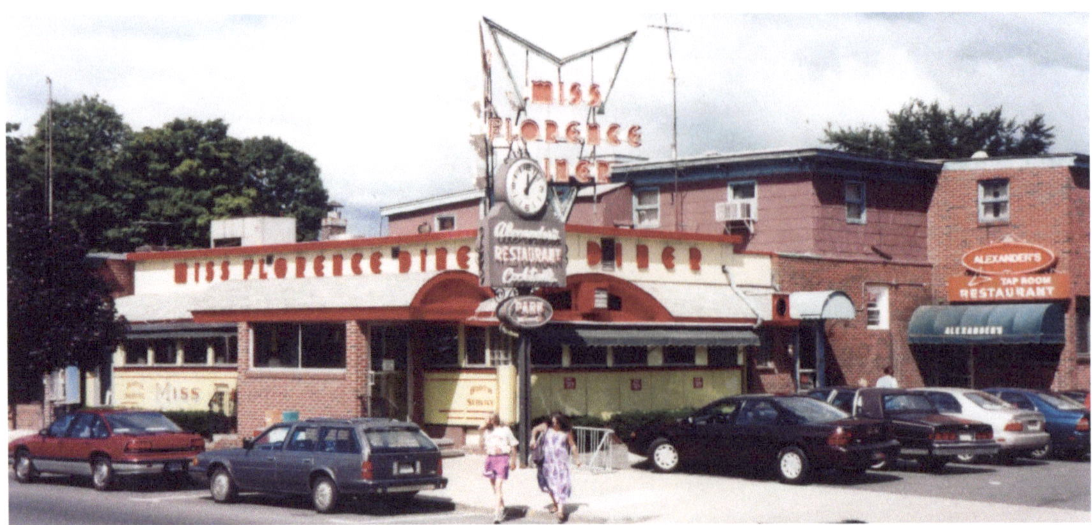

Florence, MA

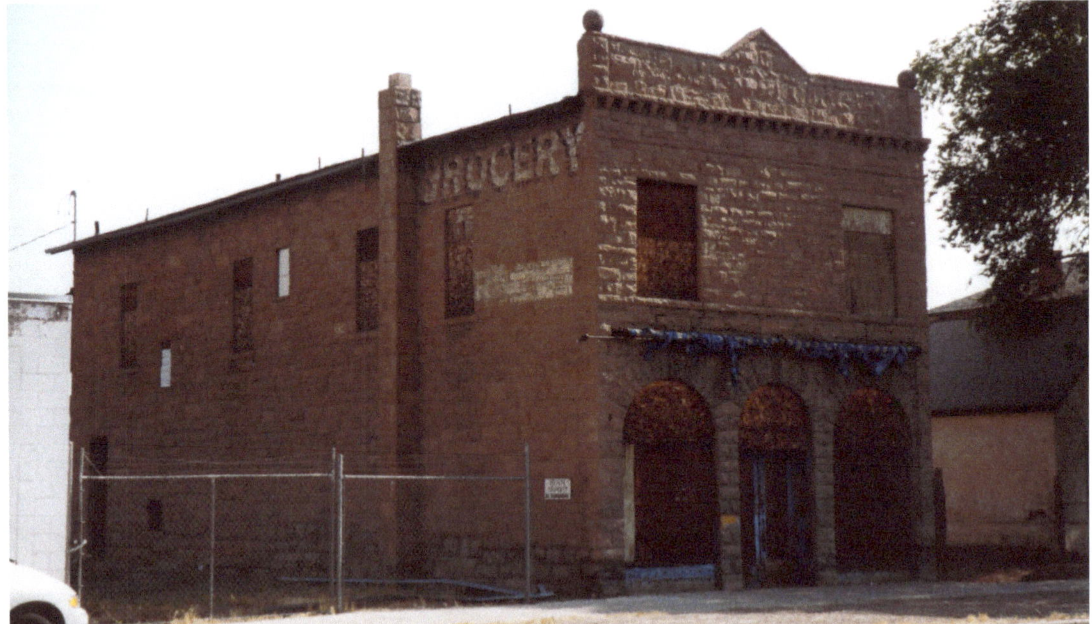

Grand Junction, CO

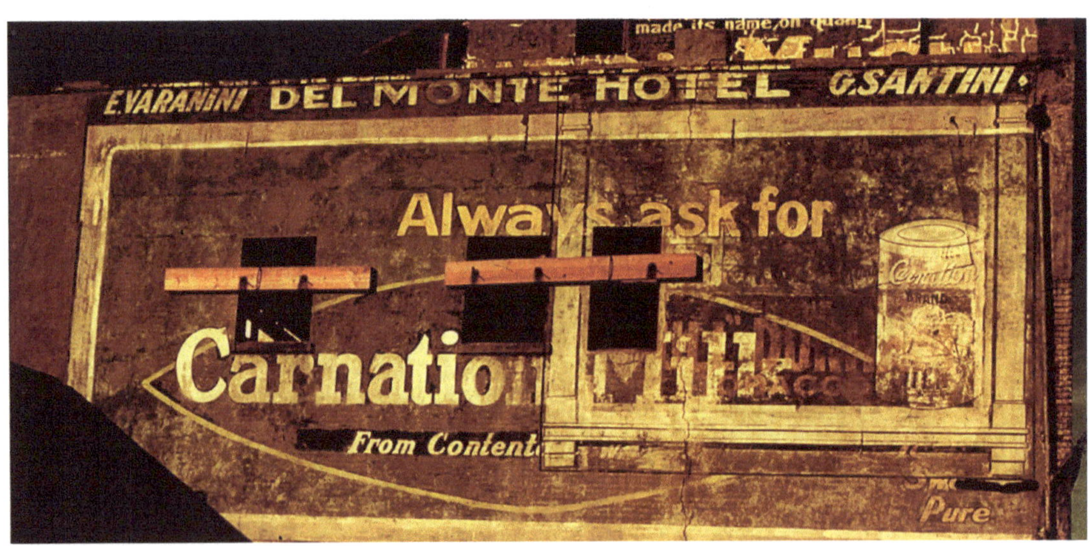

Monterey, CA

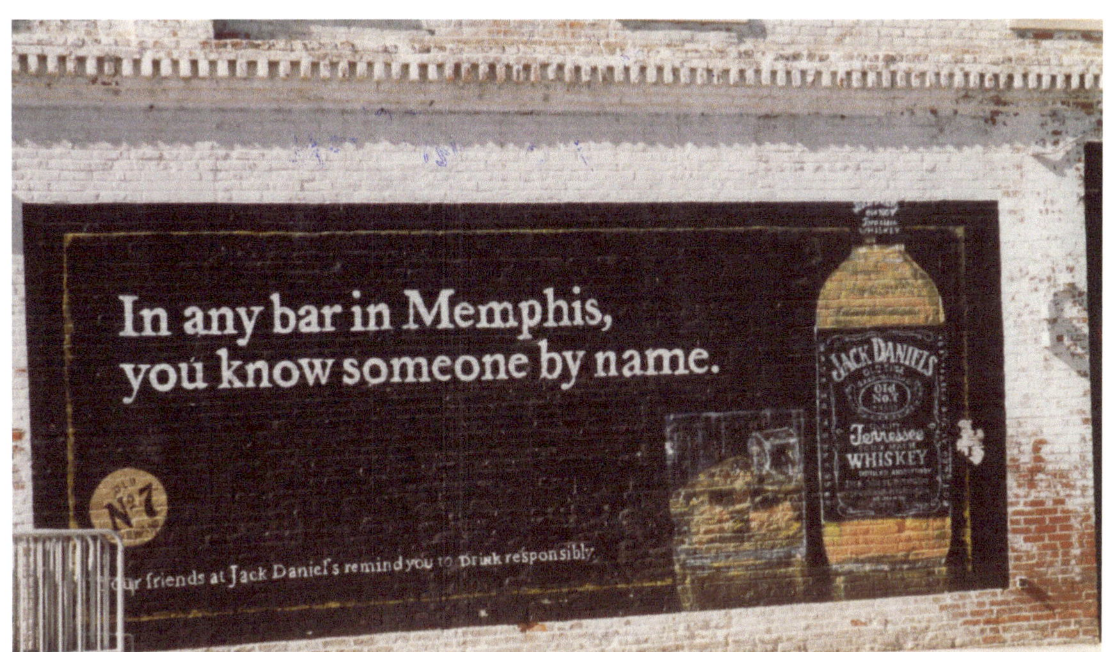

Memphis, TN

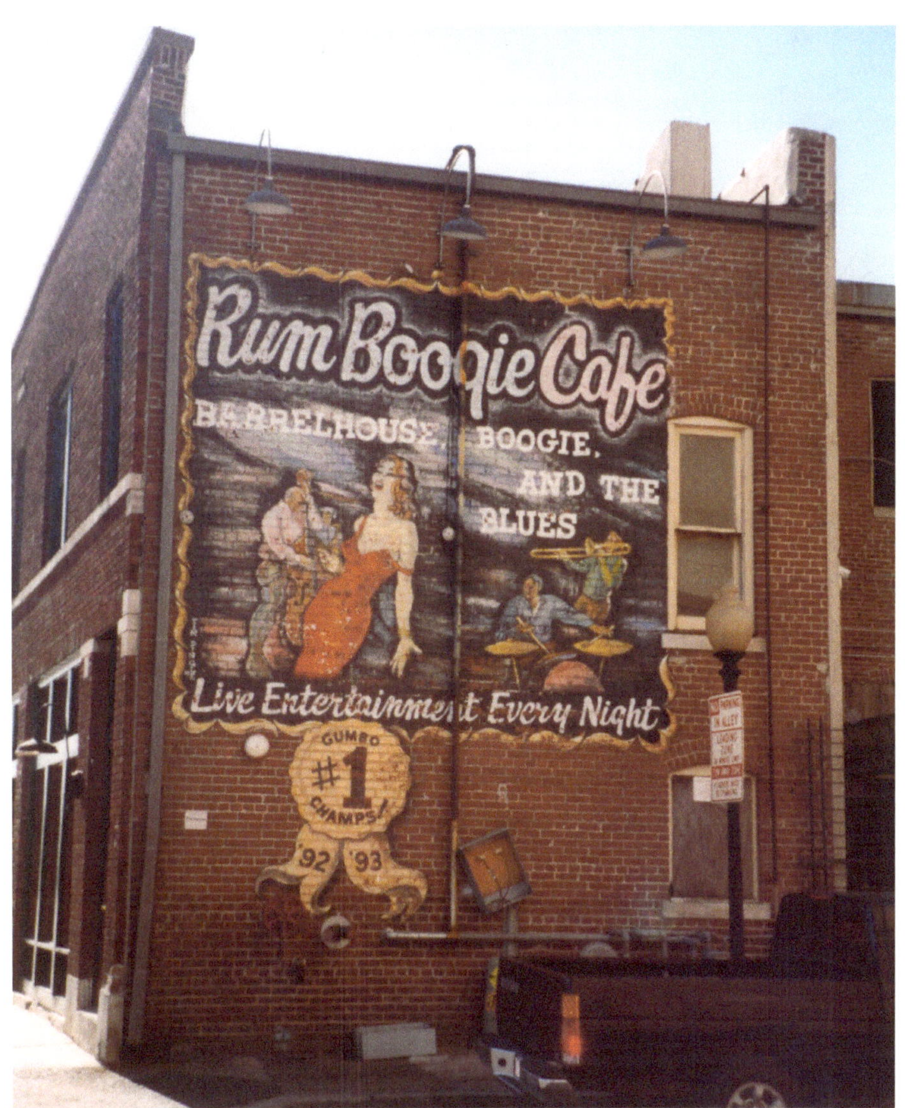

Memphis, TN

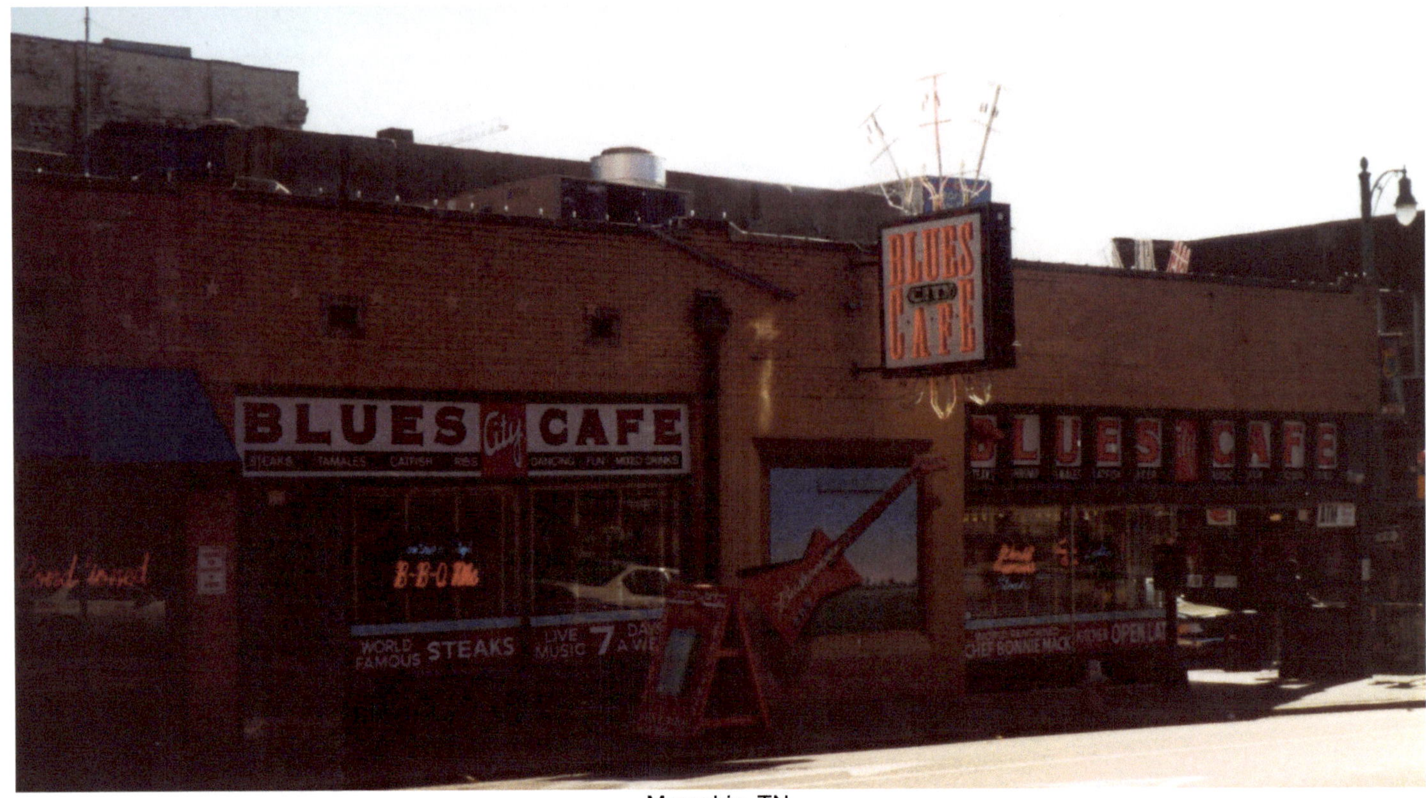

Memphis, TN

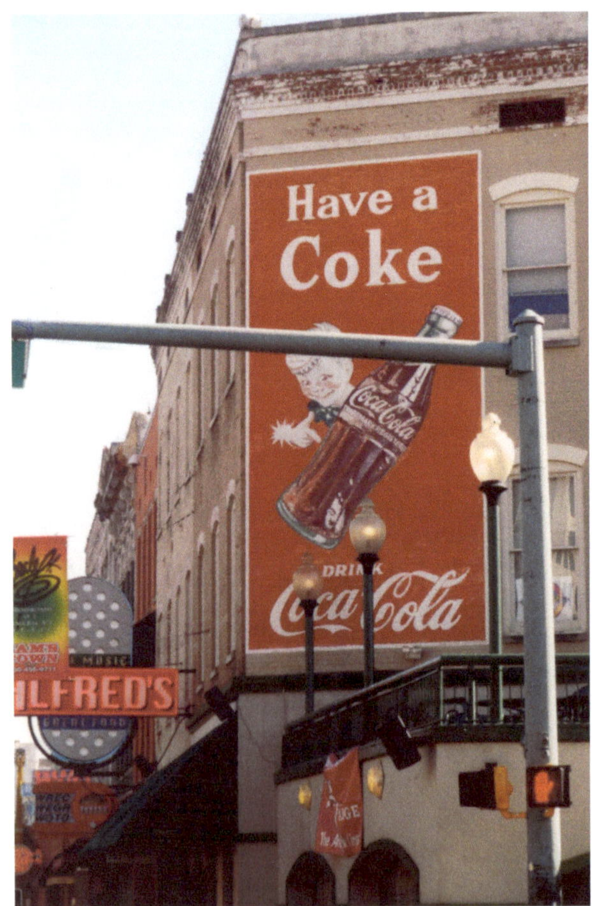

Memphis, TN

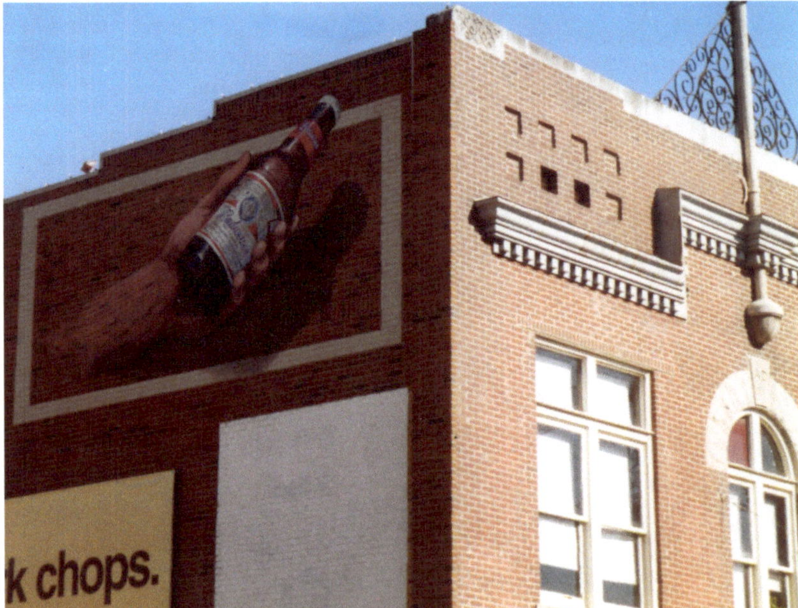

Memphis, TN

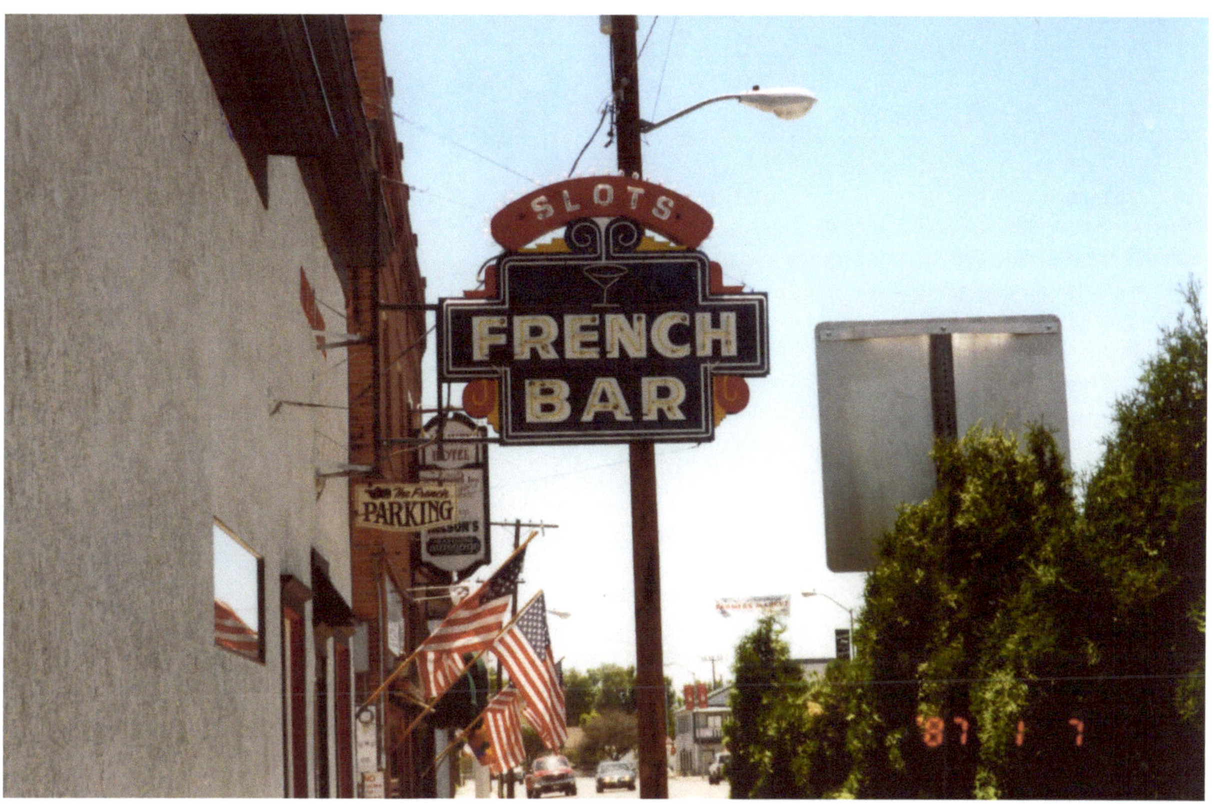

Minden, NV

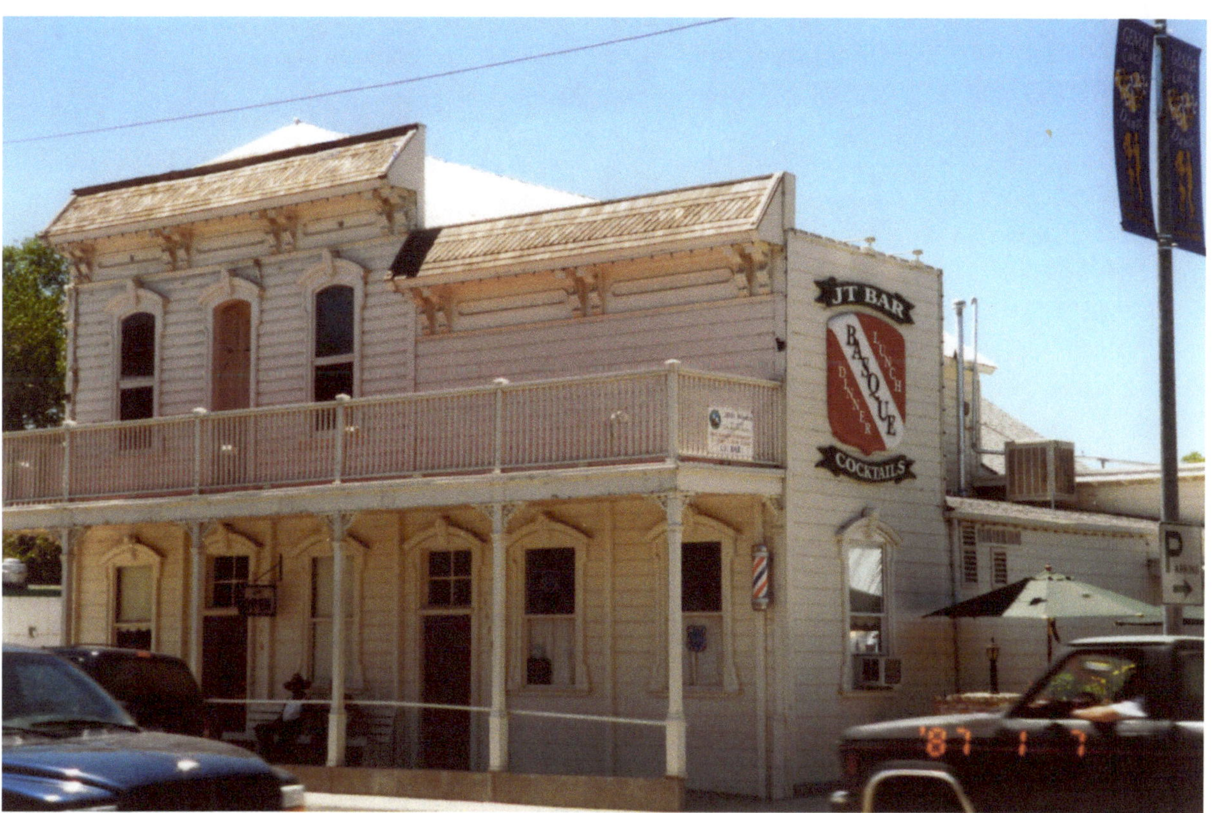

Minden, NV

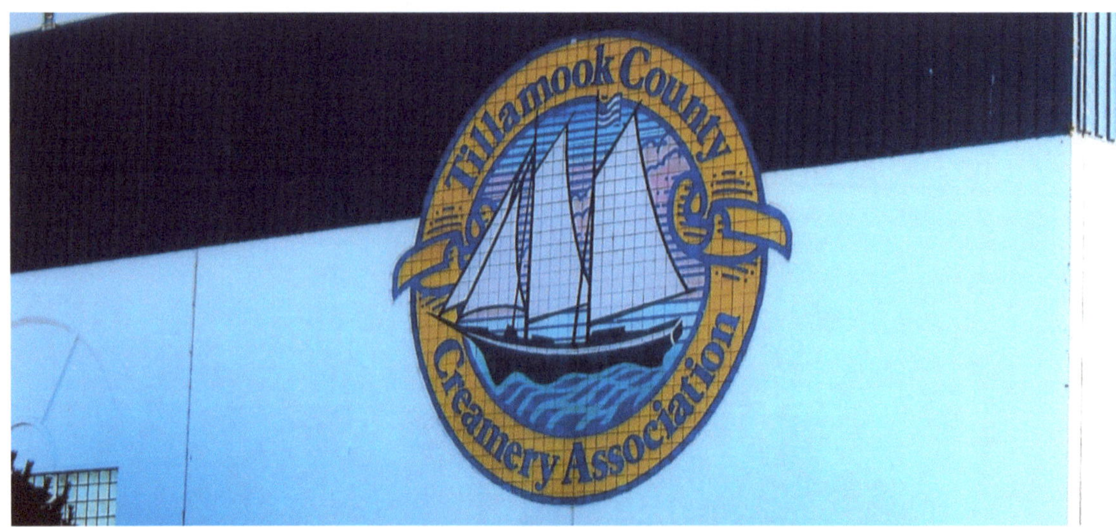

Tillamook, OR

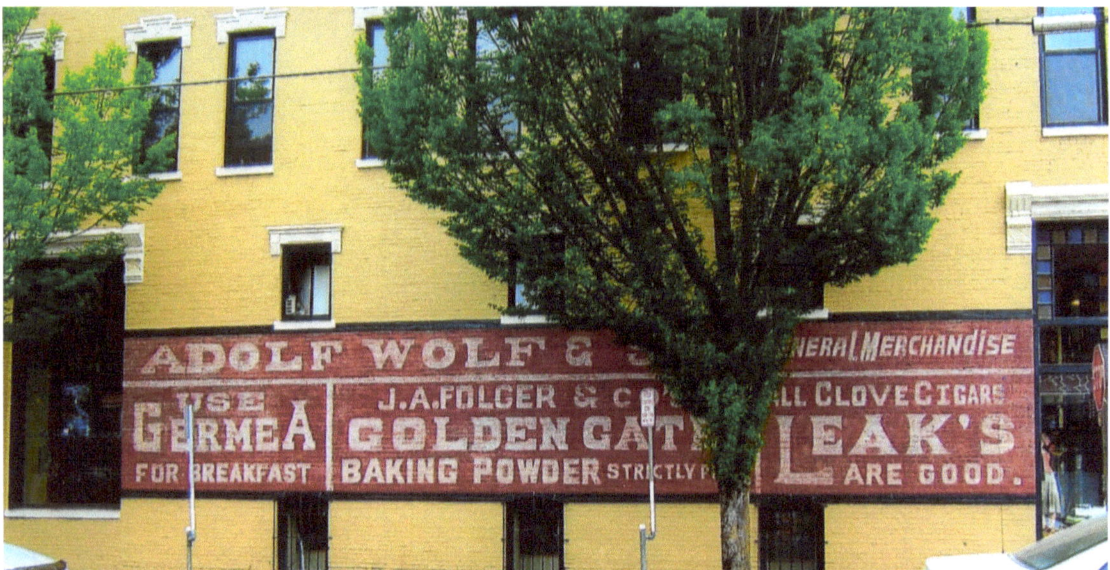

Tillamook, OR

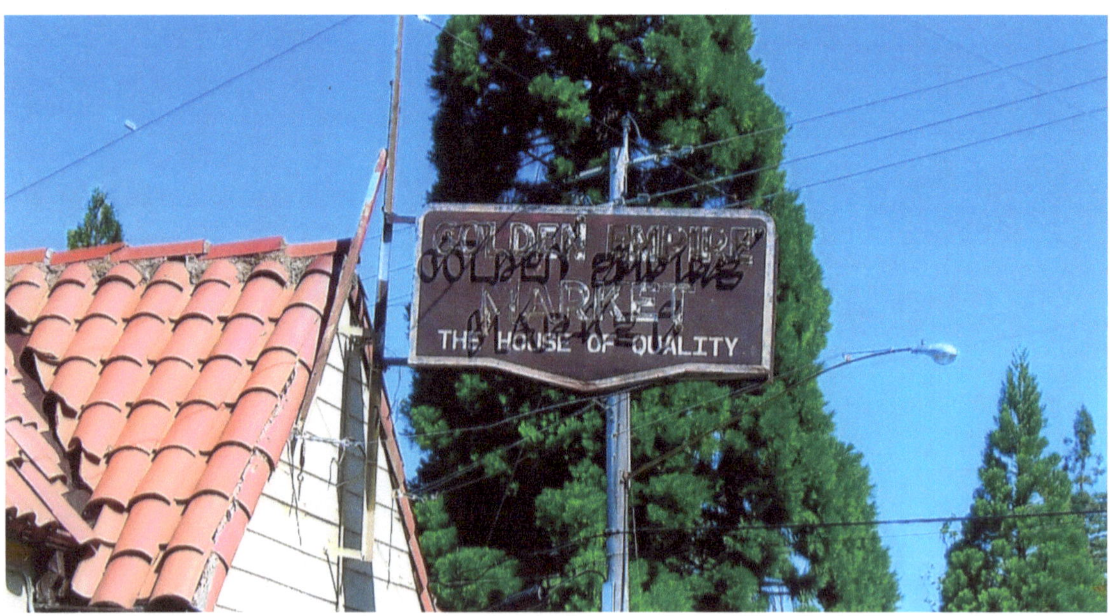

Grass Valley, CA

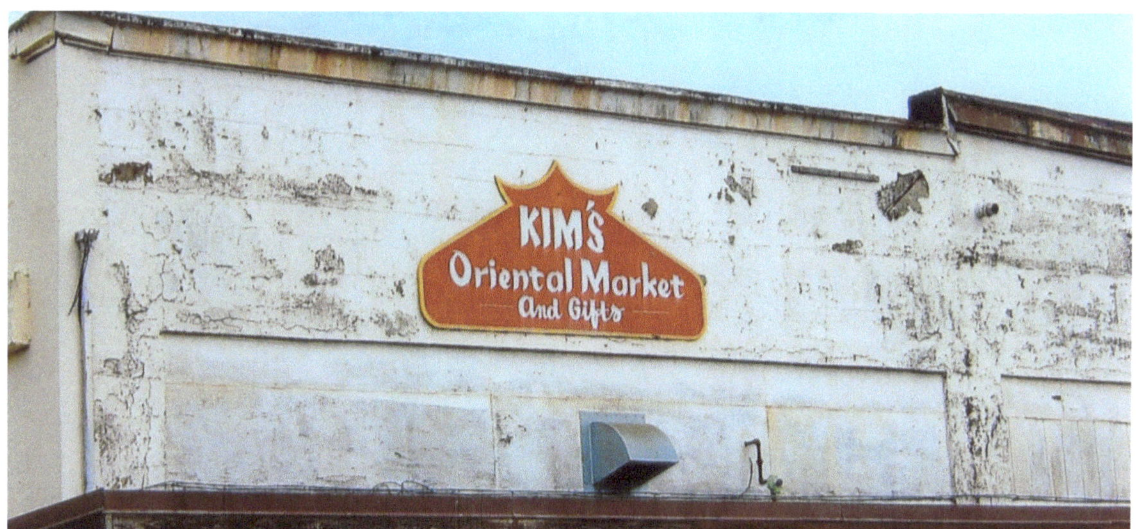

Coos Bay, OR

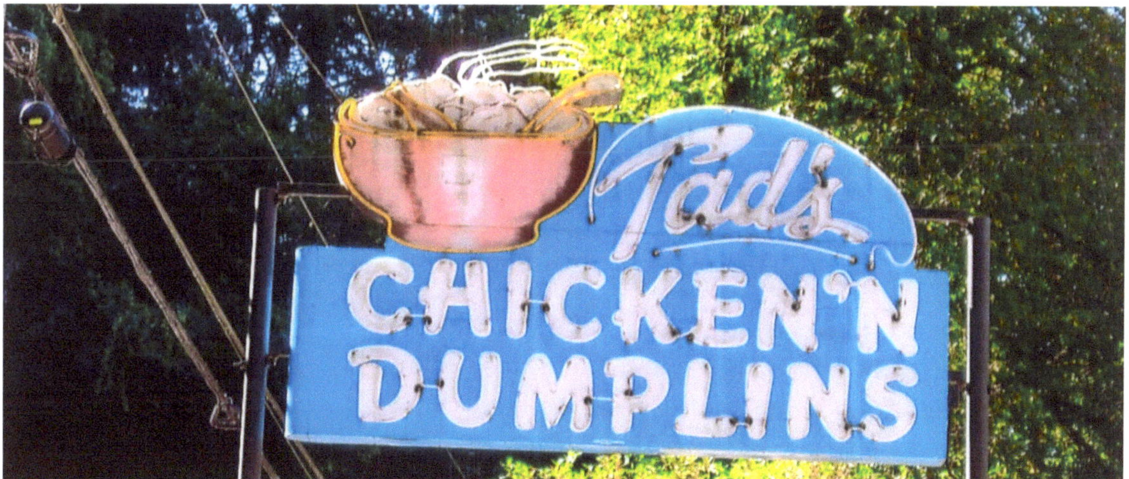

Troutdale, OR

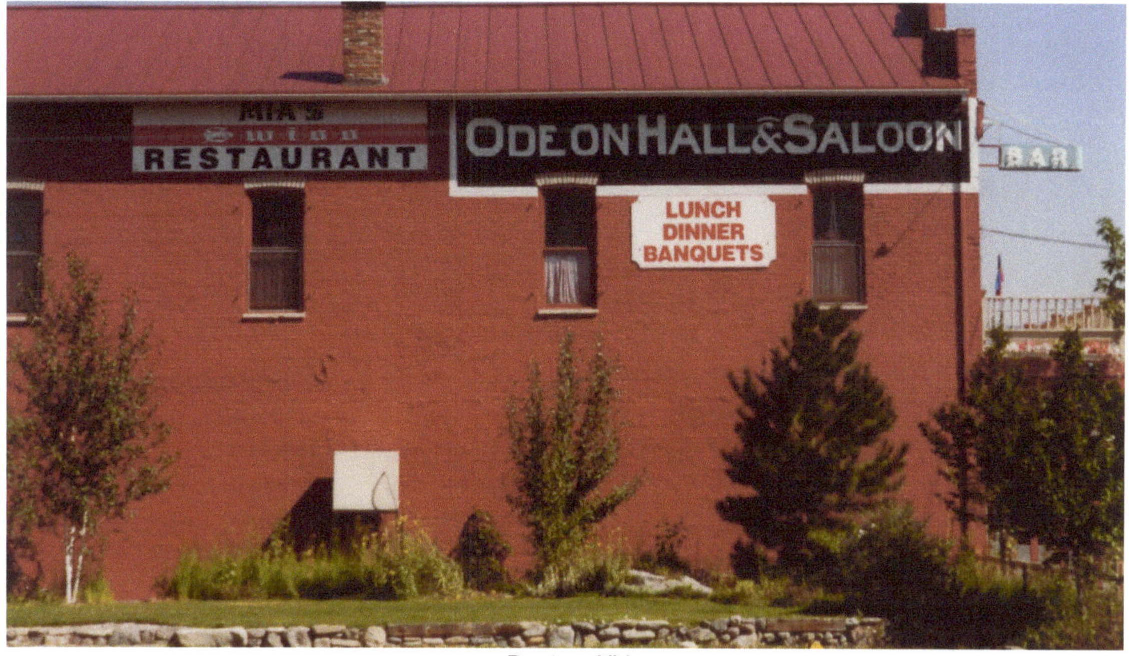

Dayton, NV

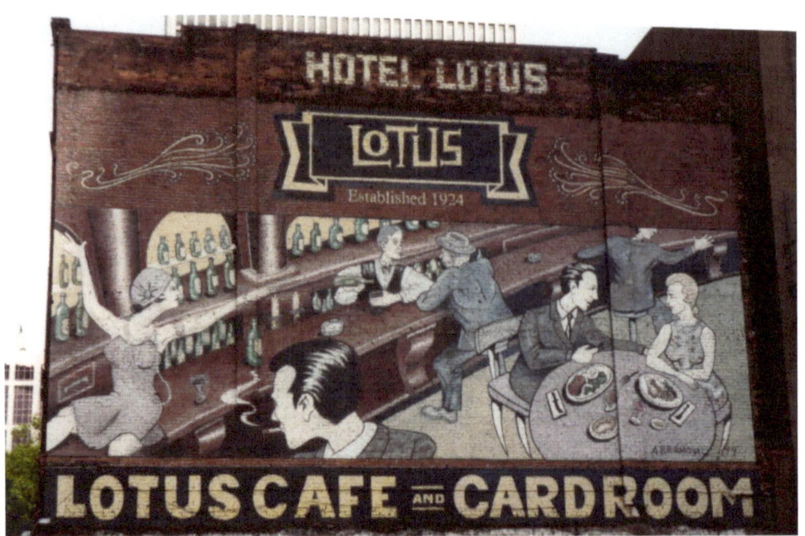

Portland, OR

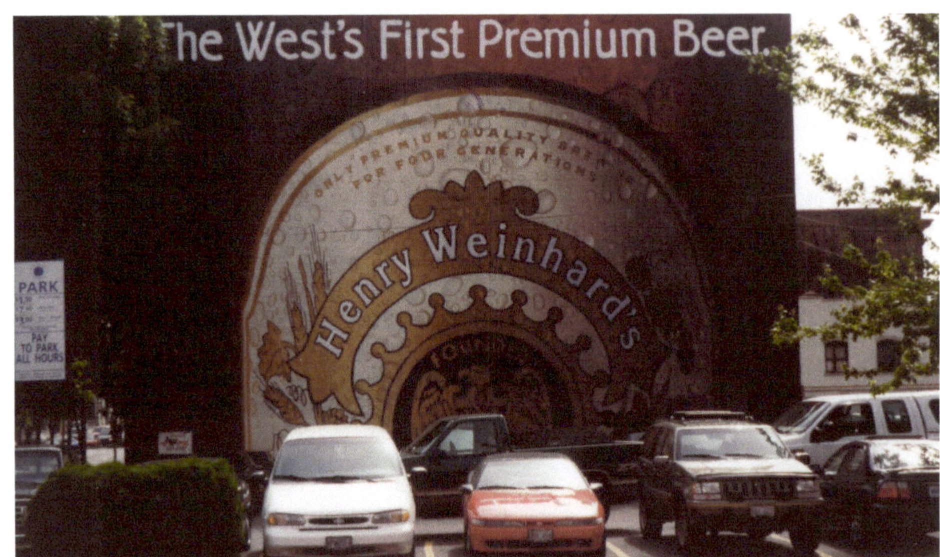

Portland, OR

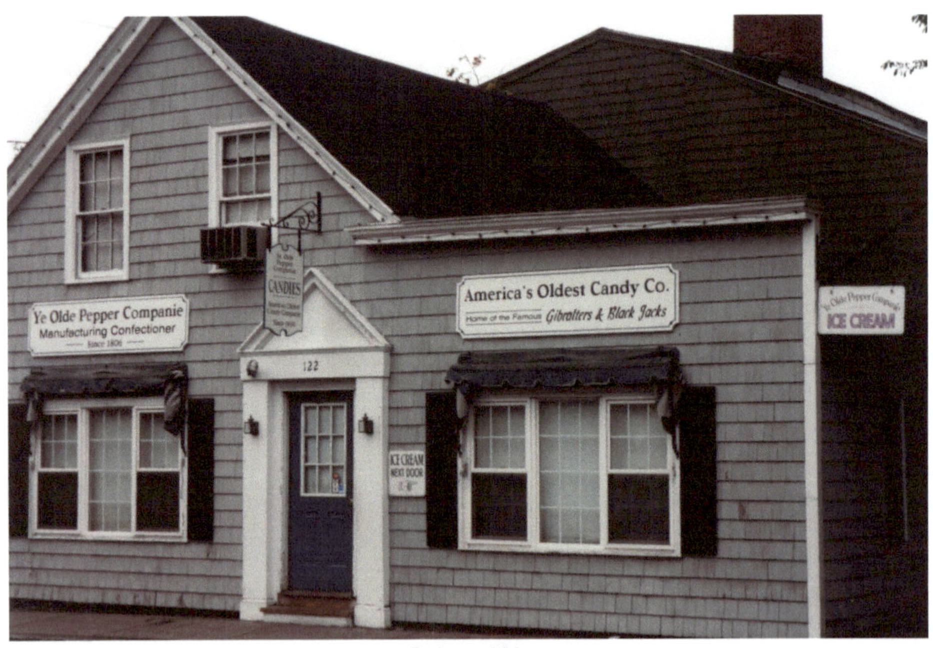

Salem, MA

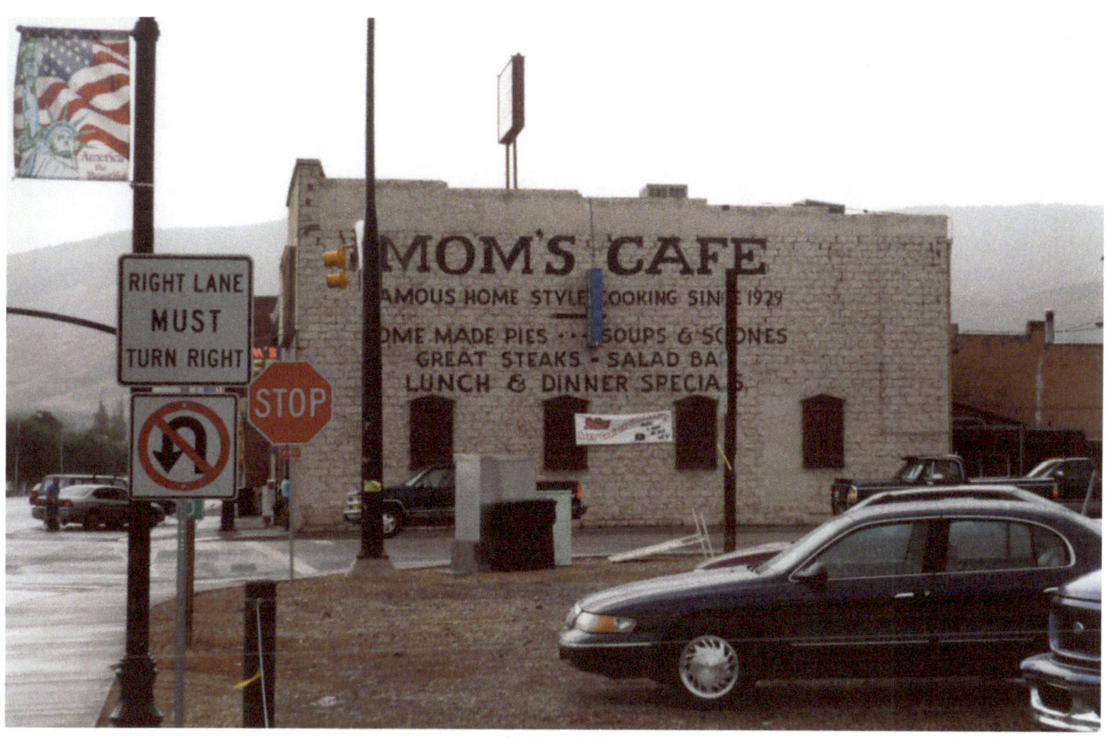

Salina, UT

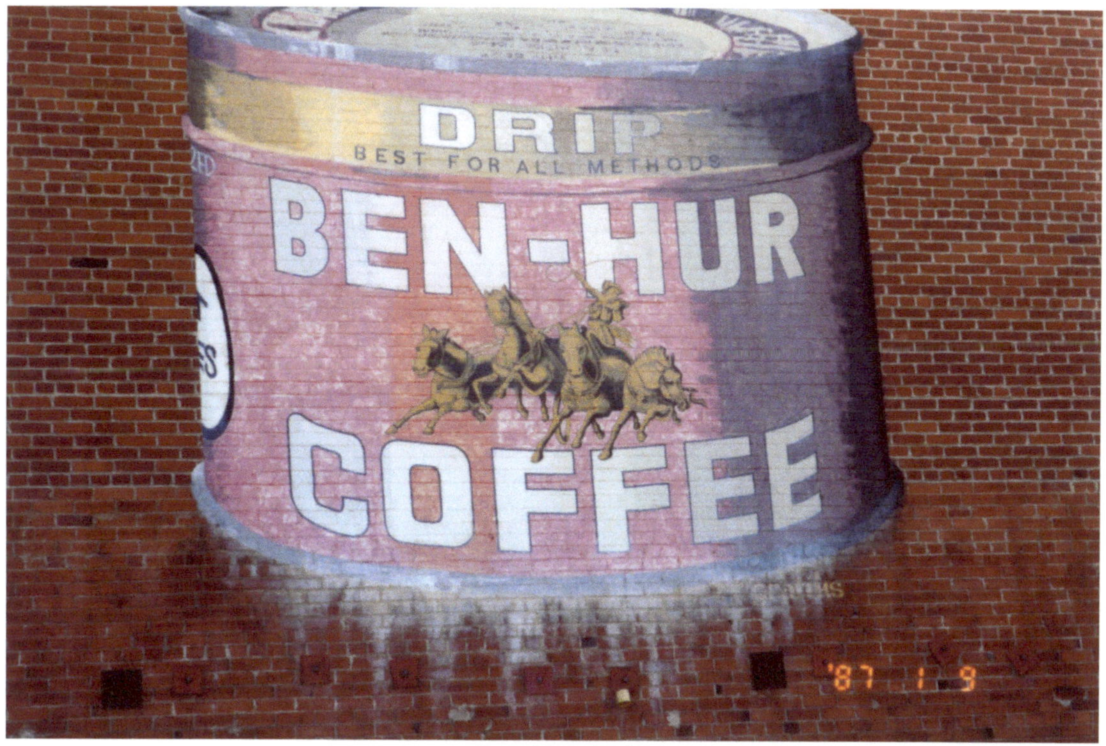

San Diego, CA

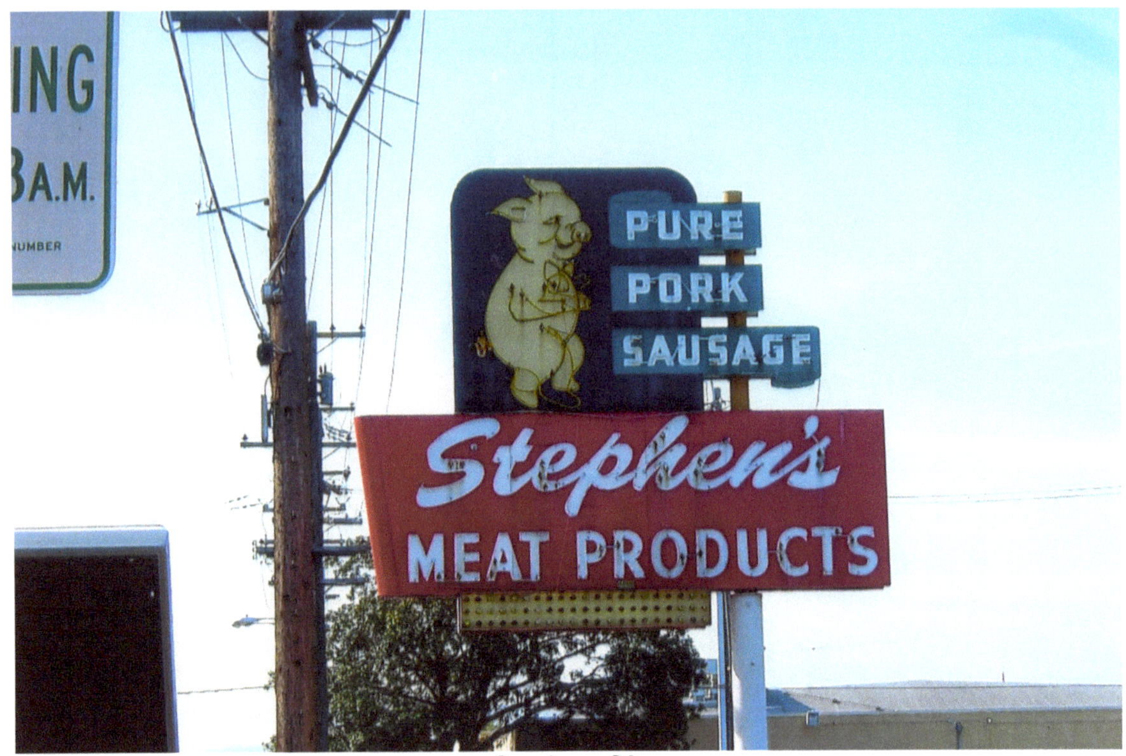

San Jose, CA

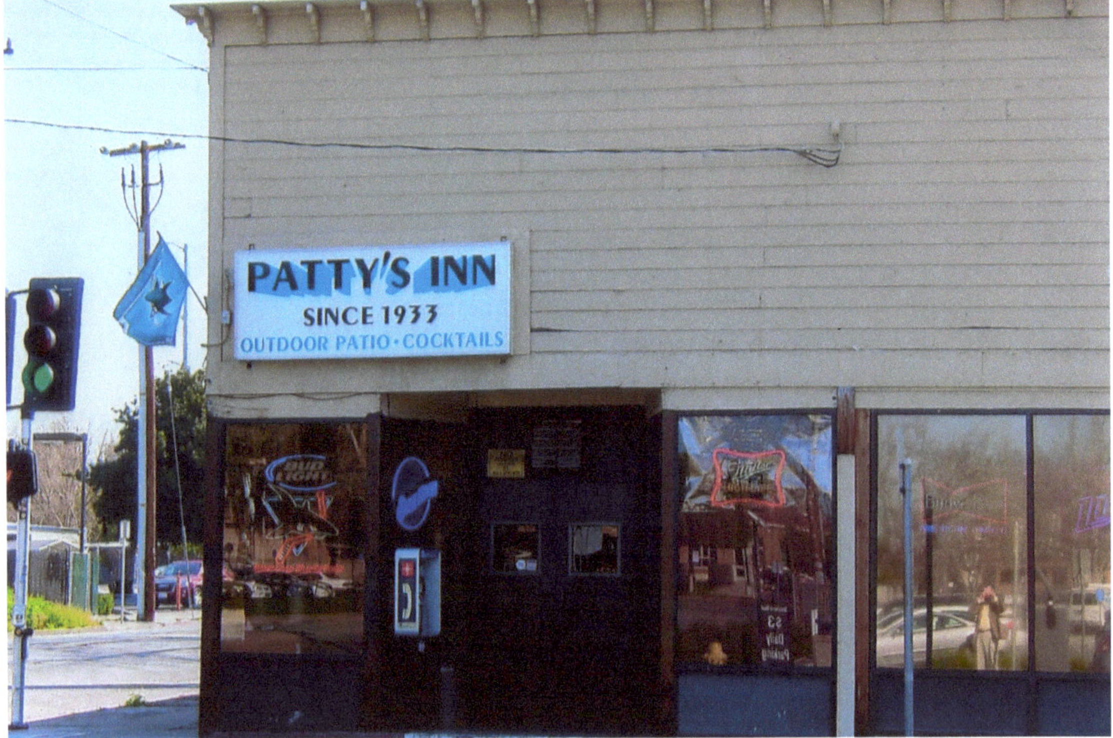

San Jose, CA

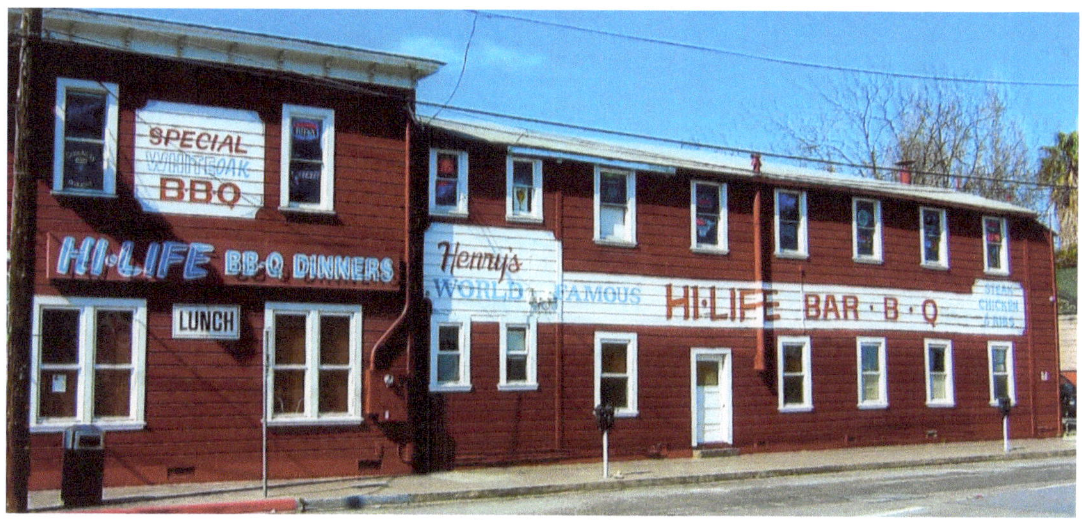

San Jose, CA

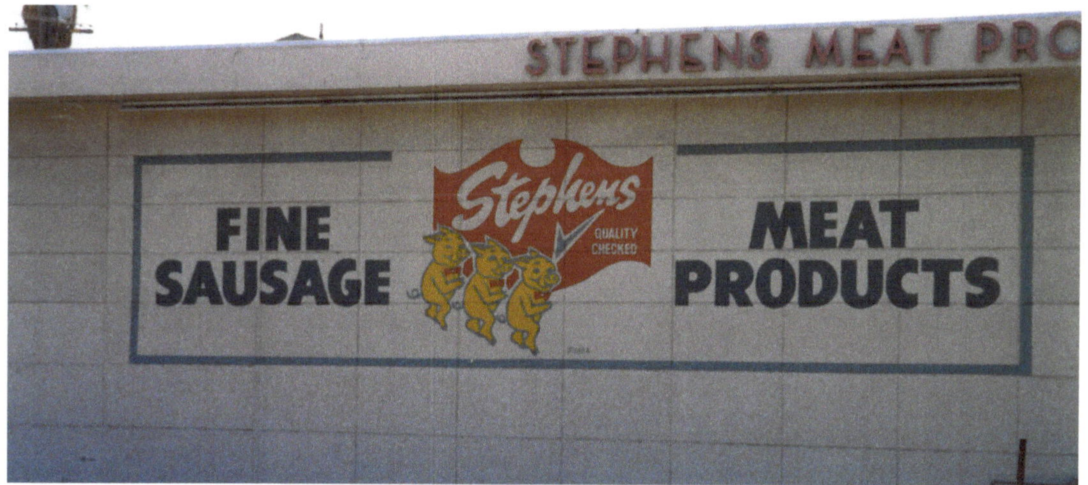

San Jose, CA

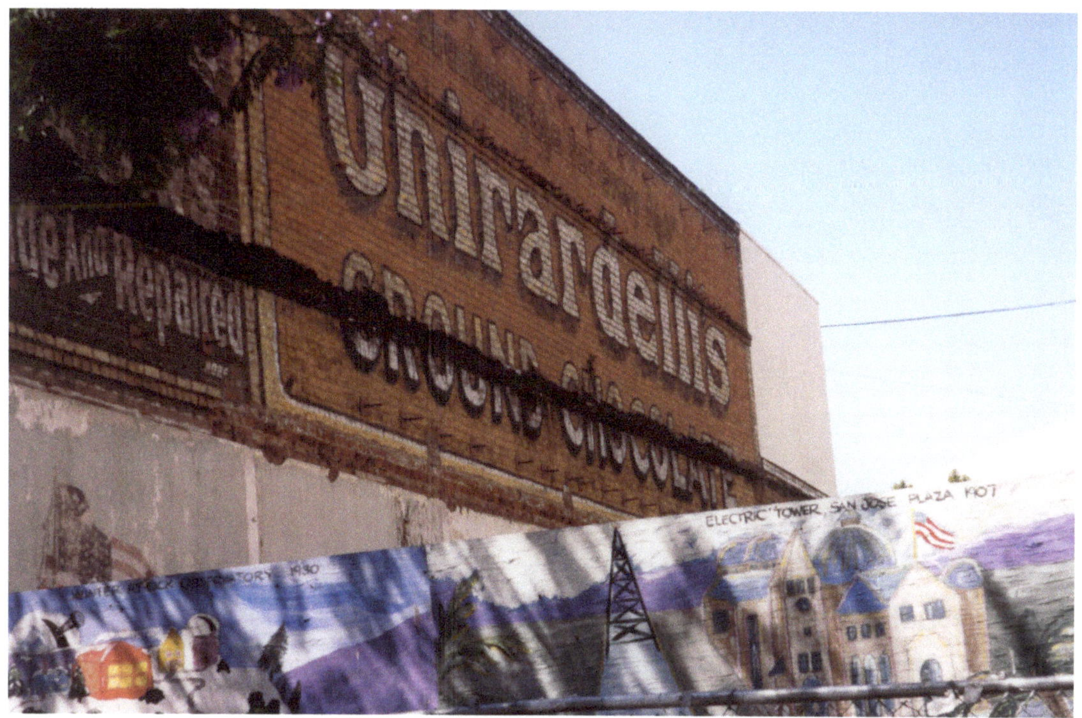

San Jose, CA

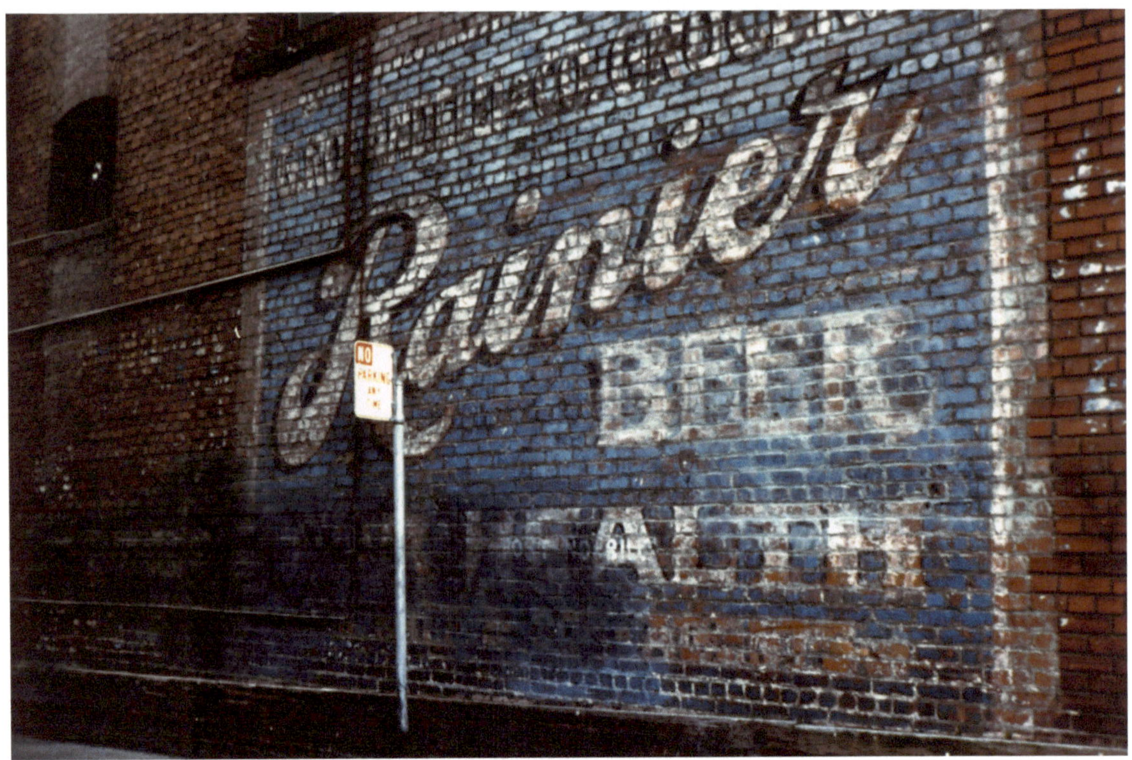

San Francisco, CA

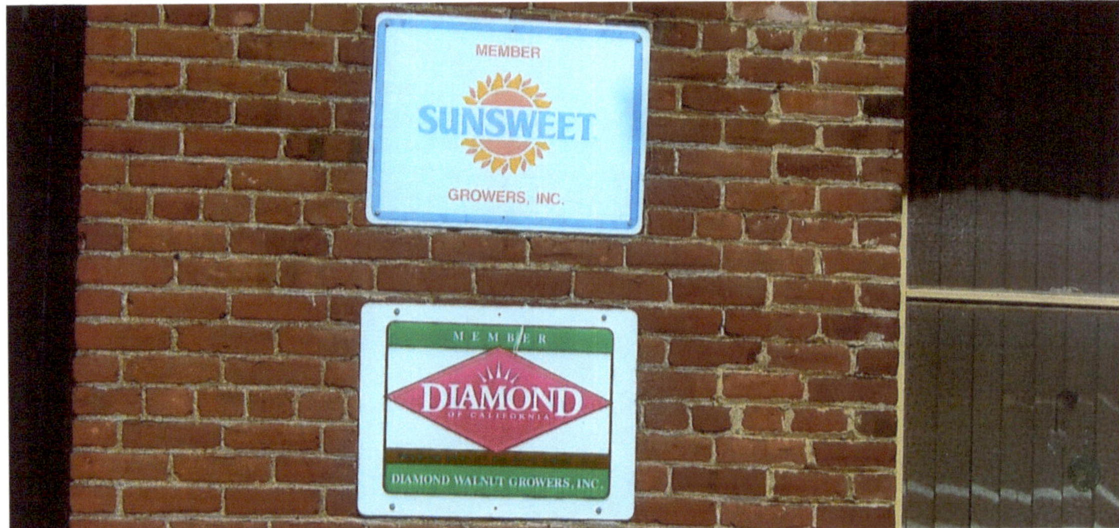

Unknown location

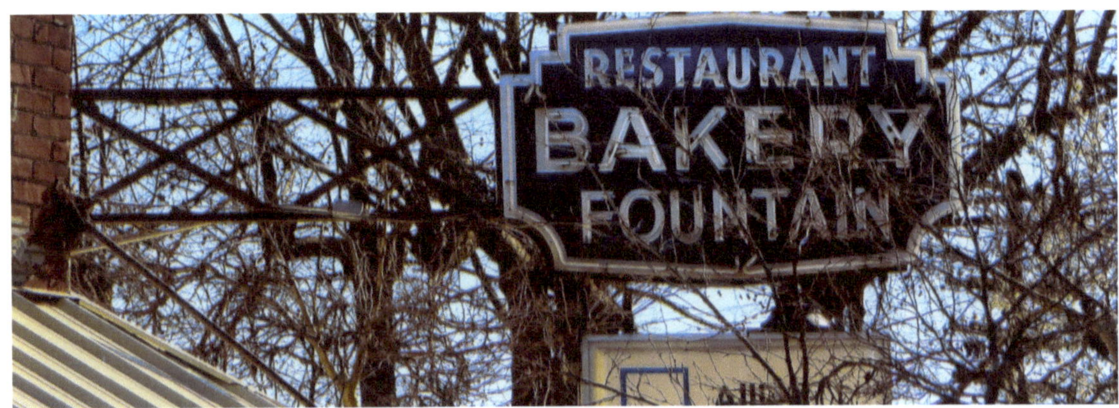

Unknown location

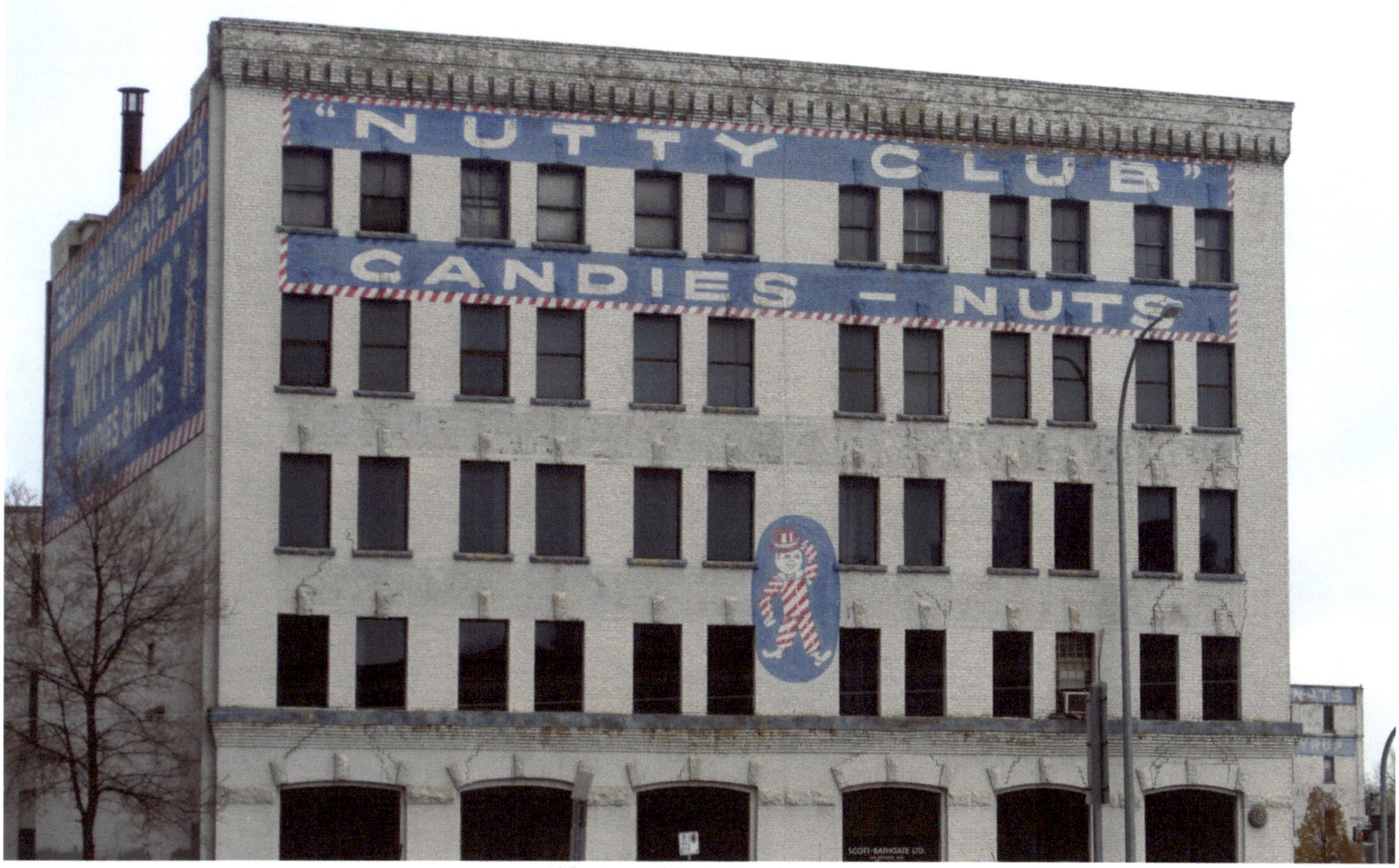

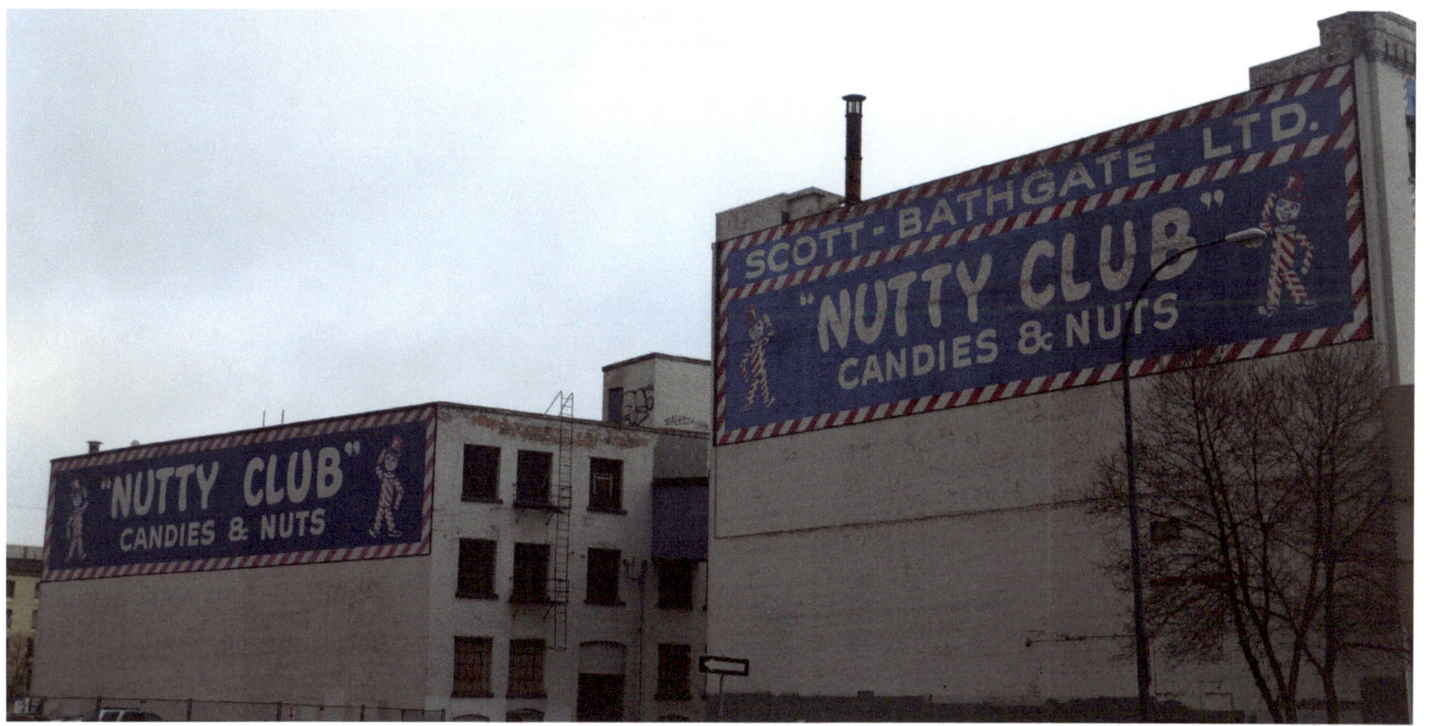

Winnipeg, Manitoba, Canada

Winnipeg, Manitoba, Canada

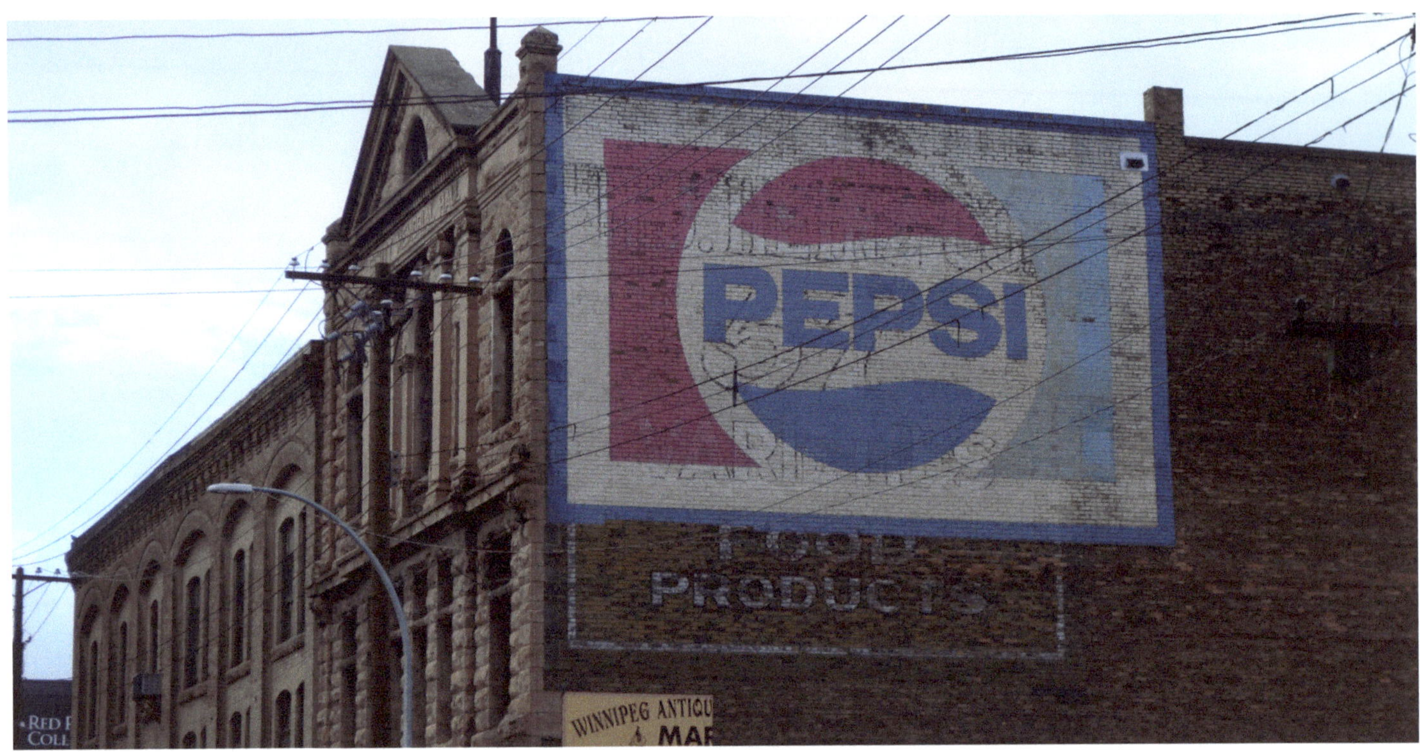

Winnipeg, Manitoba, Canada

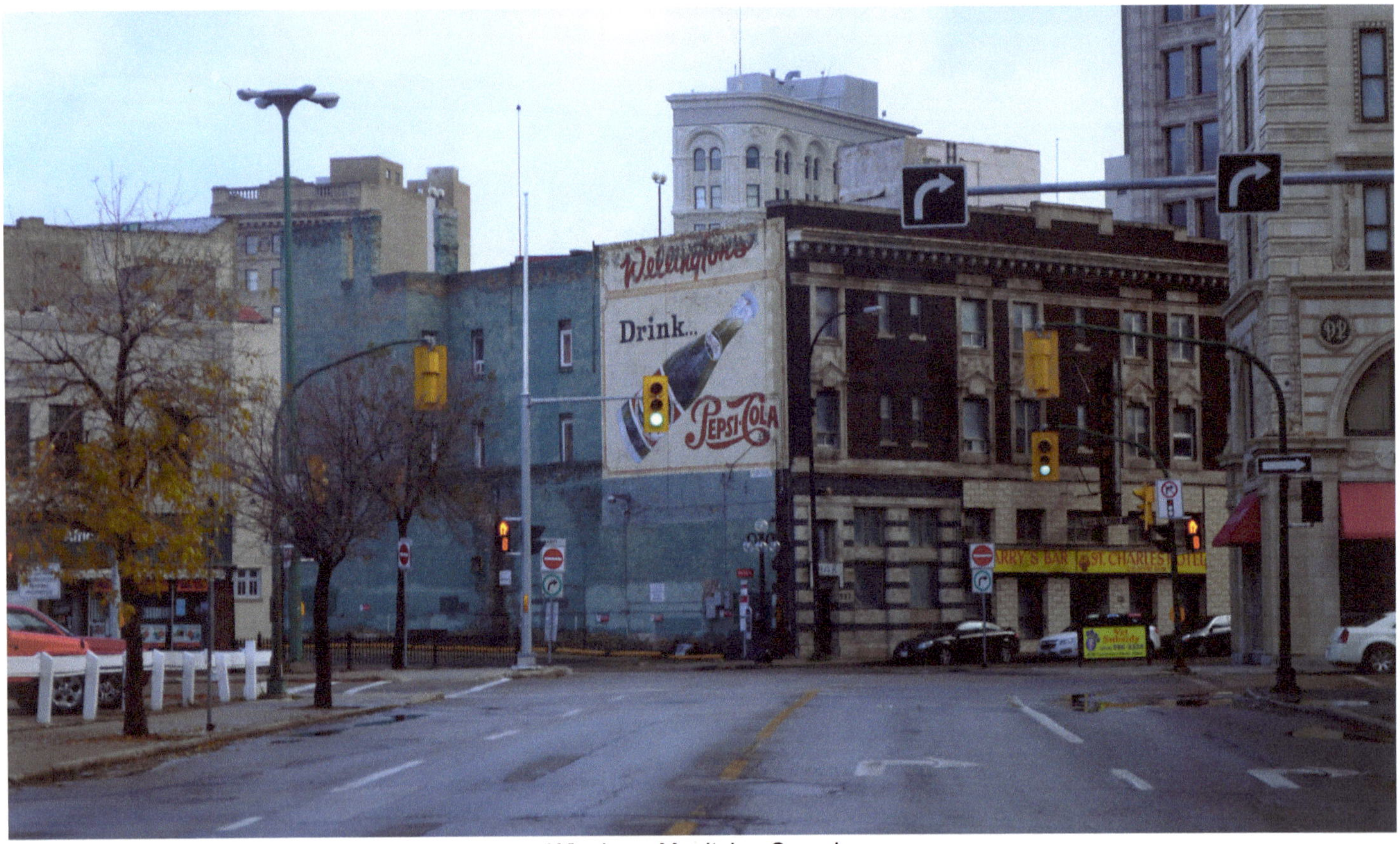

Winnipeg, Manitoba, Canada

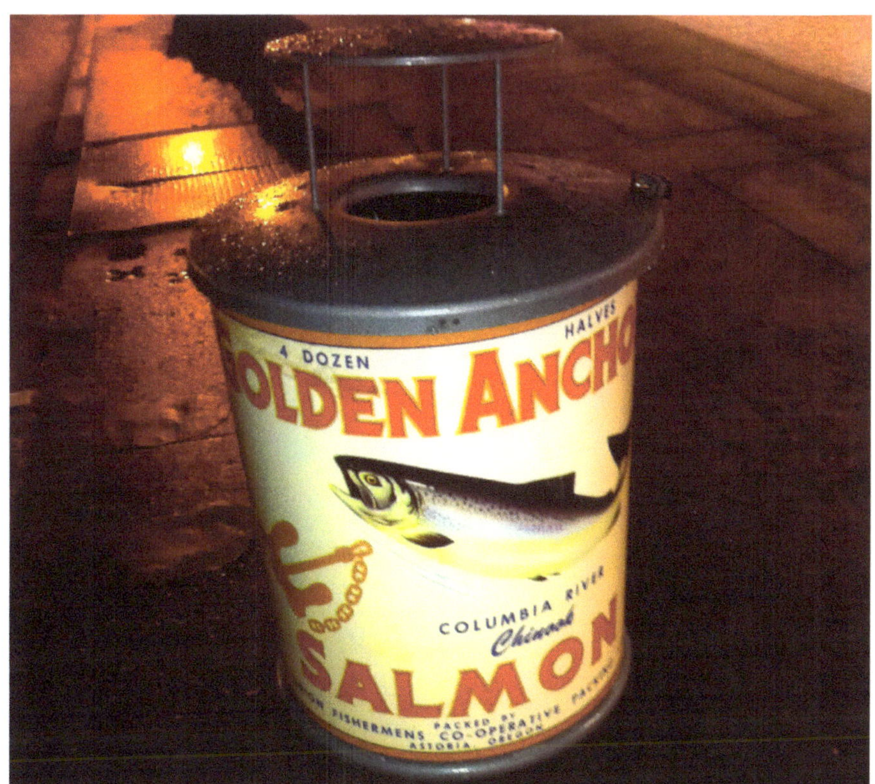

Astoria, OR

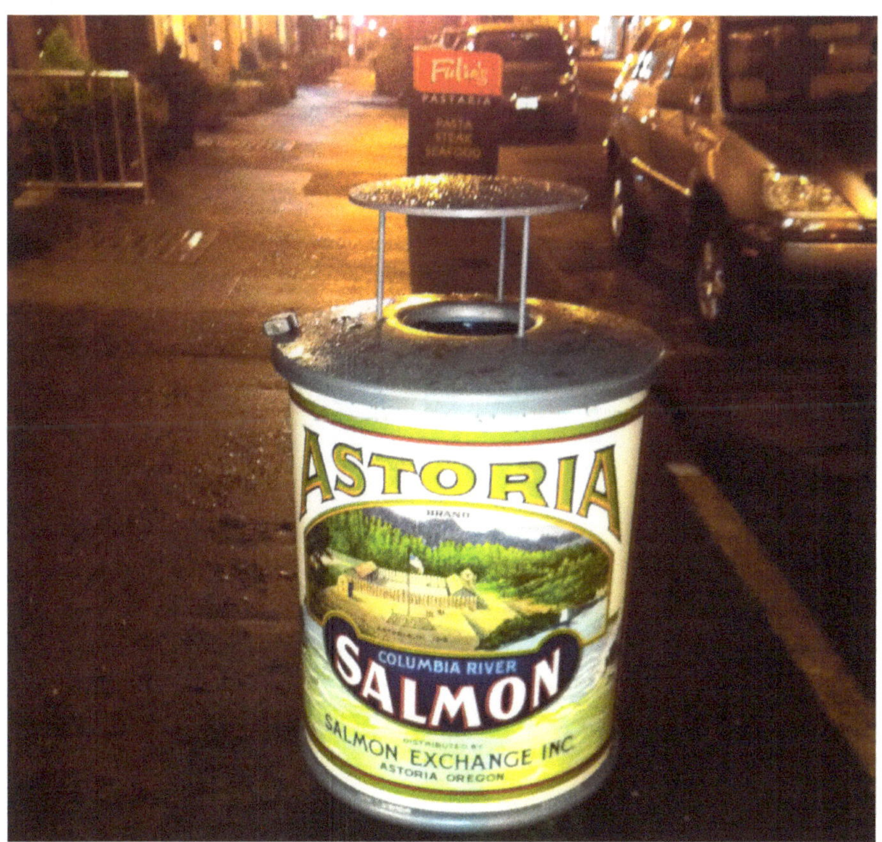

Astoria, OR

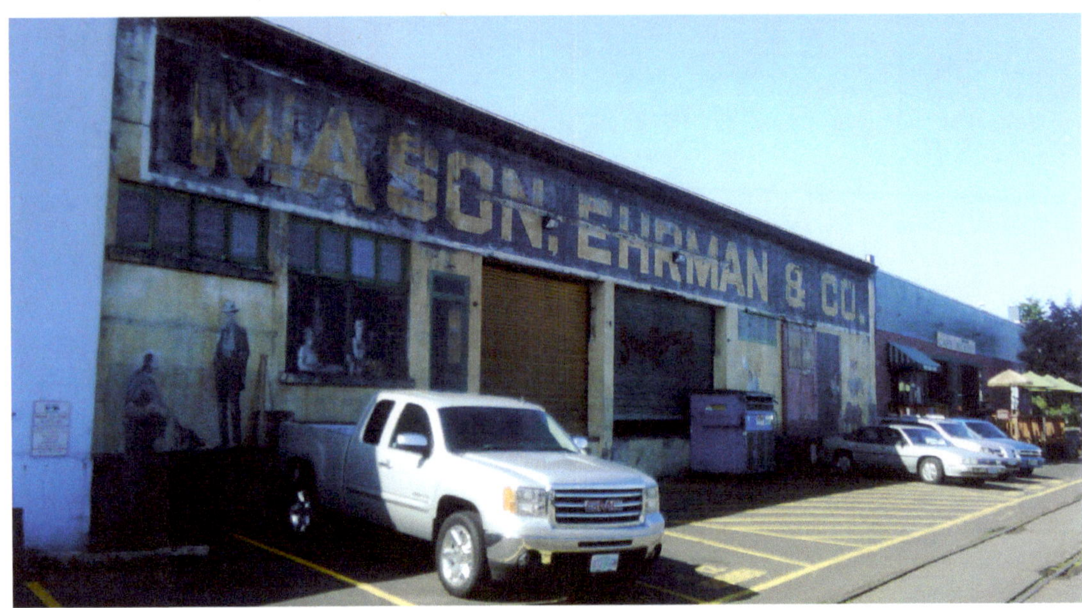

Astoria, OR

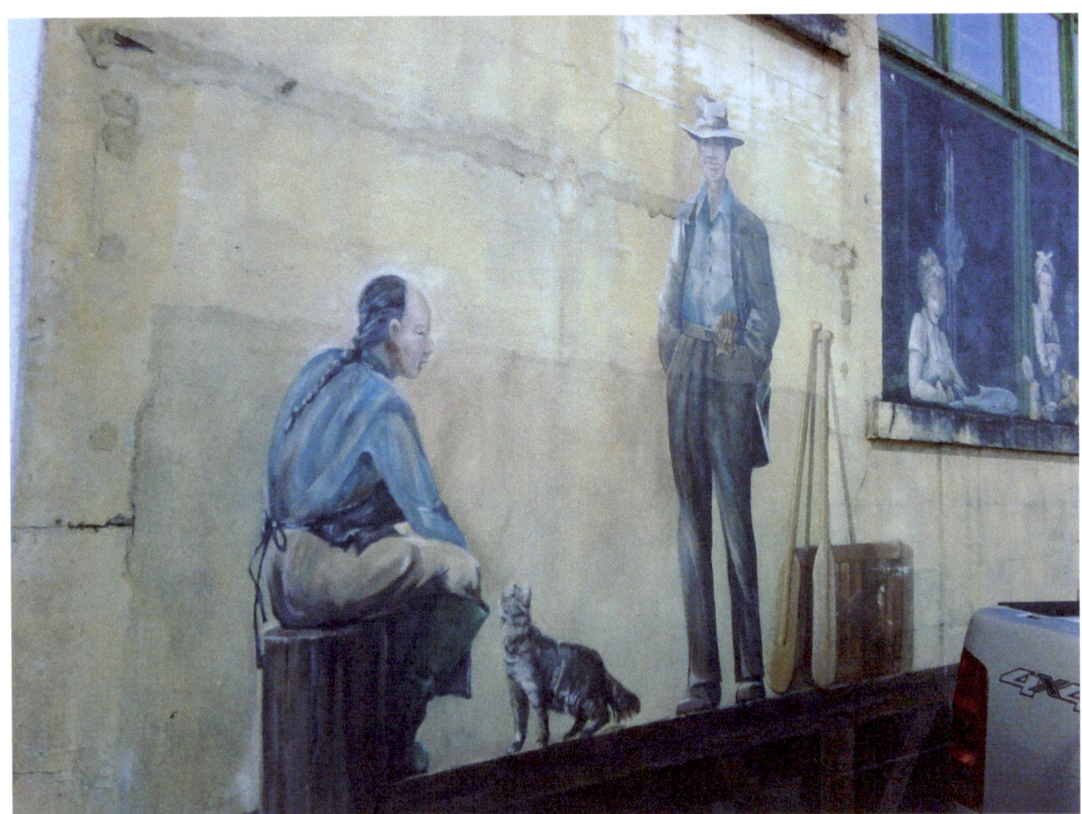

Astoria, OR

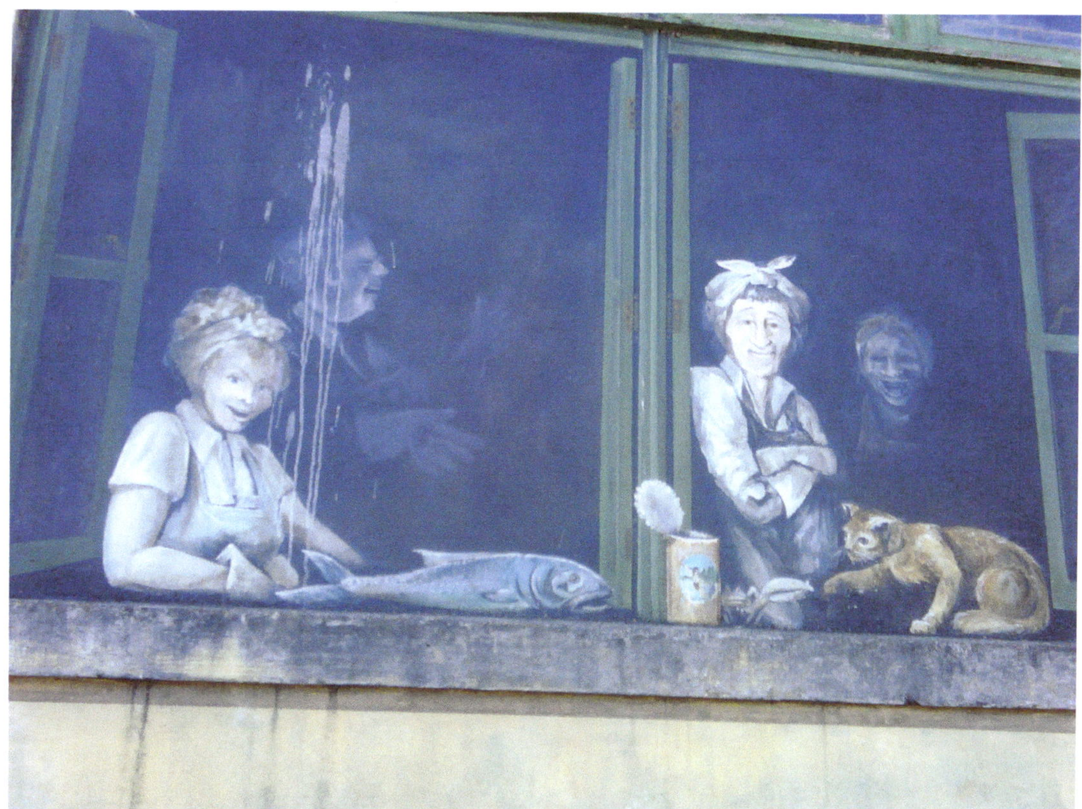

Astoria, OR

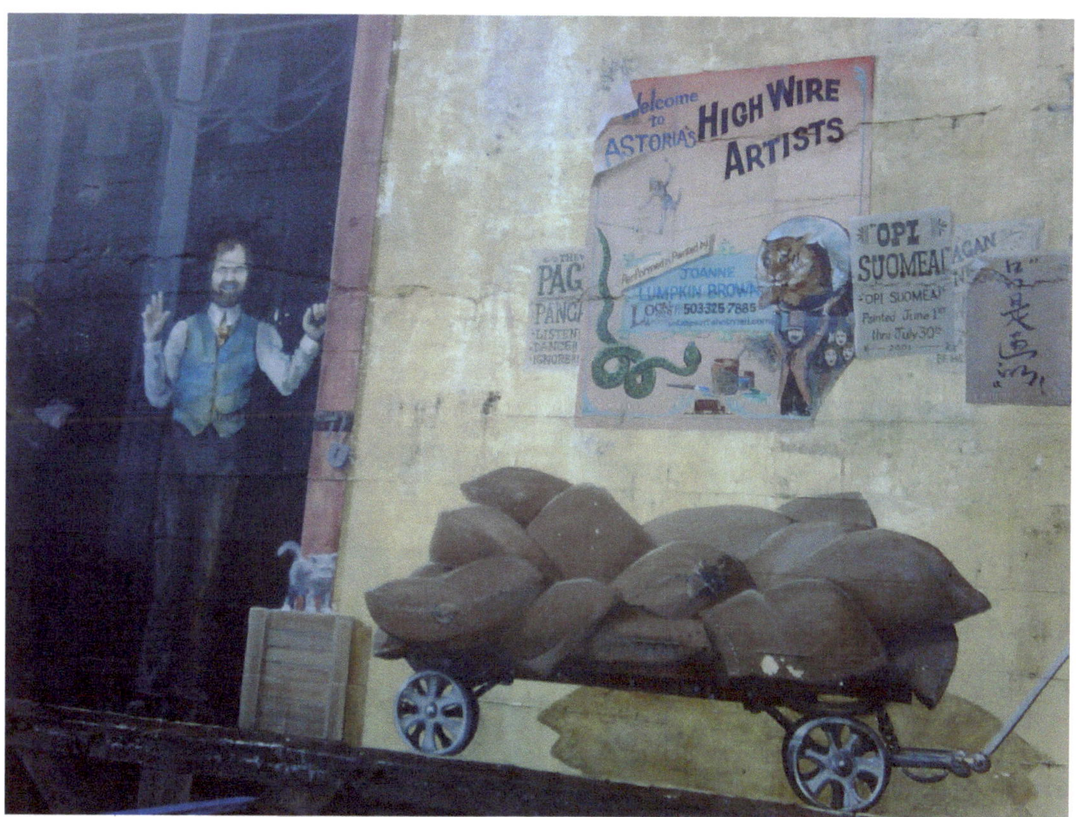

Astoria, OR

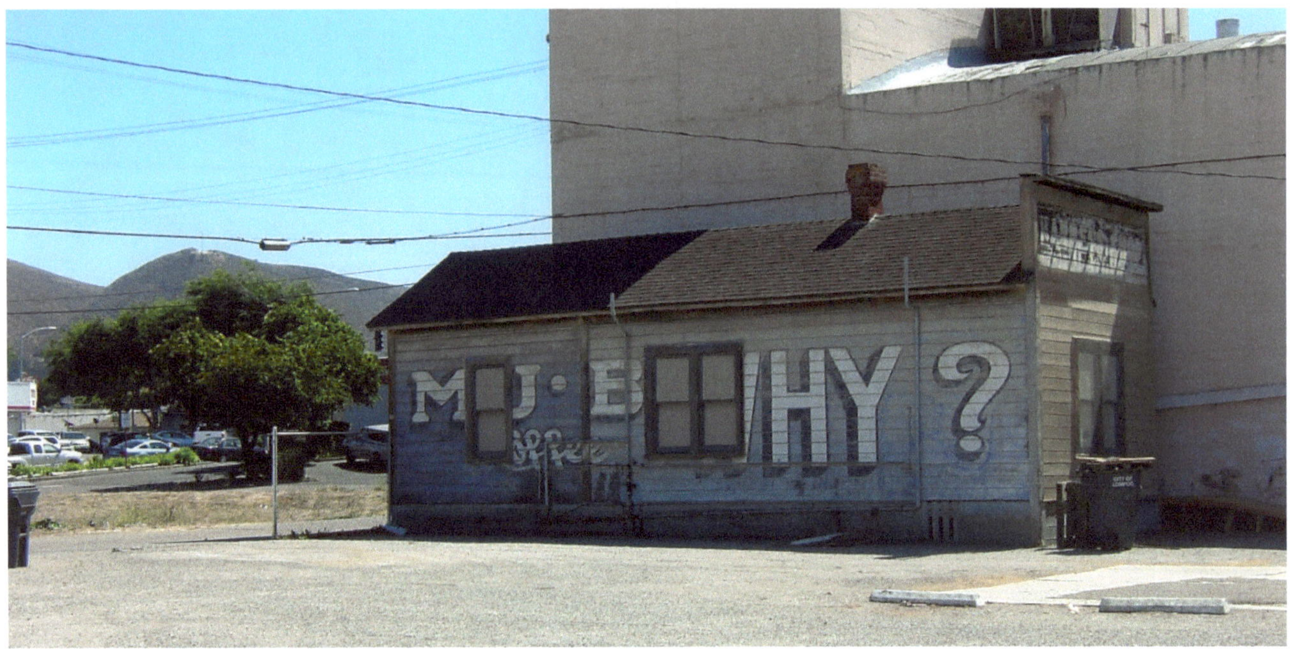

Lompoc, CA

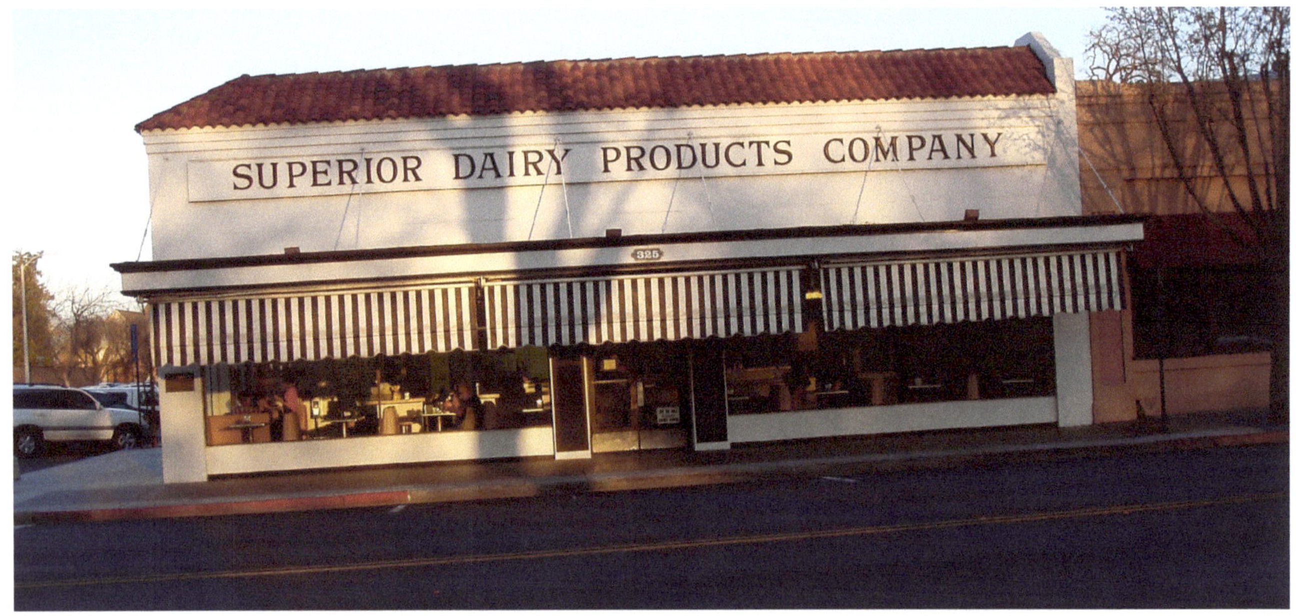

Hanford, CA

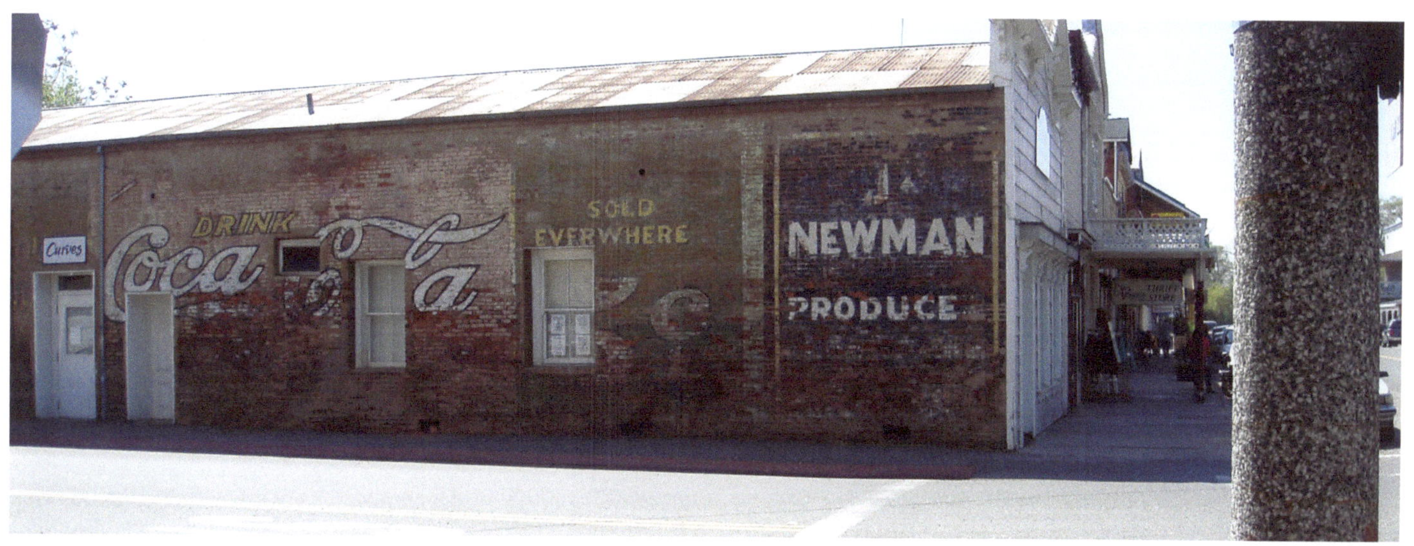

Ione, CA

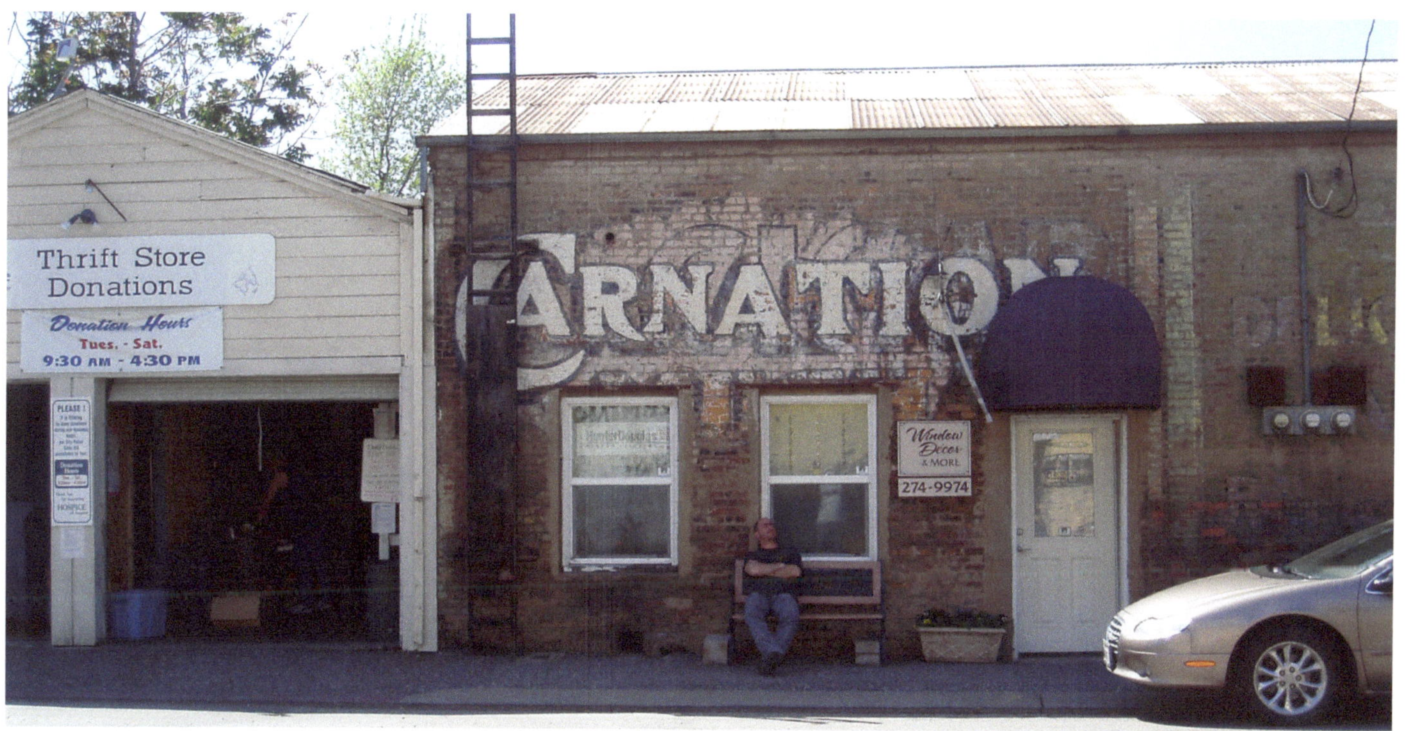

Ione, CA

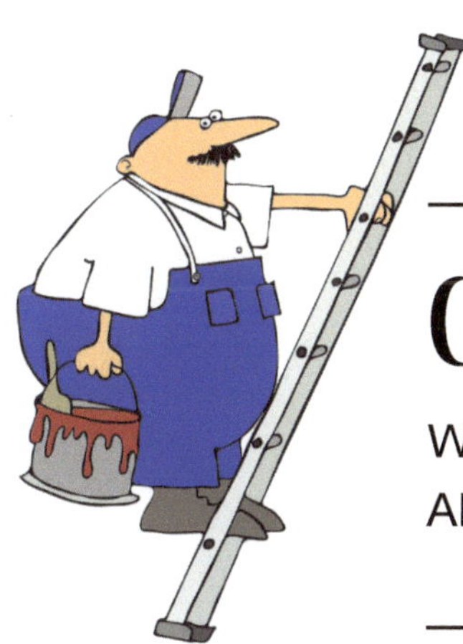

Cigars and Tobacco-related signs

White Owl Cigars, first produced in 1887, are machine made in Alabama, and contain a blend of tobaccos from five countries.

CIGARS LIVE MUSIC MARTINI BAR
CIGAR ROLLER HUMIDORS ACCESSORIES
AND PRIVATE CIGAR CLUB
LA Casa DE LA
HABANA
Cigars & Martini
LOUNGE
PARADISE
VALLEY
PARADISE VALLEY
MARTINI HABANA LOUNGE
La Casa
HABANA
CAMACHO
Martini Cigar Lounge
PREMIUM HABANA CIGARS
Casa
HABANA
Cigars

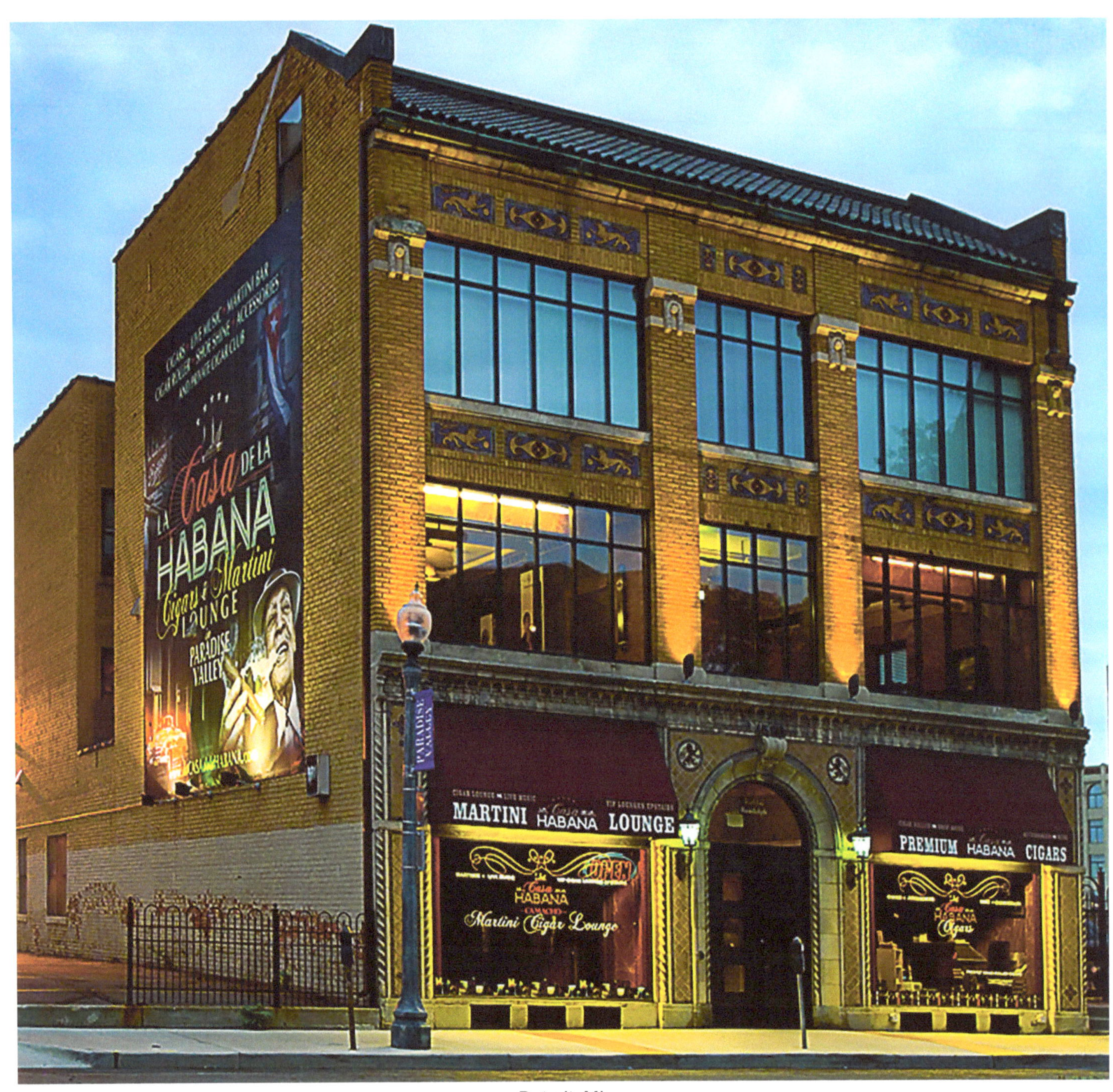

Detroit, MI

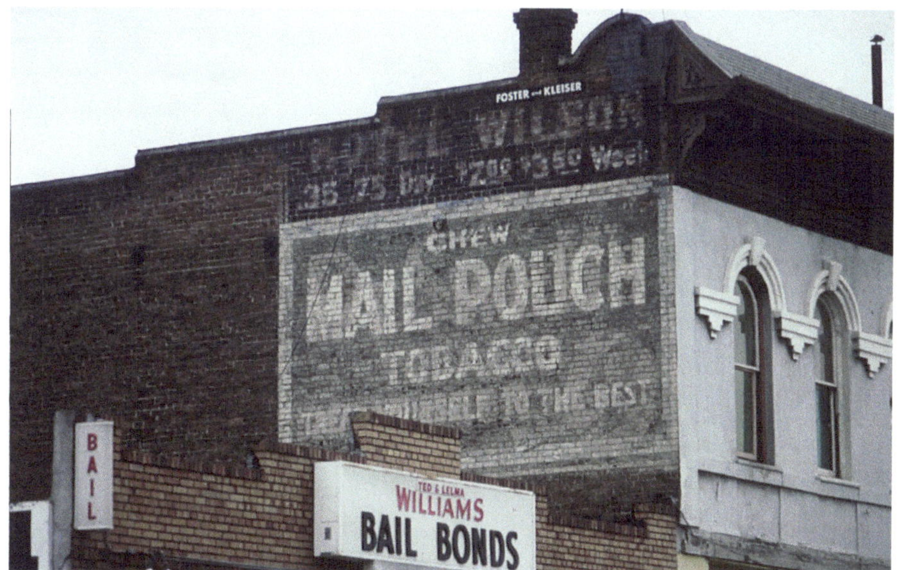

Oakland, CA

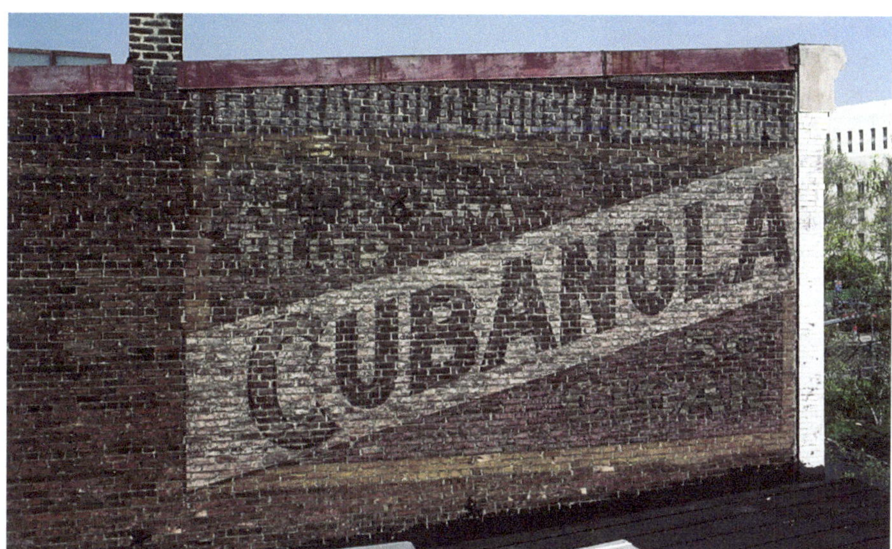

Washington, DC

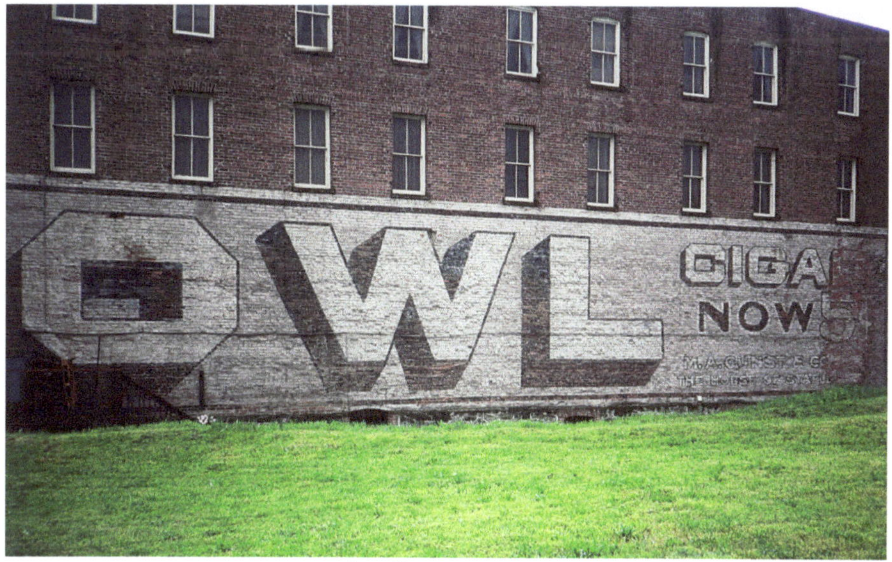

Port Townsend, WA

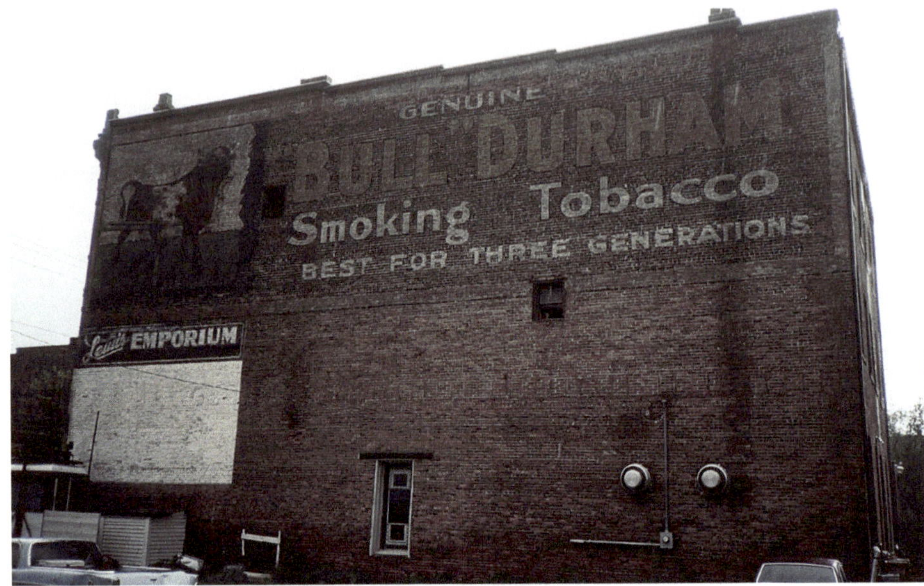

Port Townsend, WA

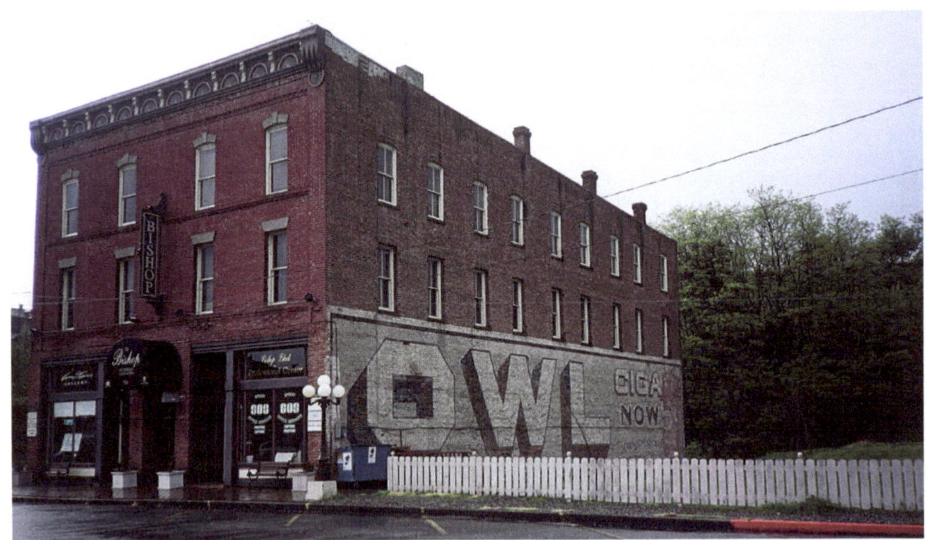

Port Townsend, WA

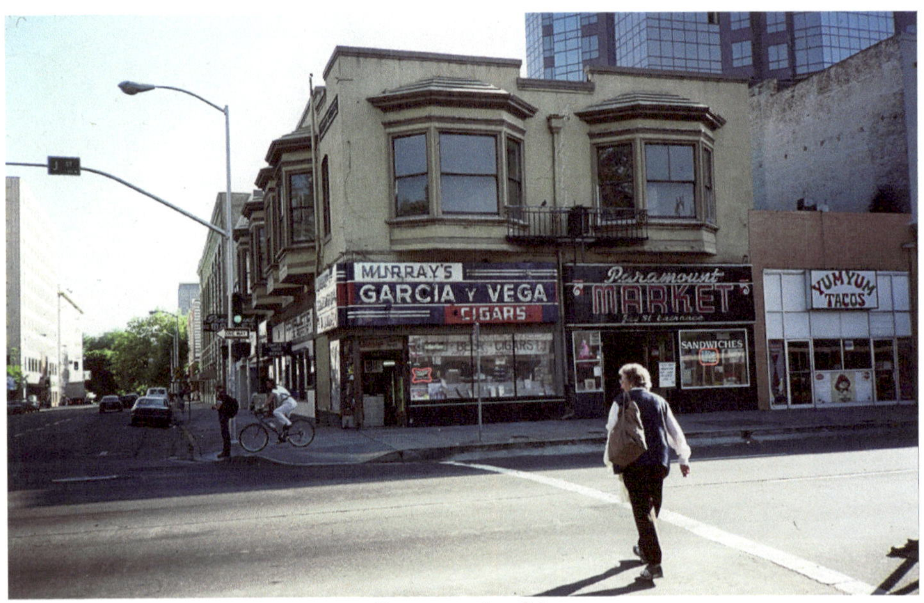

Sacramento, CA

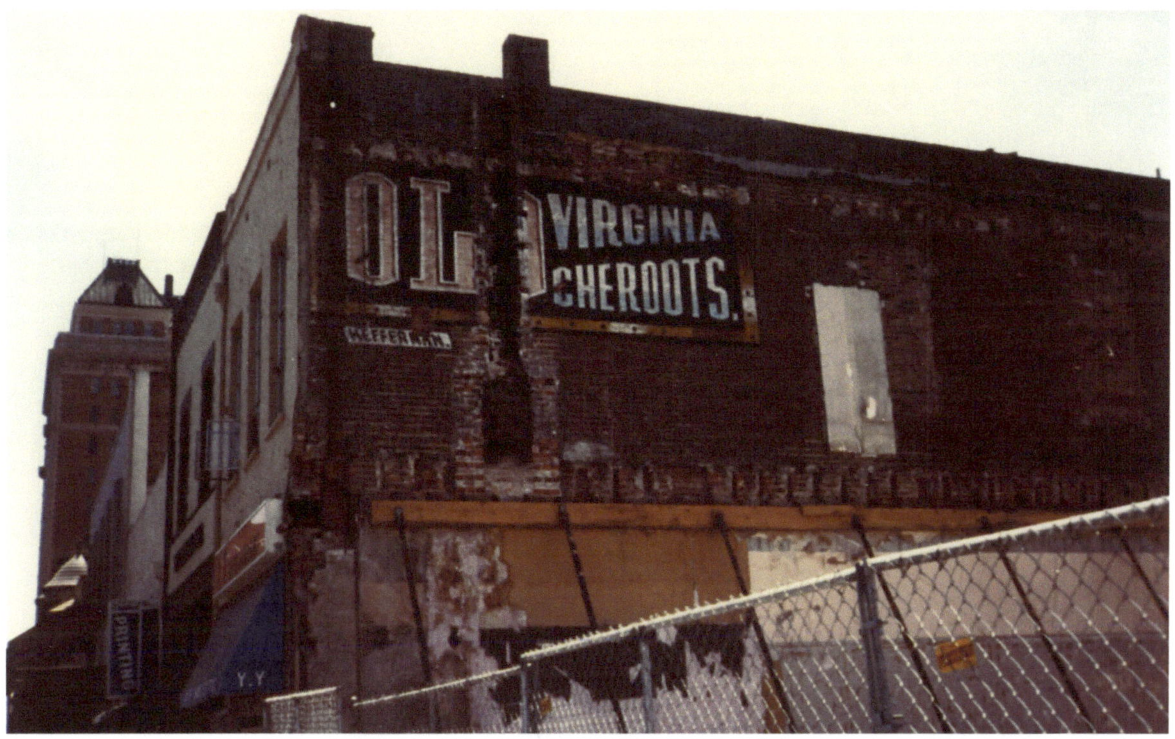

Sacramento, CA

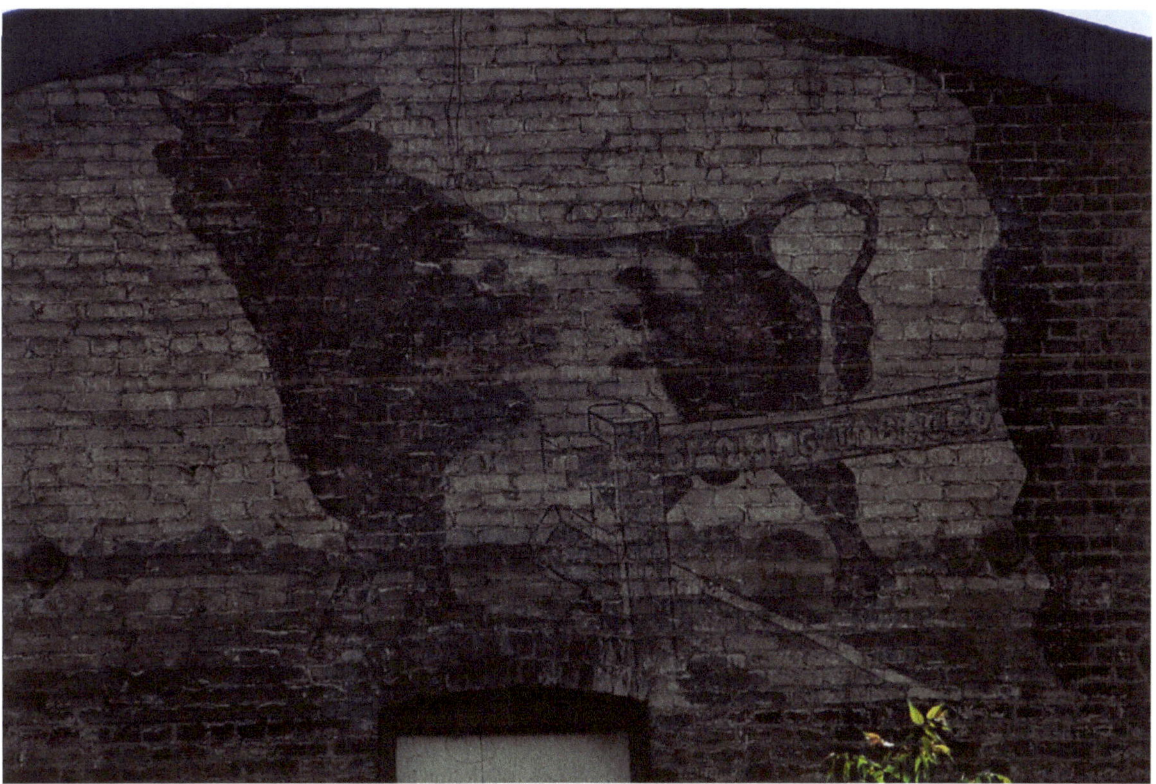

Port Townsend, WA

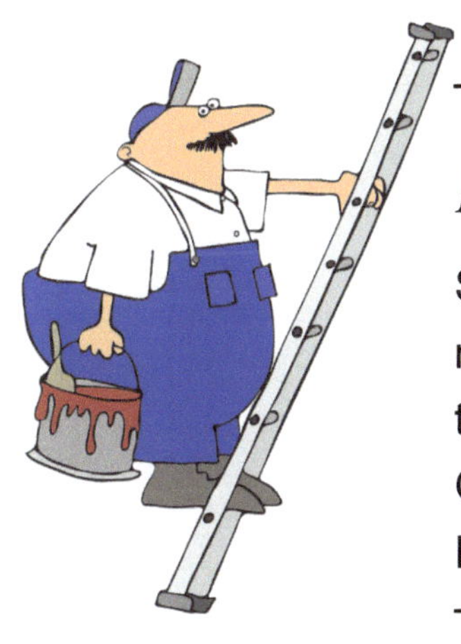

Automotive and Travel-related signs

Steve McQueen, an actor known for his wild ride in a Ford Mustang in the movie "Bullitt", drove a 1953 Hudson; "Billy" Crapo Durant, fired the second time by General Motors, ended production of his Durant in 1932; and Oilzum Motor Oil, developed in 1905 was advertised as "The Cream of Pure Pennsylvania Oil."

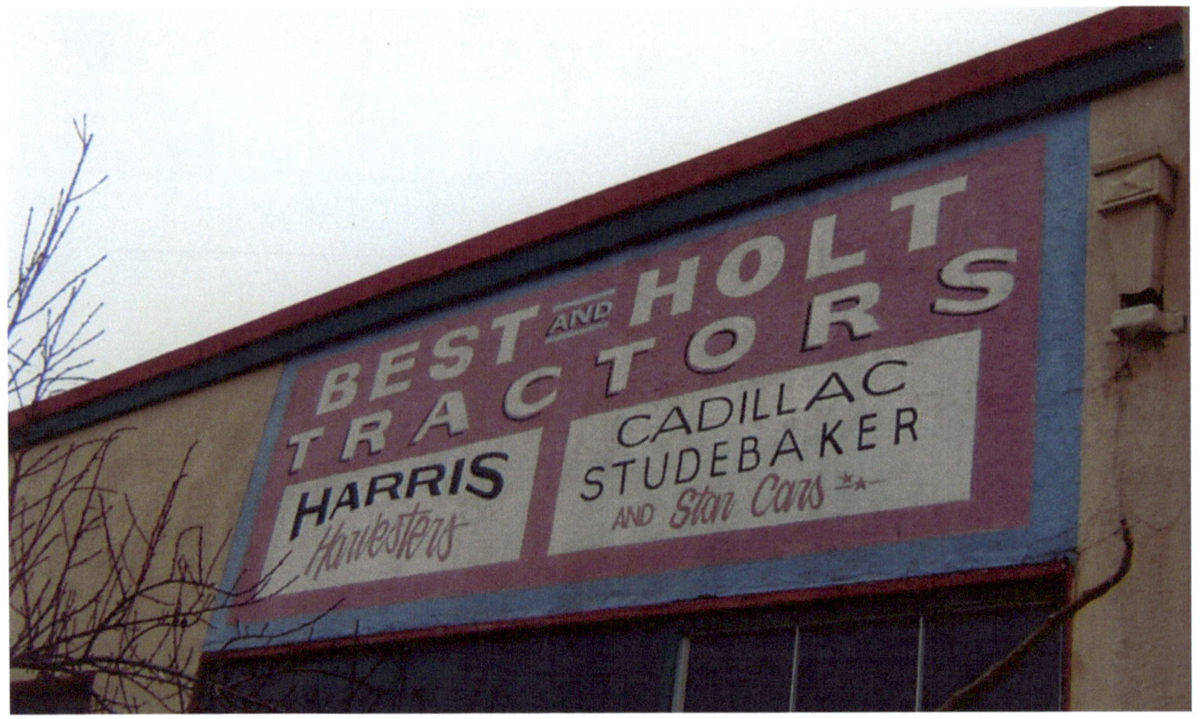

Colusa, CA

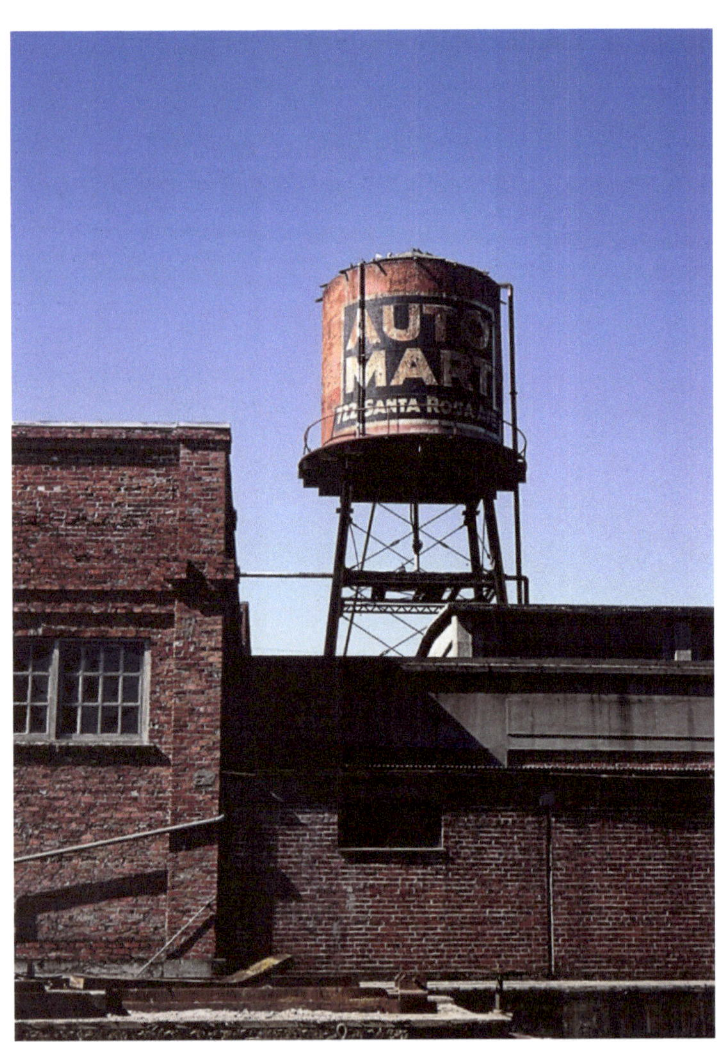

Santa Rosa, CA

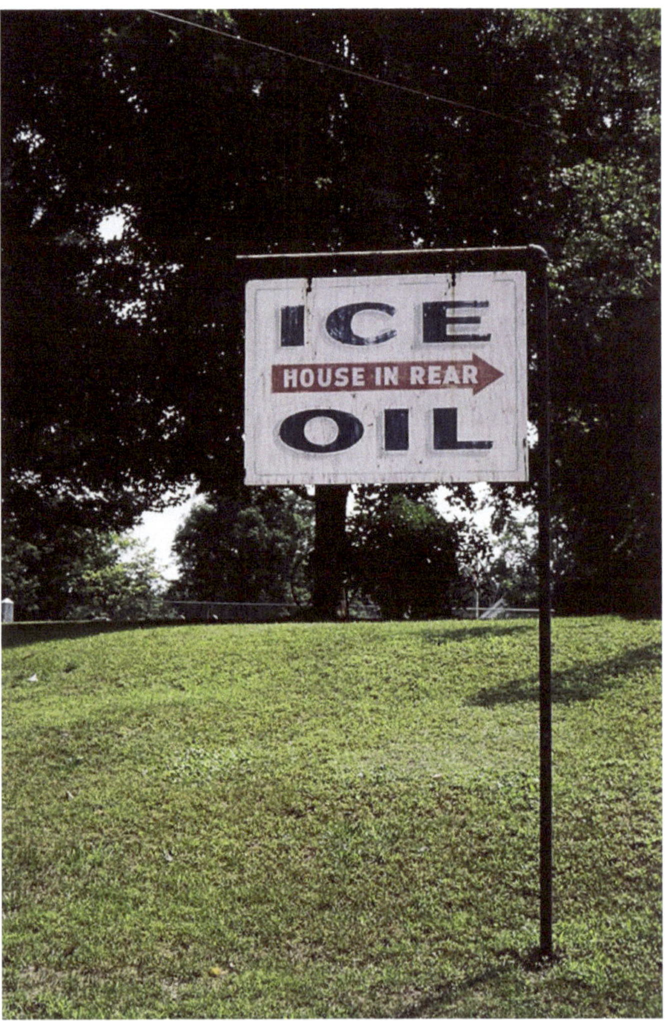

New England

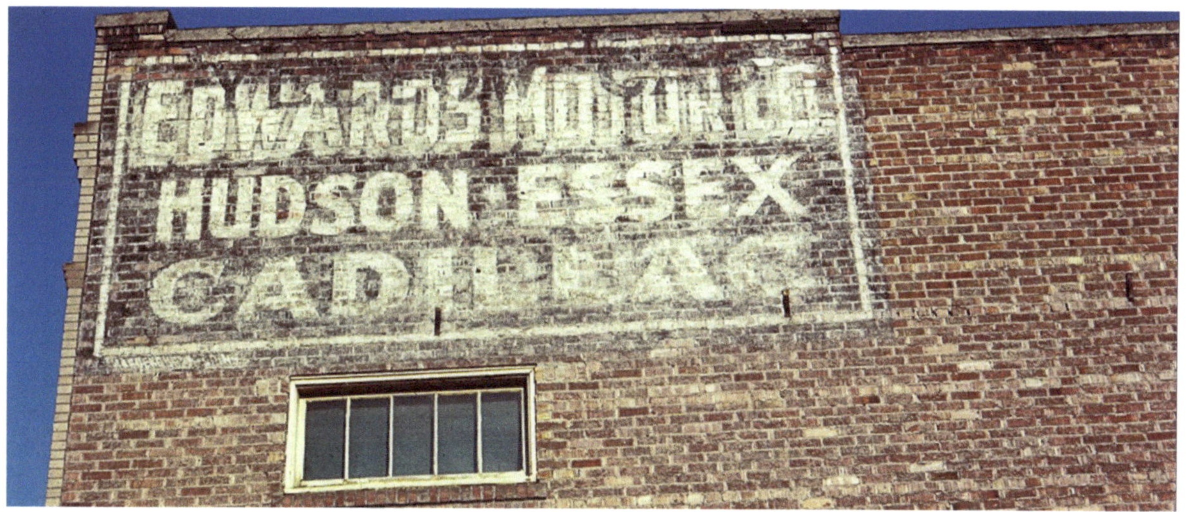

Missoula, MT

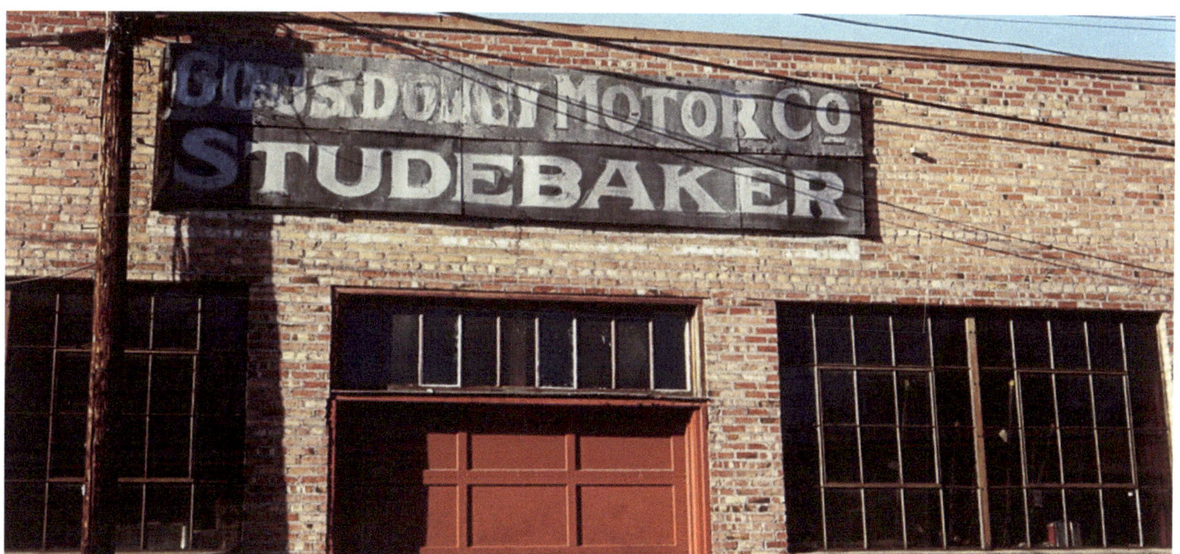

Missoula, MT

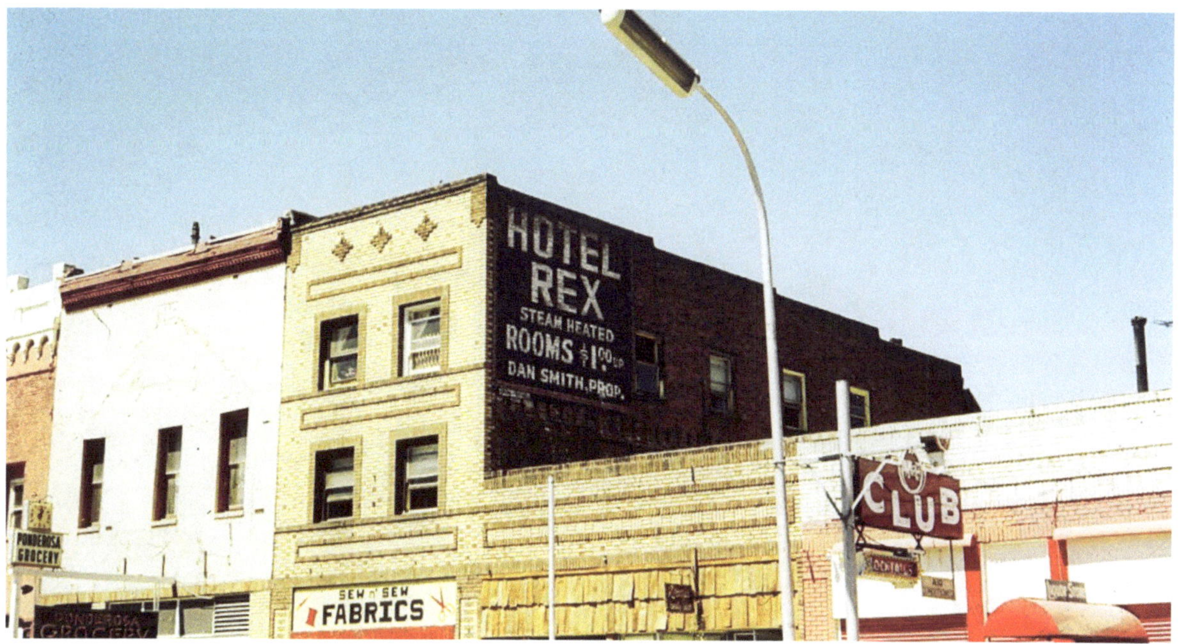

Truckee, CA

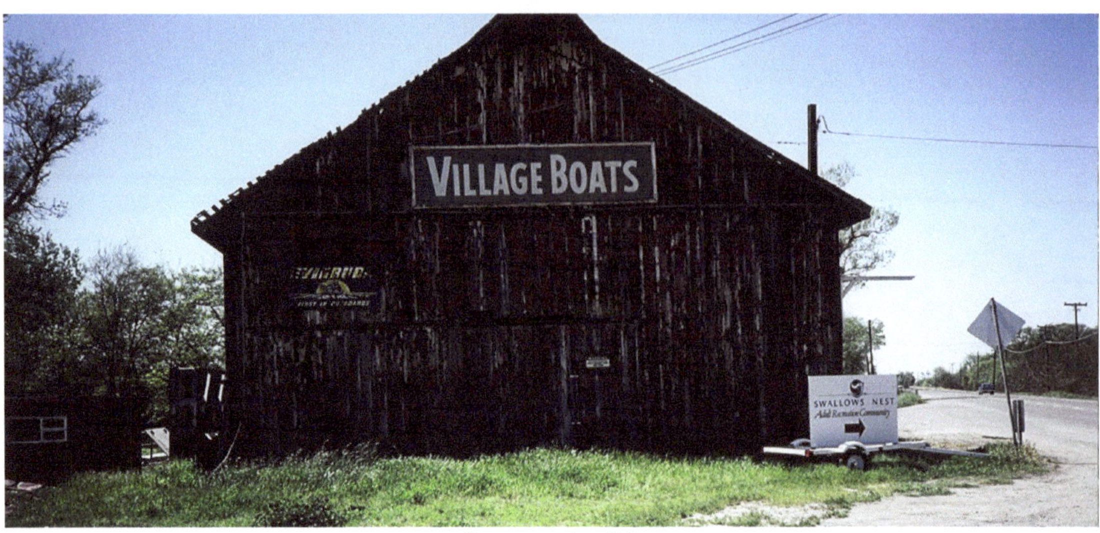

Sacramento, CA

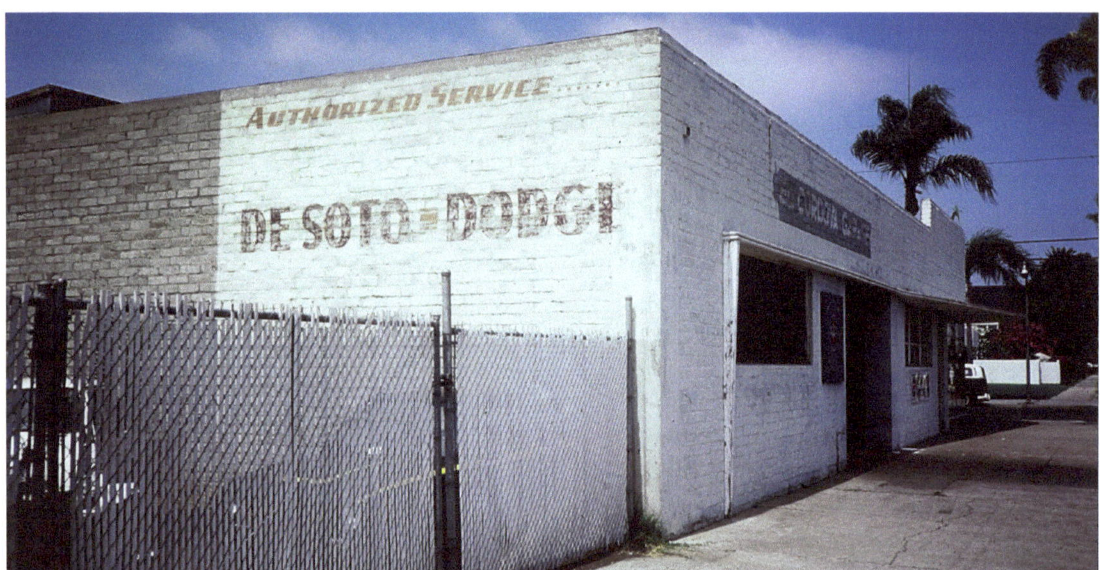

Coronado, CA

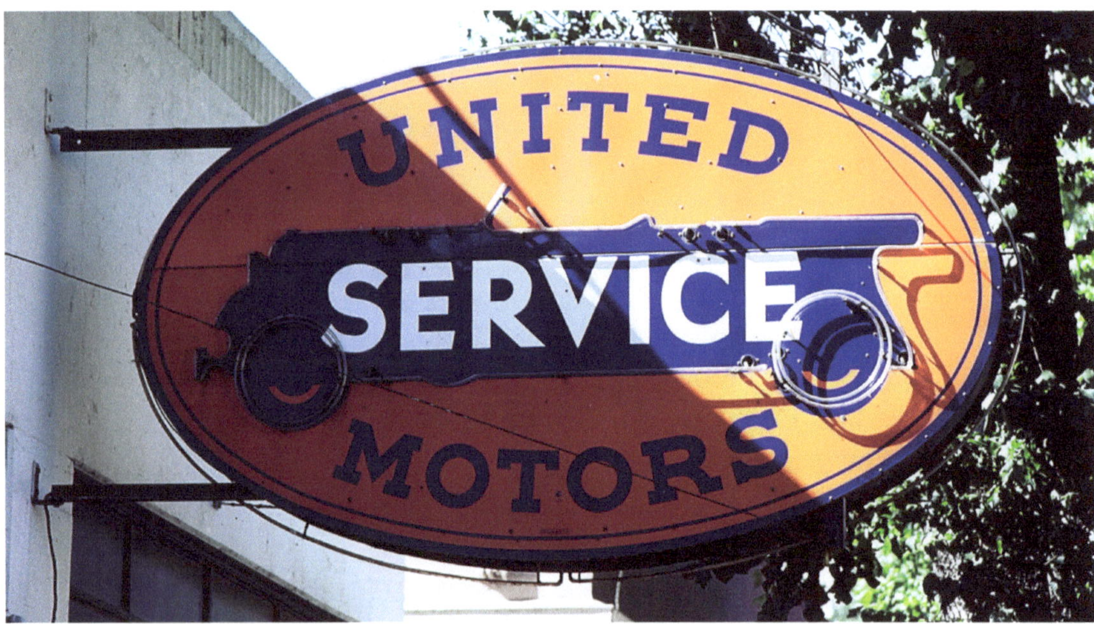

Sacramento, CA

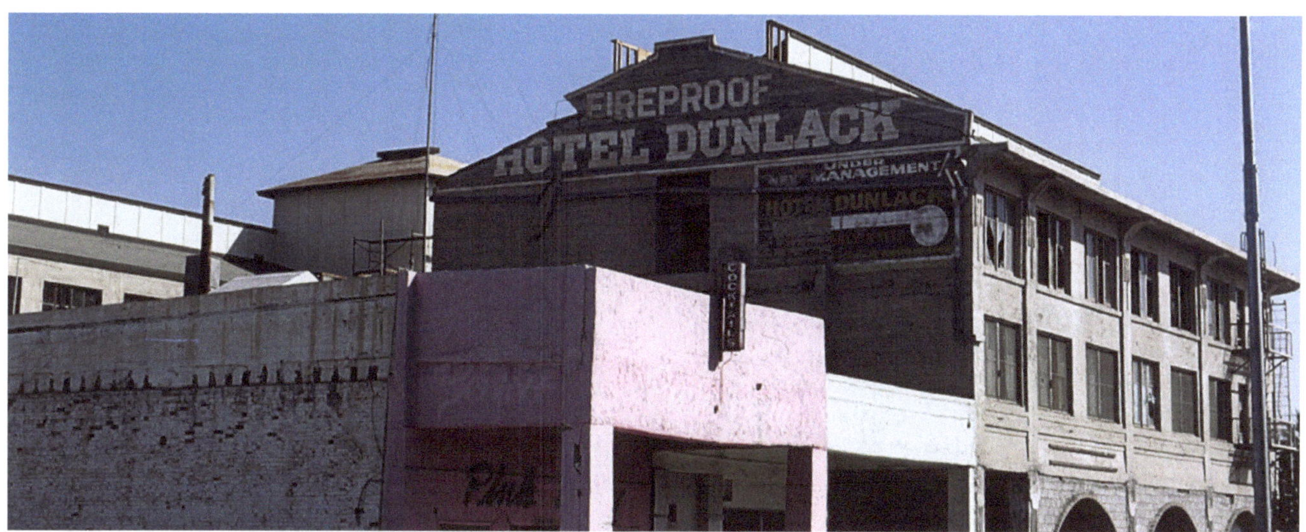

Brawley, CA

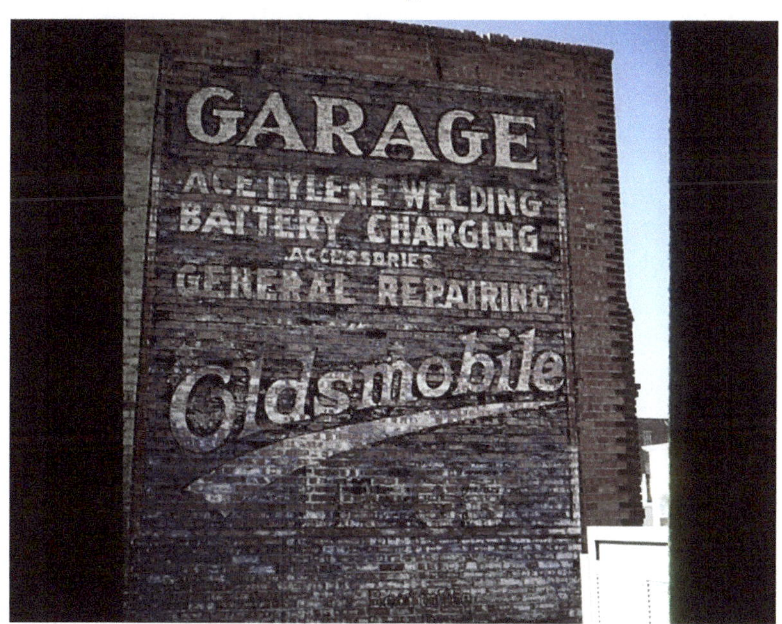

Cokeville, WY

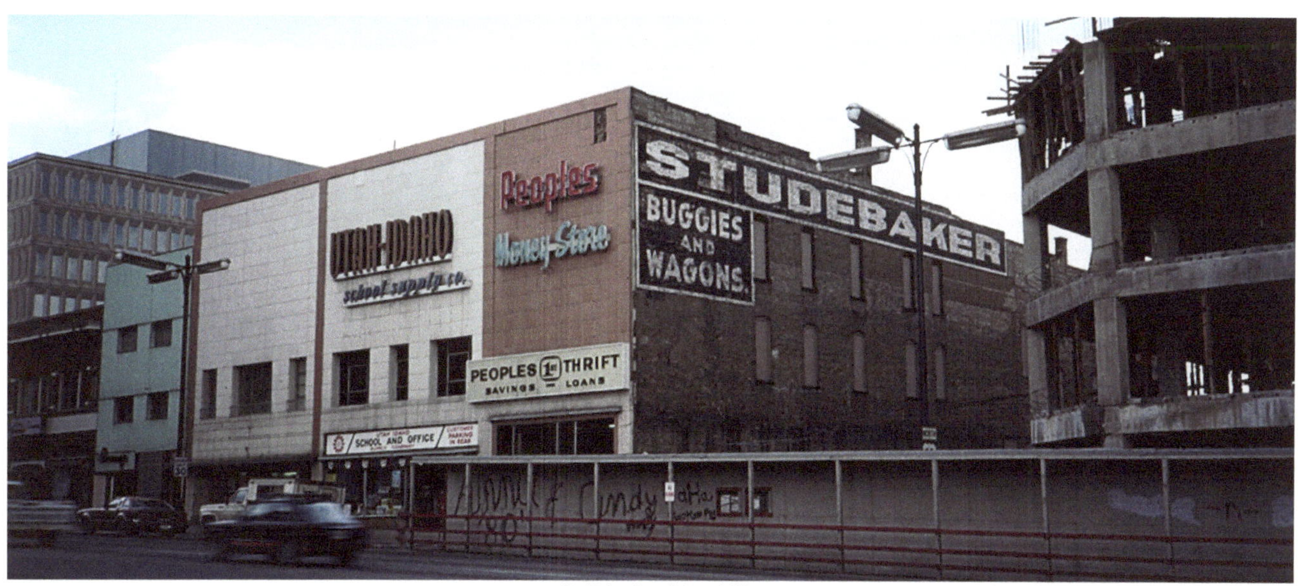

Salt Lake City, UT

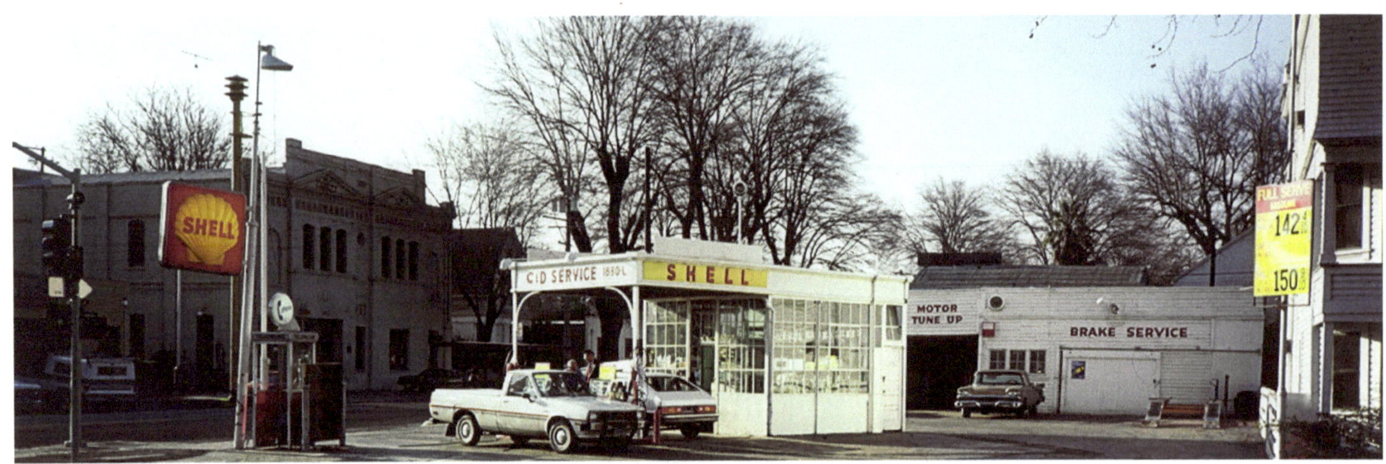

Sacramento, CA

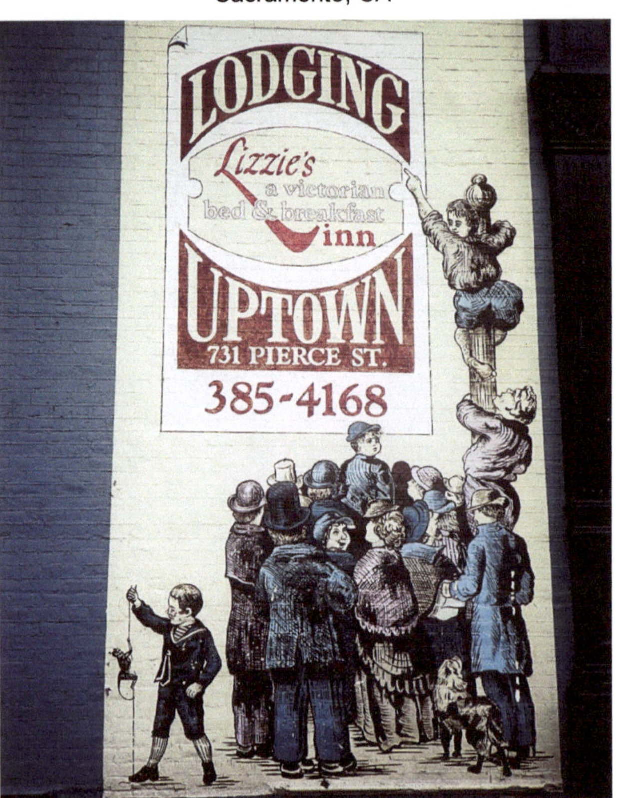

Seattle, WA

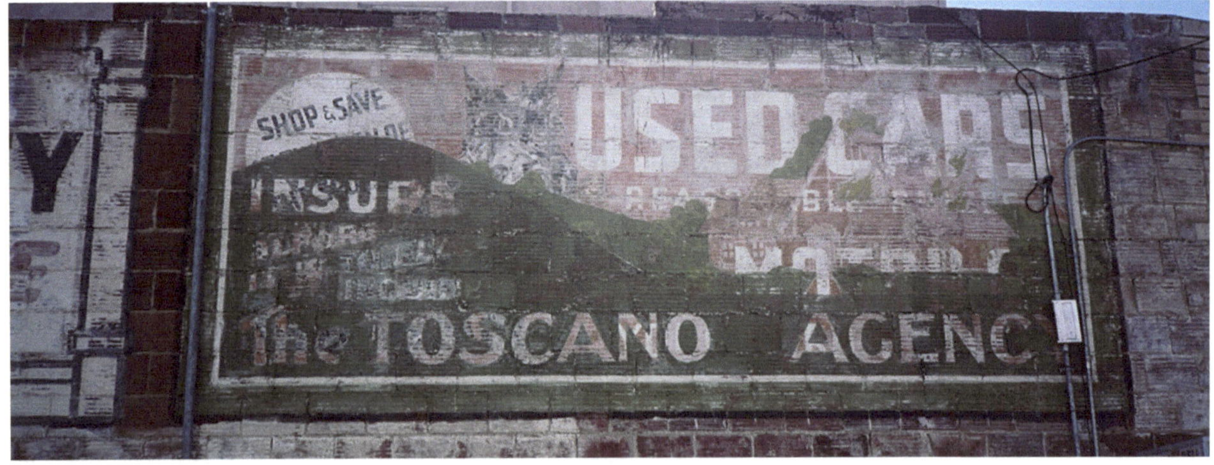

Los Banos, CA

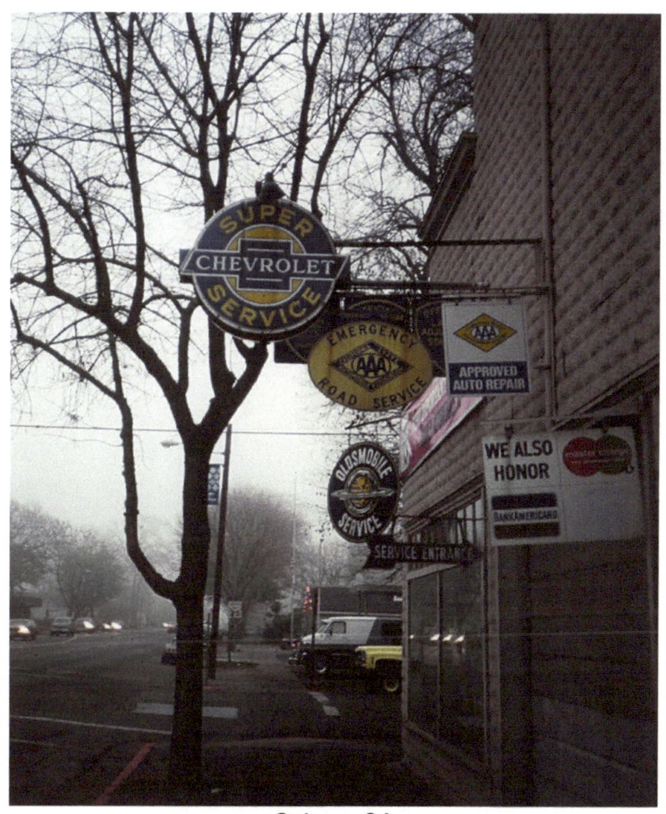

Colusa, CA

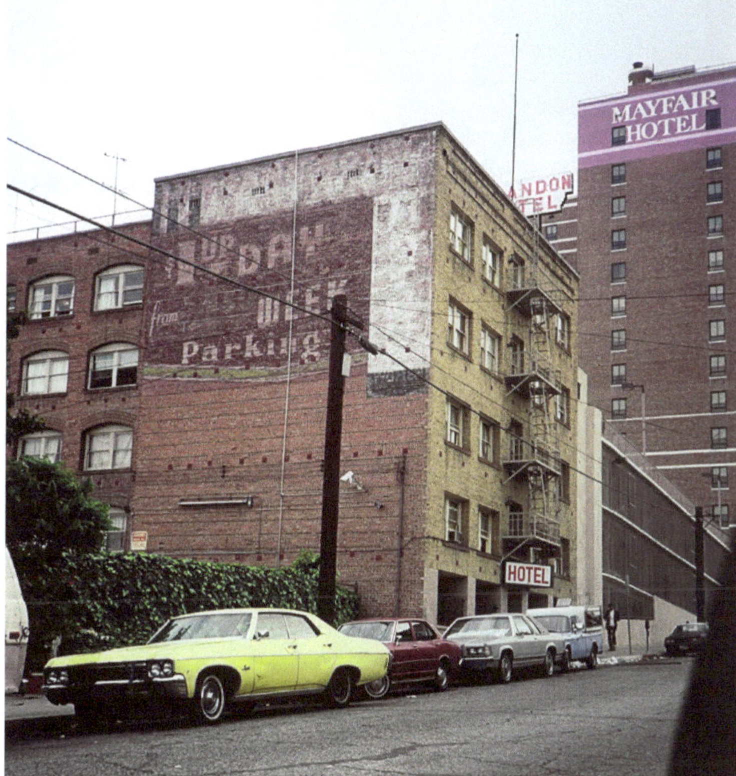

Los Angeles, CA

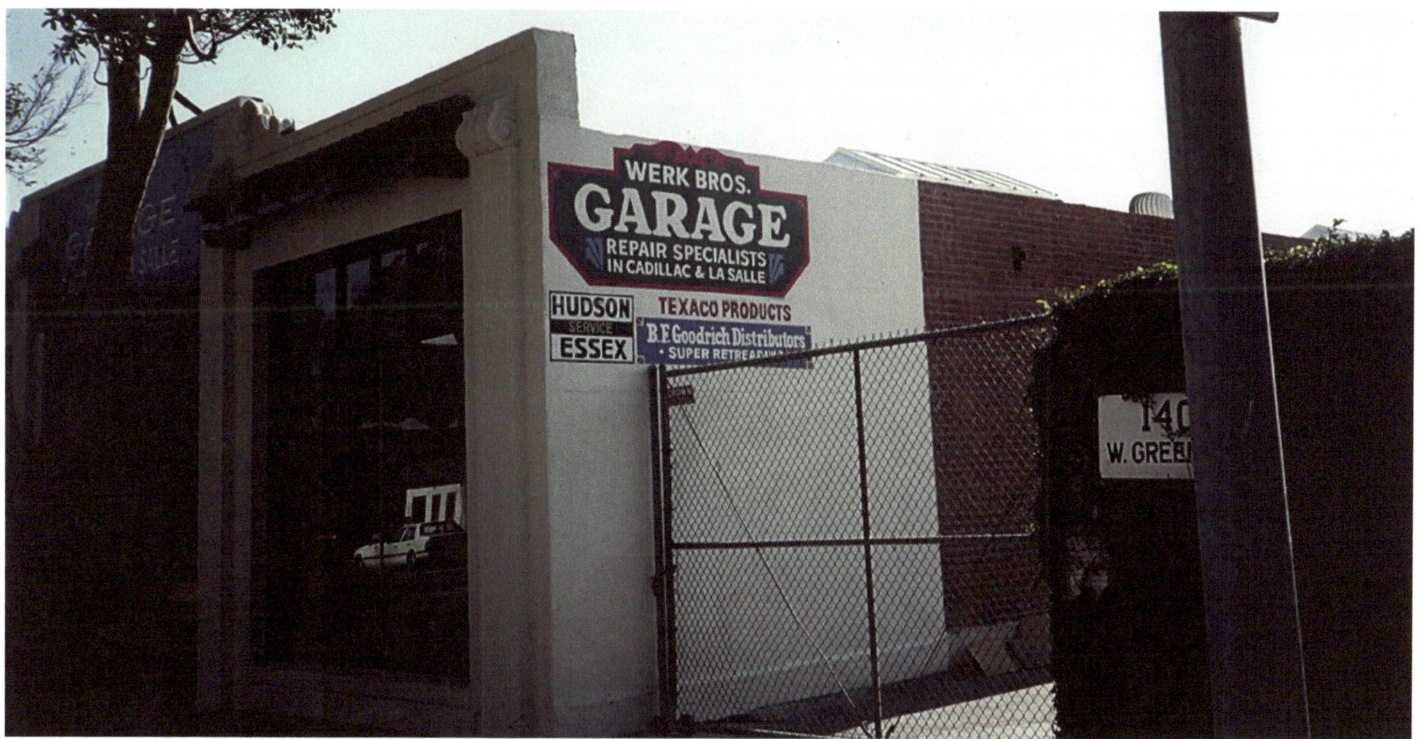

Pasadena, CA

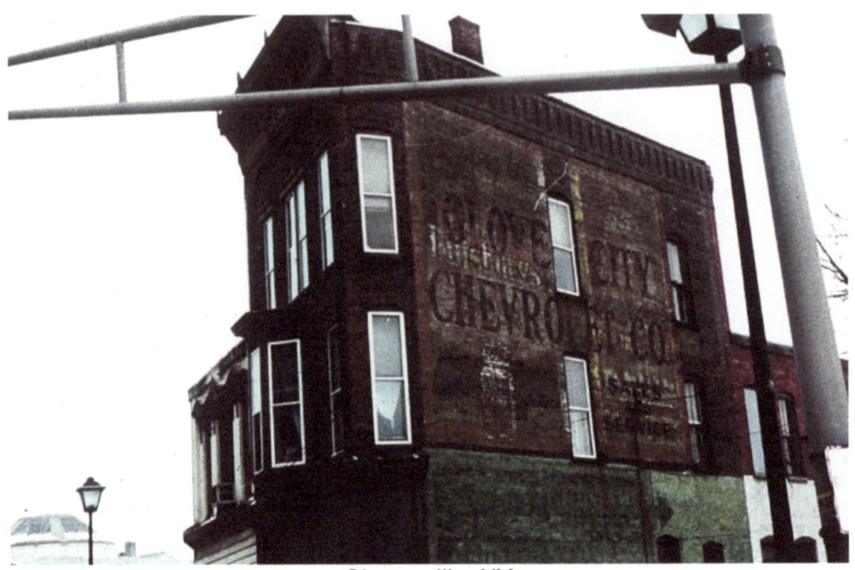

Gloversville, NY

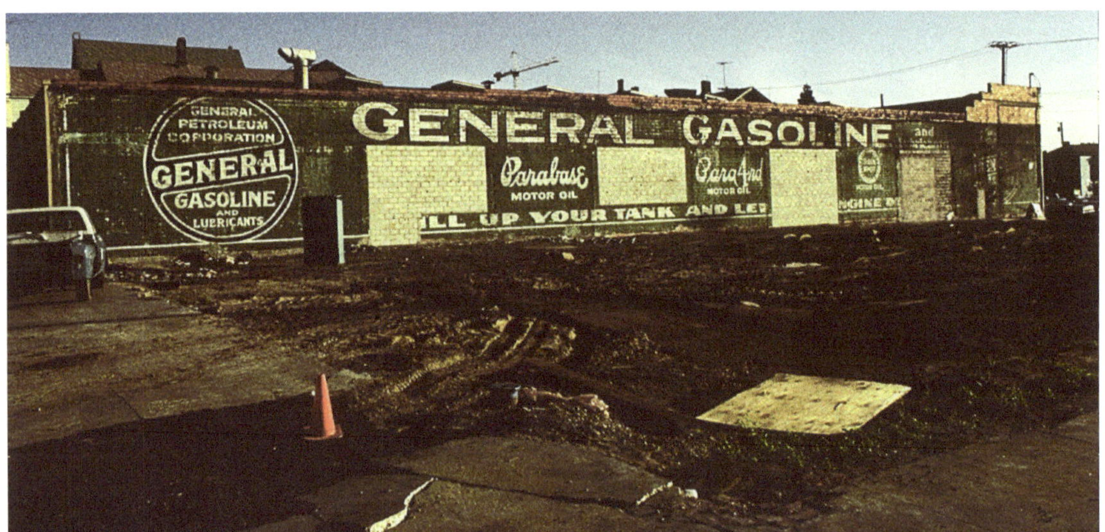

Oakland, CA

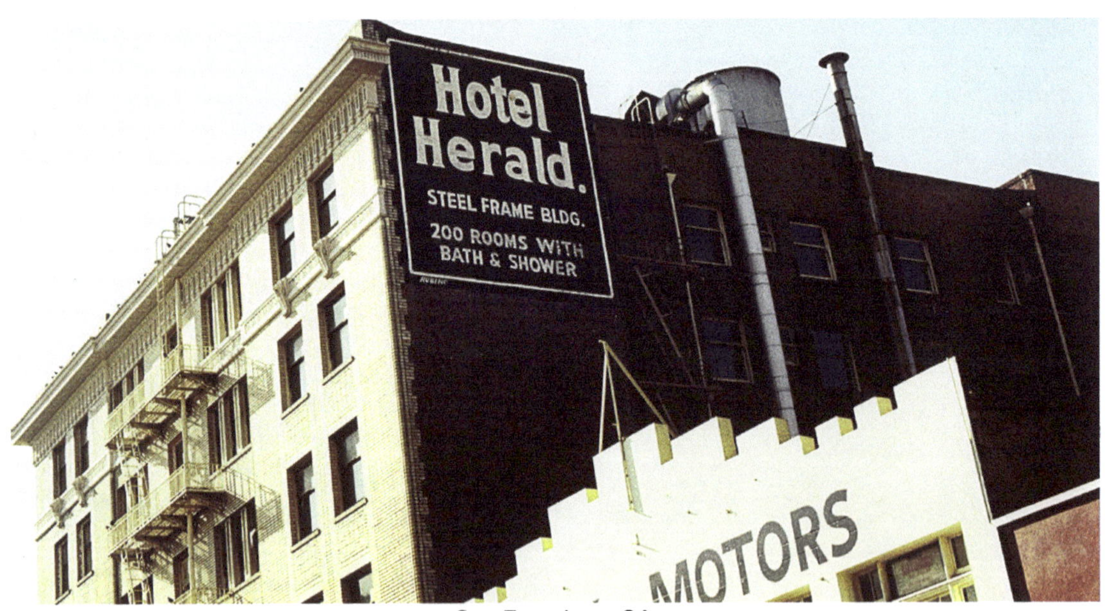

San Francisco, CA

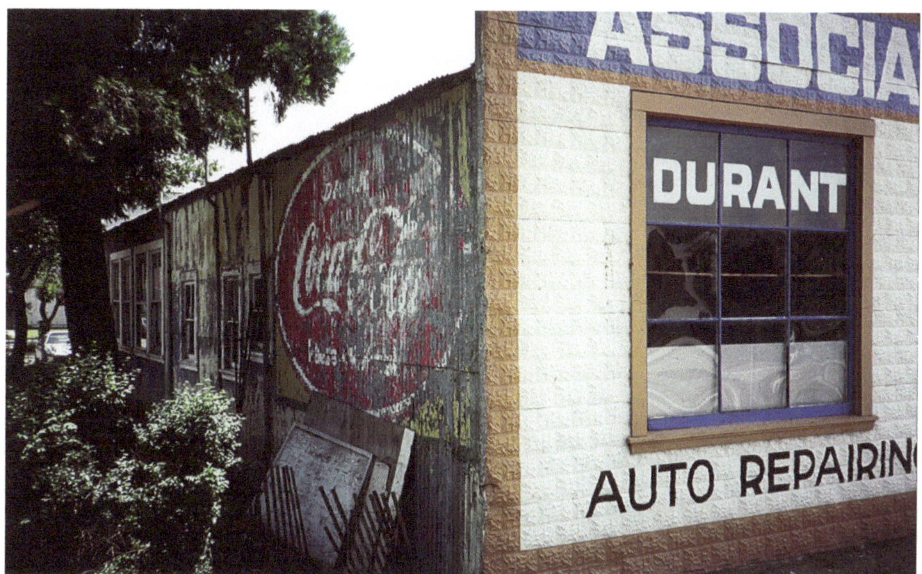

Livermore, CA

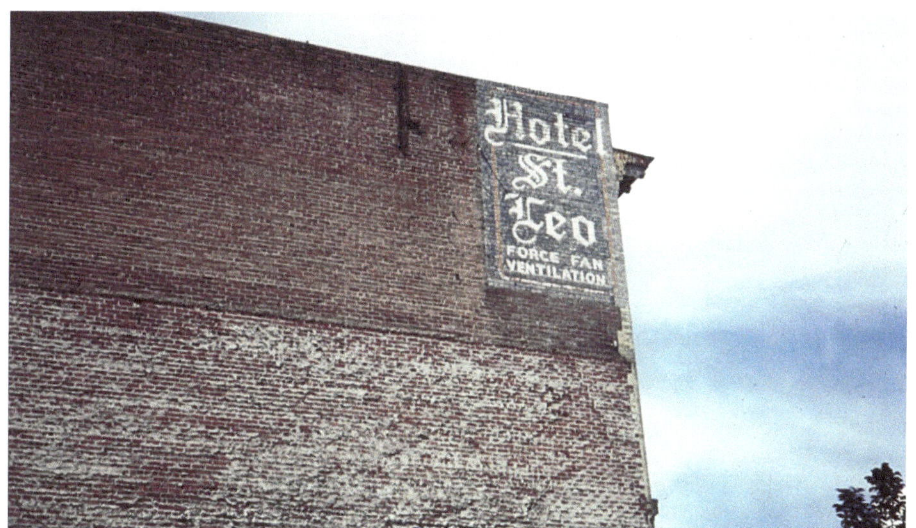

Stockton, CA

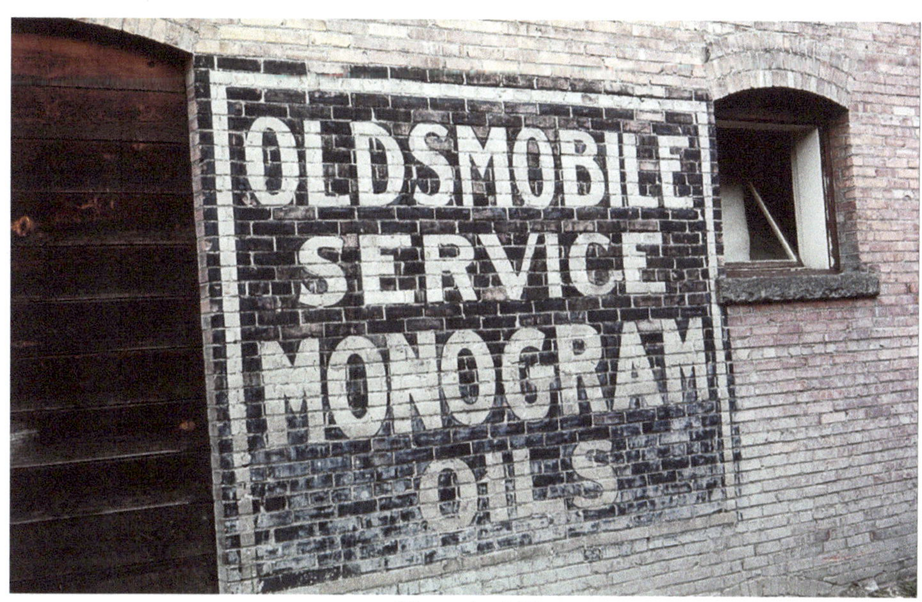

Missoula, MT

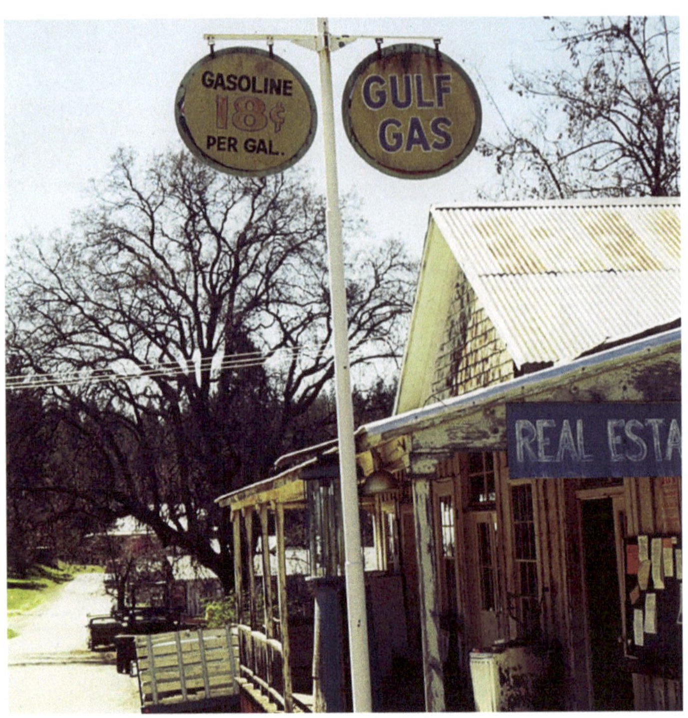

Sheepranch, CA

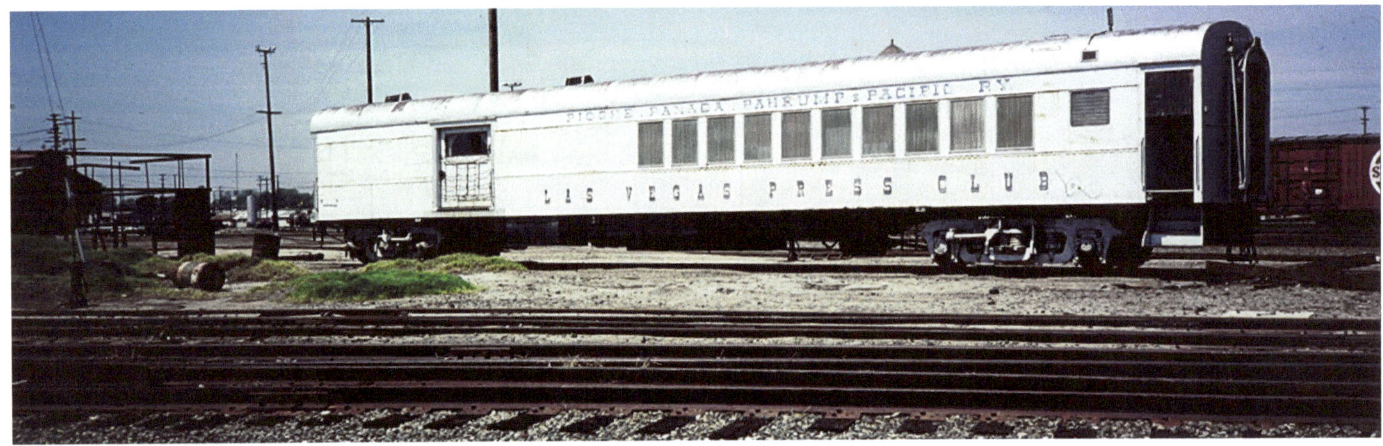

Sacramento, CA

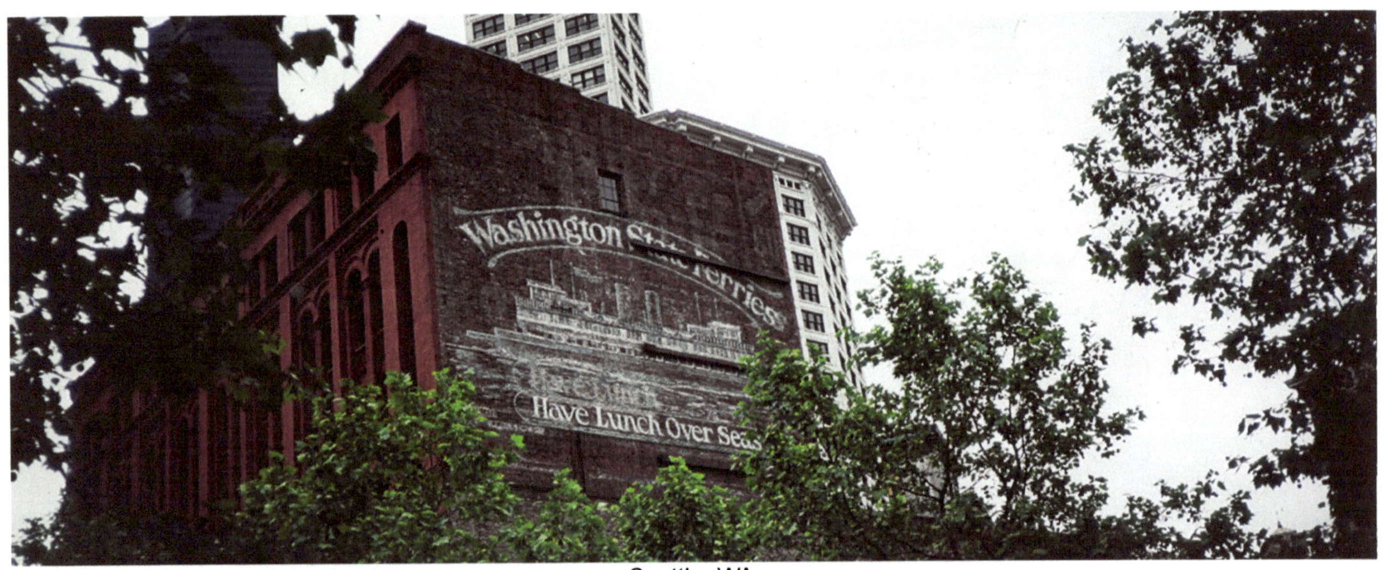

Seattle, WA

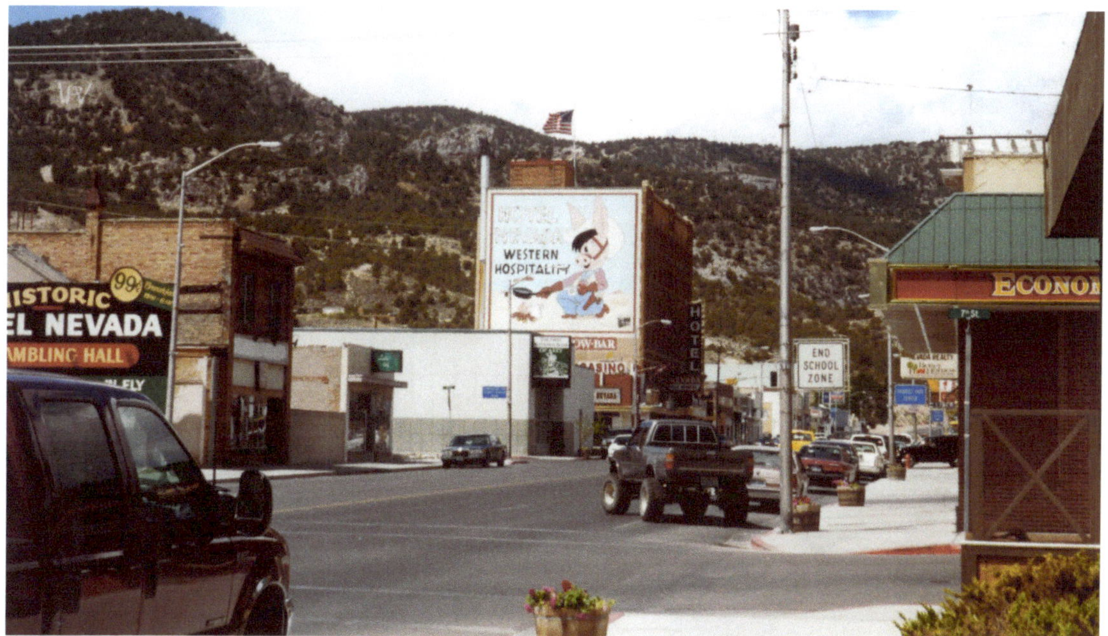

Ely, NV

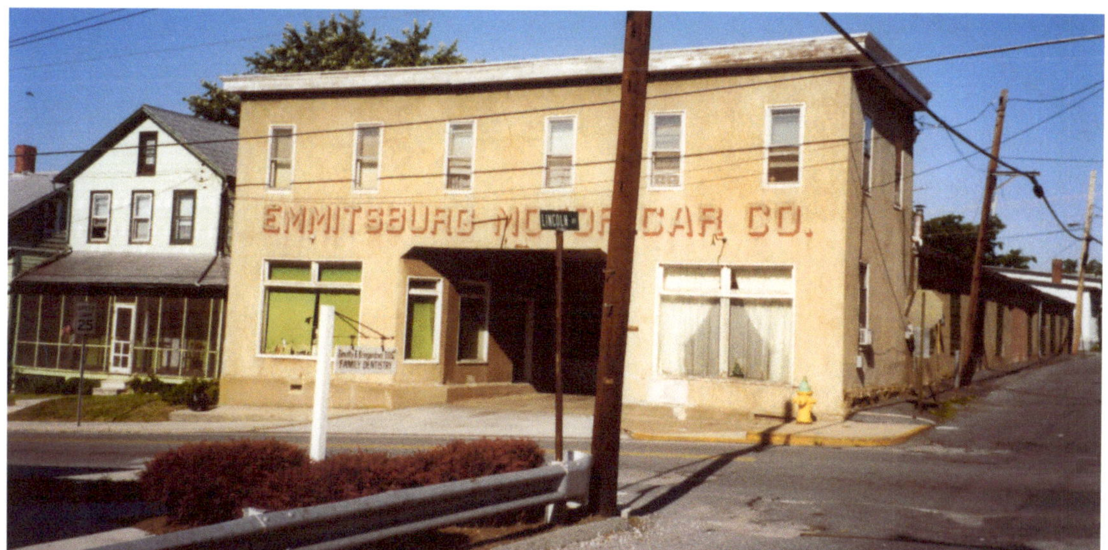

Emmitsburg, MD

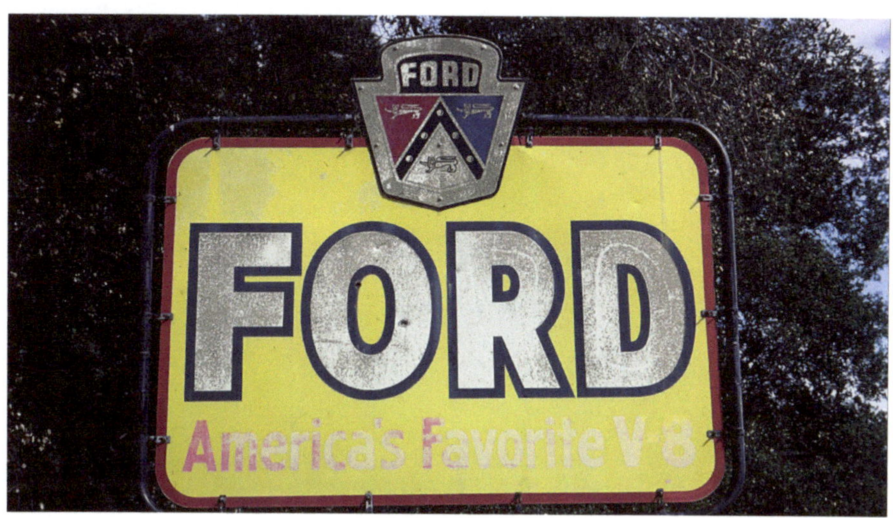

Geyserville, CA

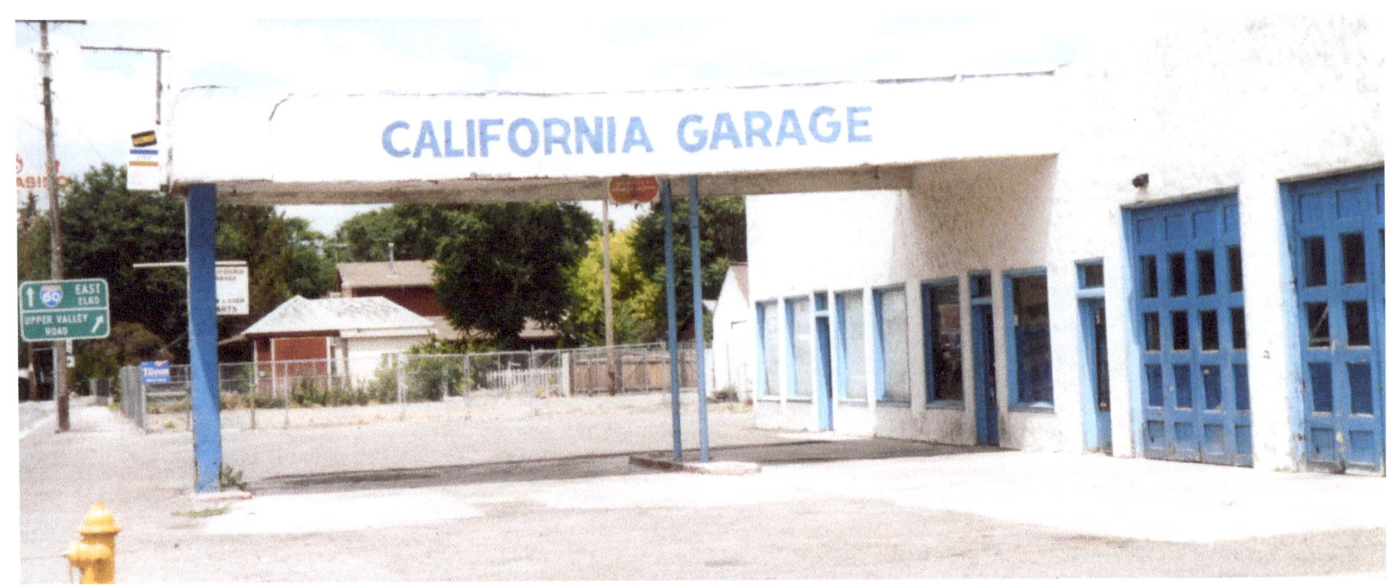

Lovelock, NV

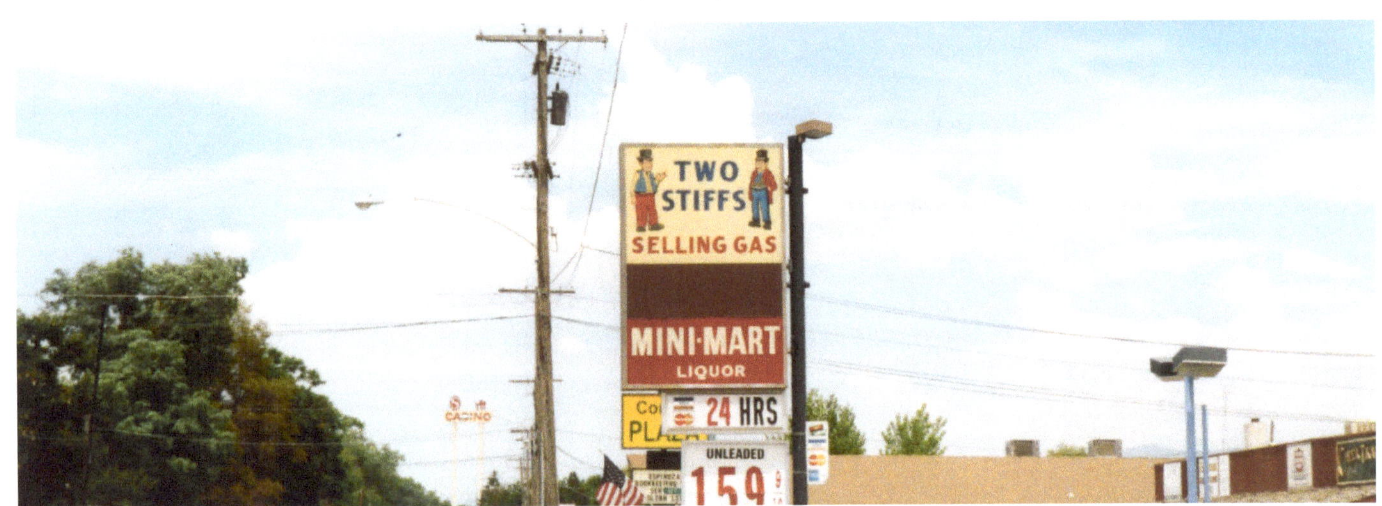

Lovelock, NV

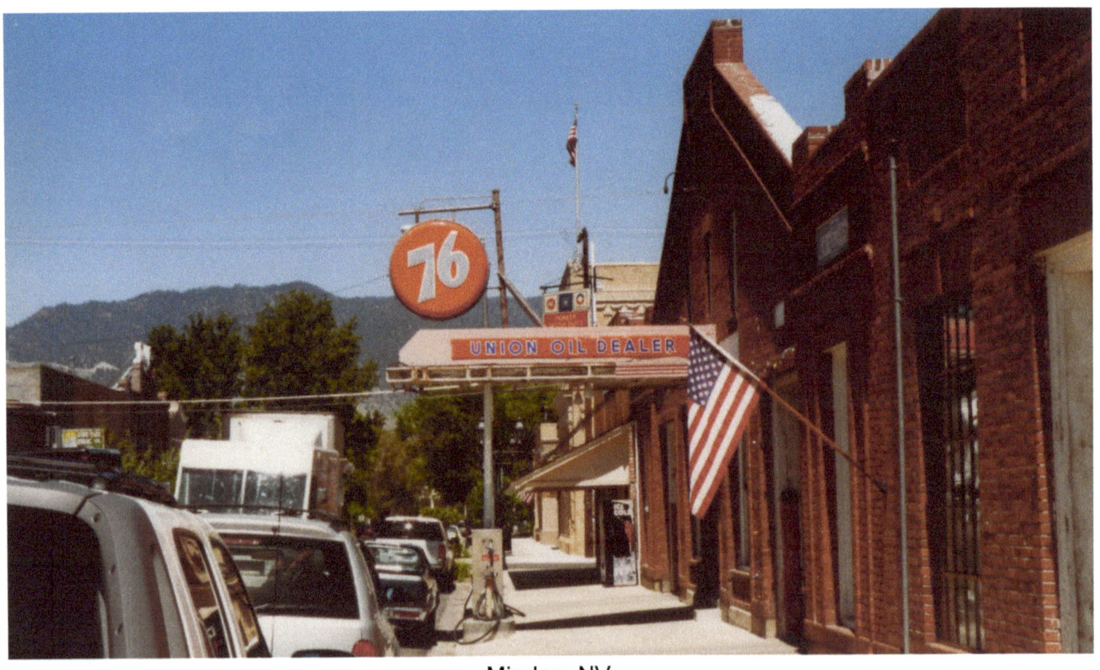

Minden, NV

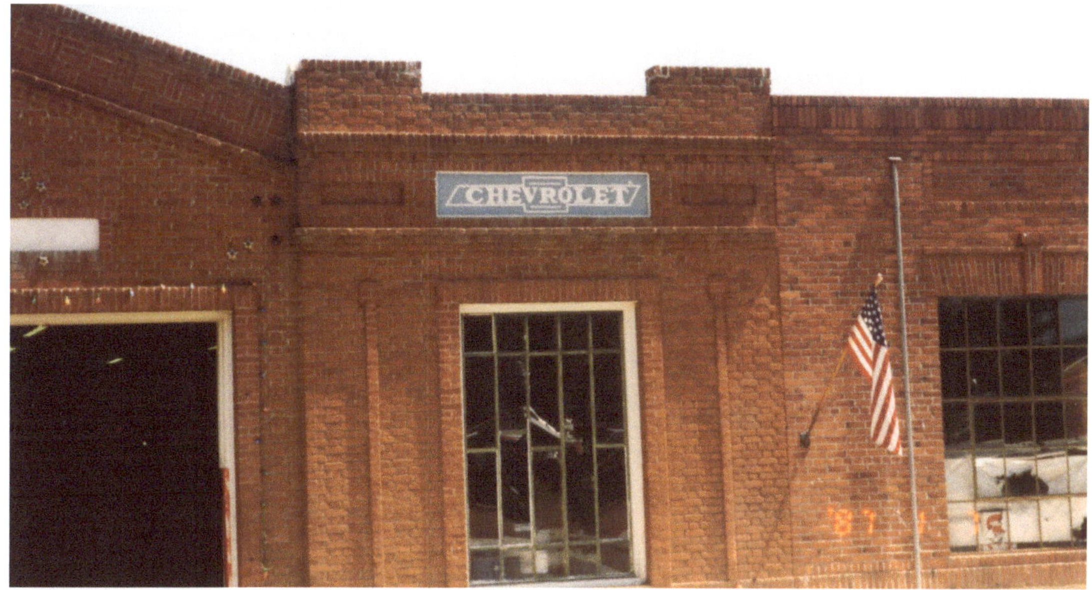

Minden, NV

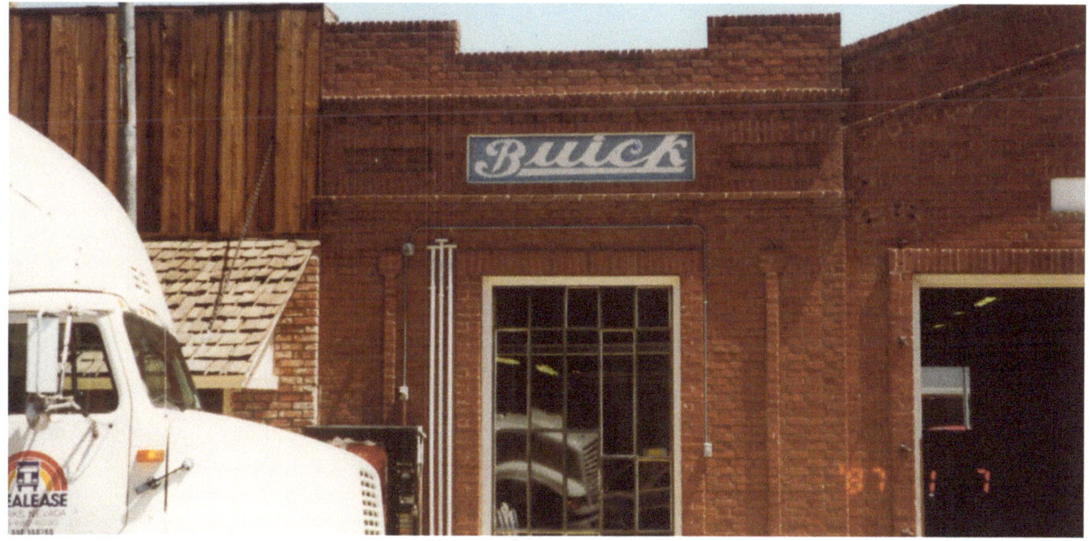

Minden, NV

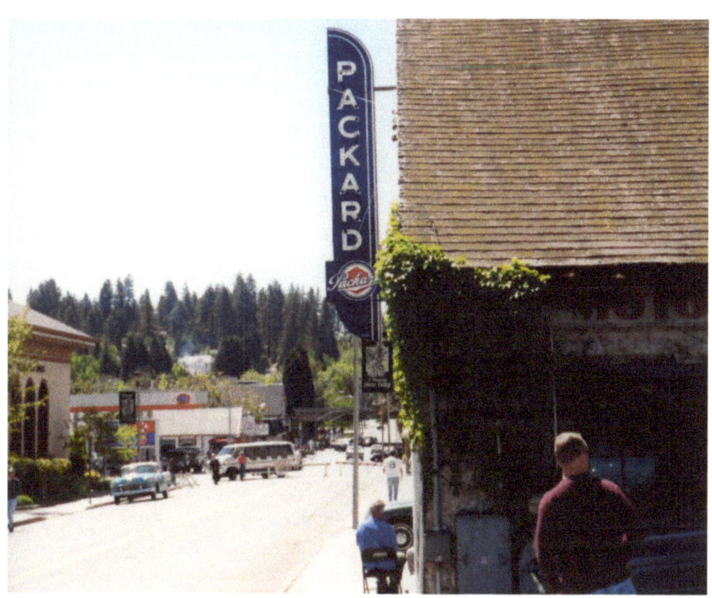

Nevada City, CA

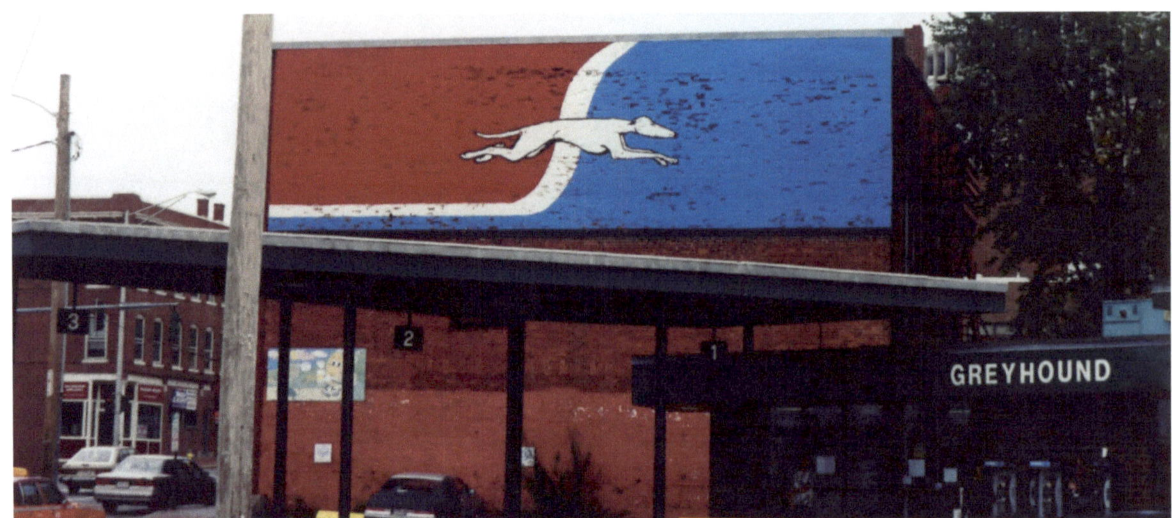

Portland, ME

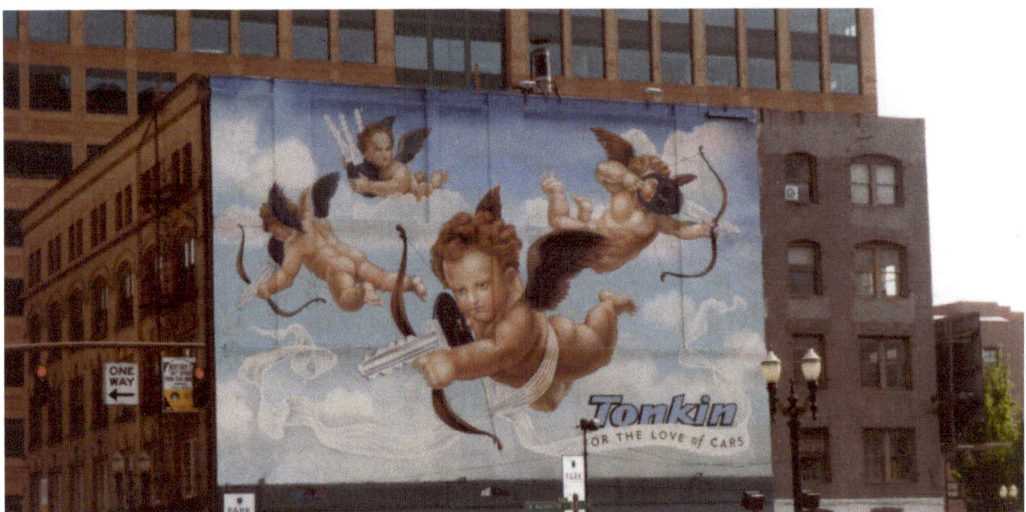

Portland, OR

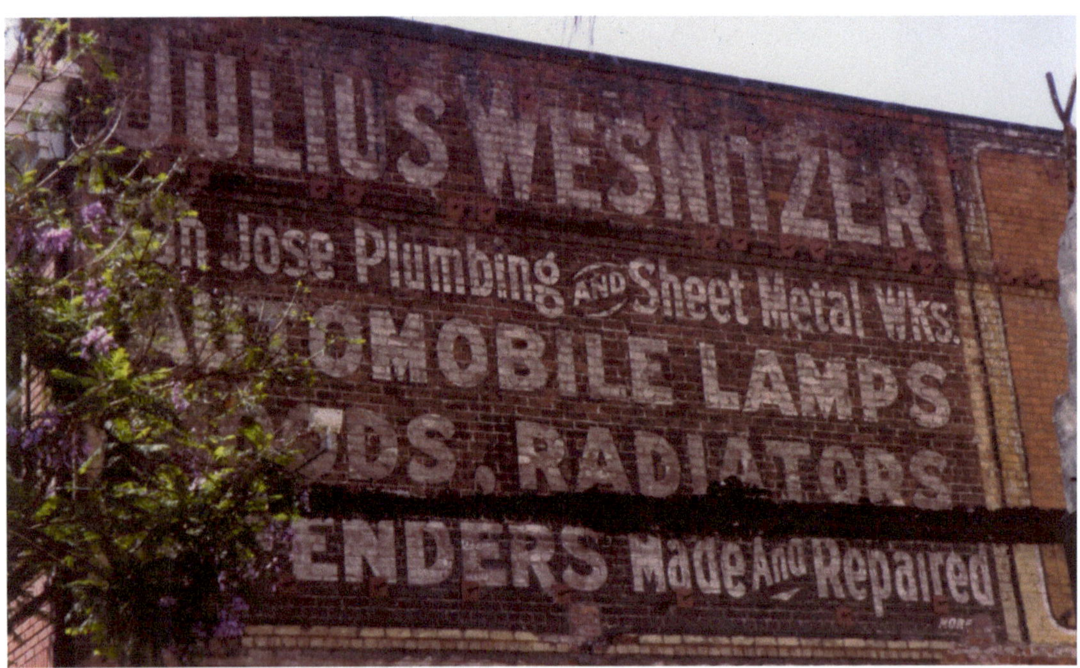

San Jose, CA

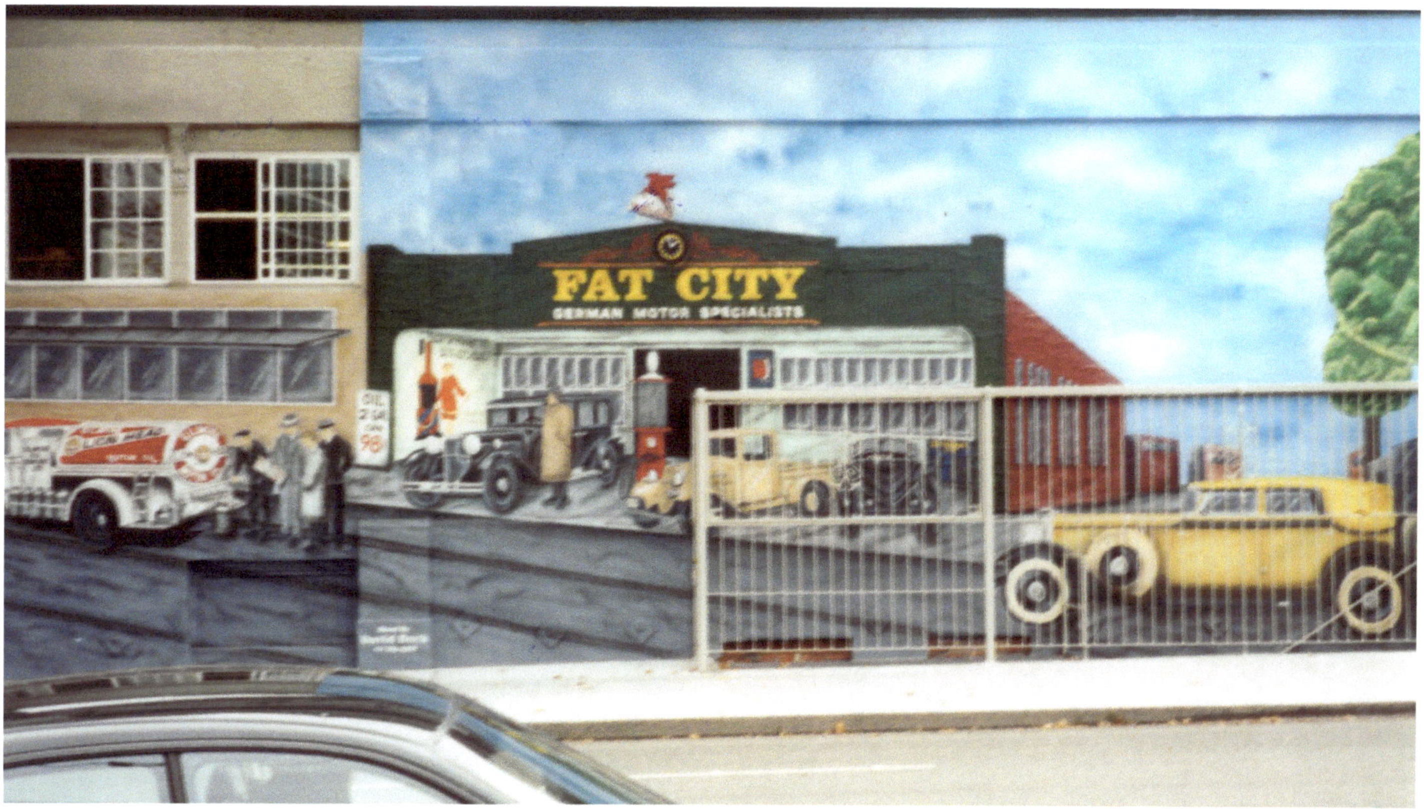

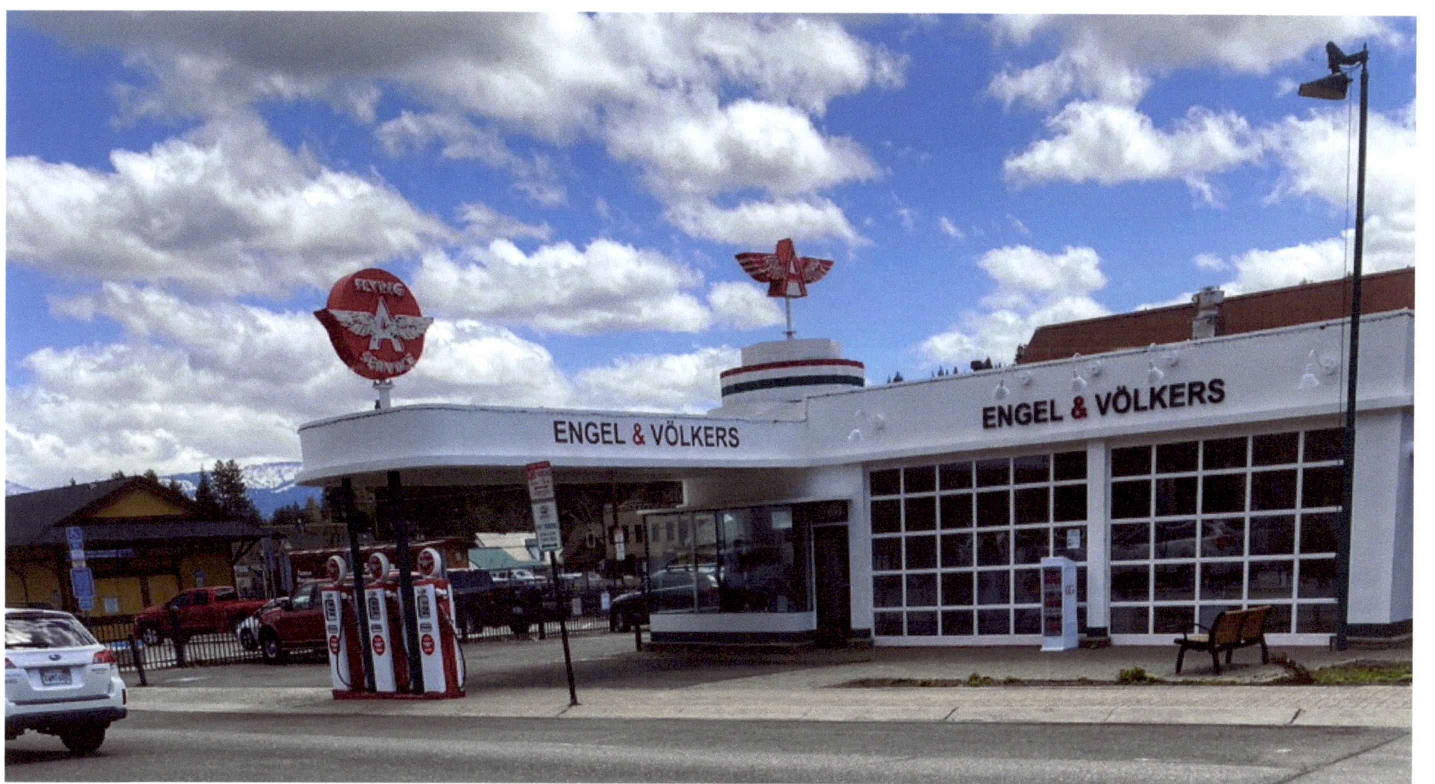

Seattle, WA

Truckee, CA

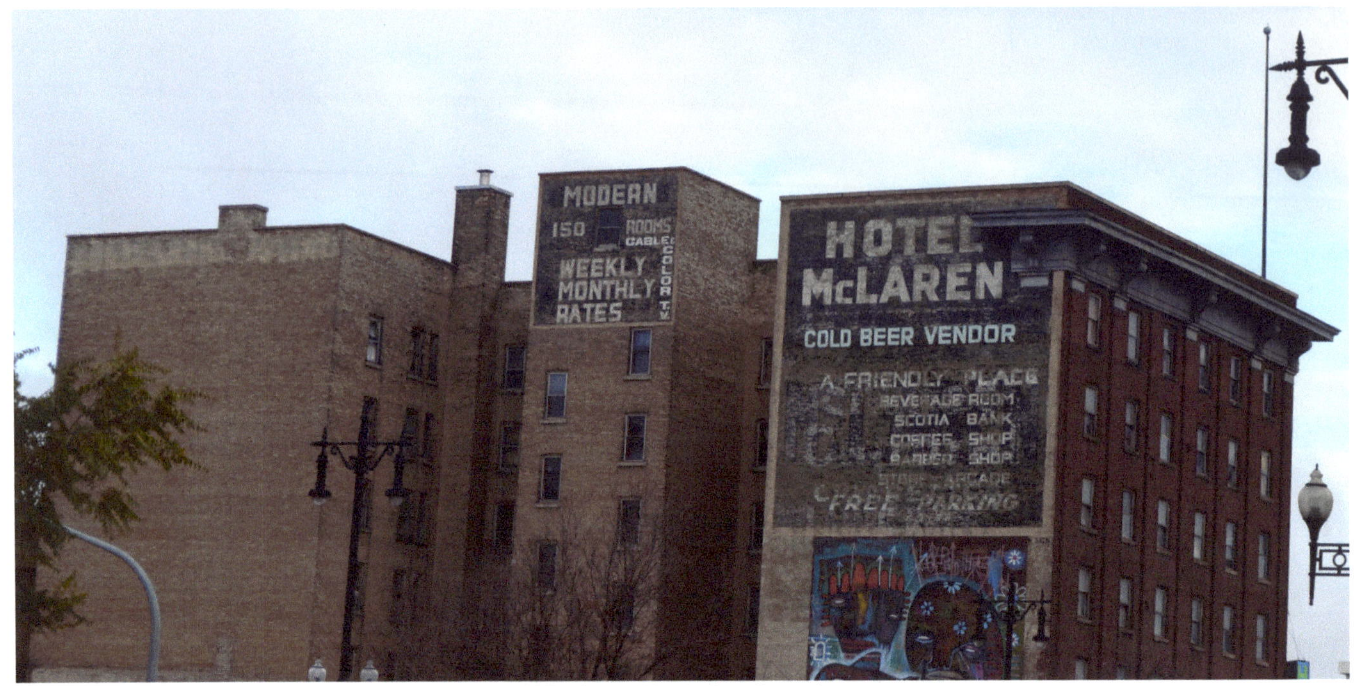

Winnipeg, Manitoba, Canada

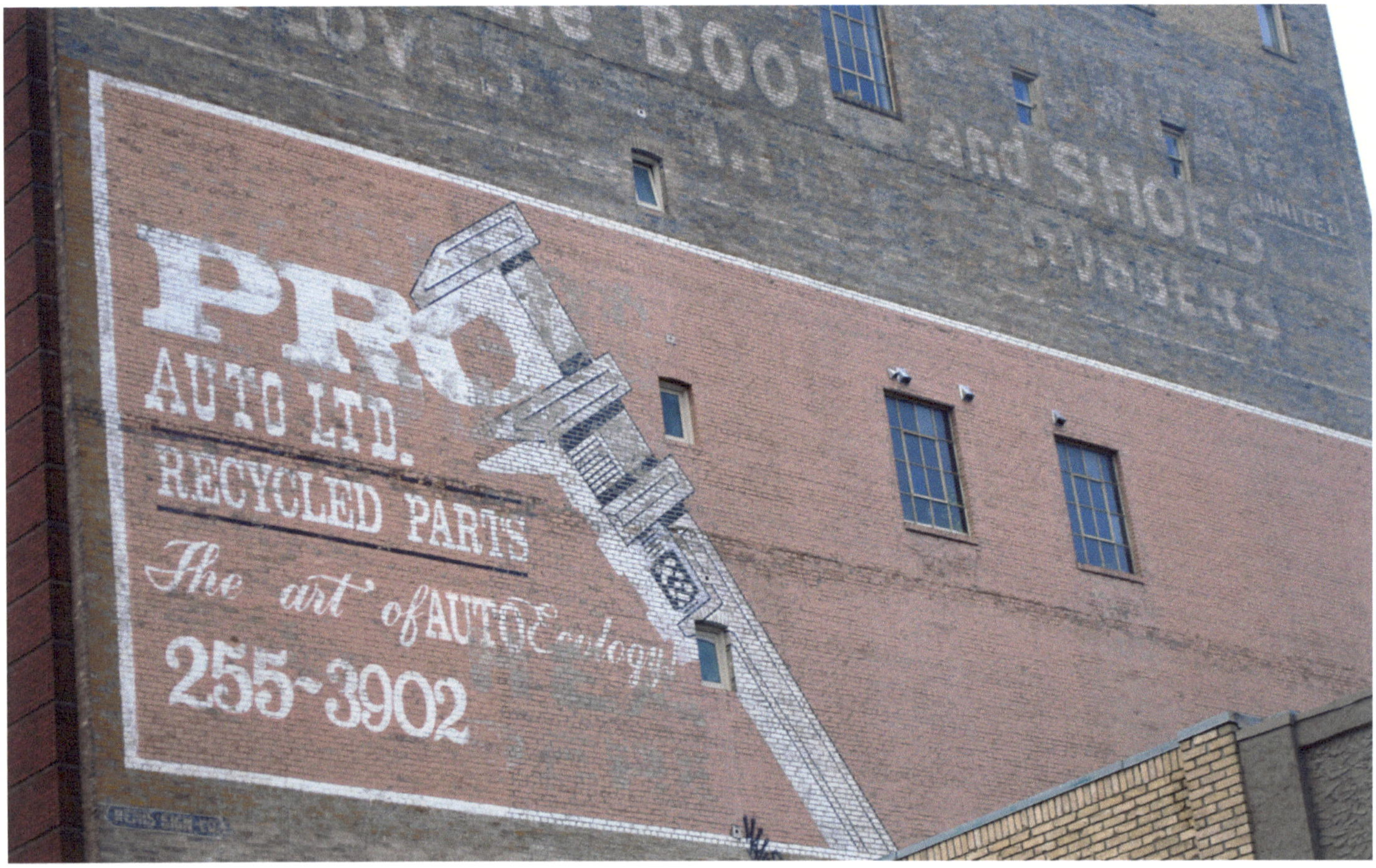

Winnipeg, Manitoba, Canada

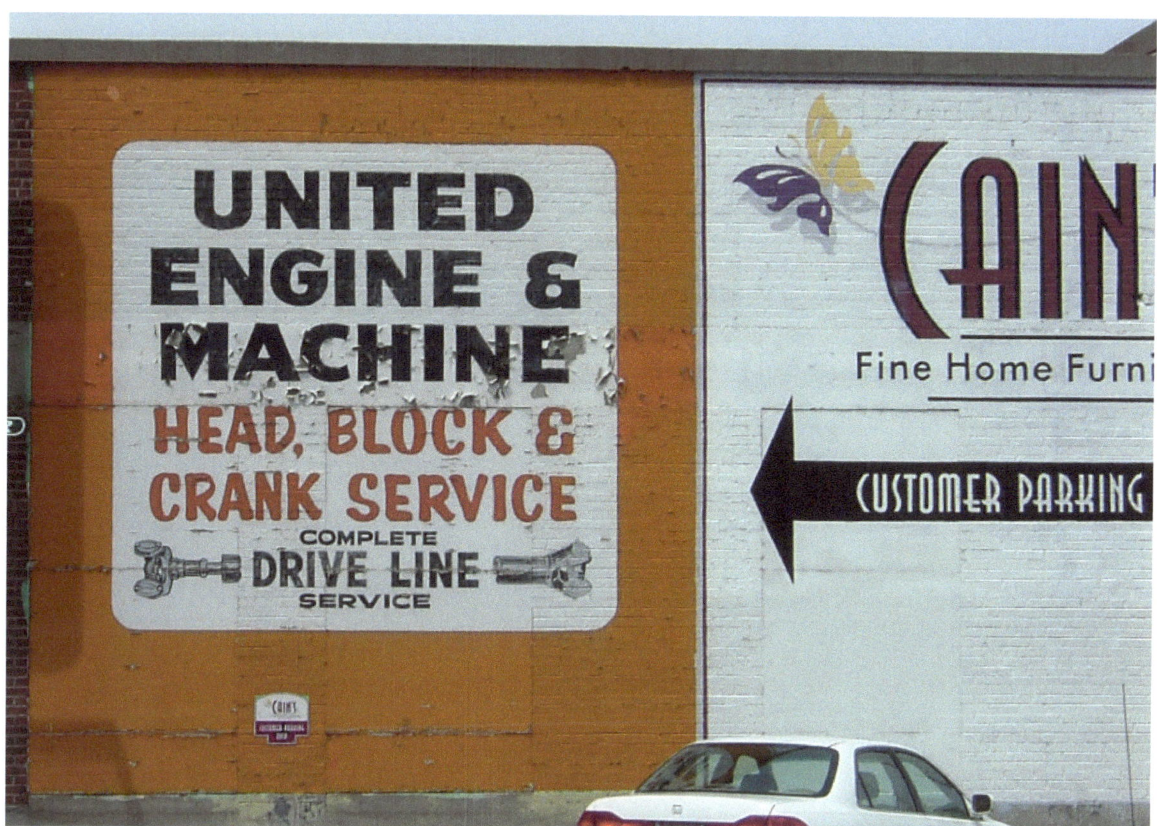

Buhl, ID

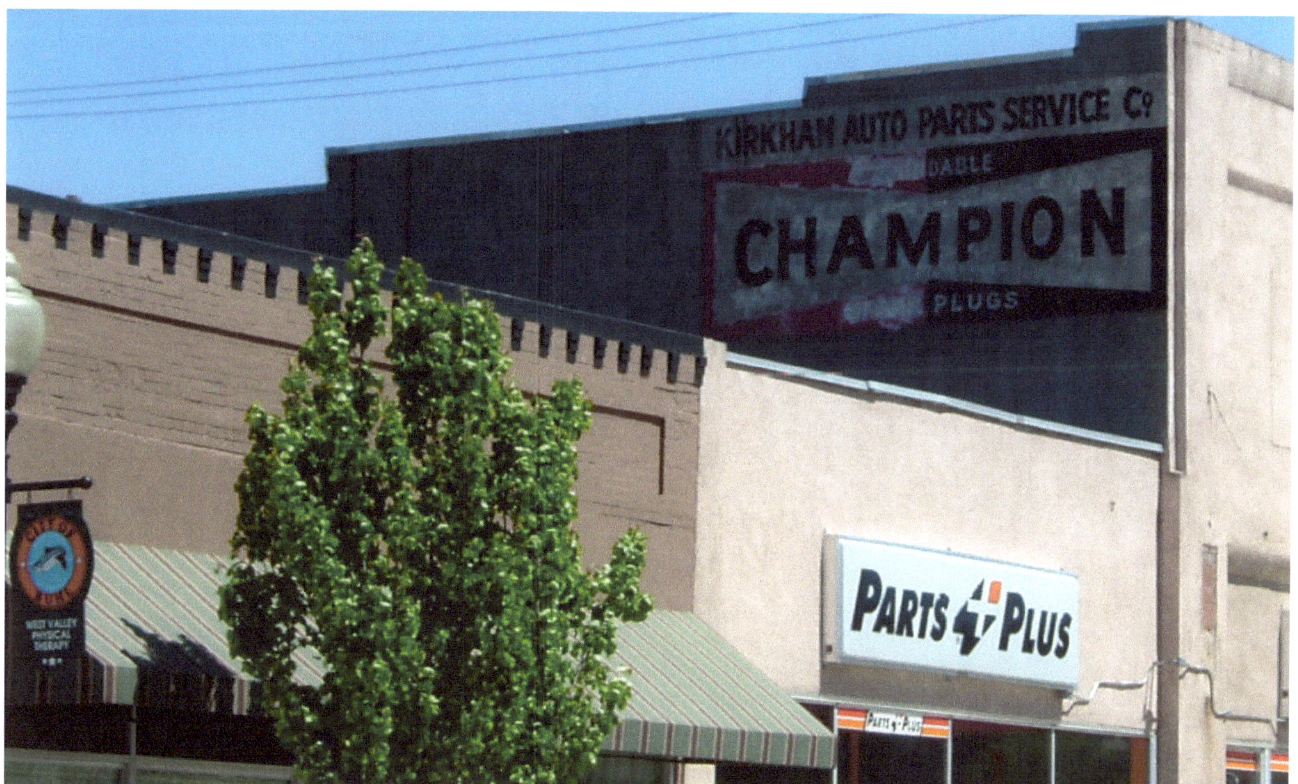

Buhl, ID

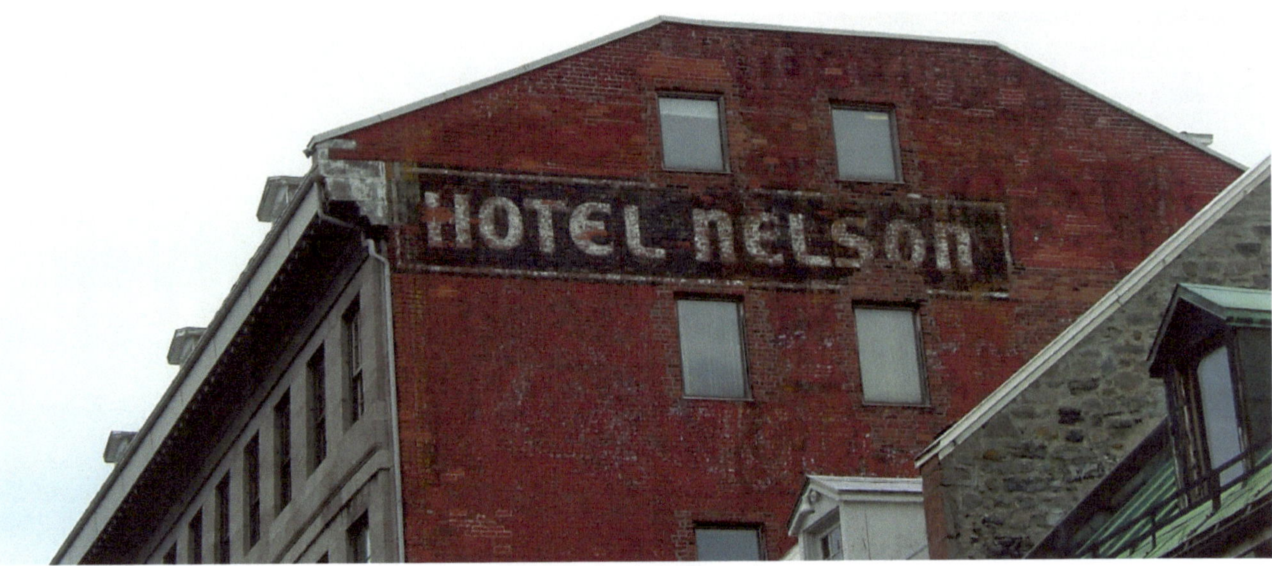

Montreal, Quebec, Canada

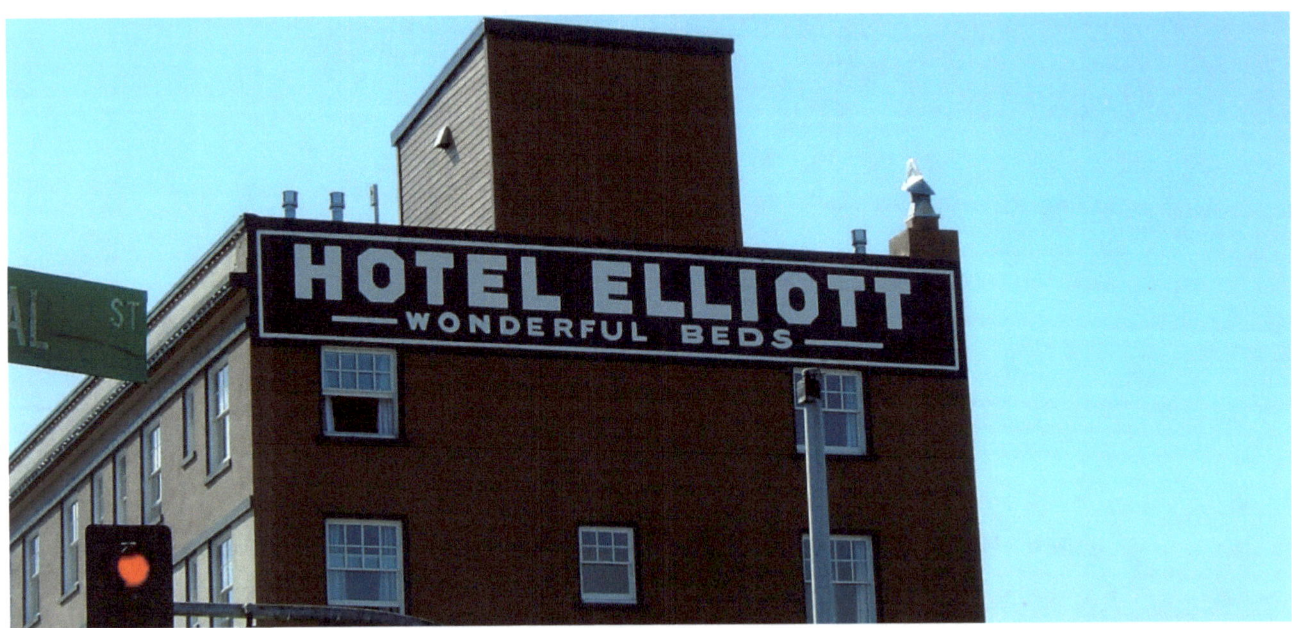

Astoria, OR

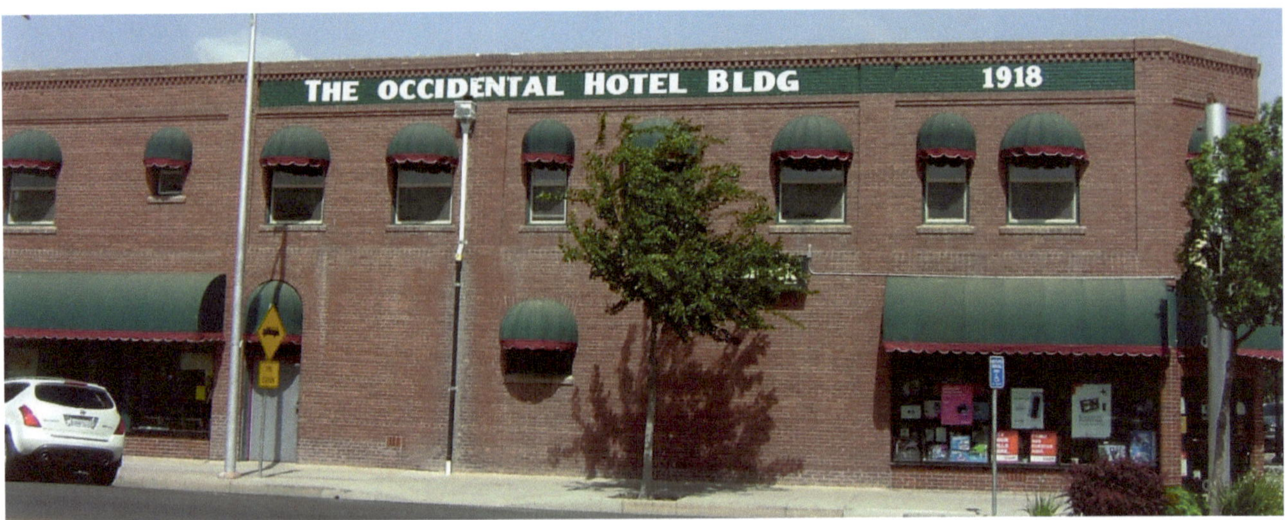

Corcoran, CA

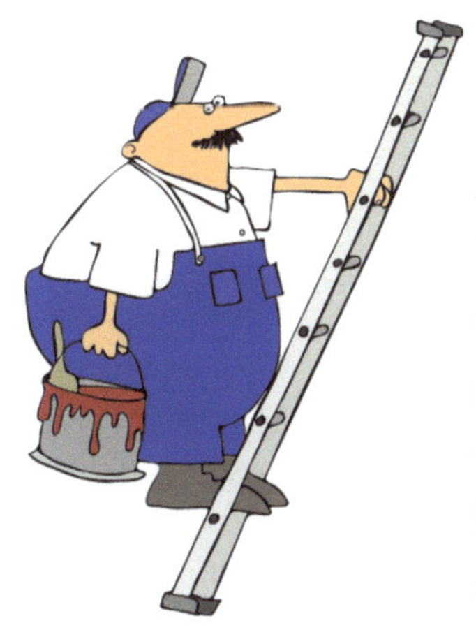

Agriculture-related signs

Adjacent to Vina, California, sits the Roman Catholic Trappist Abbey of New Clairvaux. On land formerly owned by Leland Stanford, its wines are good, but of particular interest is the rebuilt 800-year-old restored stone-by-stone chapter house purchased by William Randolph Hearst in 1925 where seven prayer services are held daily.

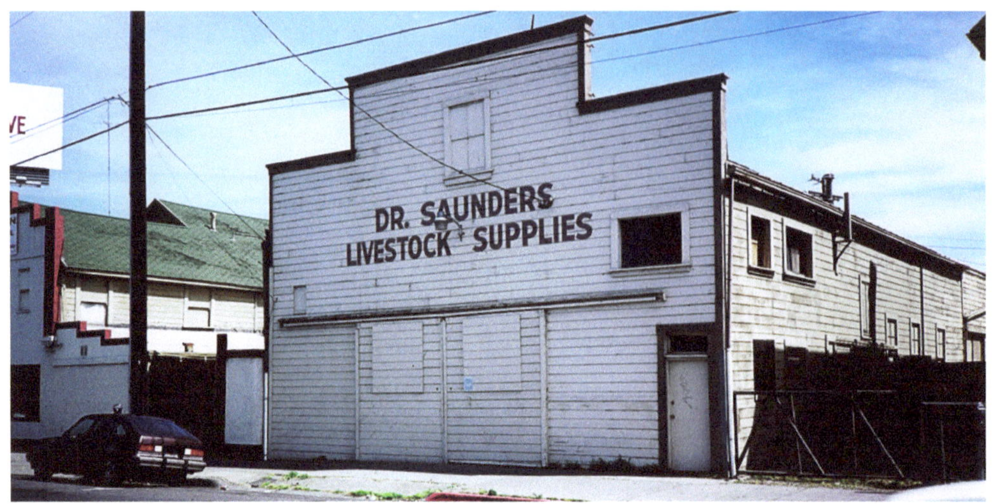

Stockton, CA

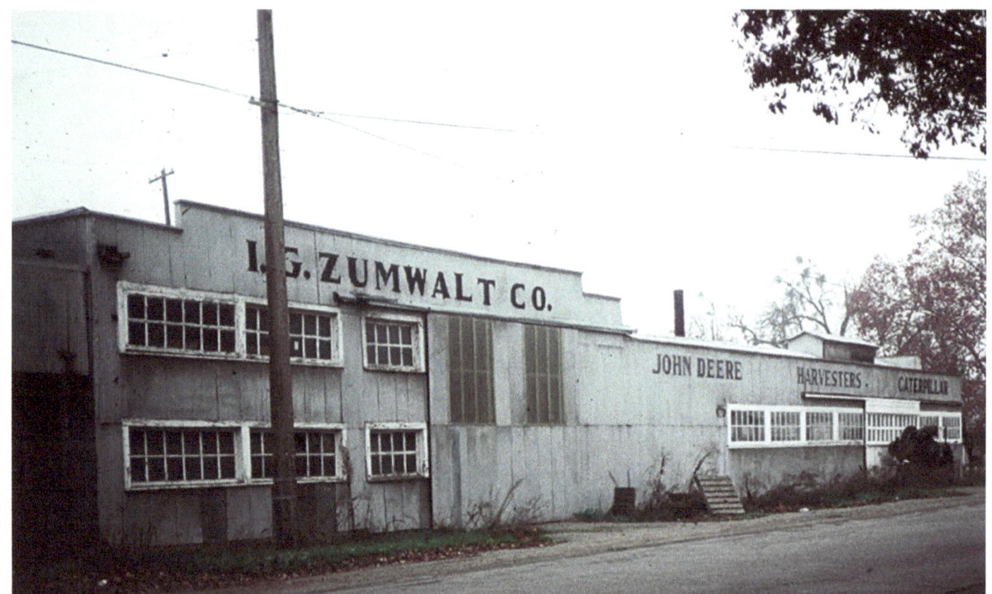

Colusa, CA

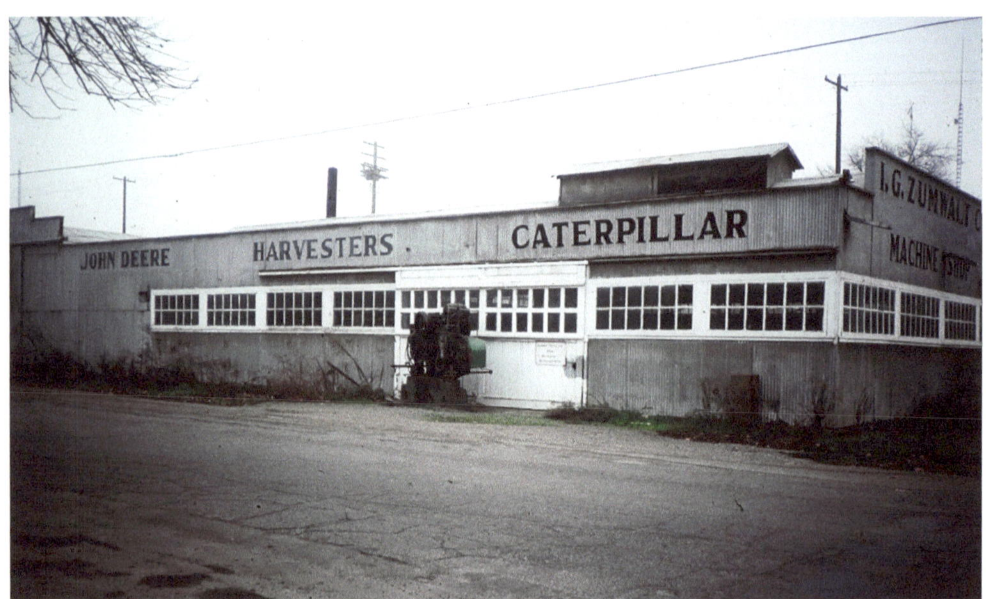

Colusa, CA

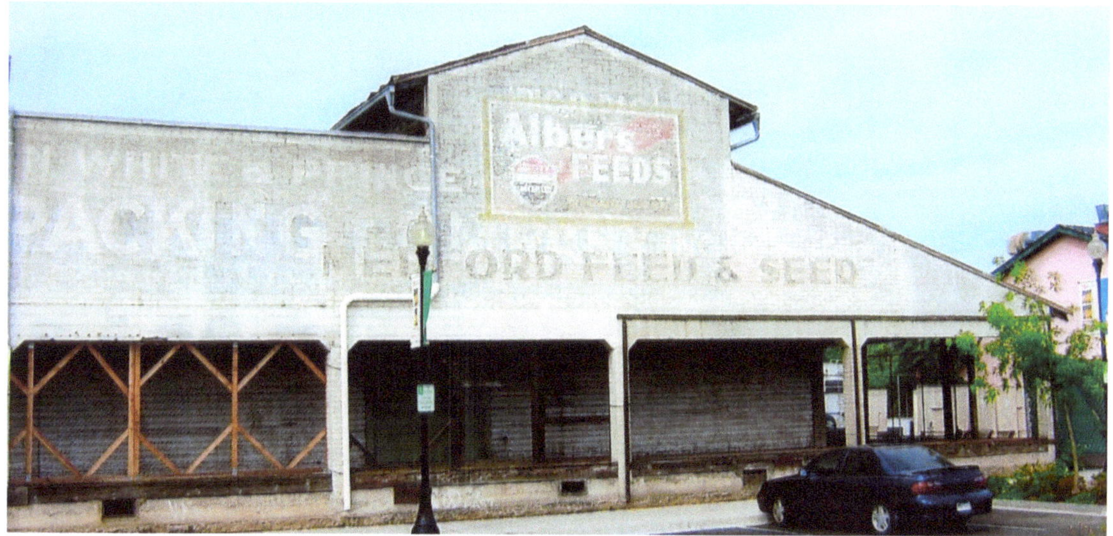

Medford, OR

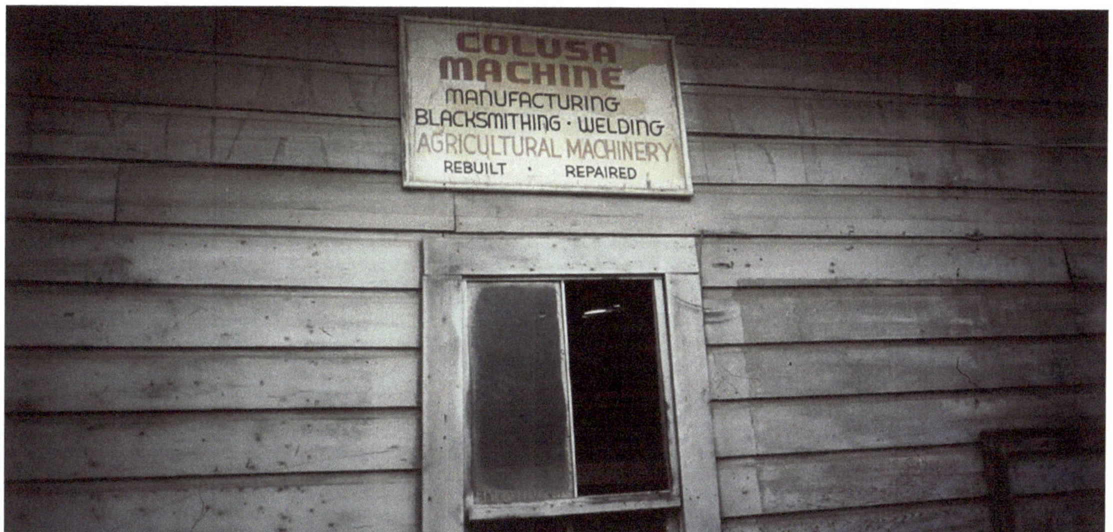

Colusa, CA

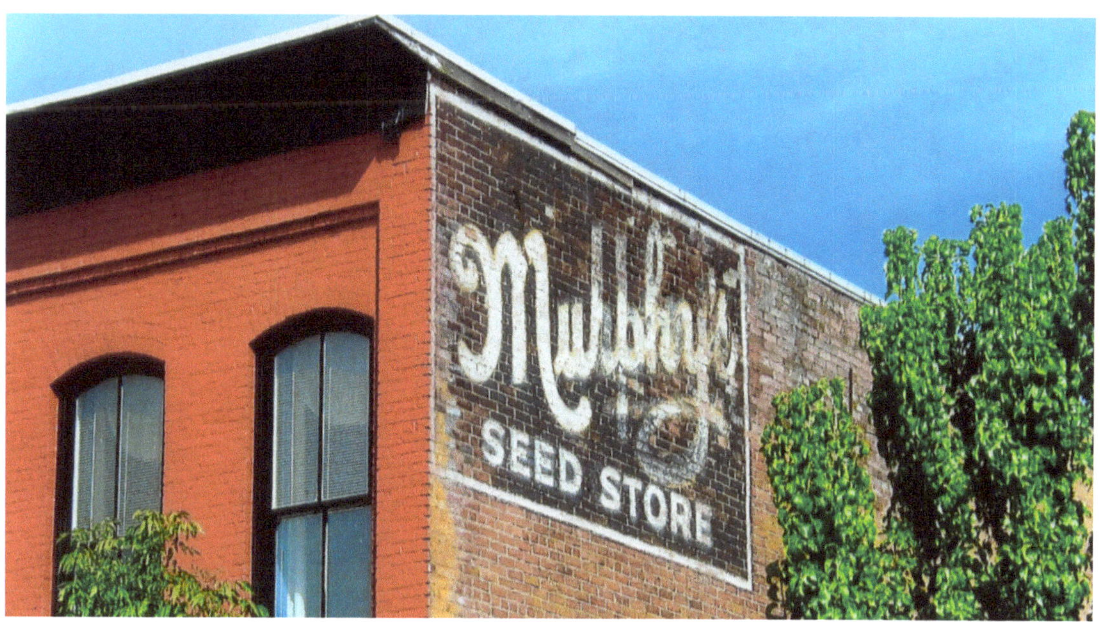

Silverton, OR

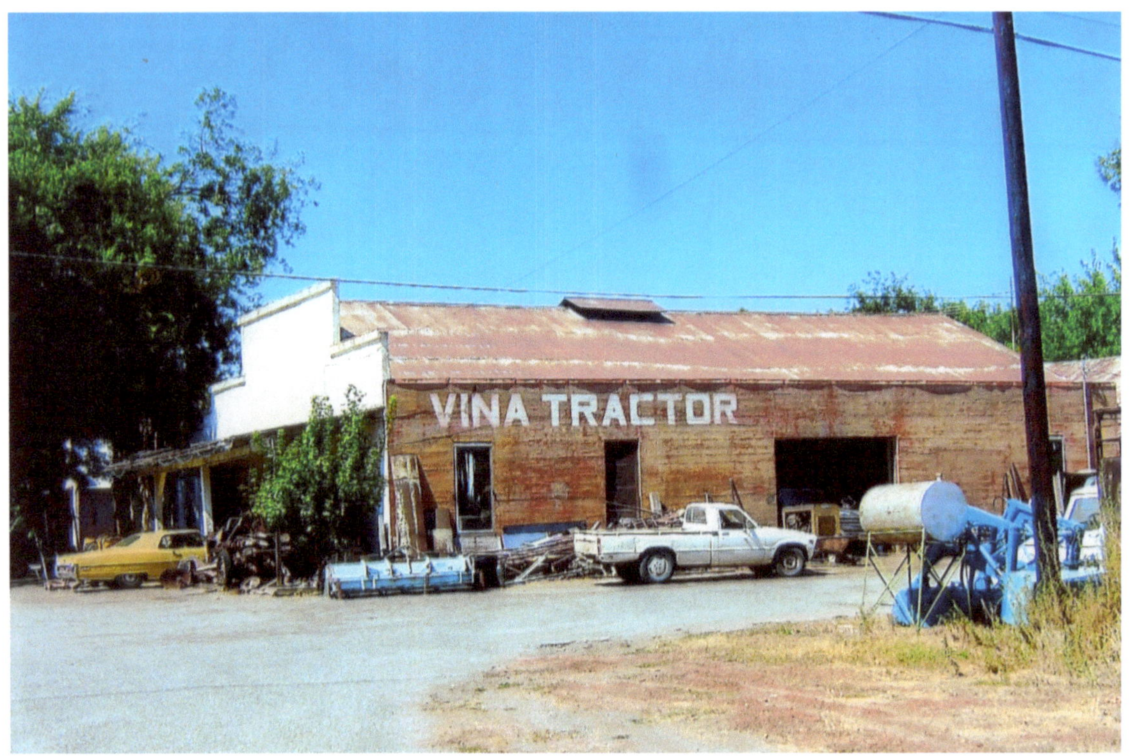

Vina, CA

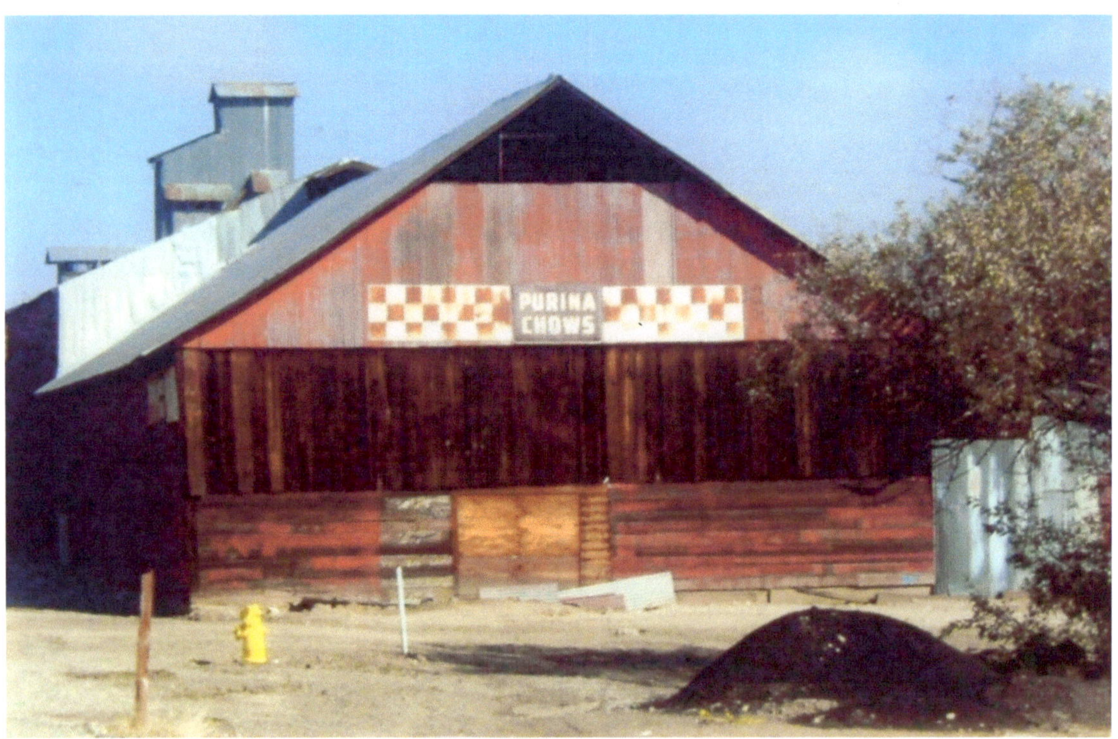

San Miguel, CA

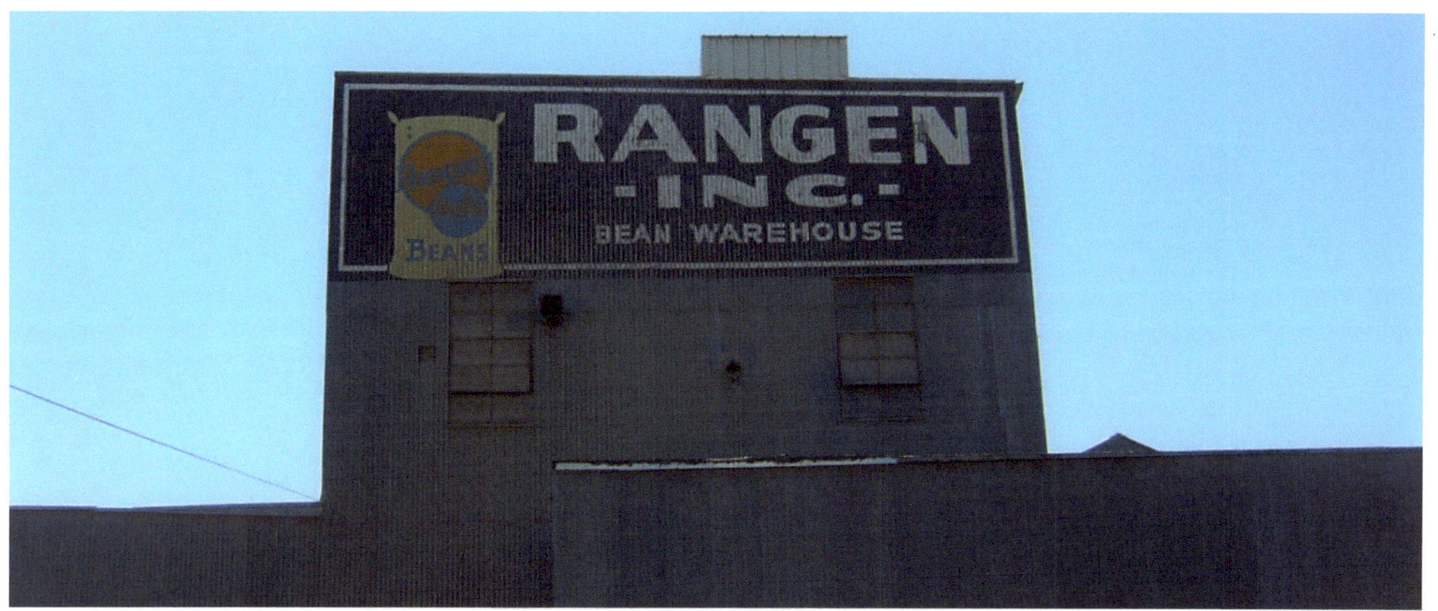

Buhl, Idaho

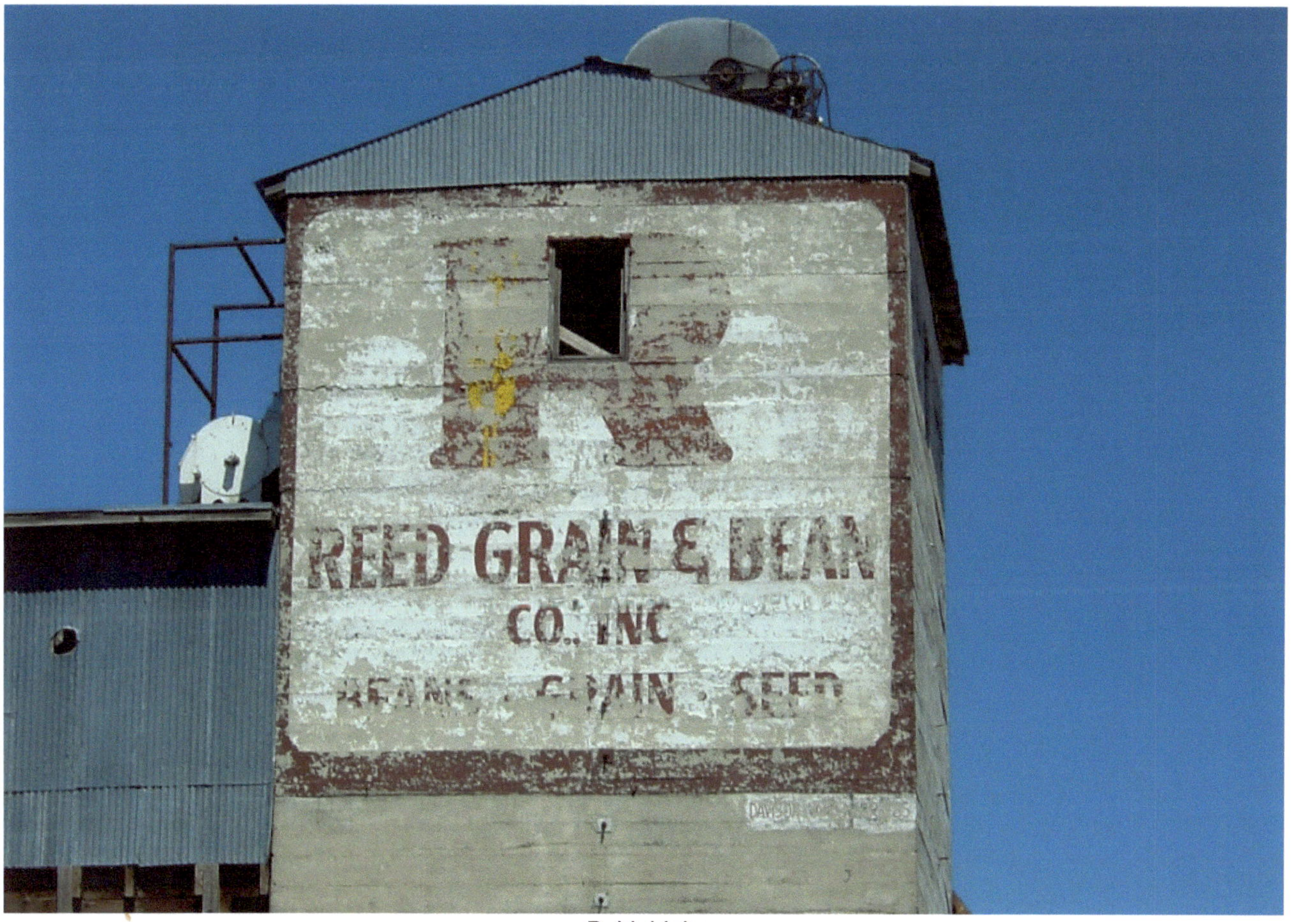

Buhl, Idaho

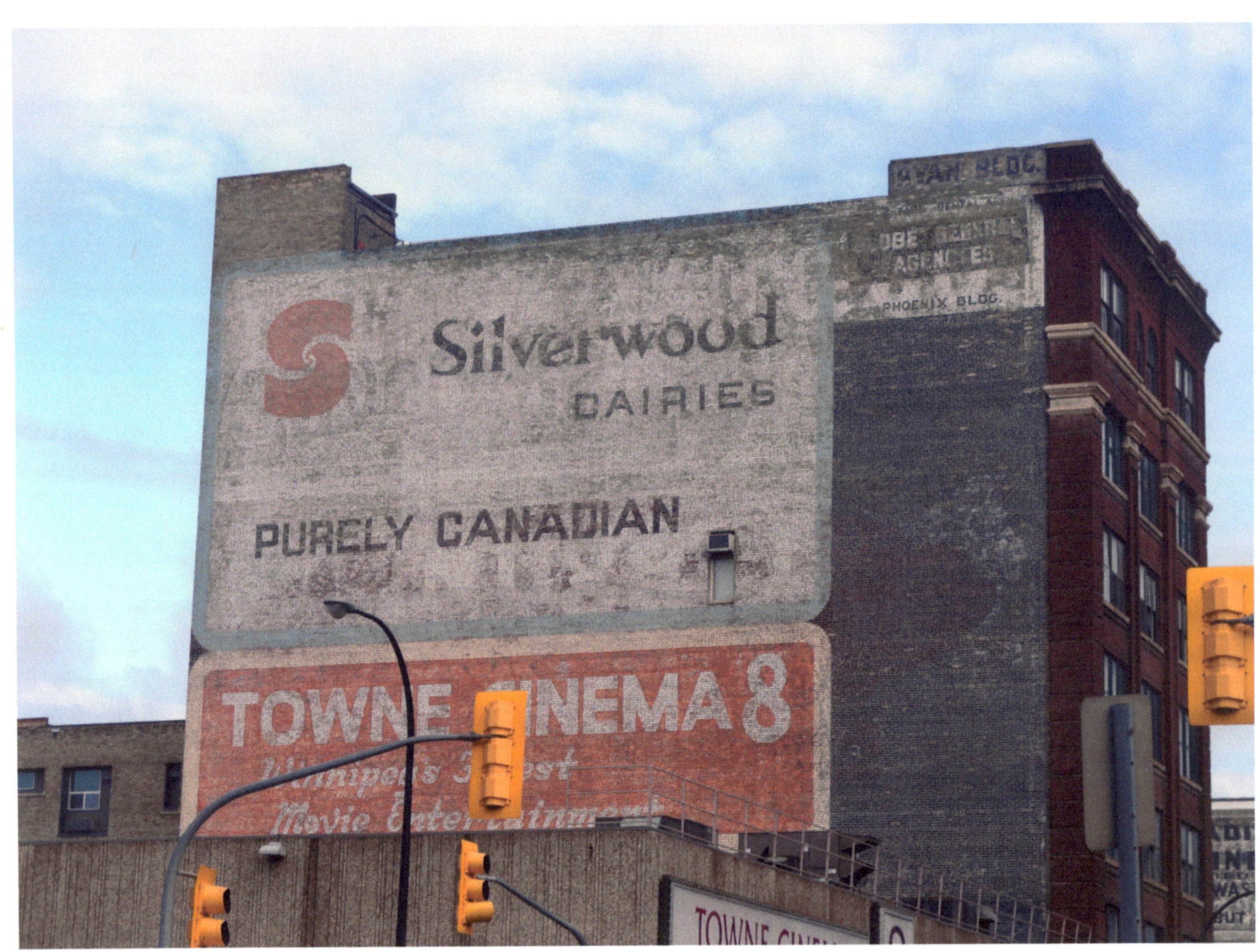

Winnipeg, Manitoba, Canada

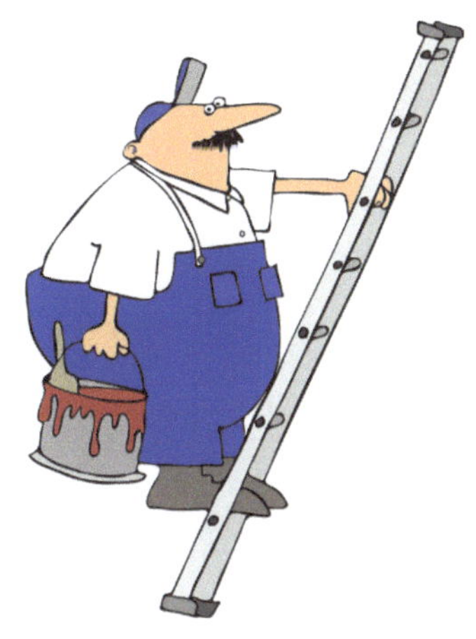

Other signs of Interest

The Key System was an interurban train system connecting San Francisco and Oakland area across the Bay Bridge. My grandfather, Wilhelm Juergens, commuted on a Key System train, and on special occasions I rode with my Grandma May to San Francisco to go Christmas shopping and have lunch at Blum's restaurant.

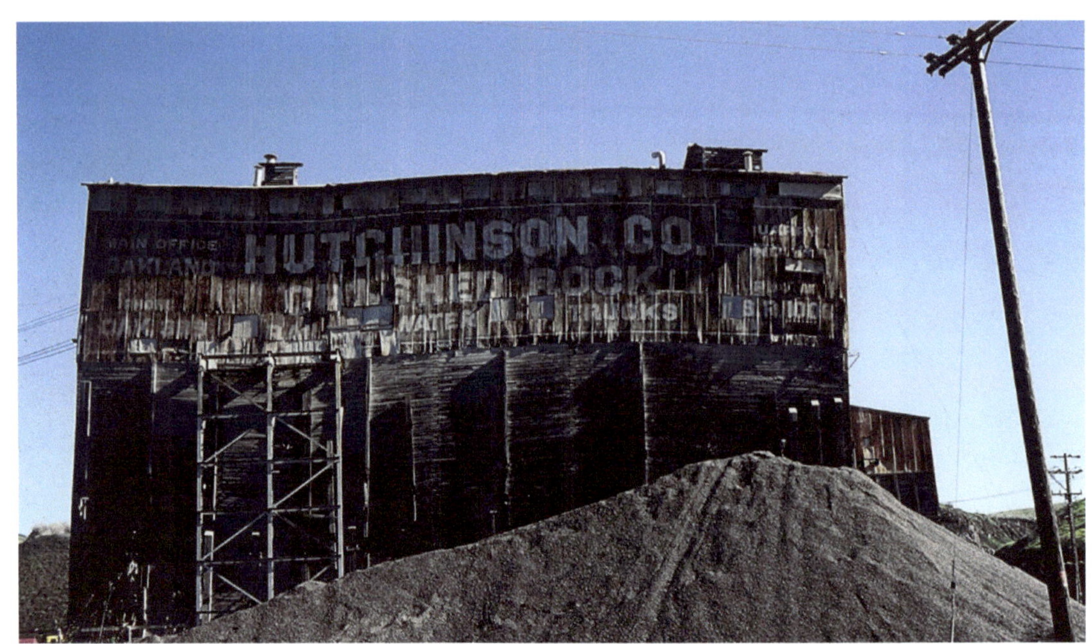

Greenbrae, CA

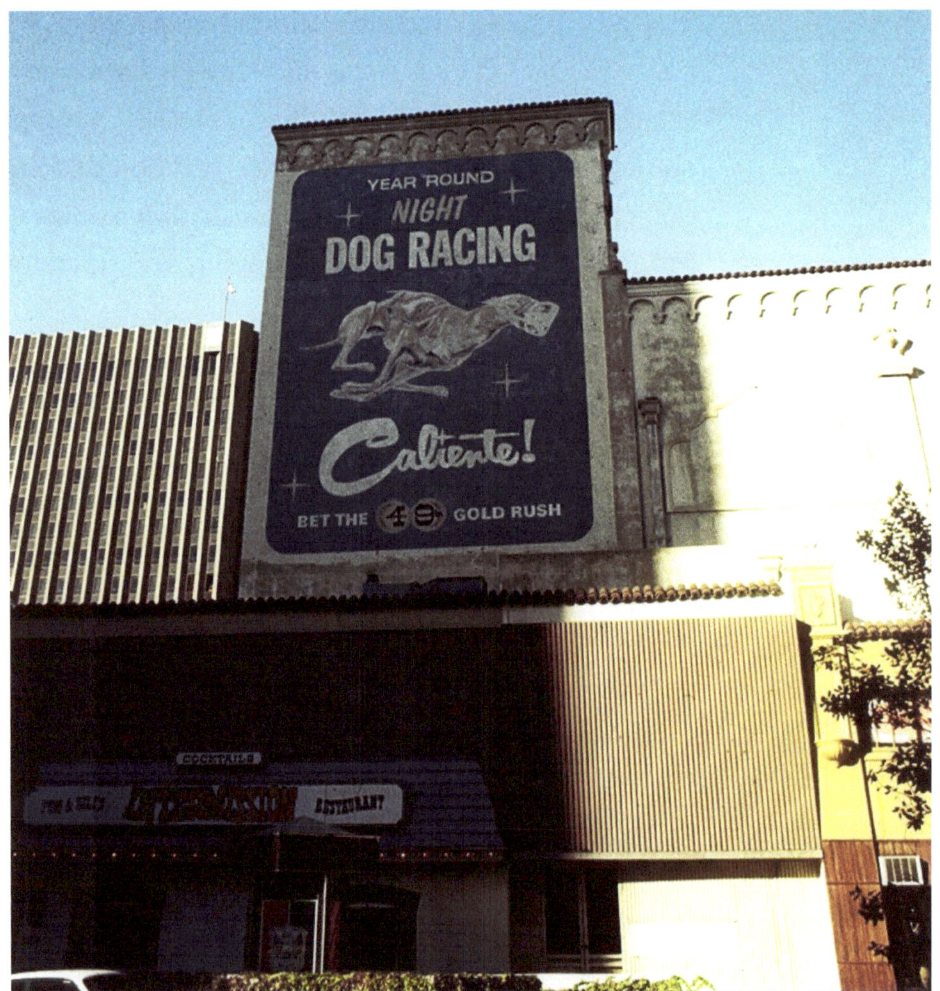

San Diego, CA

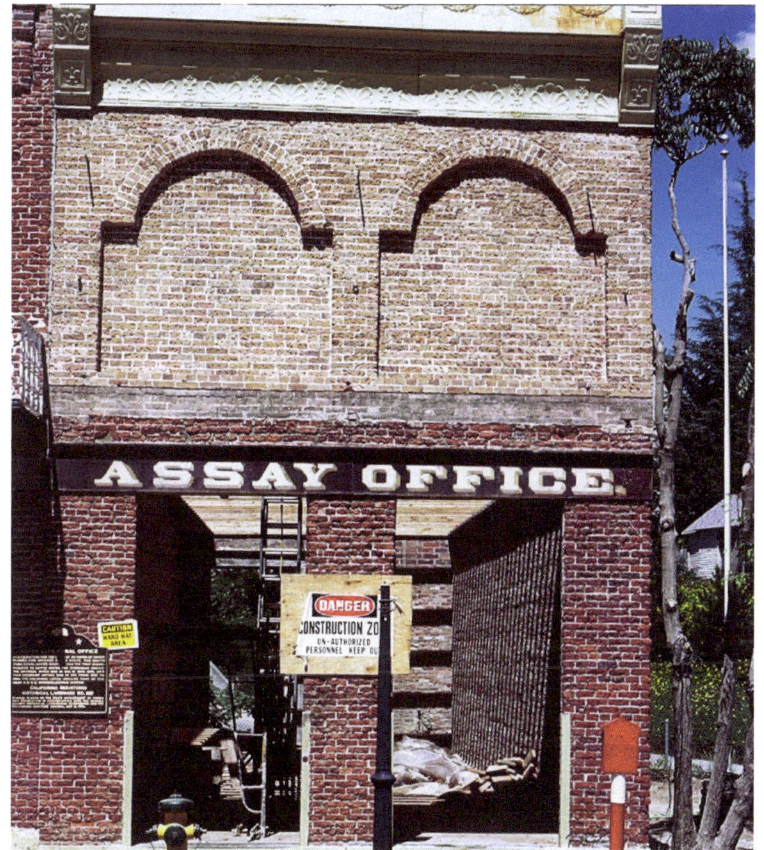

Nevada City, CA

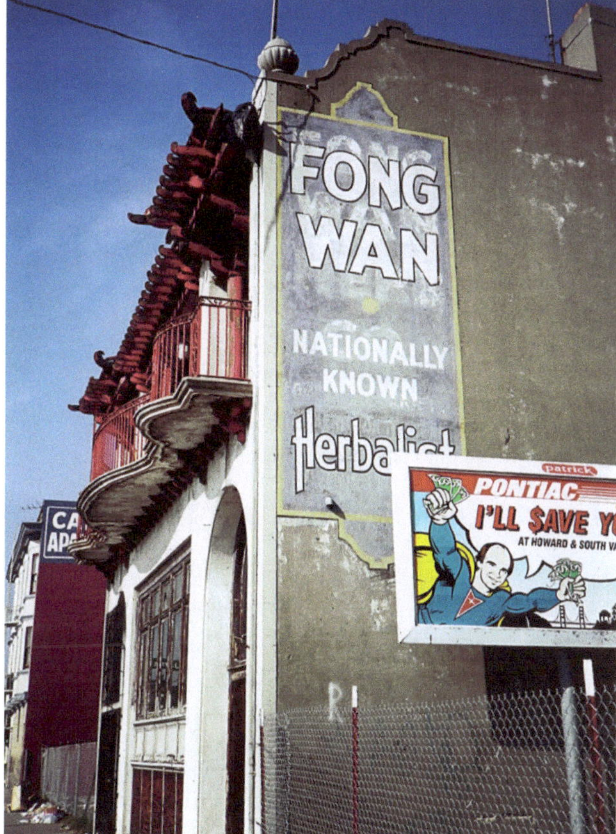

Oakland, CA

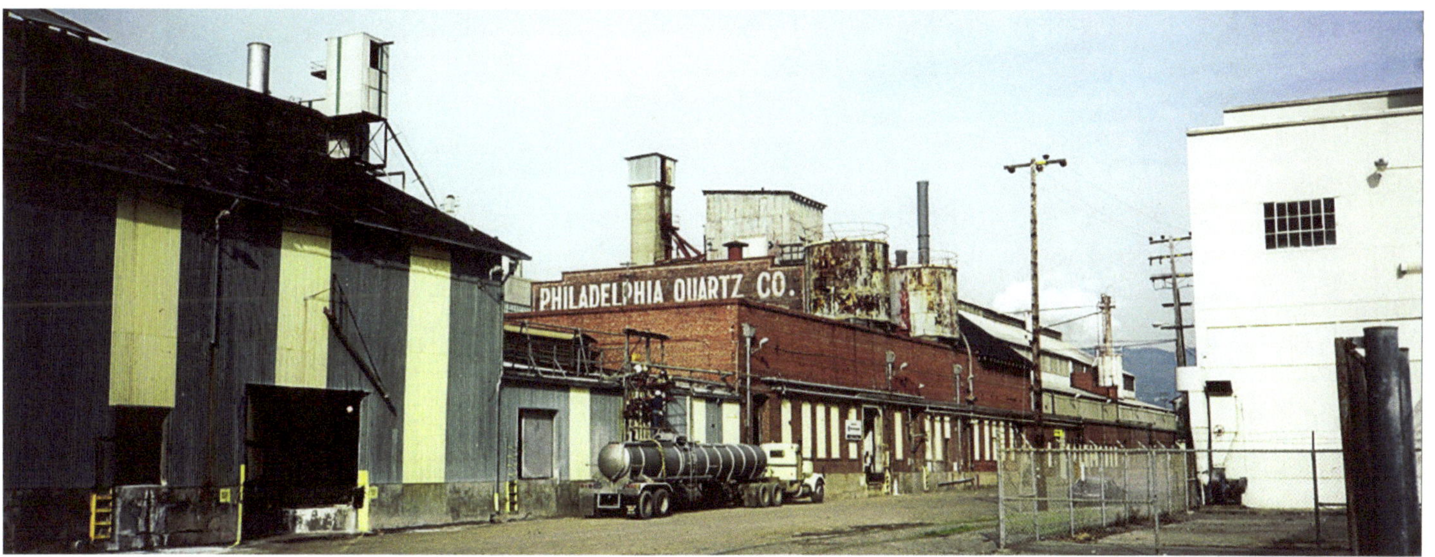

Berkeley, CA

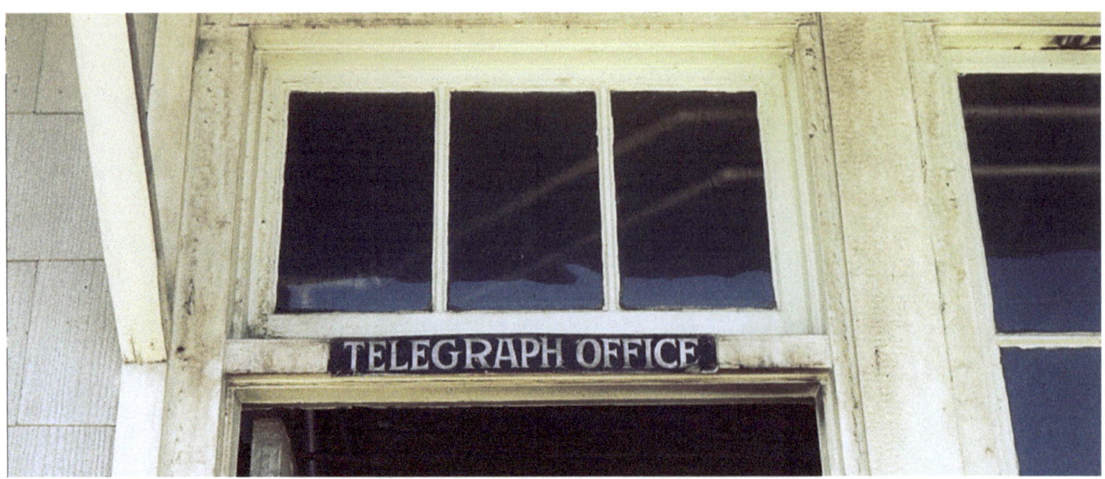

Truckee, CA

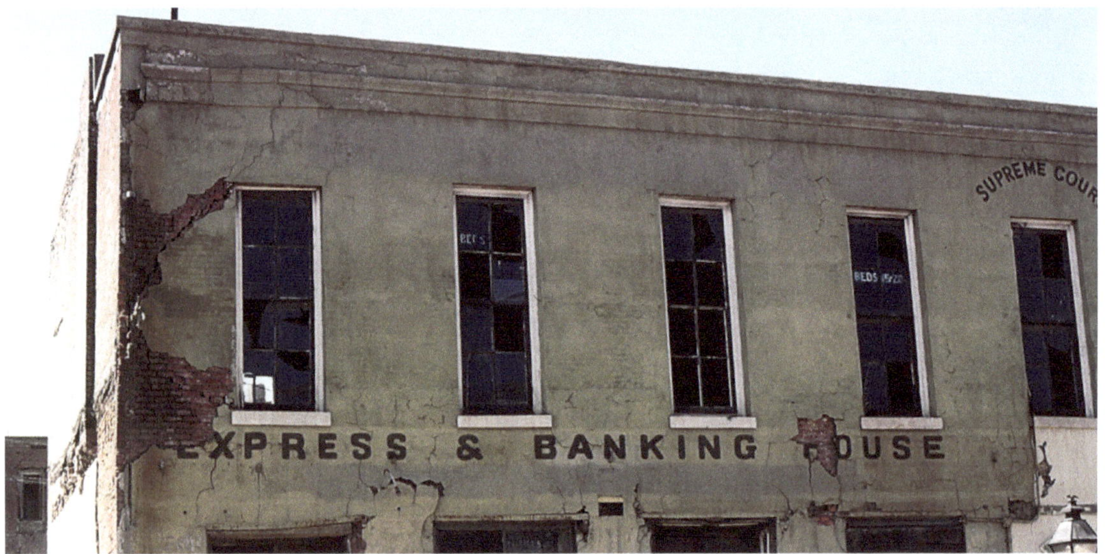

Sacramento, CA

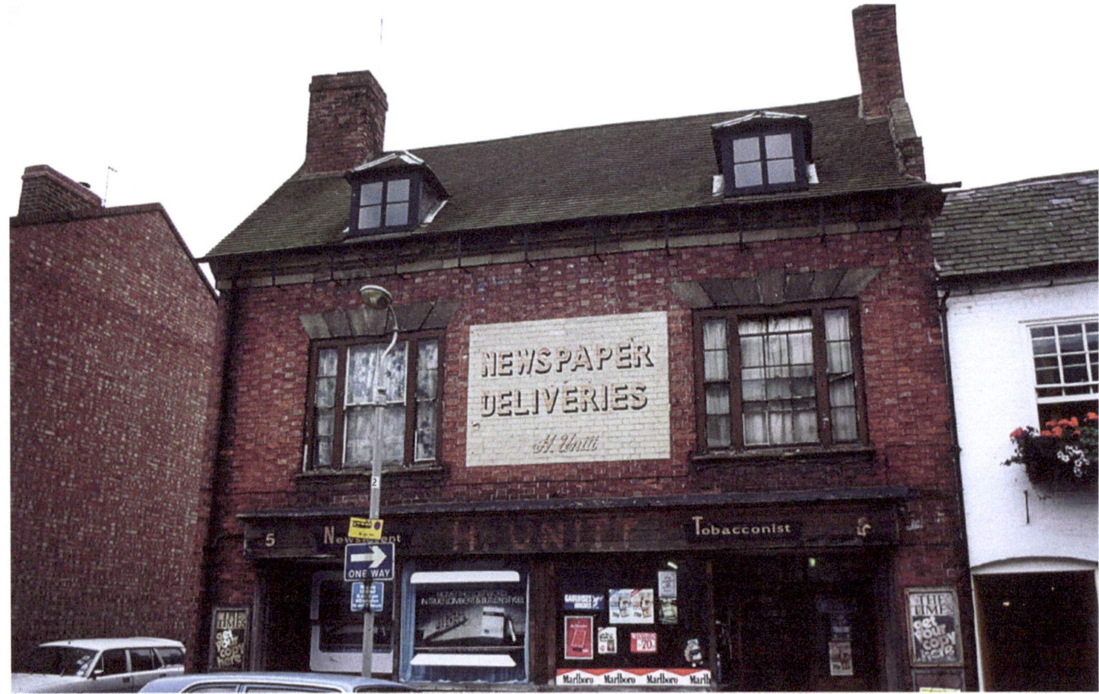

Stratford-on-Avon, England

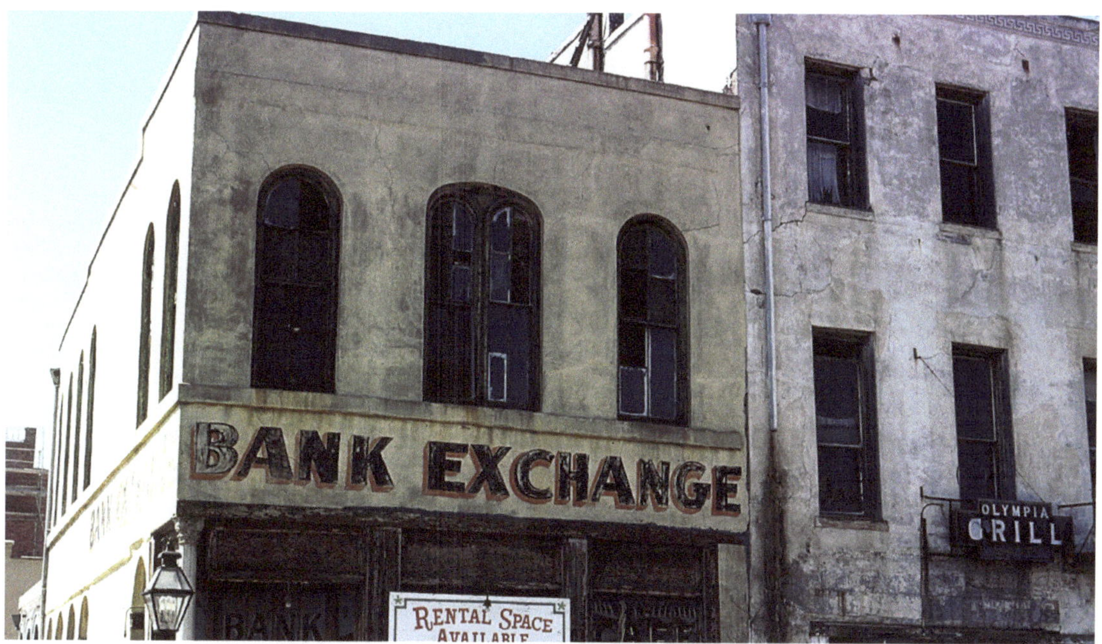

Sacramento, CA

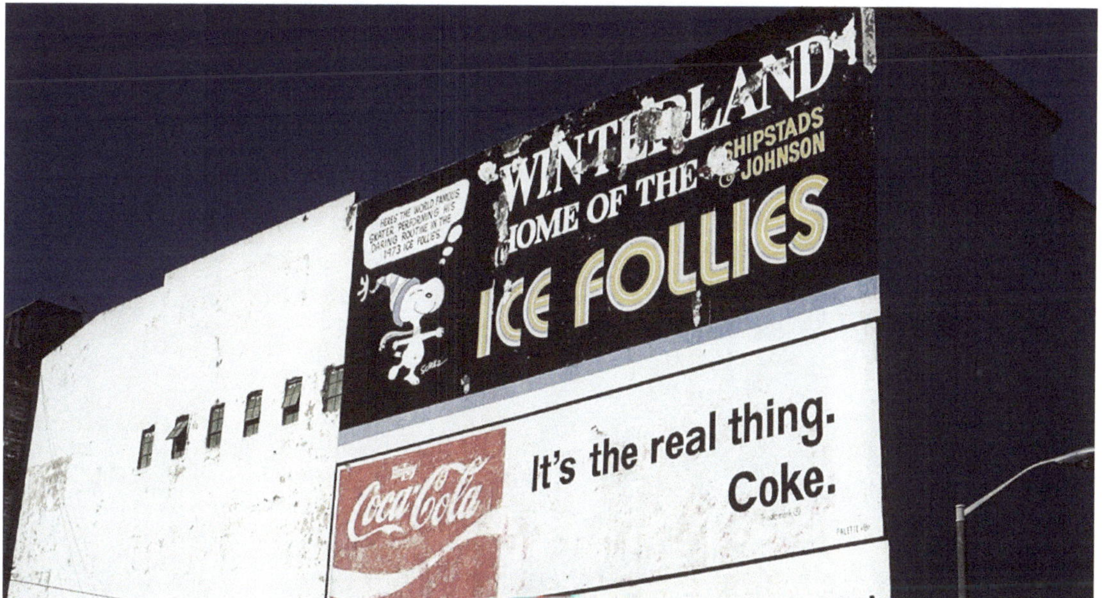

San Francisco, CA

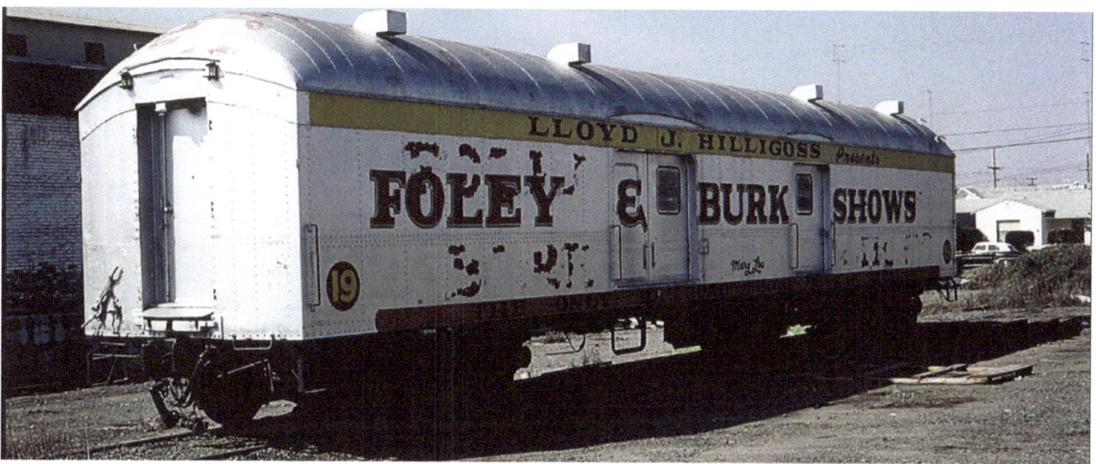

Sacramento, CA

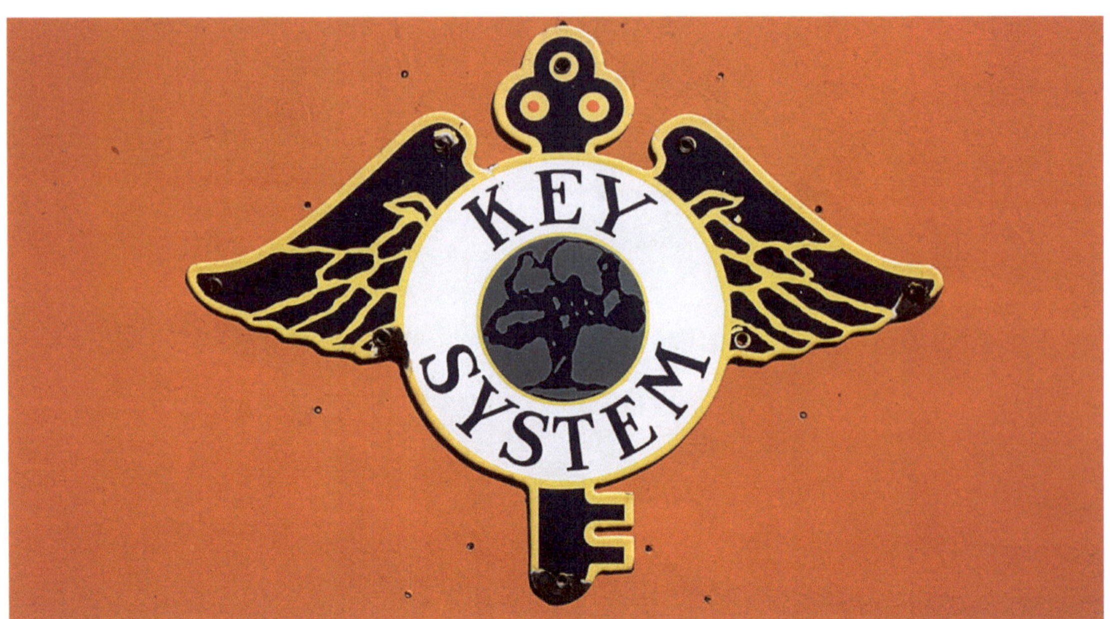

Rio Vista, CA

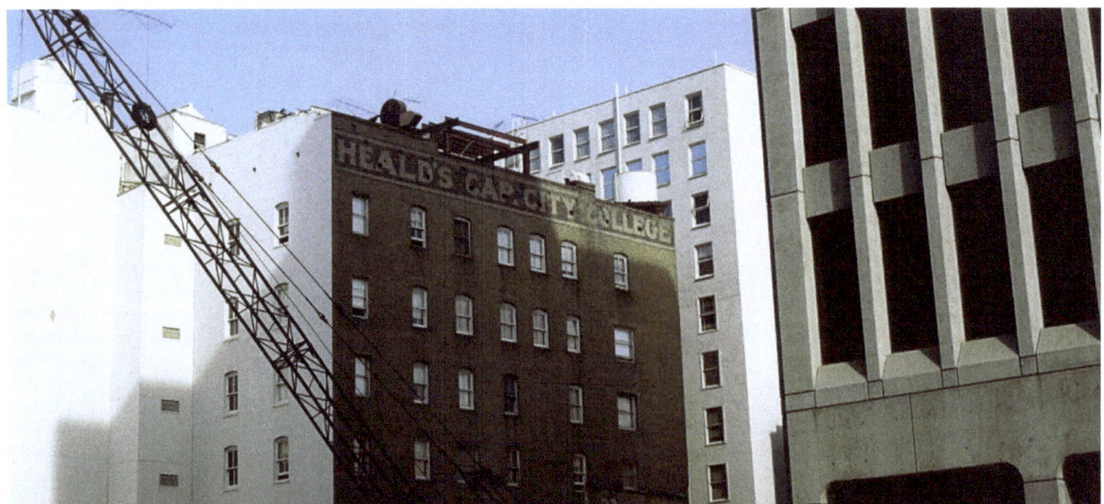

Sacramento, CA

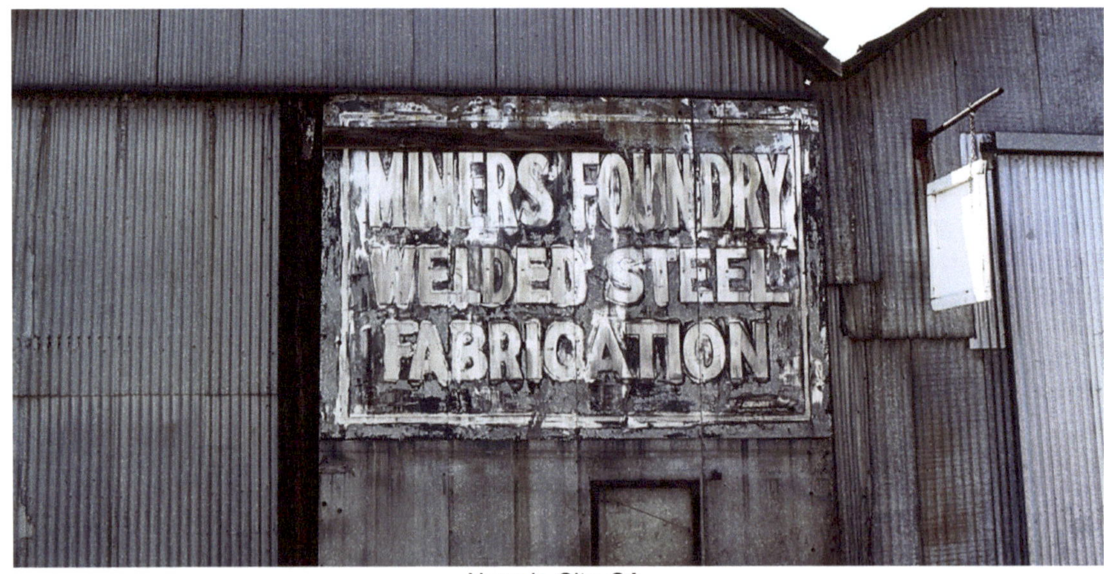

Nevada City, CA

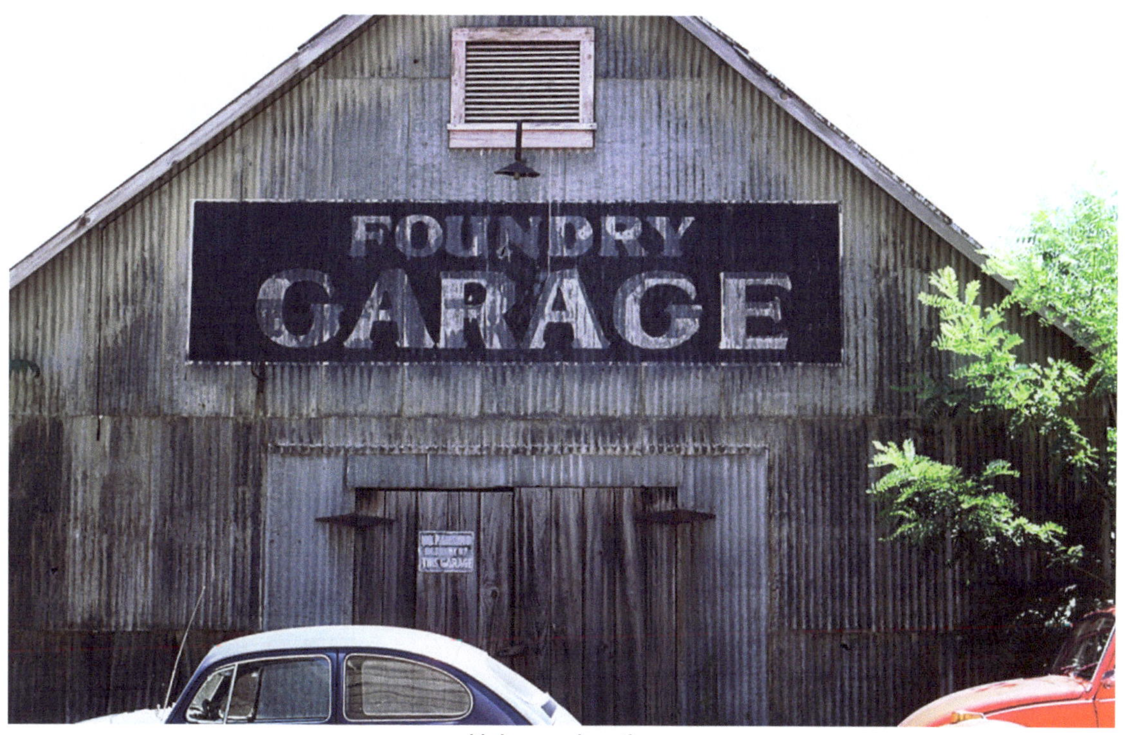

Unknown location

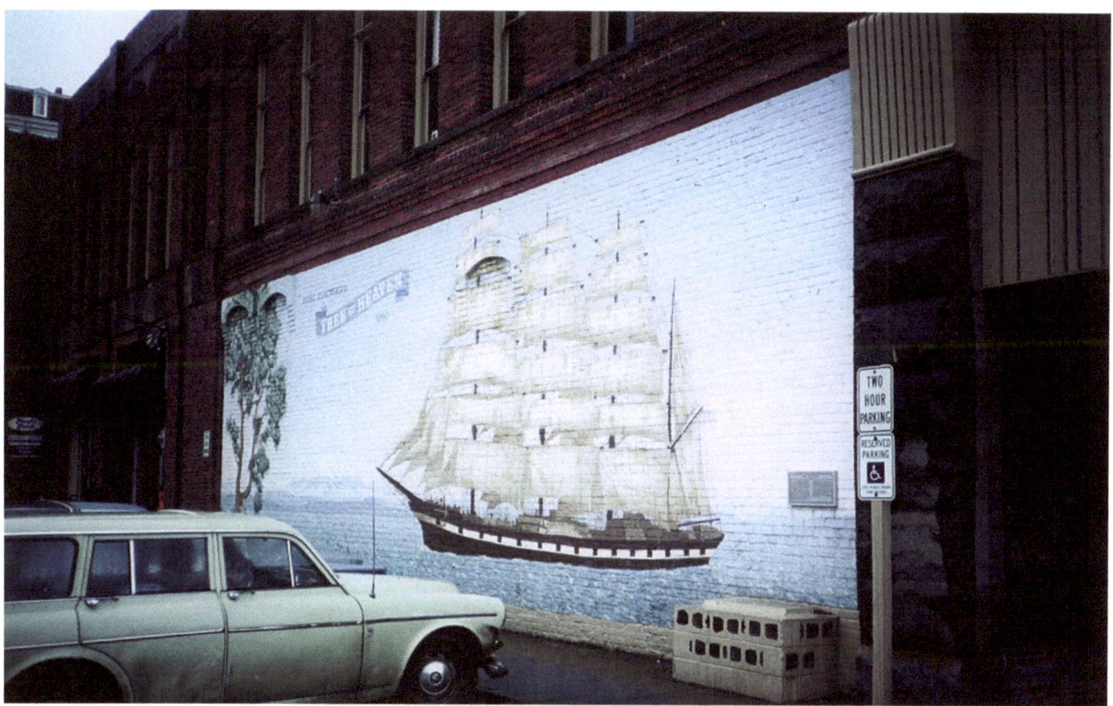

Seattle, WA

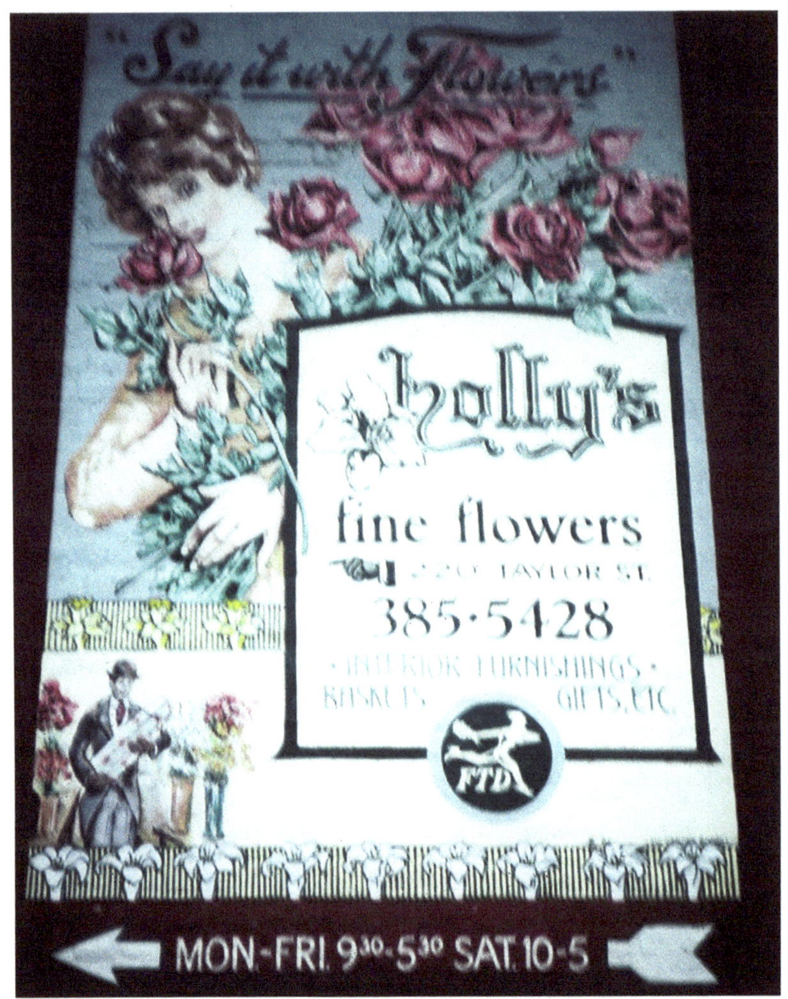

Silverton, OR

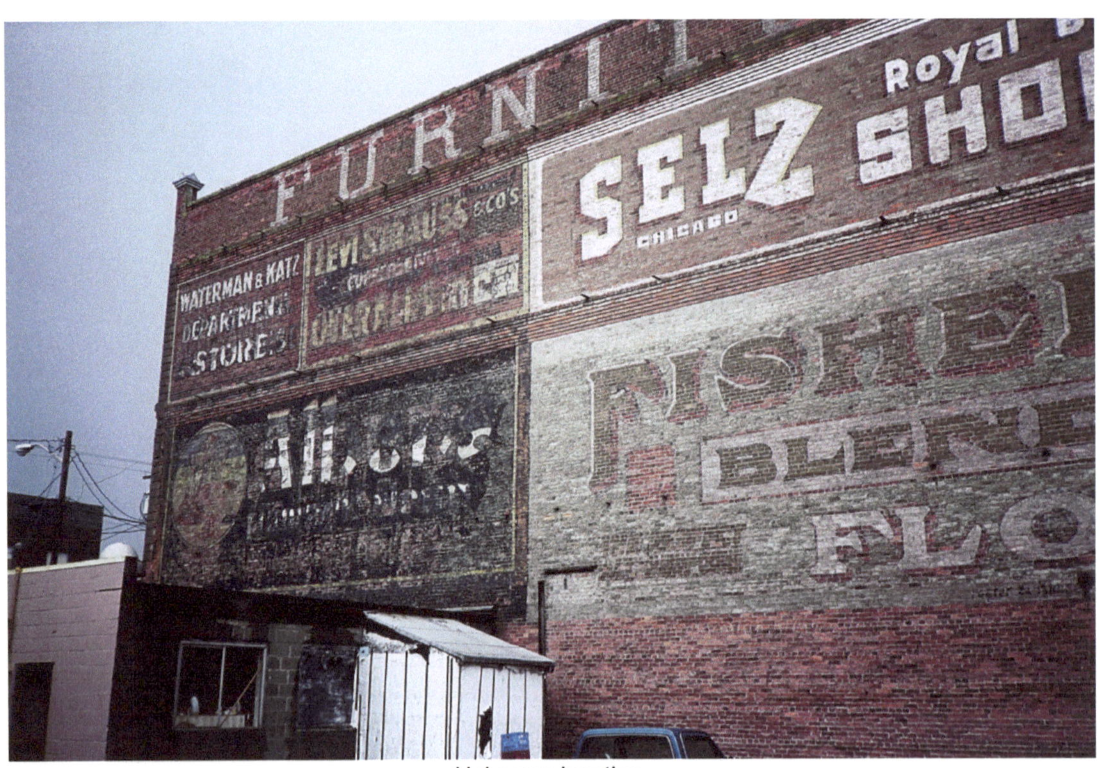

Unknown location

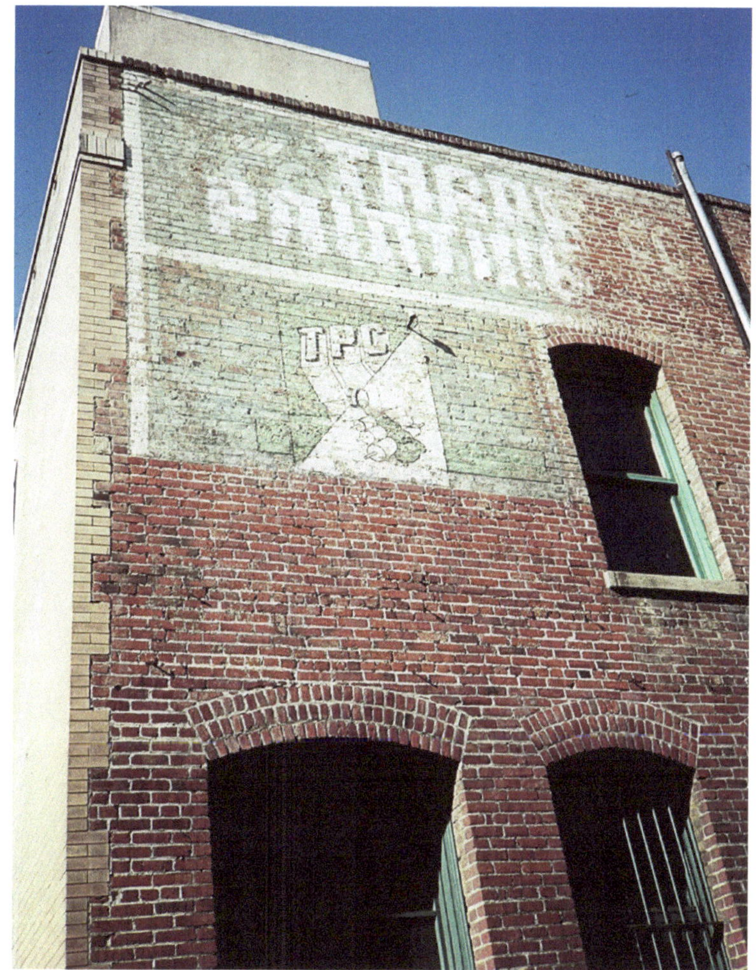

Pasadena, CA

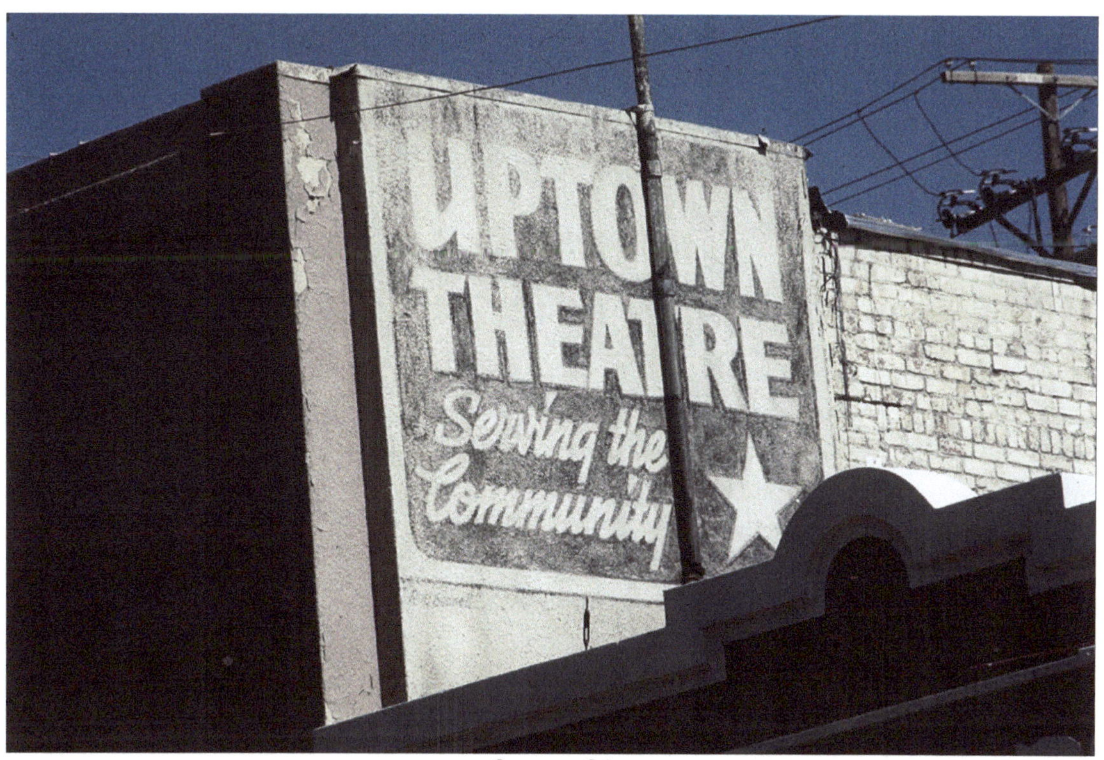

Sonora, CA

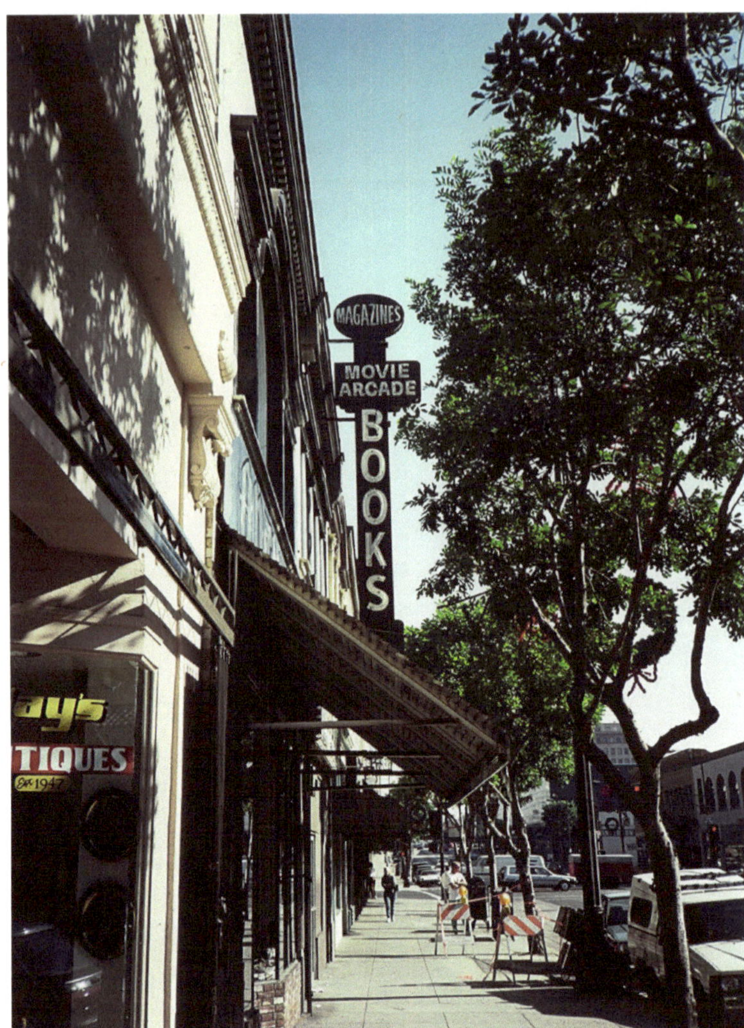

Pasadena, CA

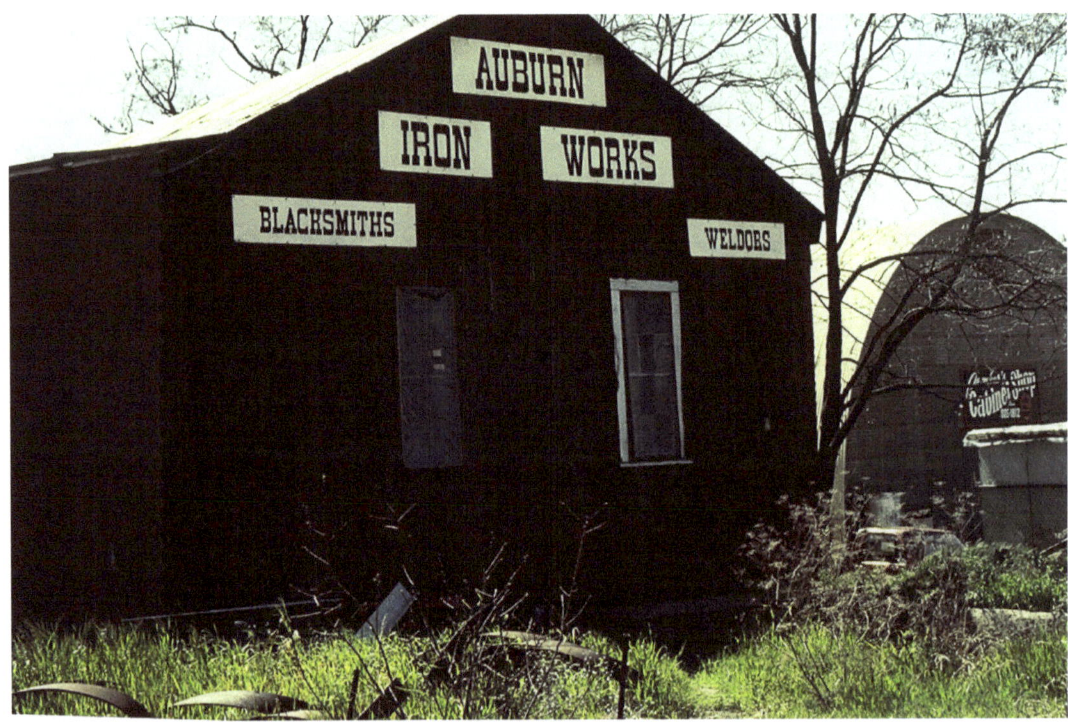

Auburn, CA

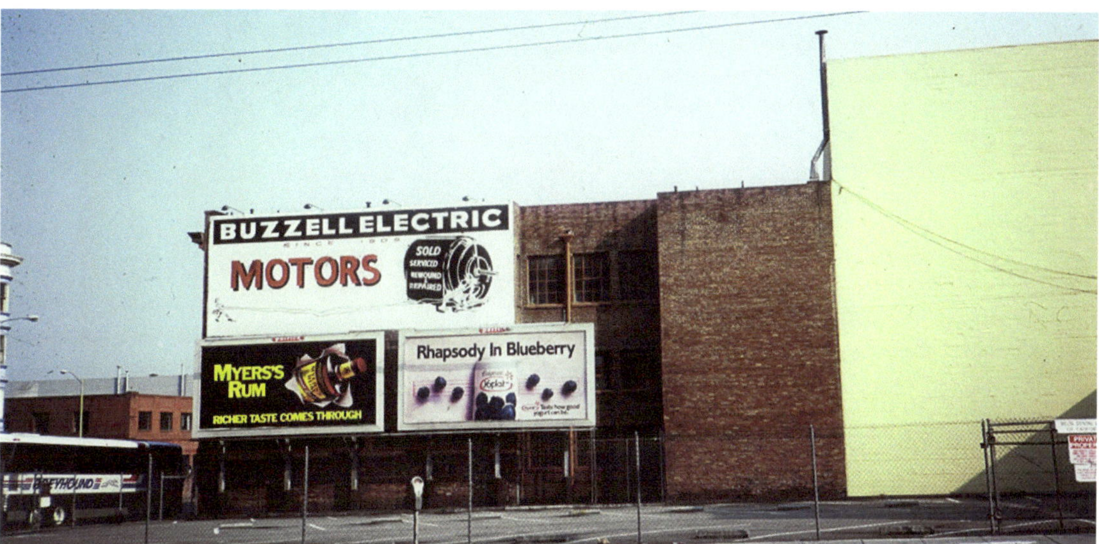

San Francisco, CA

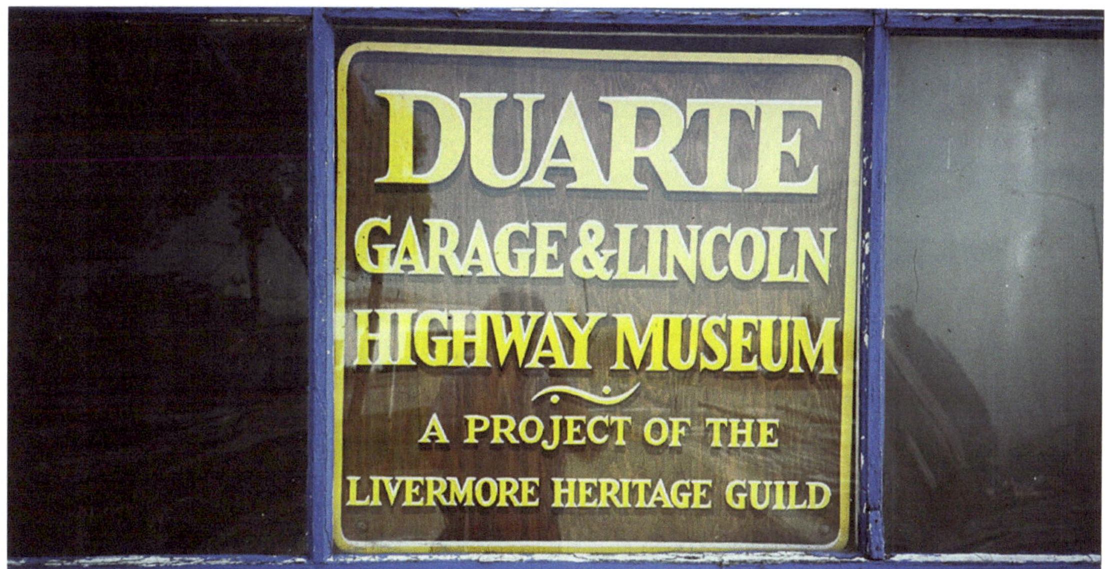

Livermore, CA

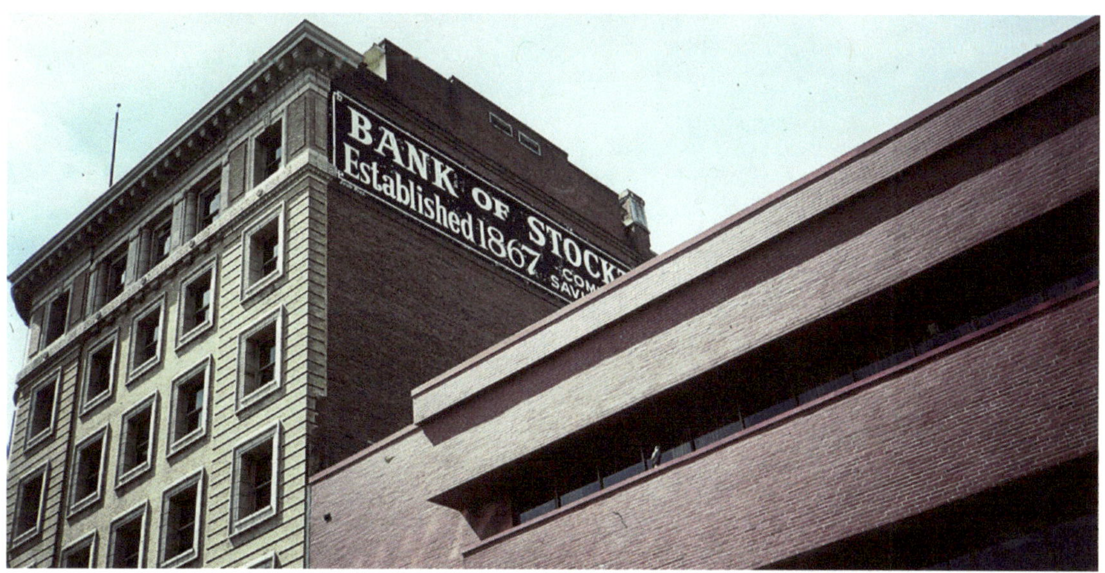

Stockton, CA

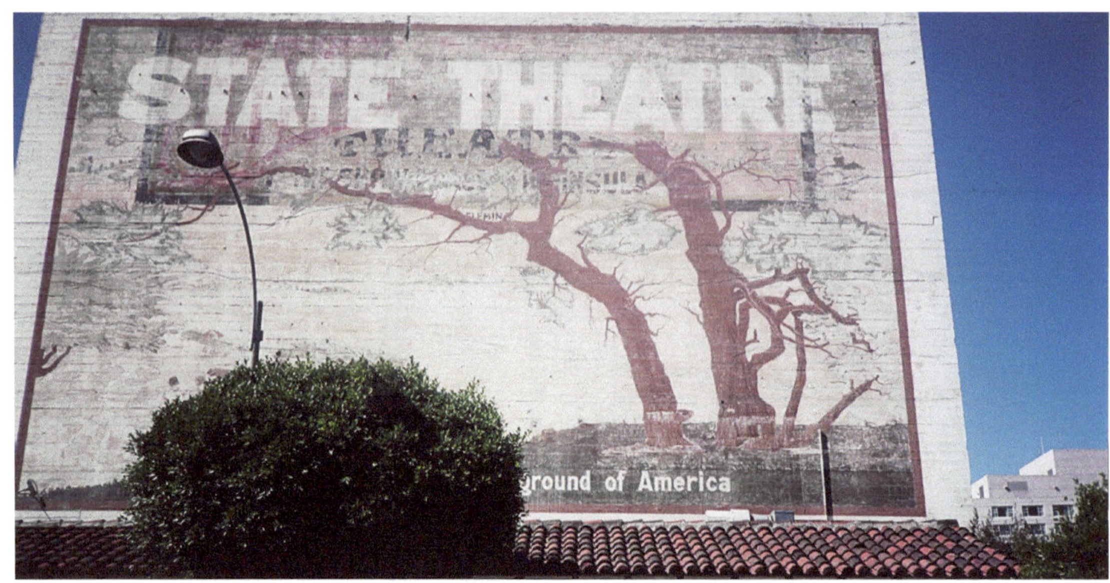

Monterey, CA

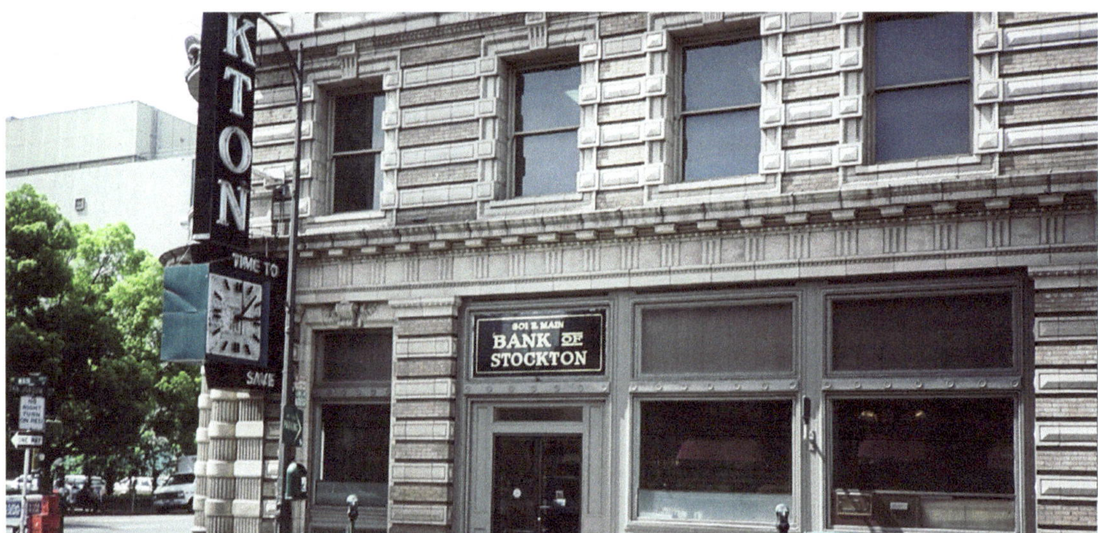

Stockton, CA

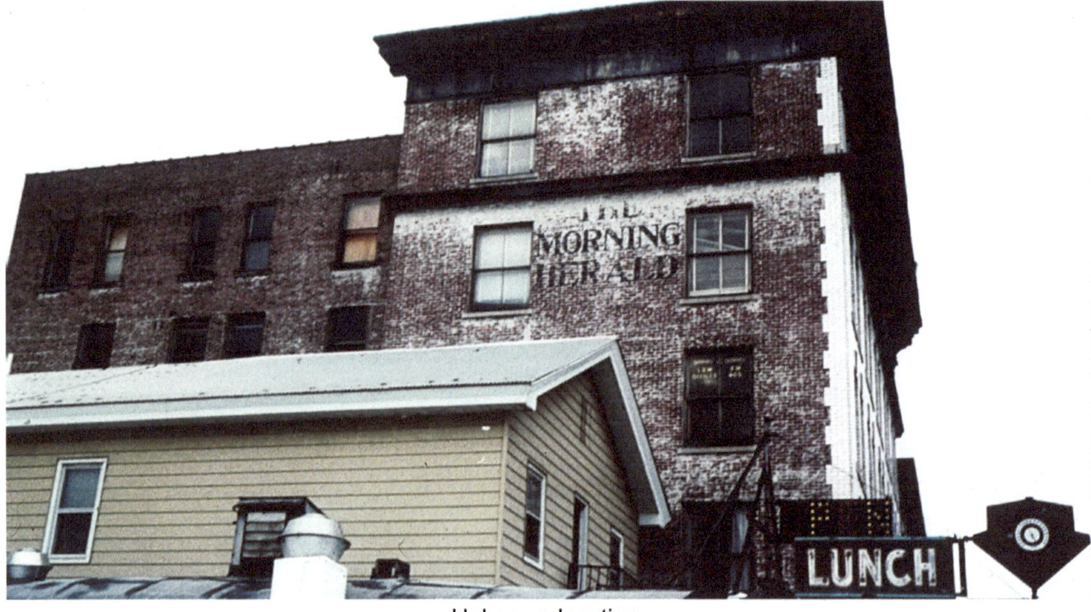

Unknown location

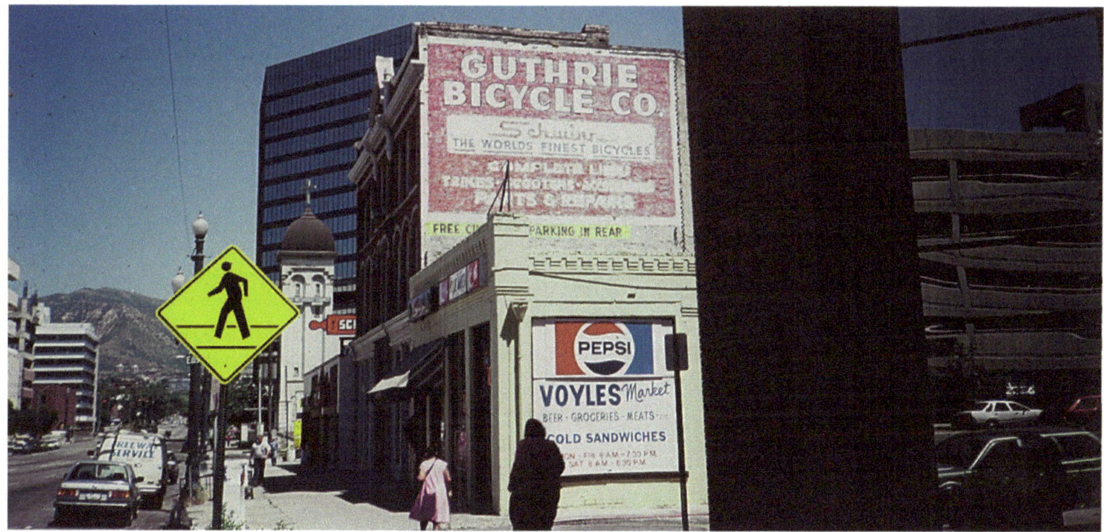

Provo, UT

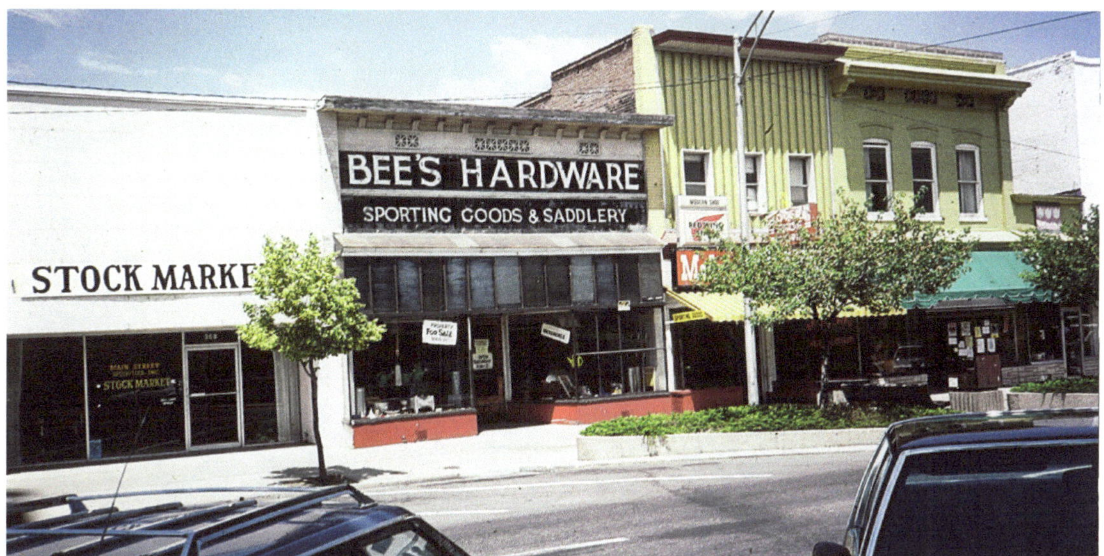

Provo, UT

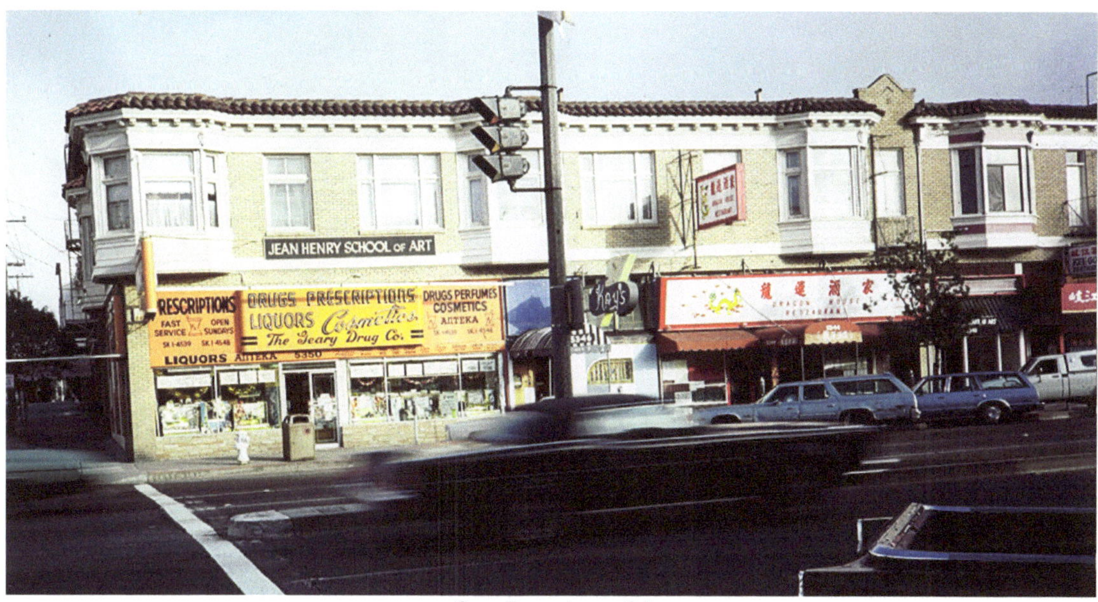

San Francisco, CA

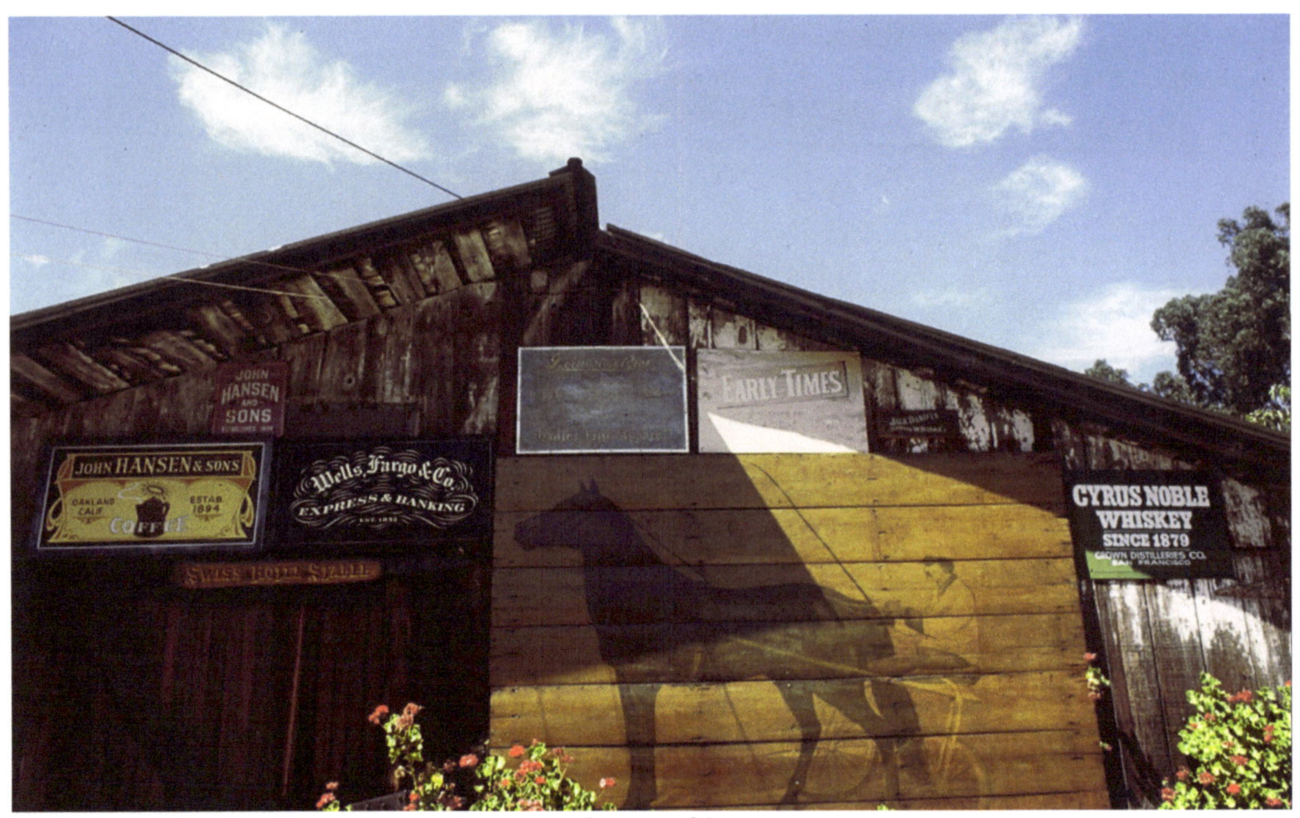

Sonoma, CA

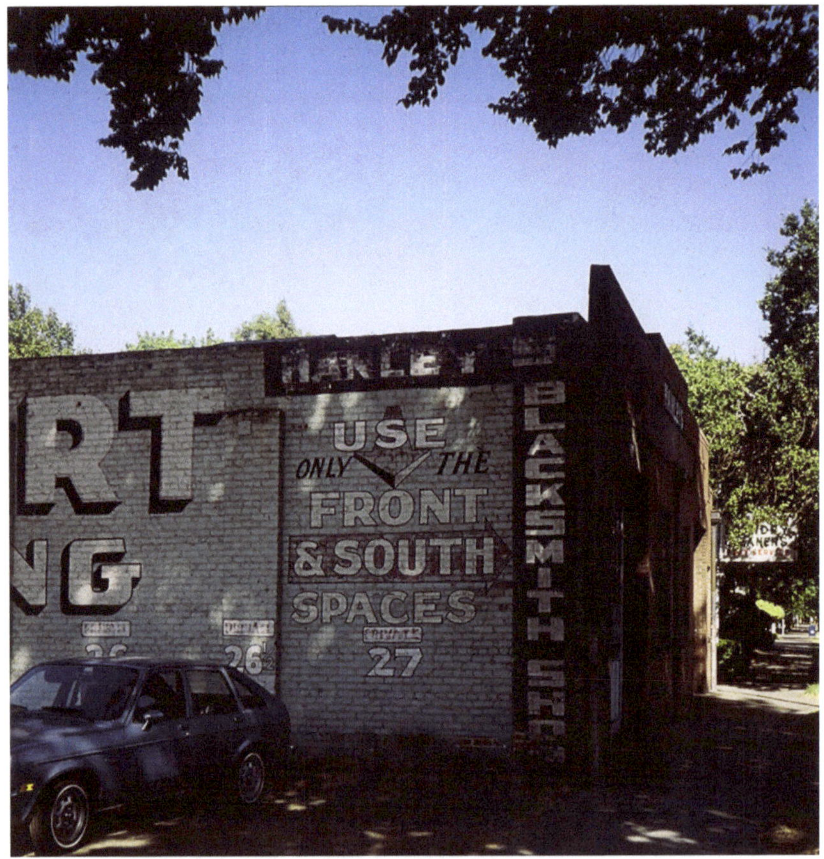

Sacramento, CA

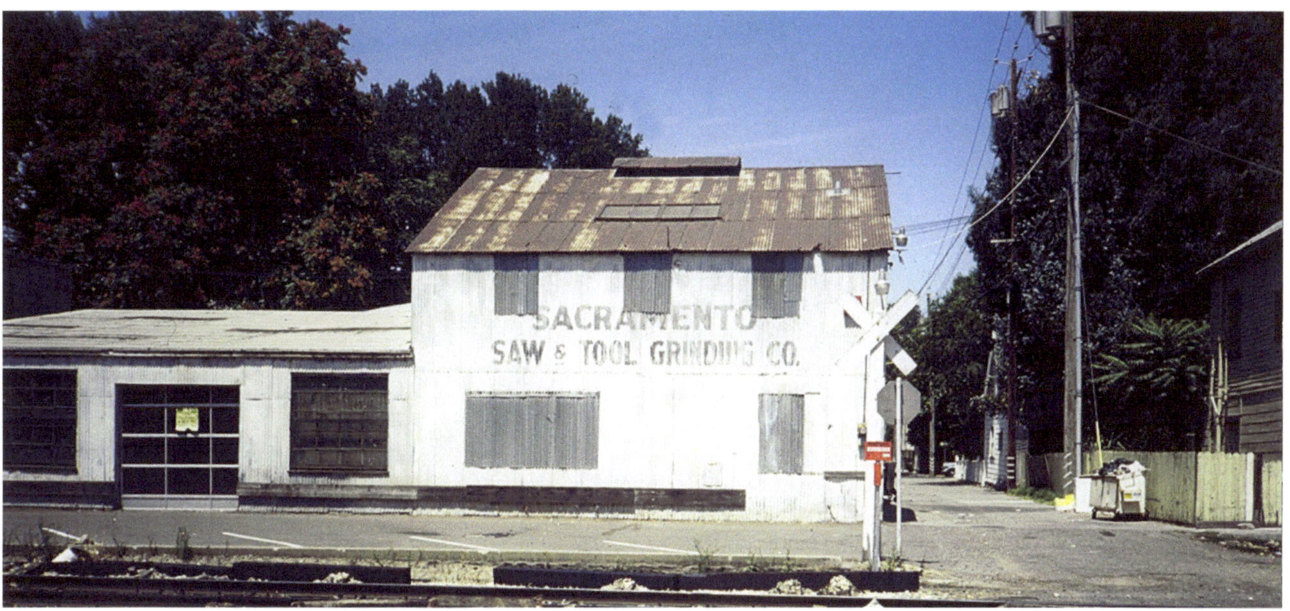

Sacramento, CA

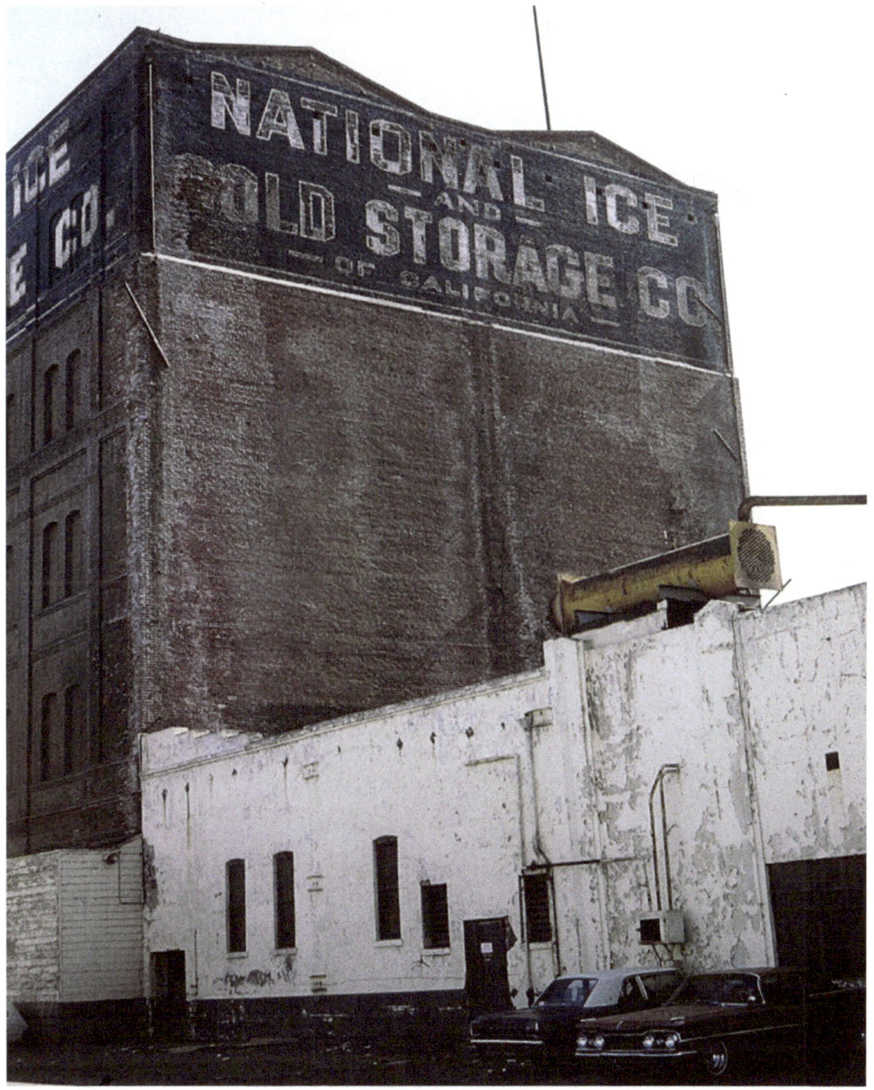

Sacramento, CA

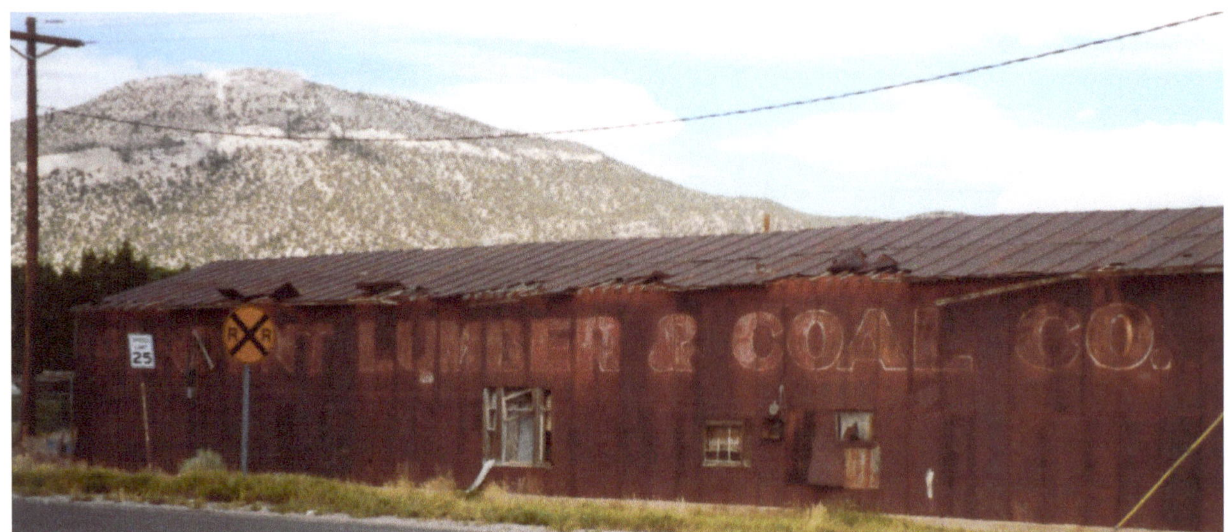

Ely, NV

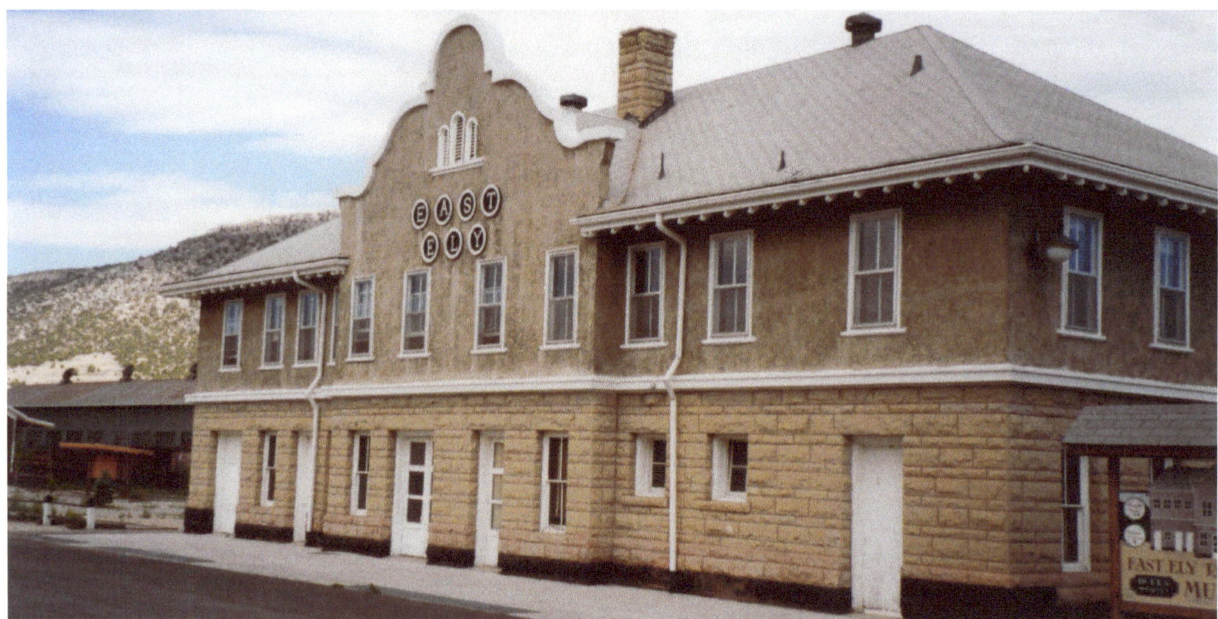

Ely, NV

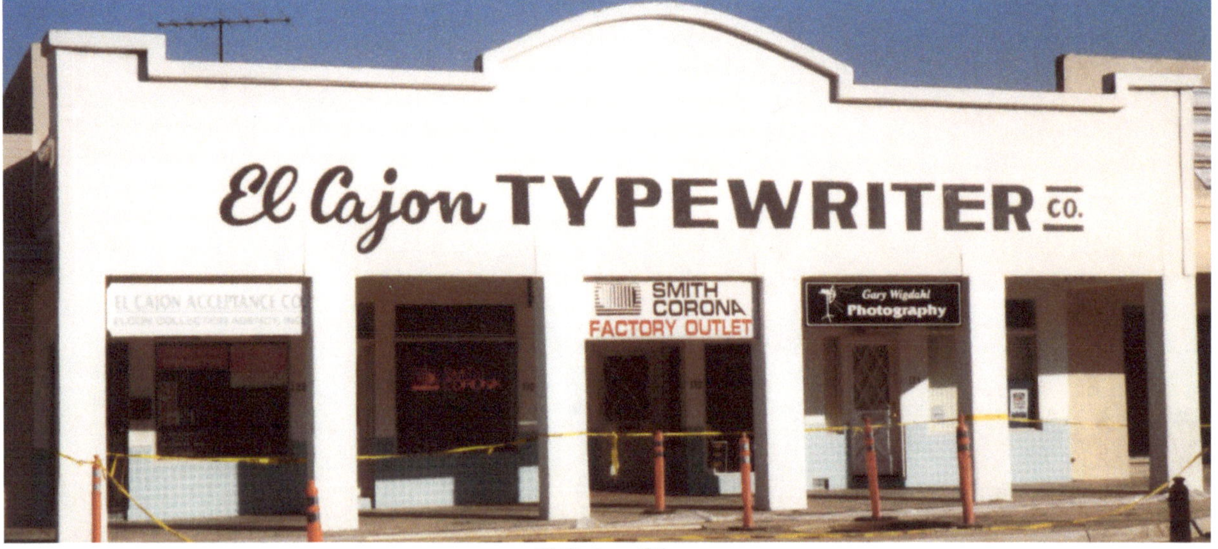

El Cajon, CA

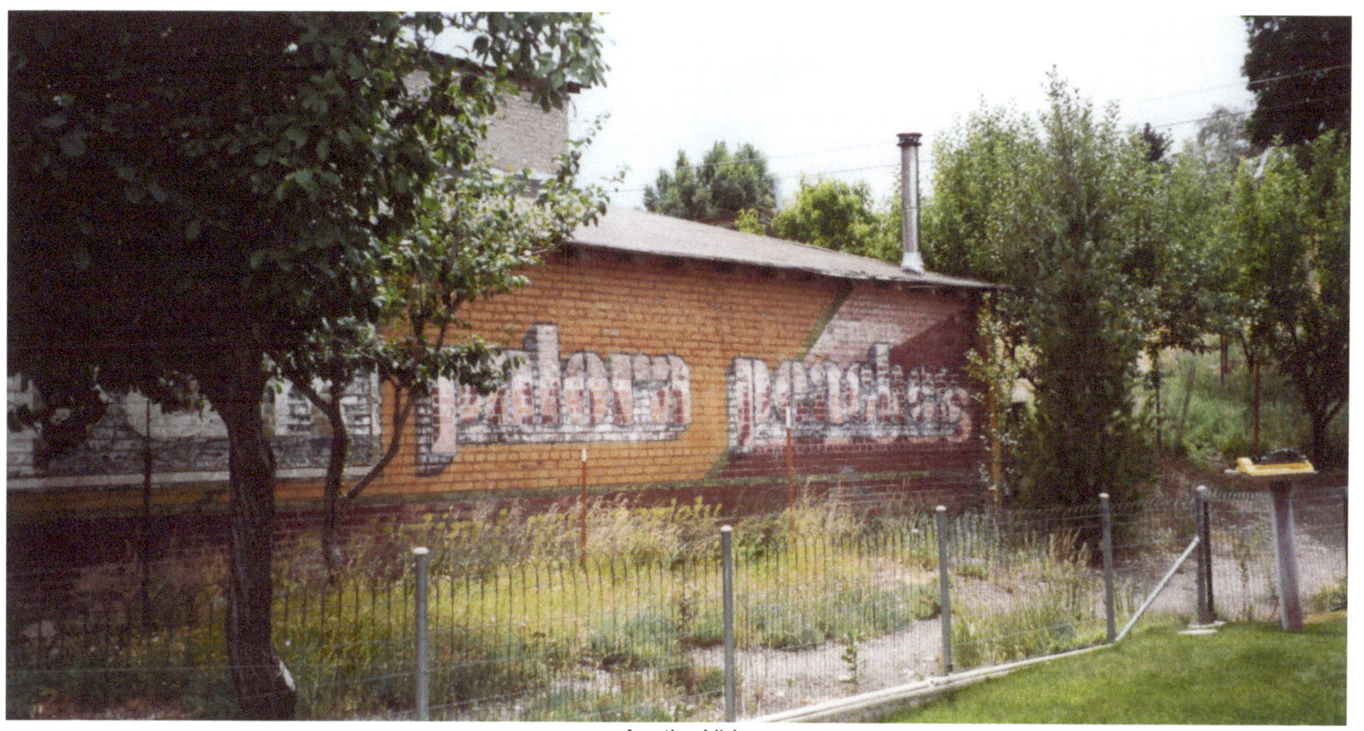

Austin, NV

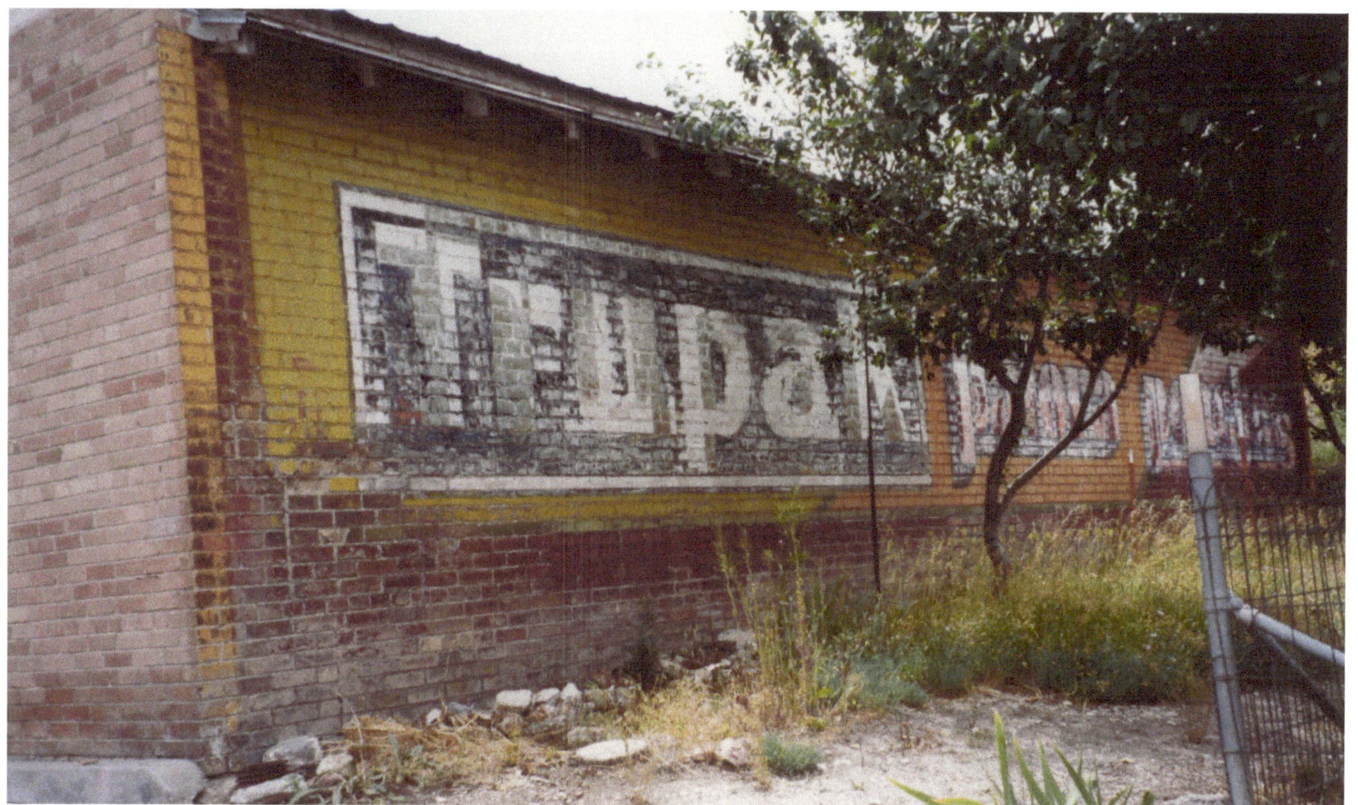

Austin, NV

CAFE·DUBARRY
"LAISSEZ CHACUN PROUVER EXCELLER L'ART QU'IL CONNAIT"
GARBER TRAVEL

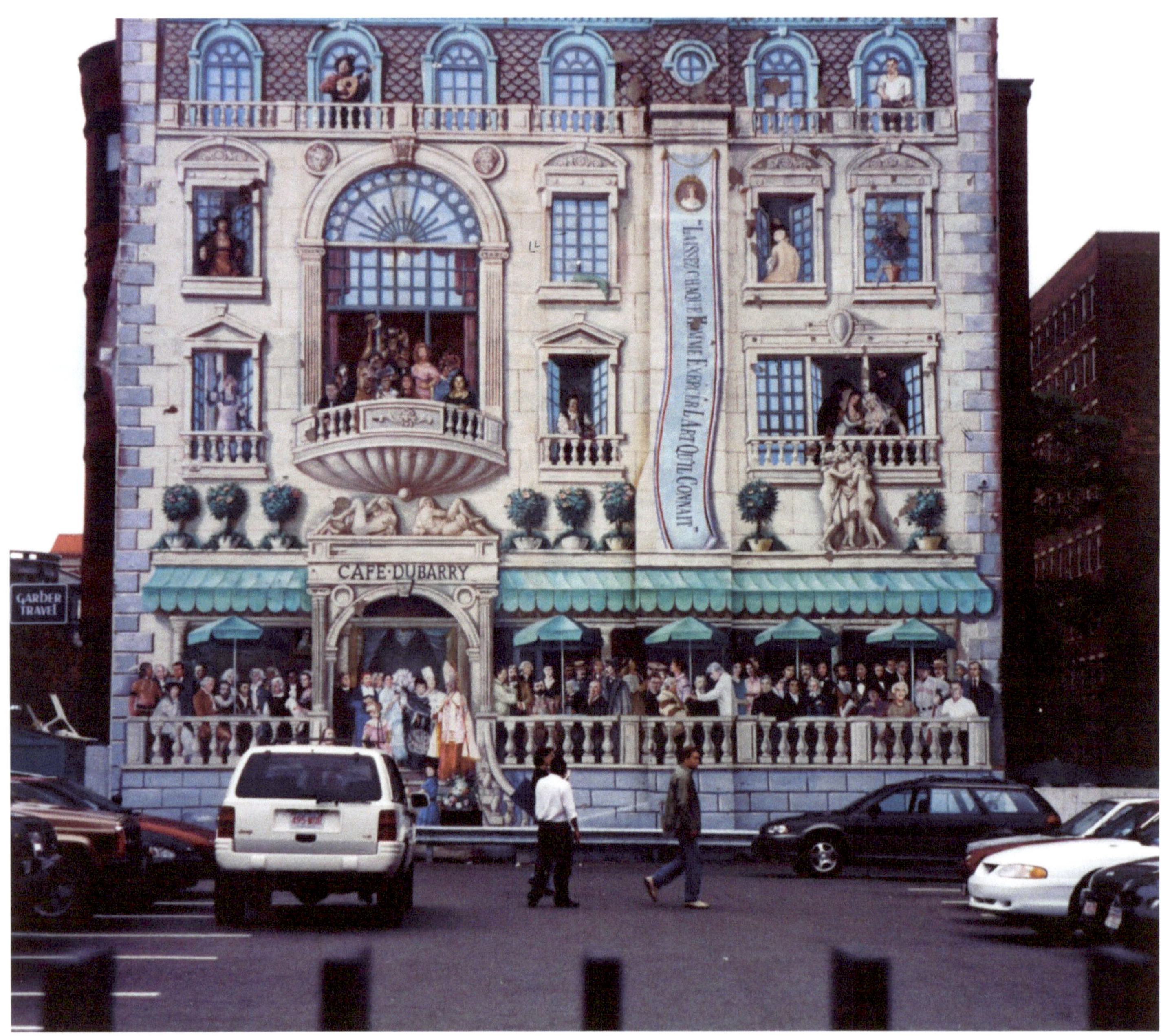

Boston, MA

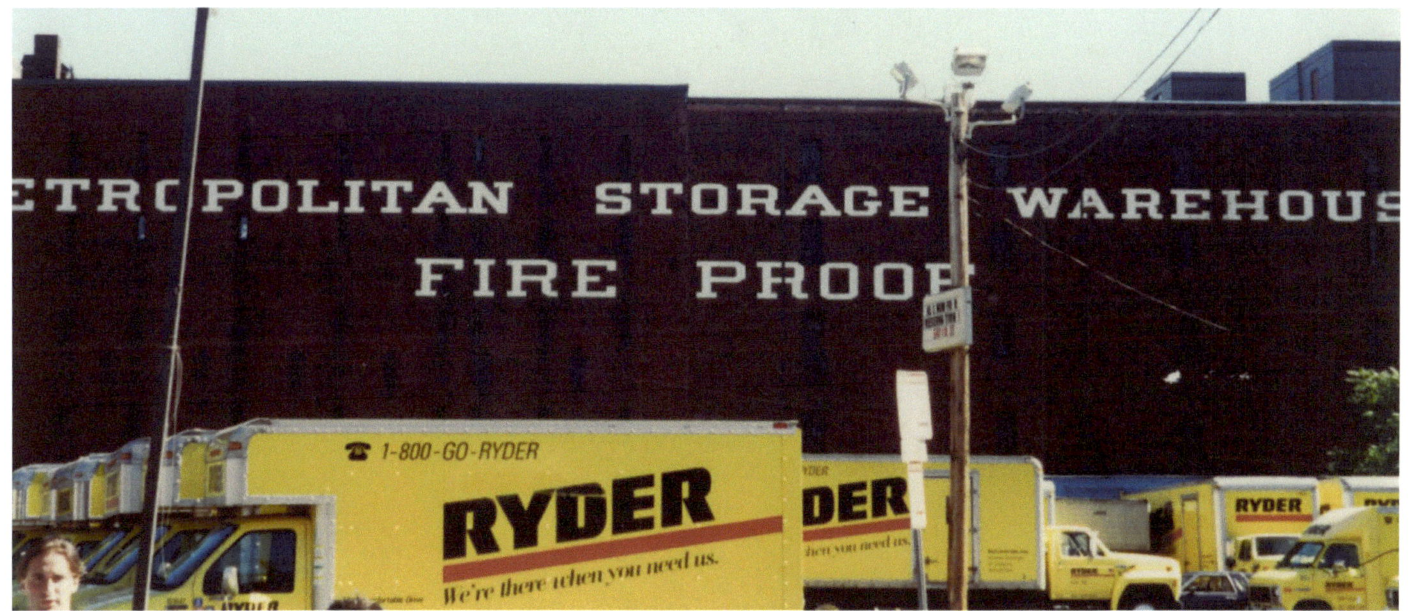

Cambridge, MA

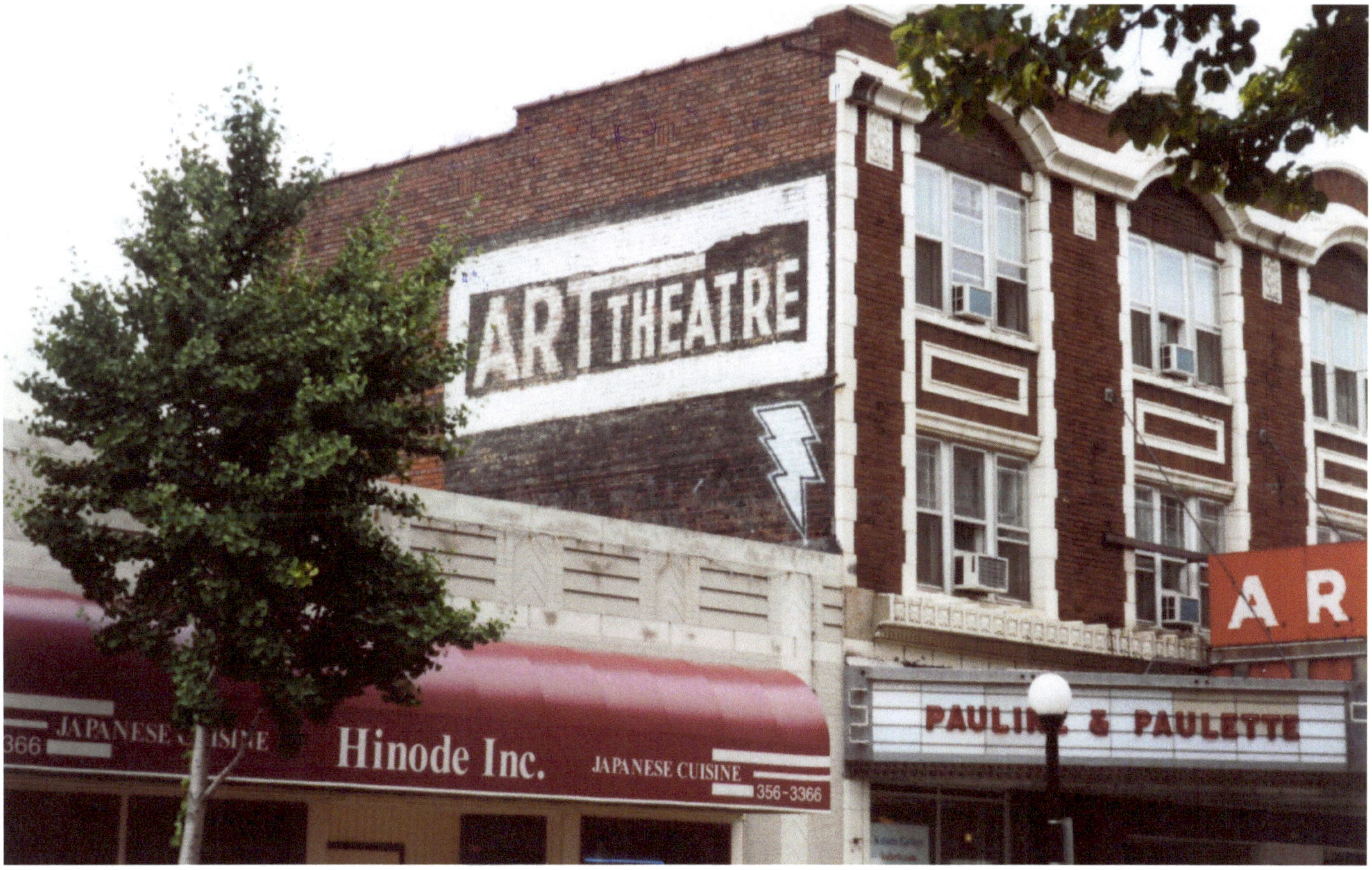

Champaign-Urbana, IL

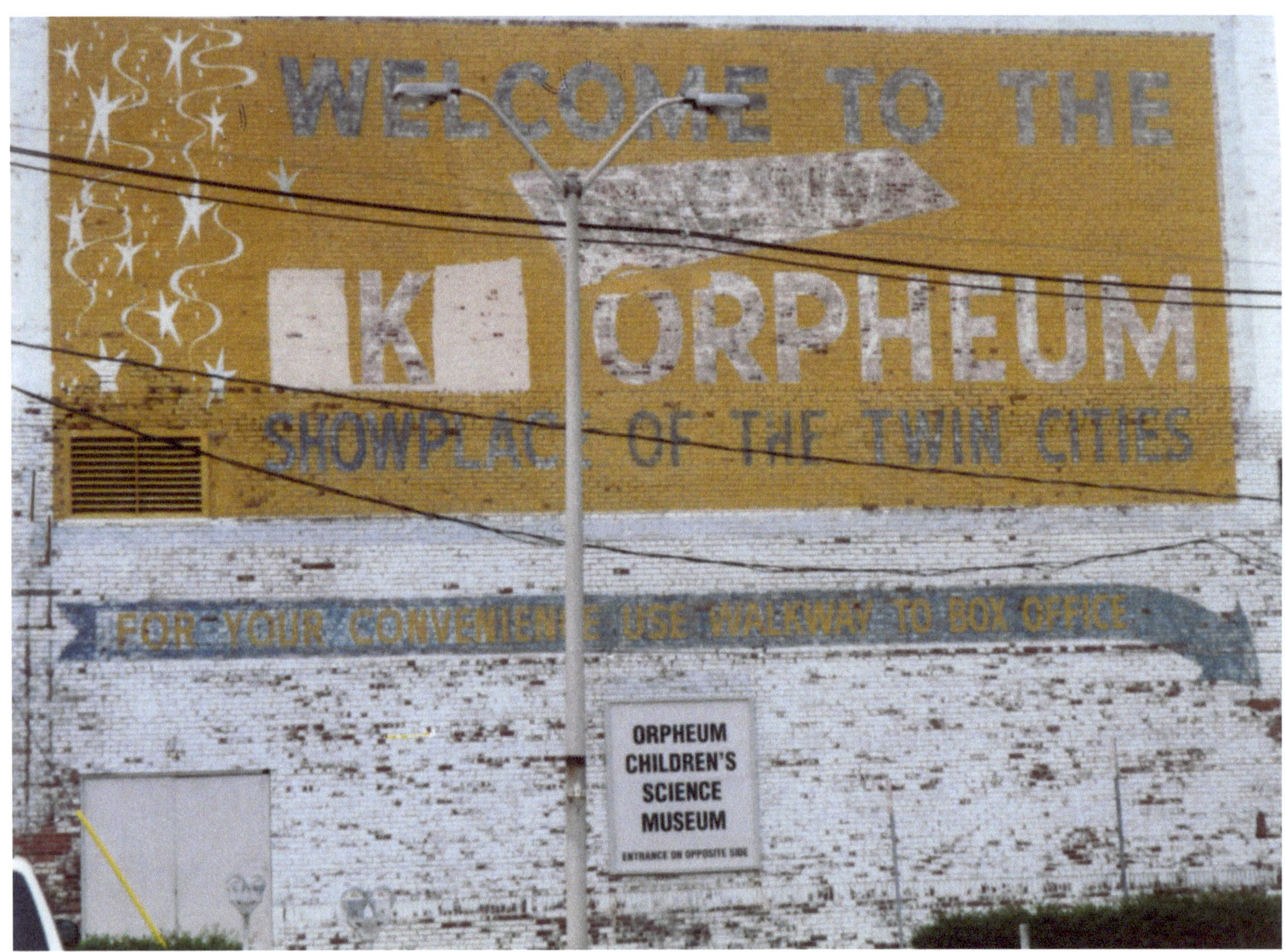

Champaign-Urbana, IL

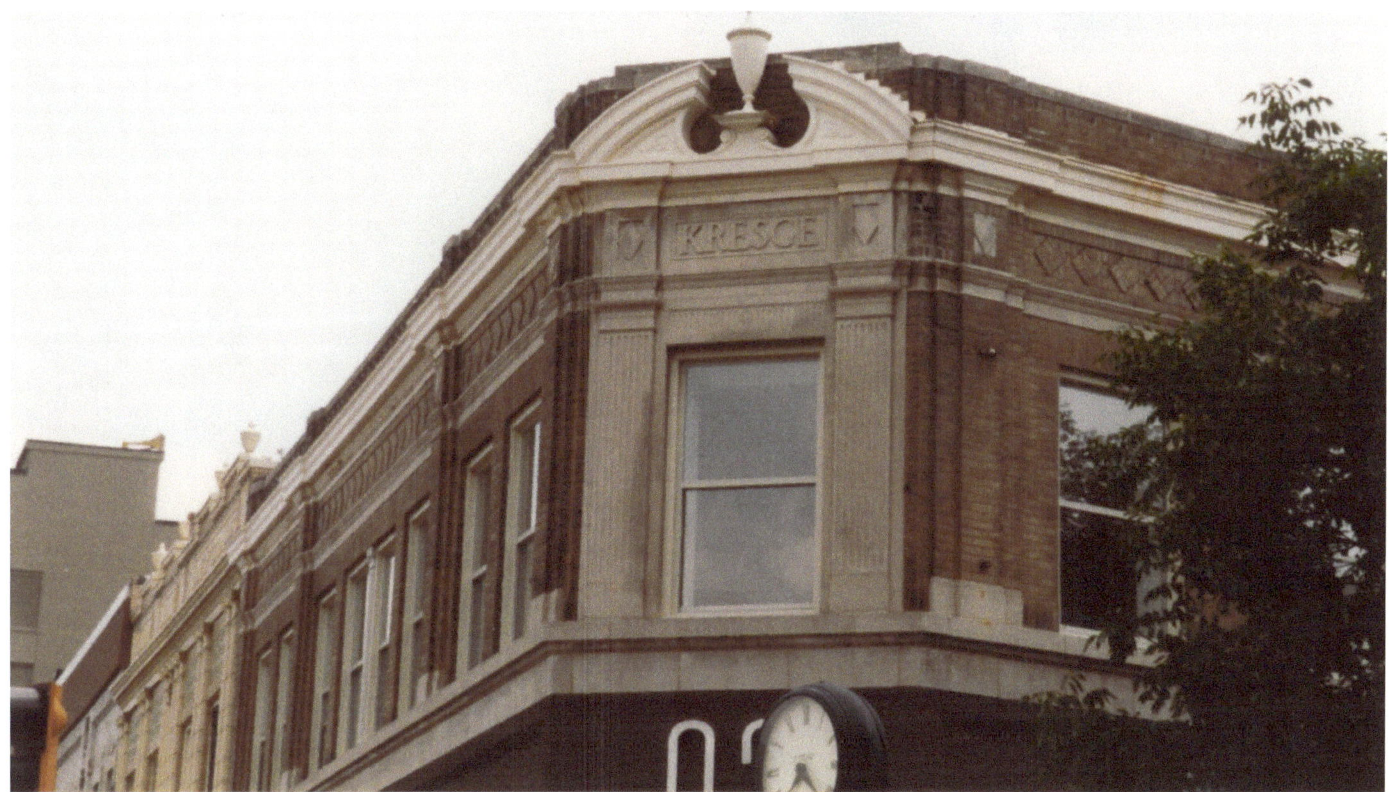

Champaign-Urbana, IL

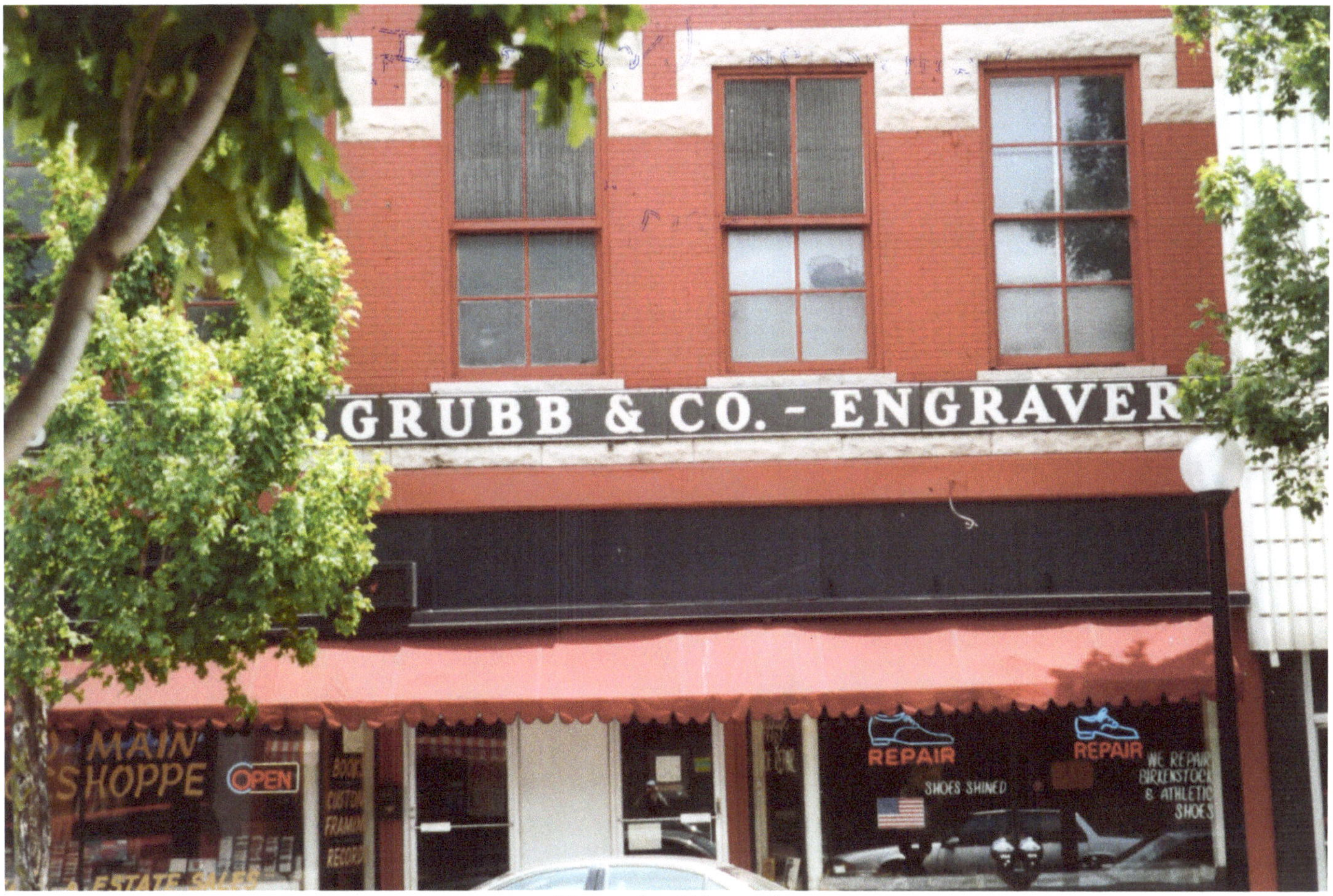

Champaign-Urbana, IL

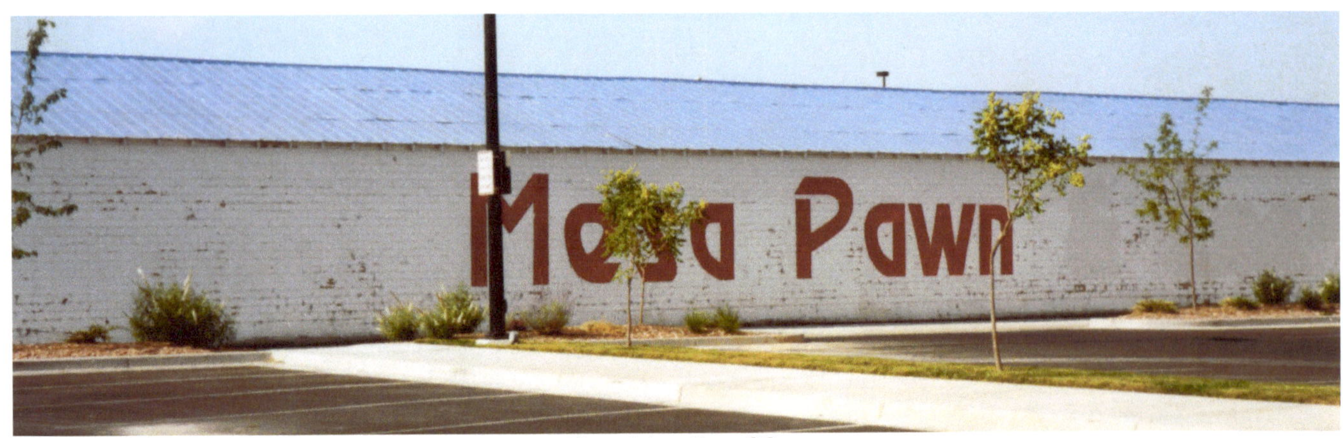

Grand Junction, CO

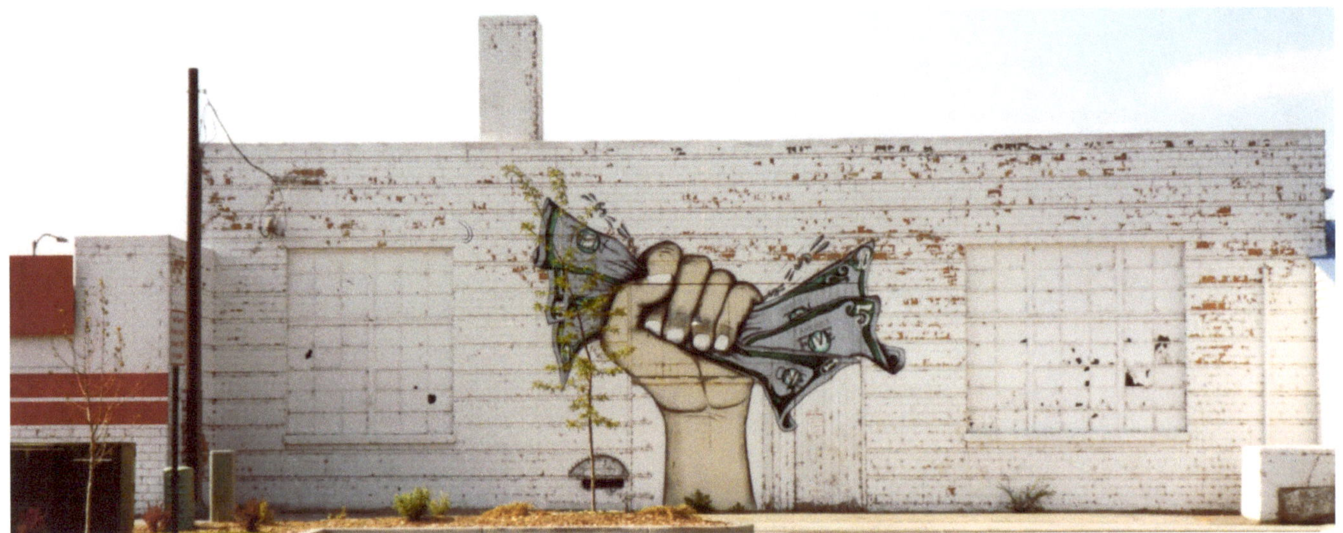

Grand Junction, CO

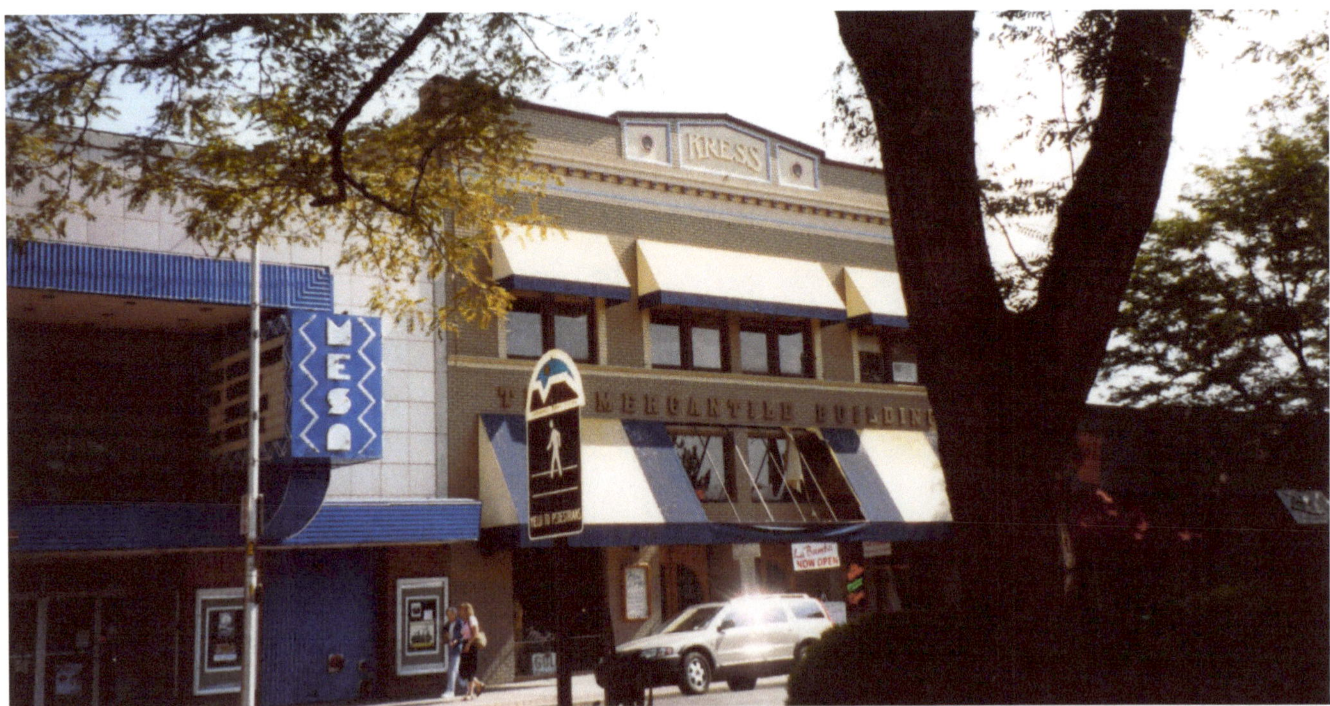

Grand Junction, CO

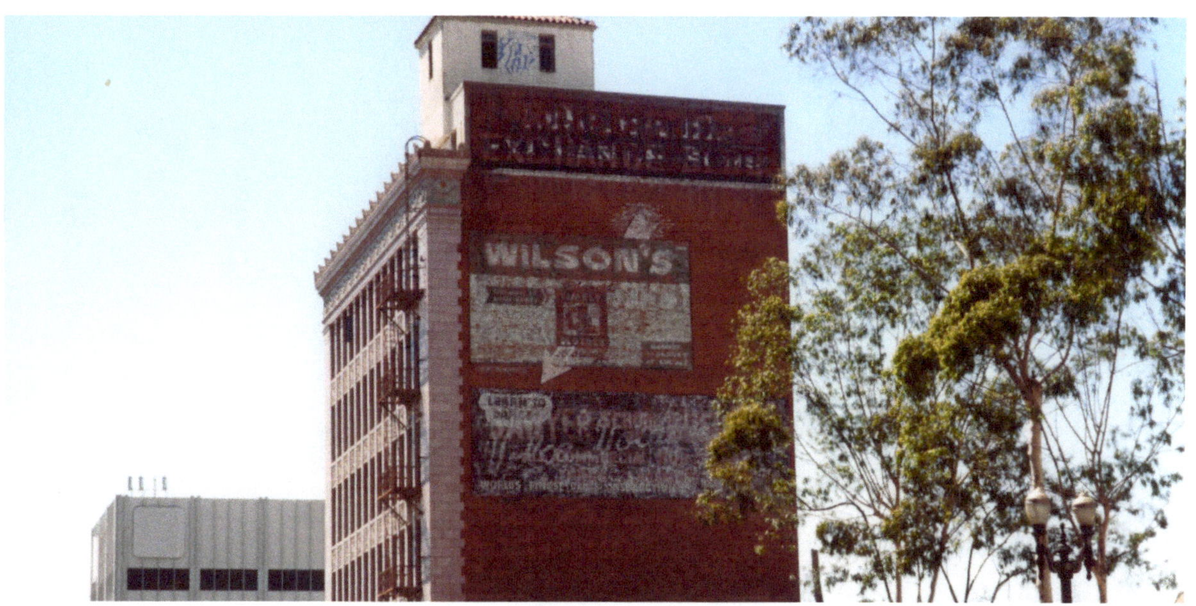

Long Beach, CA

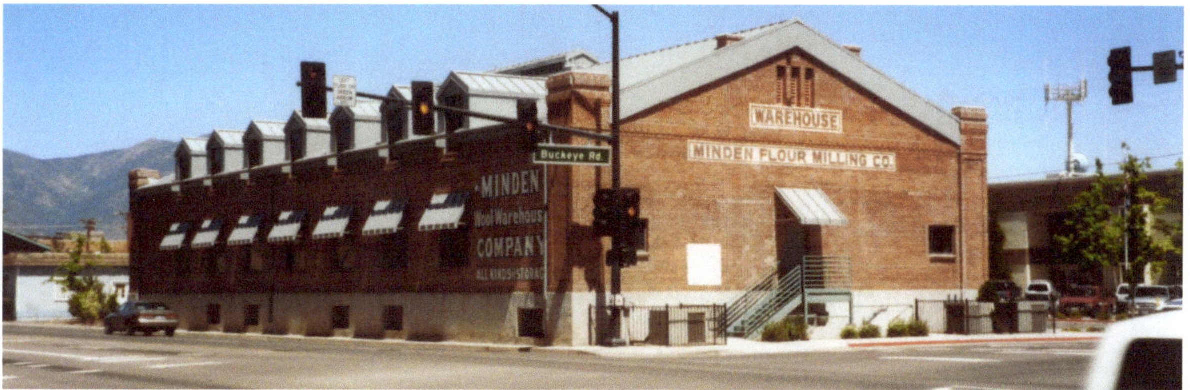

Minden, NV

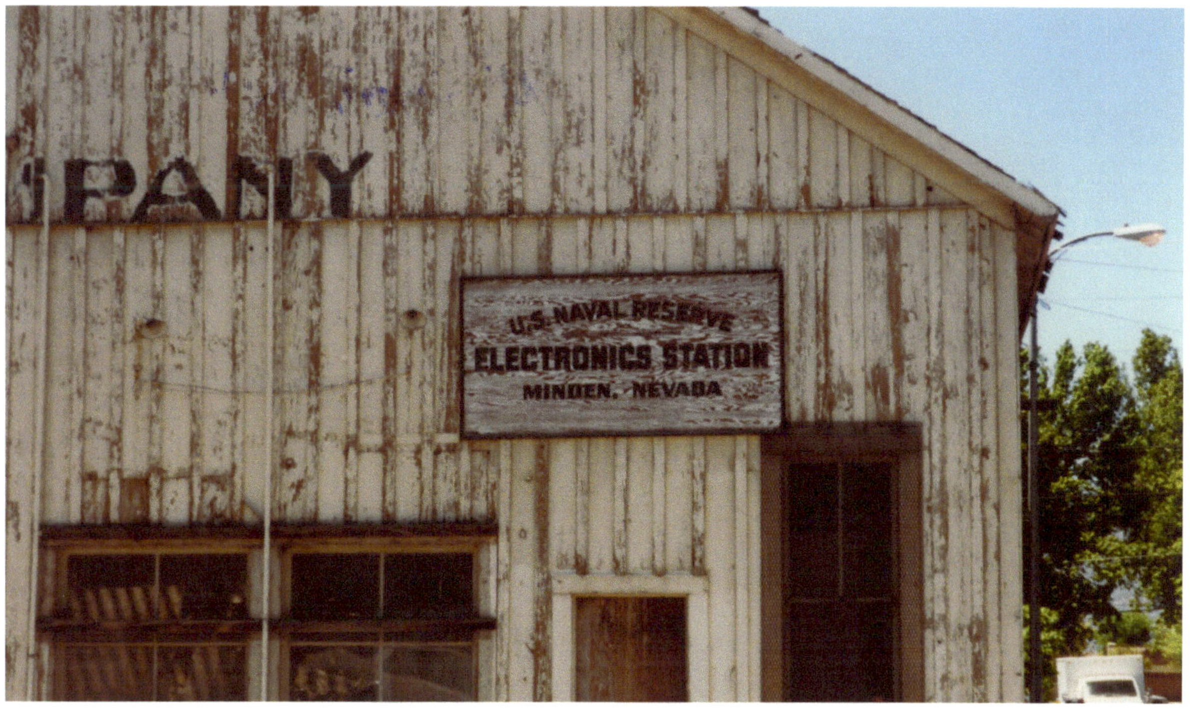

Minden, NV

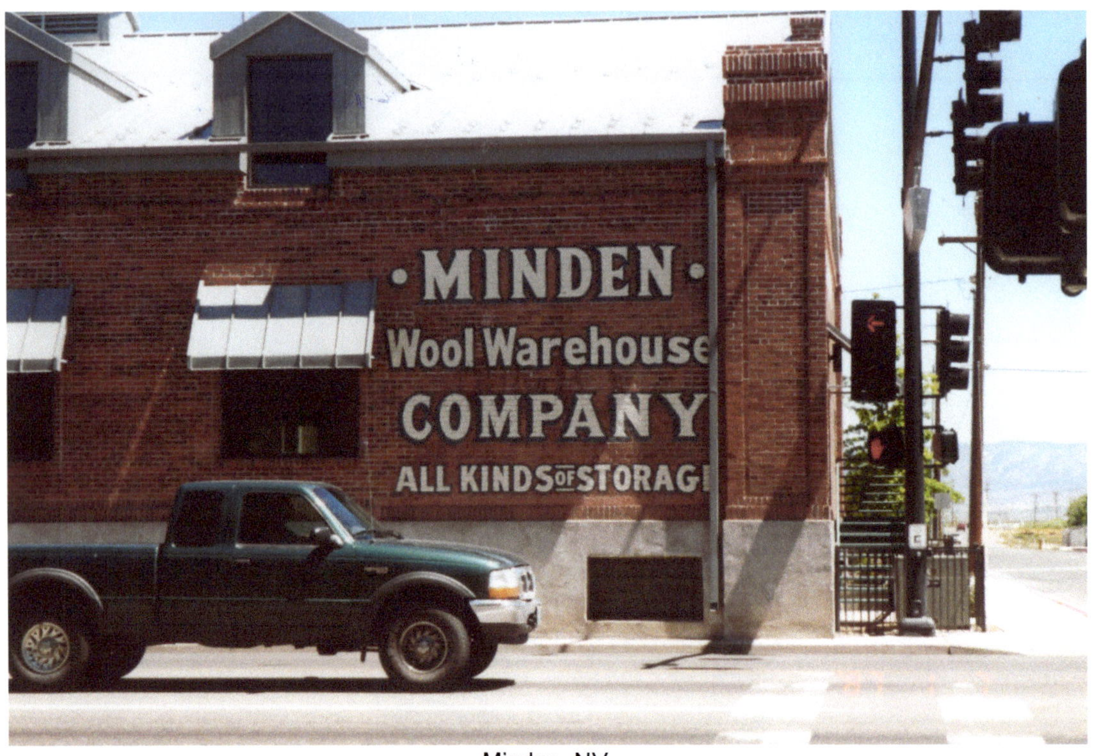

Minden, NV

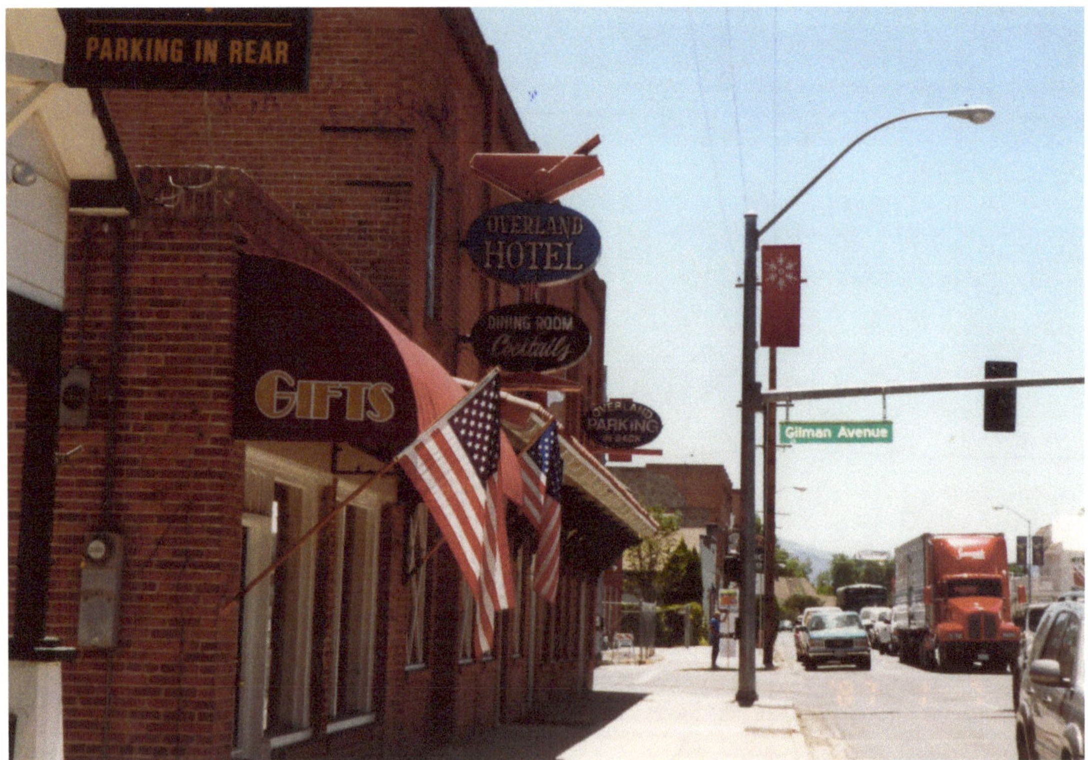

Minden, NV

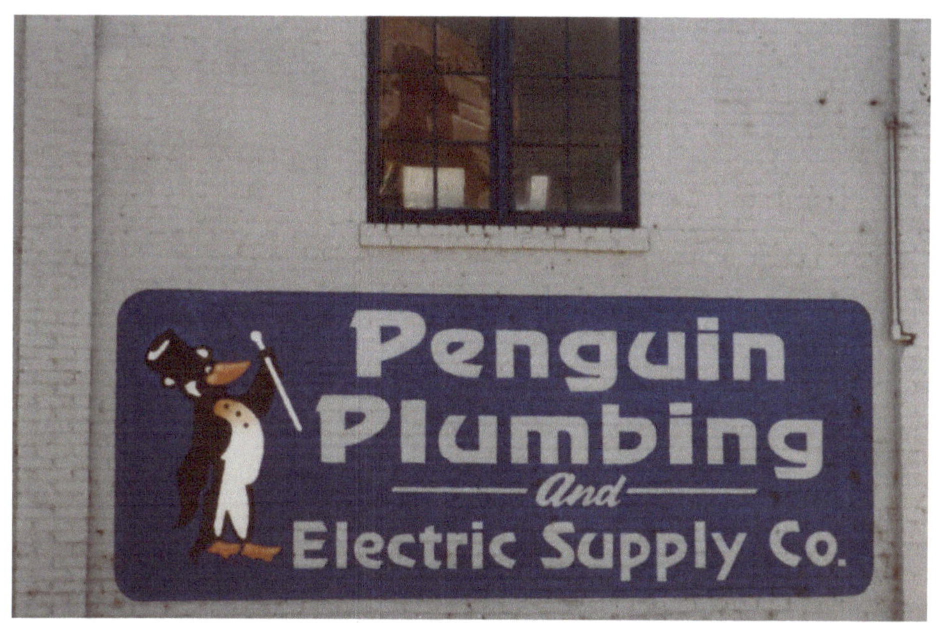

Minden, NV

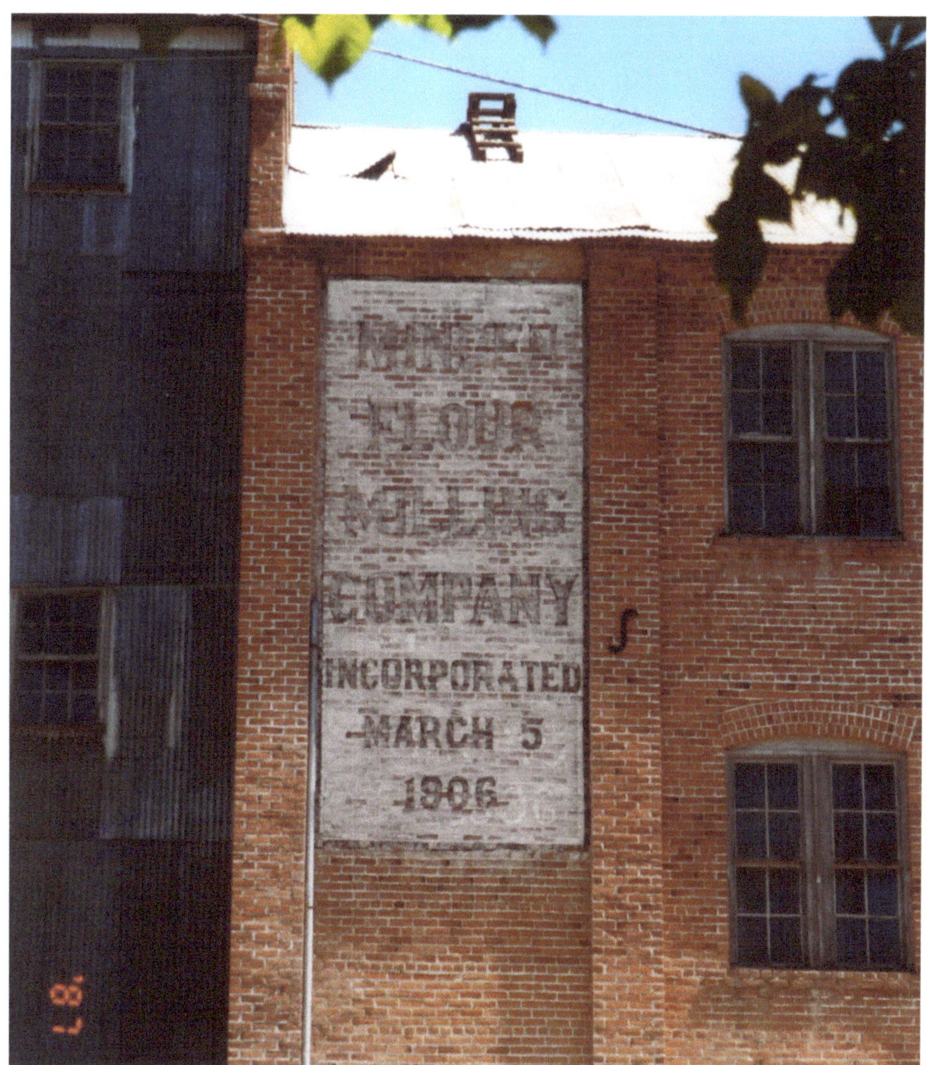

Minden, NV

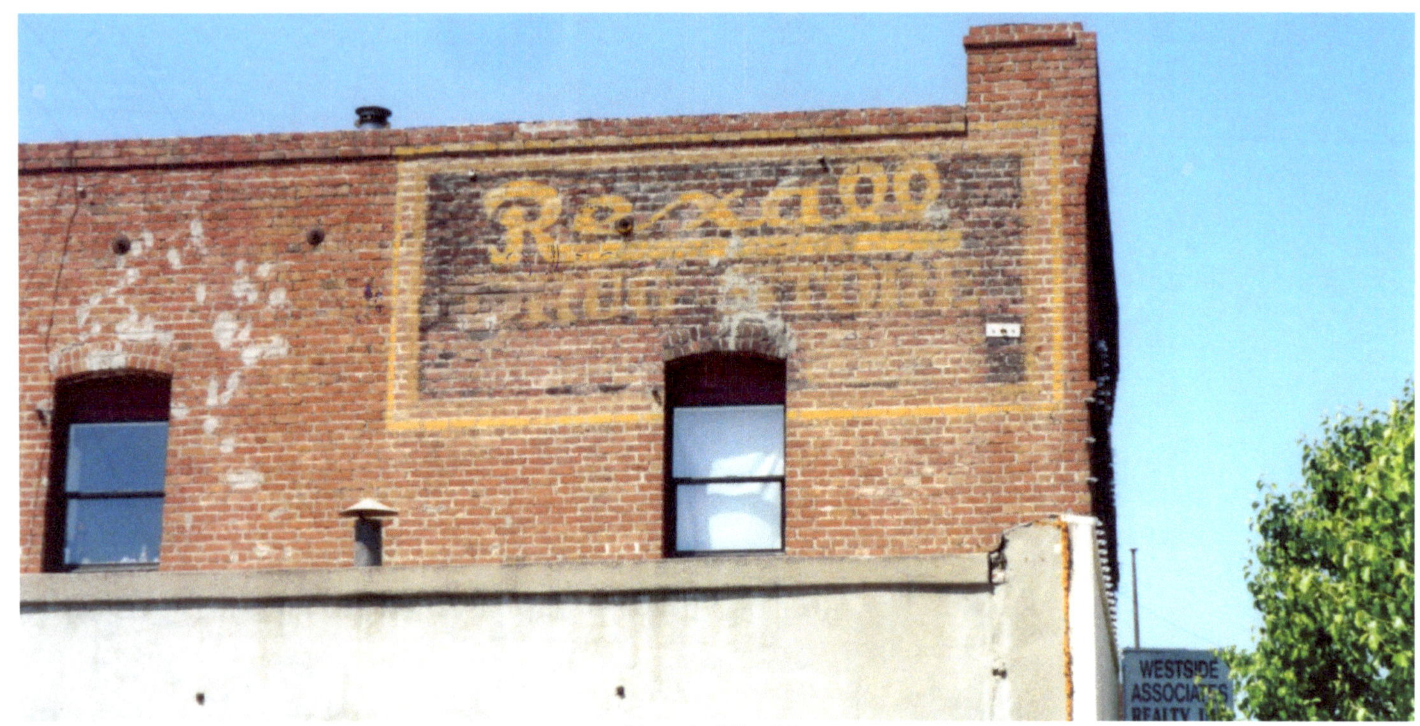

Nevada City, CA

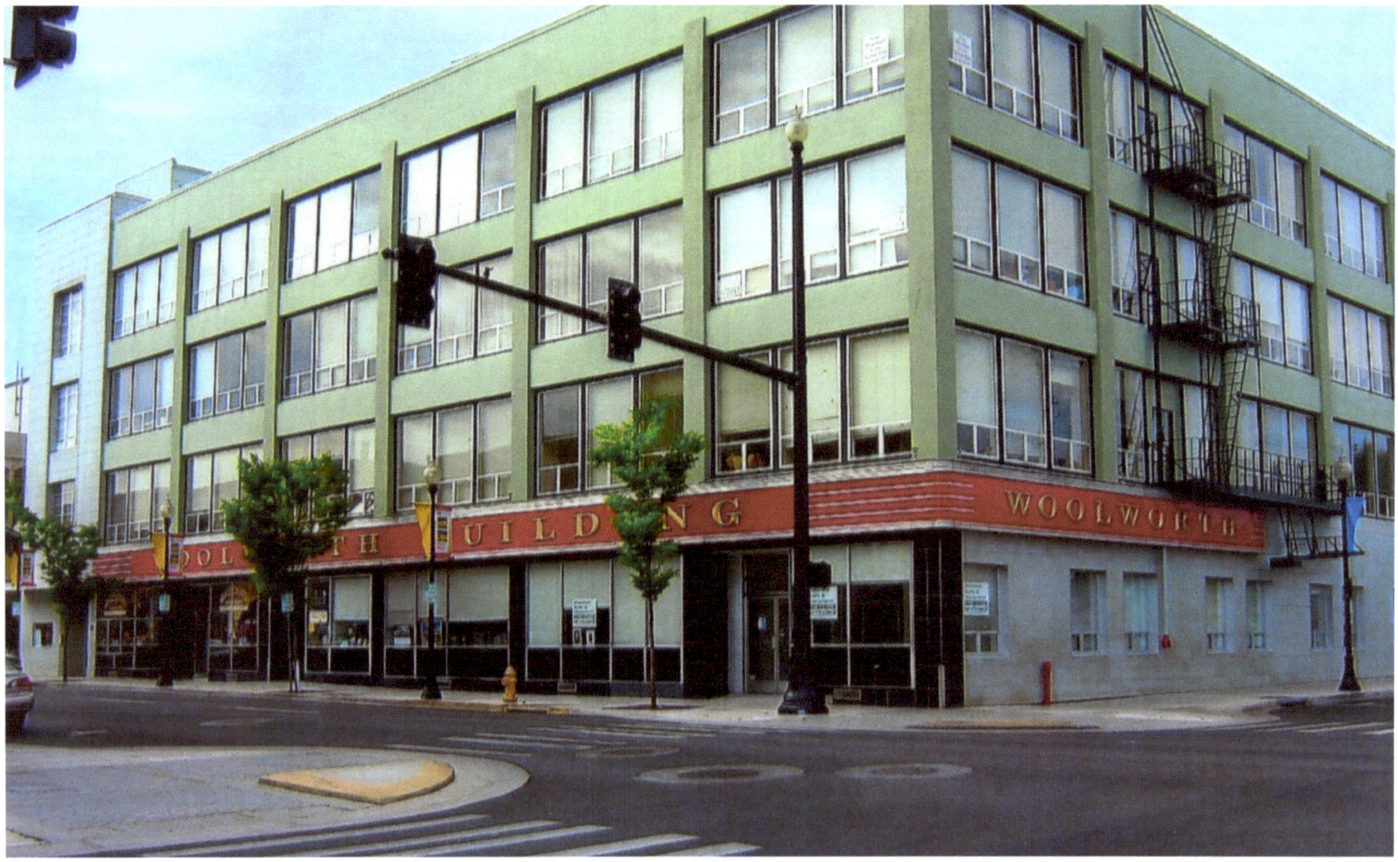

Medford, OR

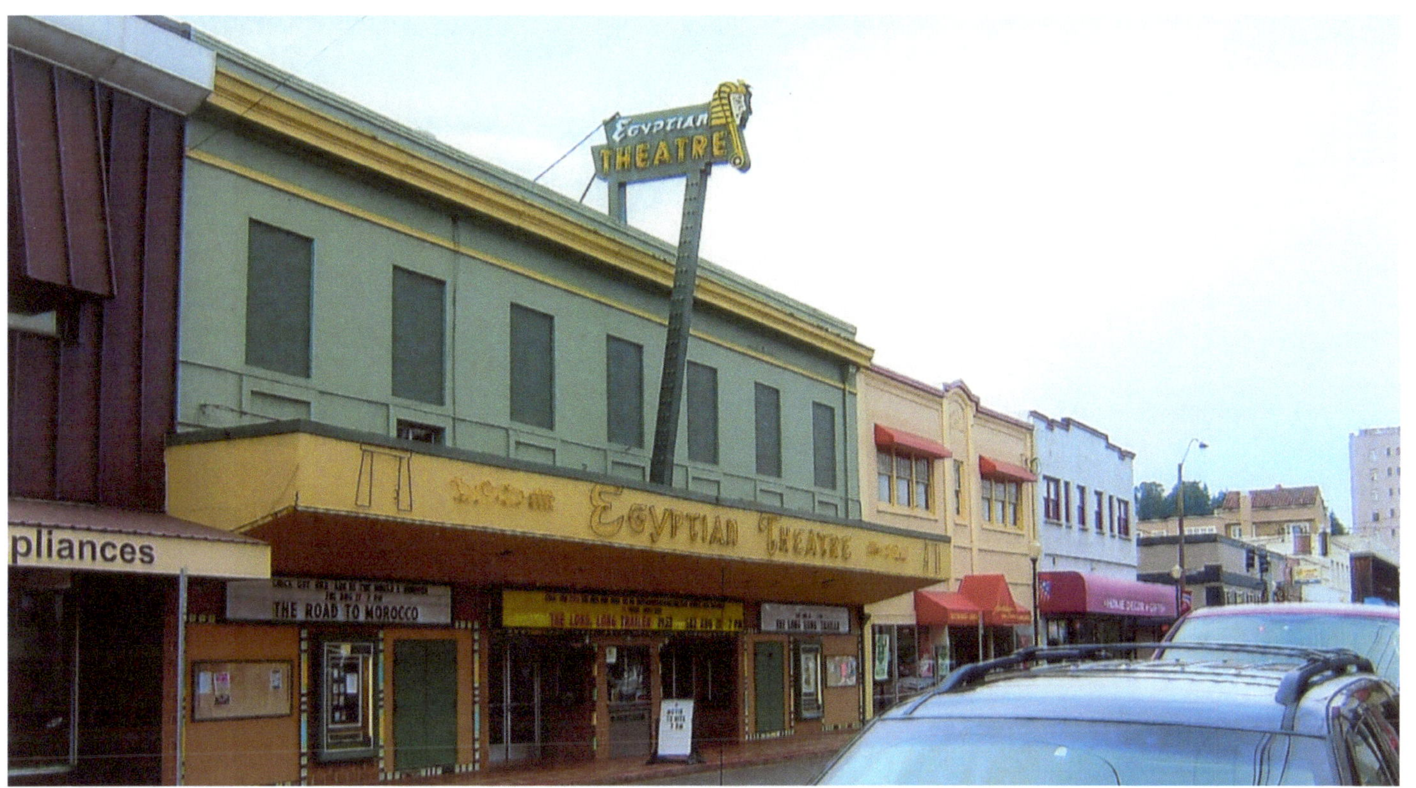

Coos Bay, OR

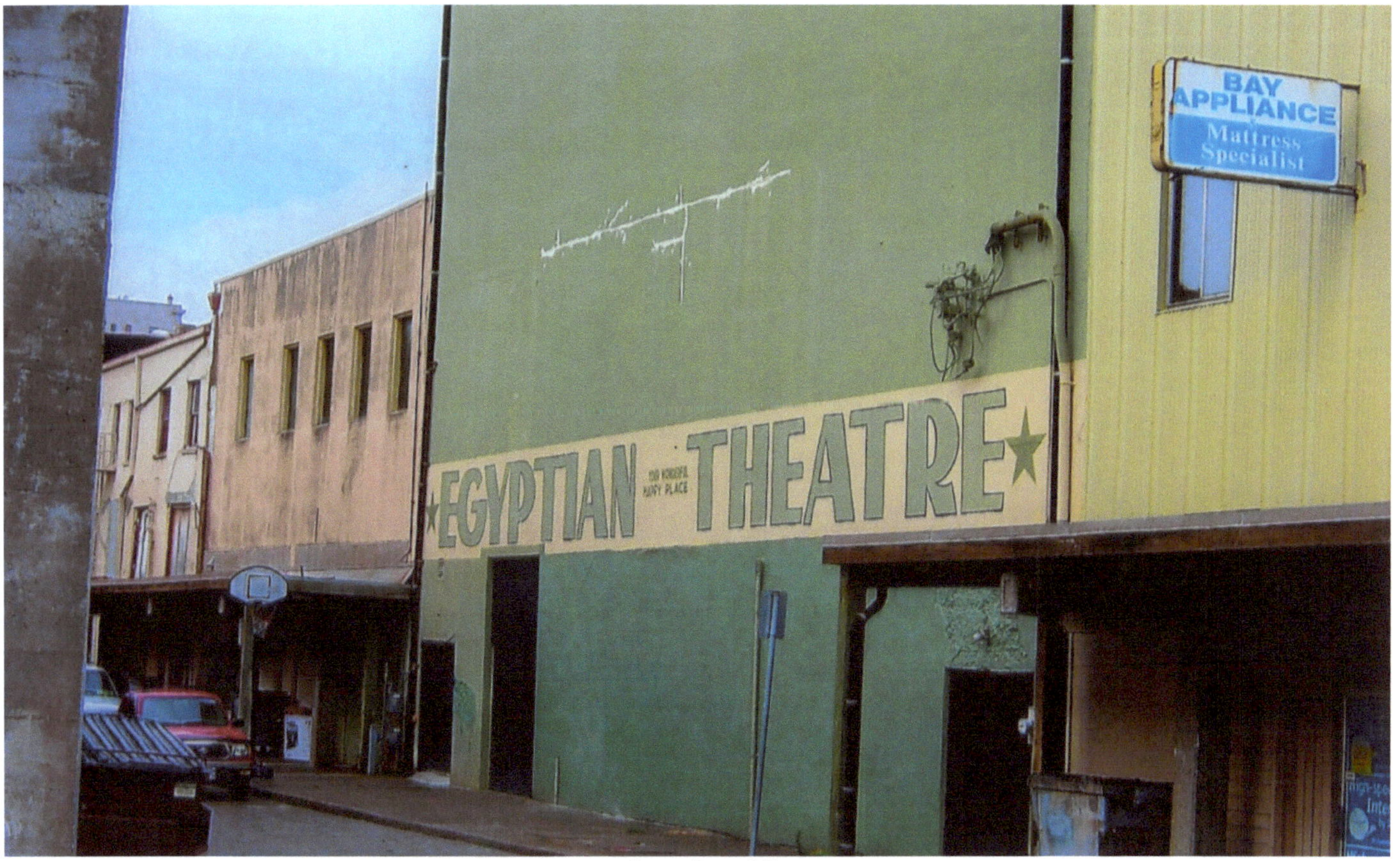

Coos Bay, OR

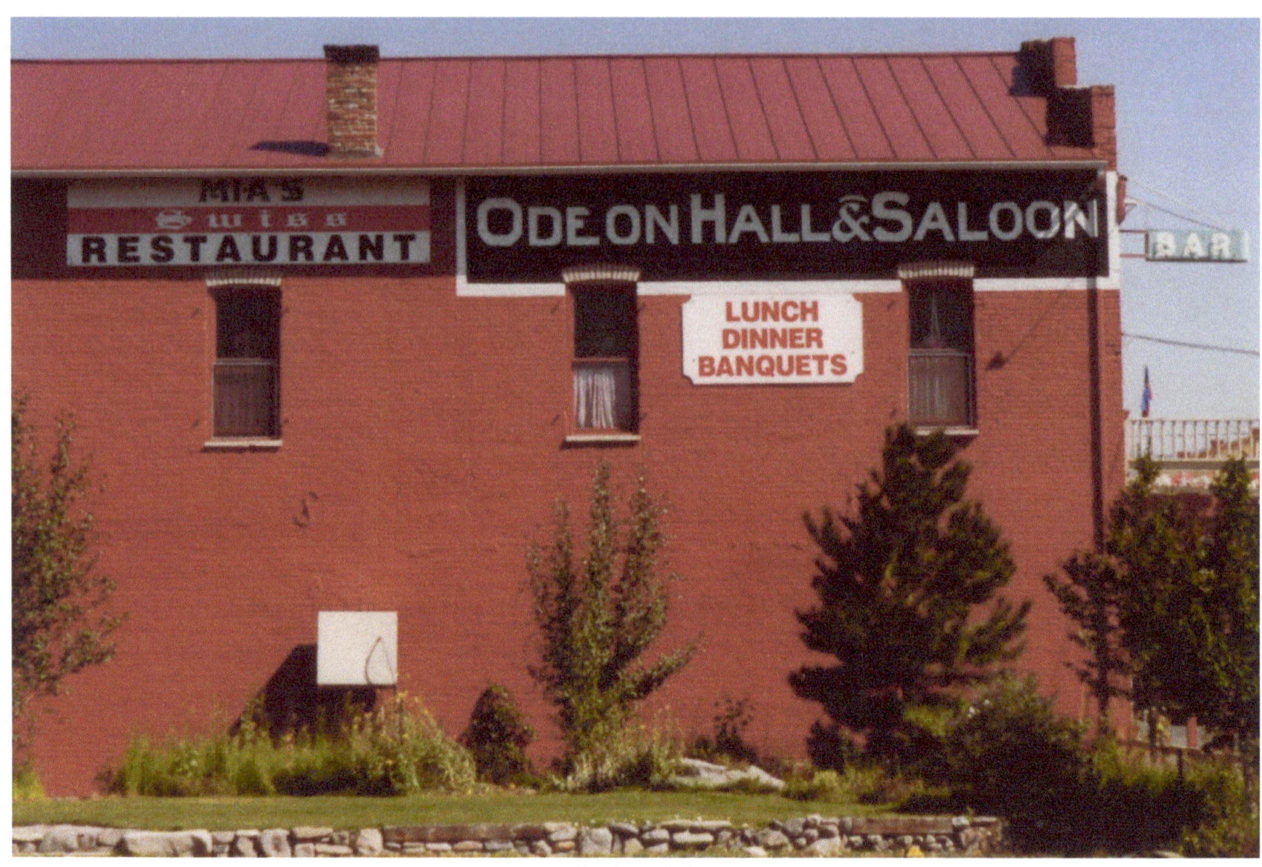

Dayton, NV

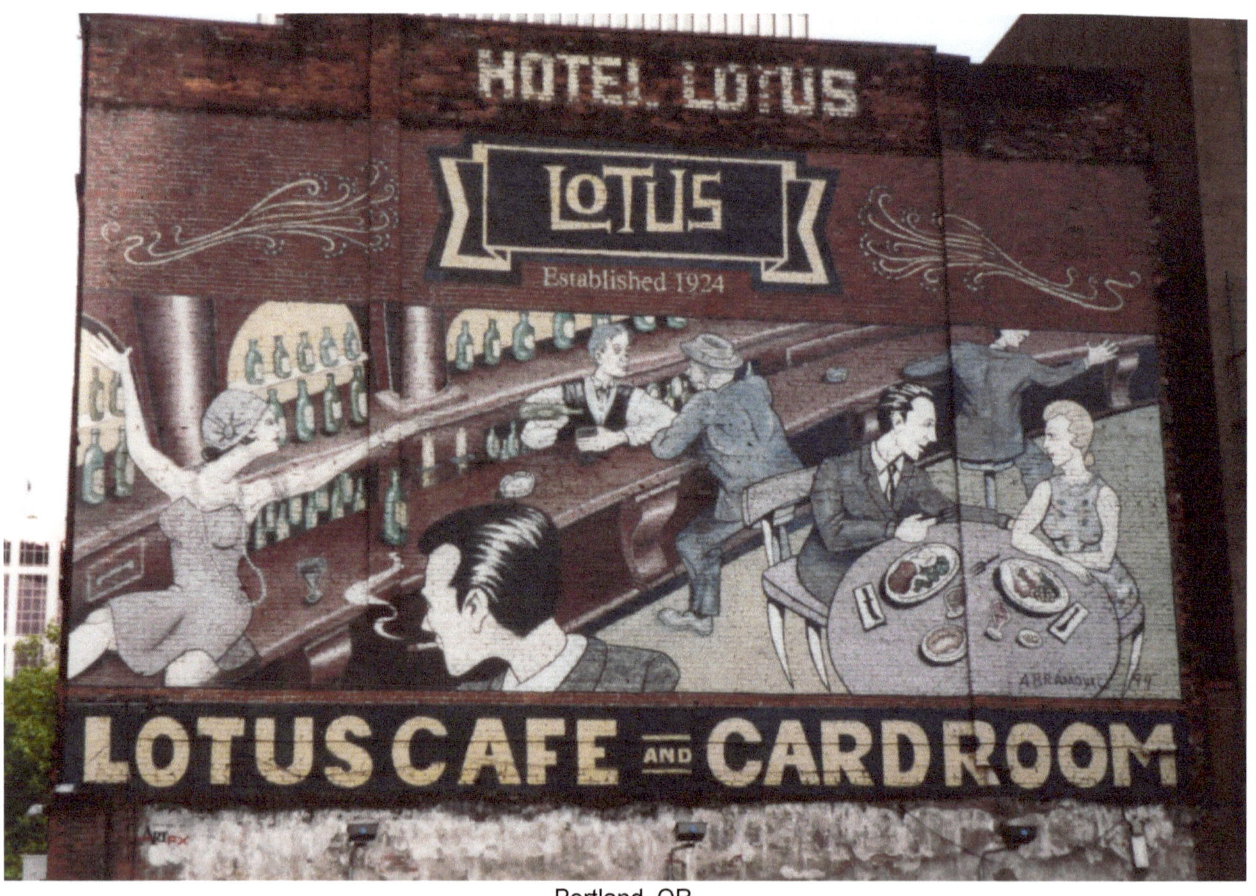

Portland, OR

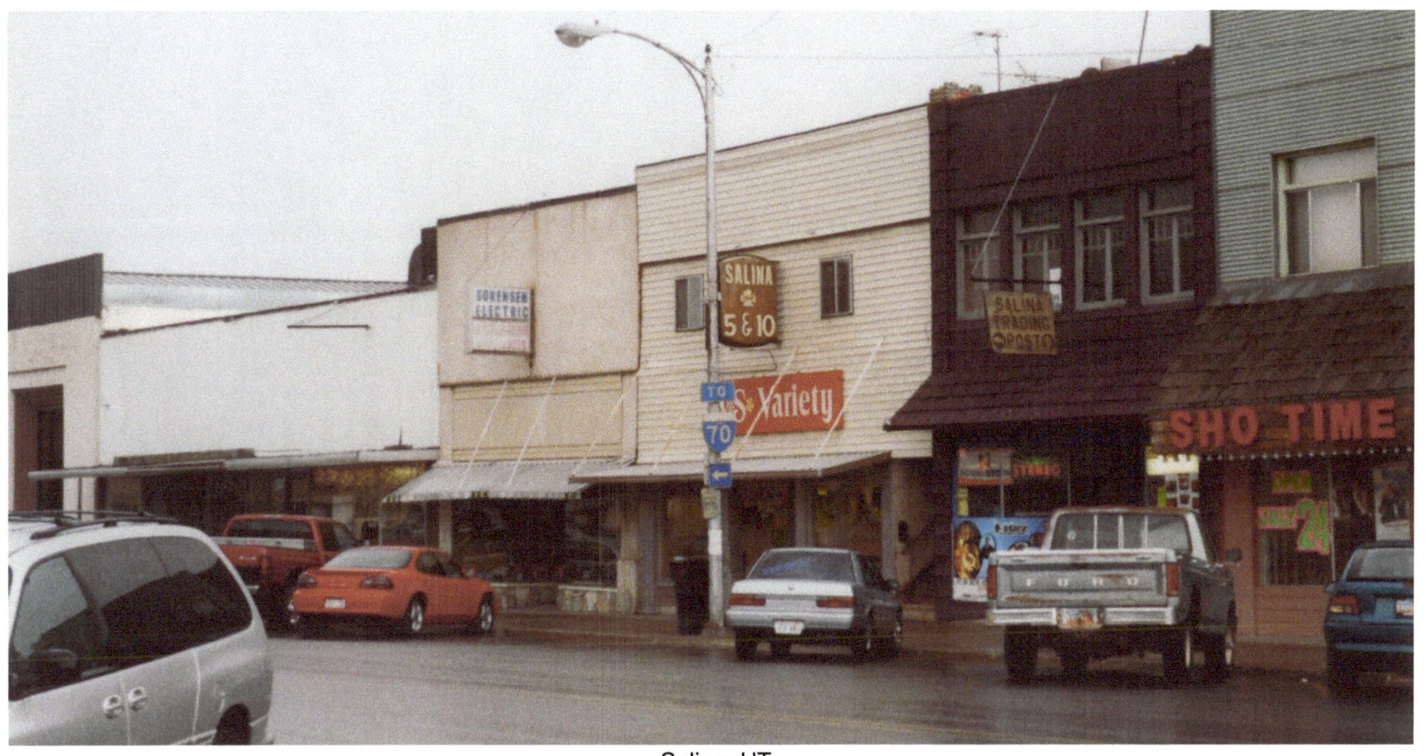

Salina, UT

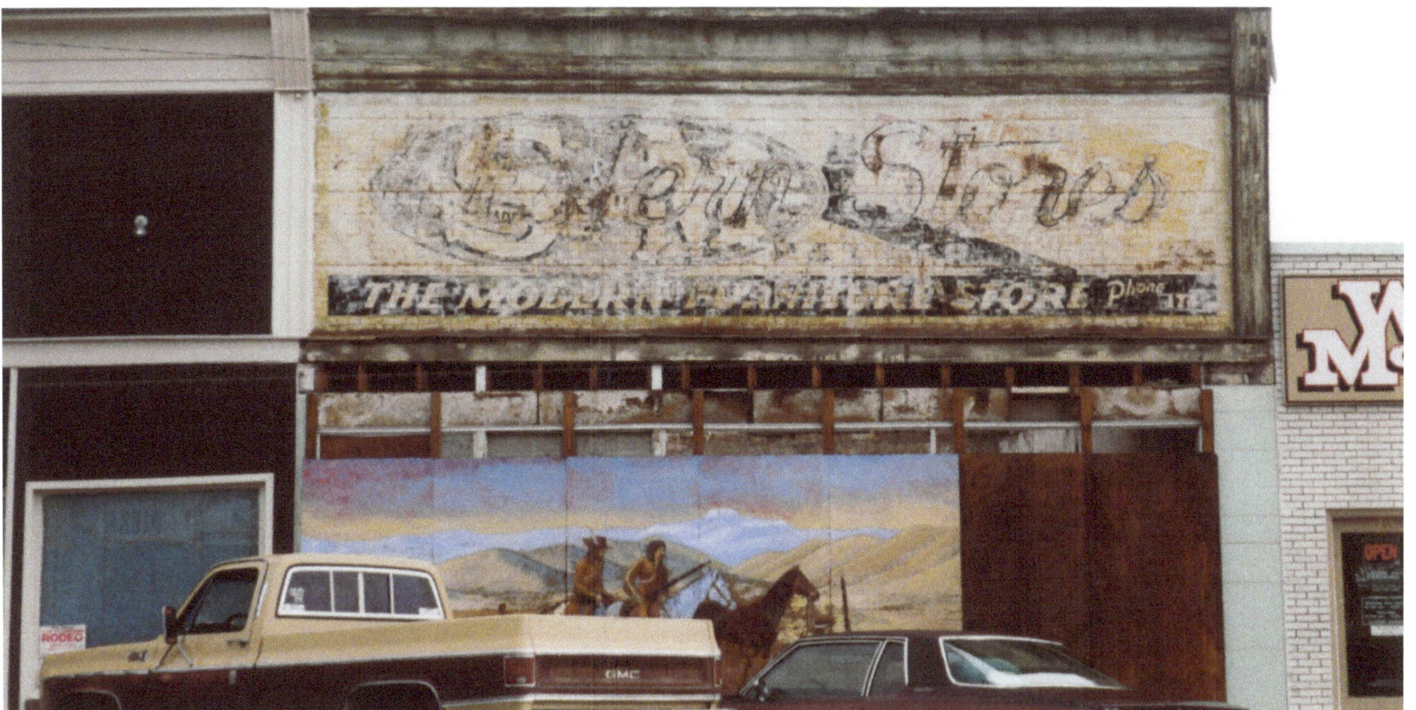

Salina, UT

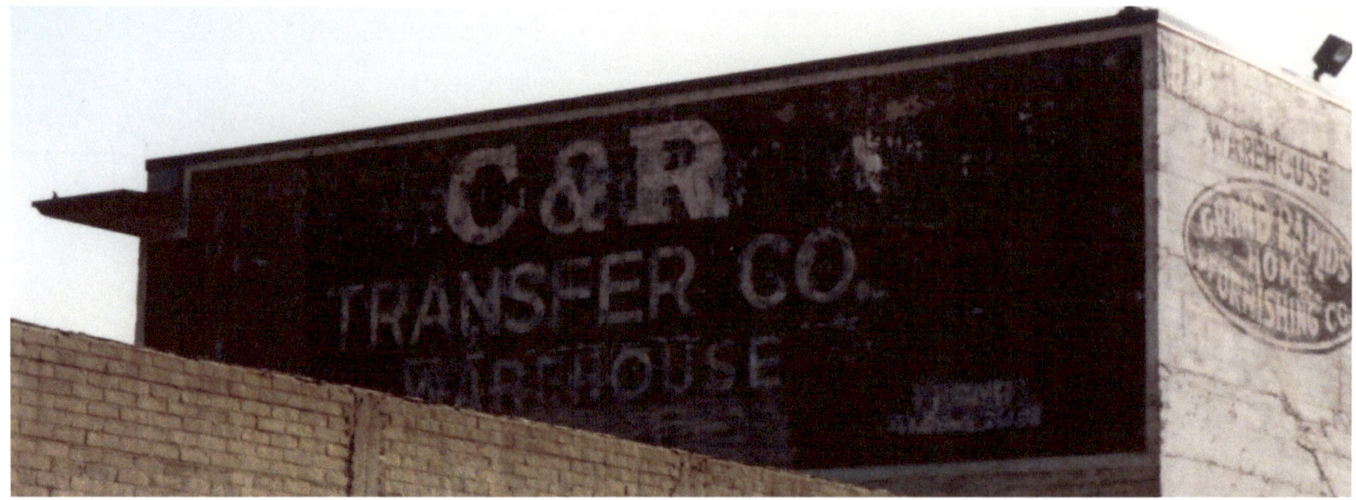

San Diego, CA

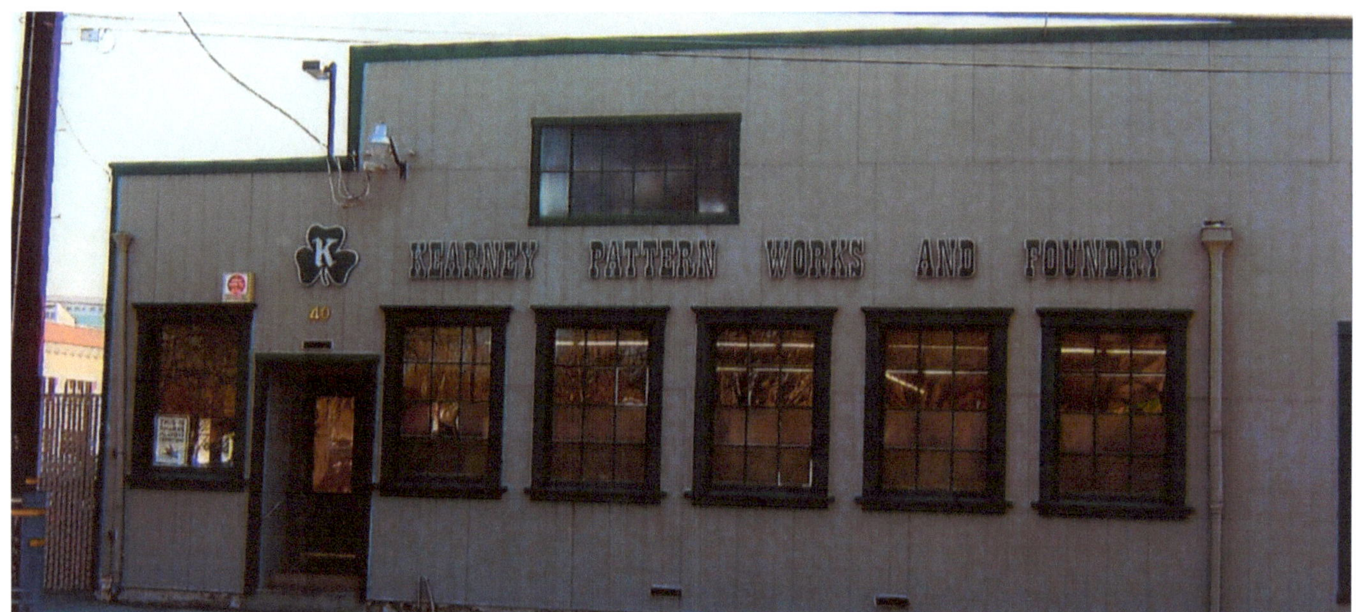

San Jose, CA

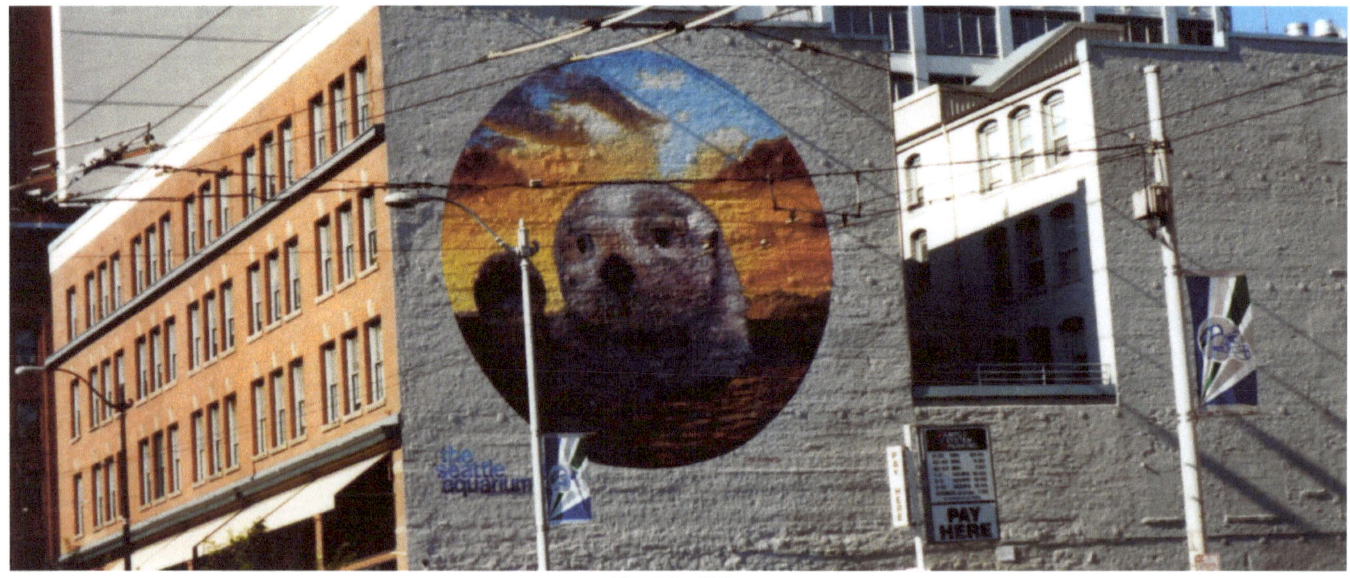

Seattle, WA

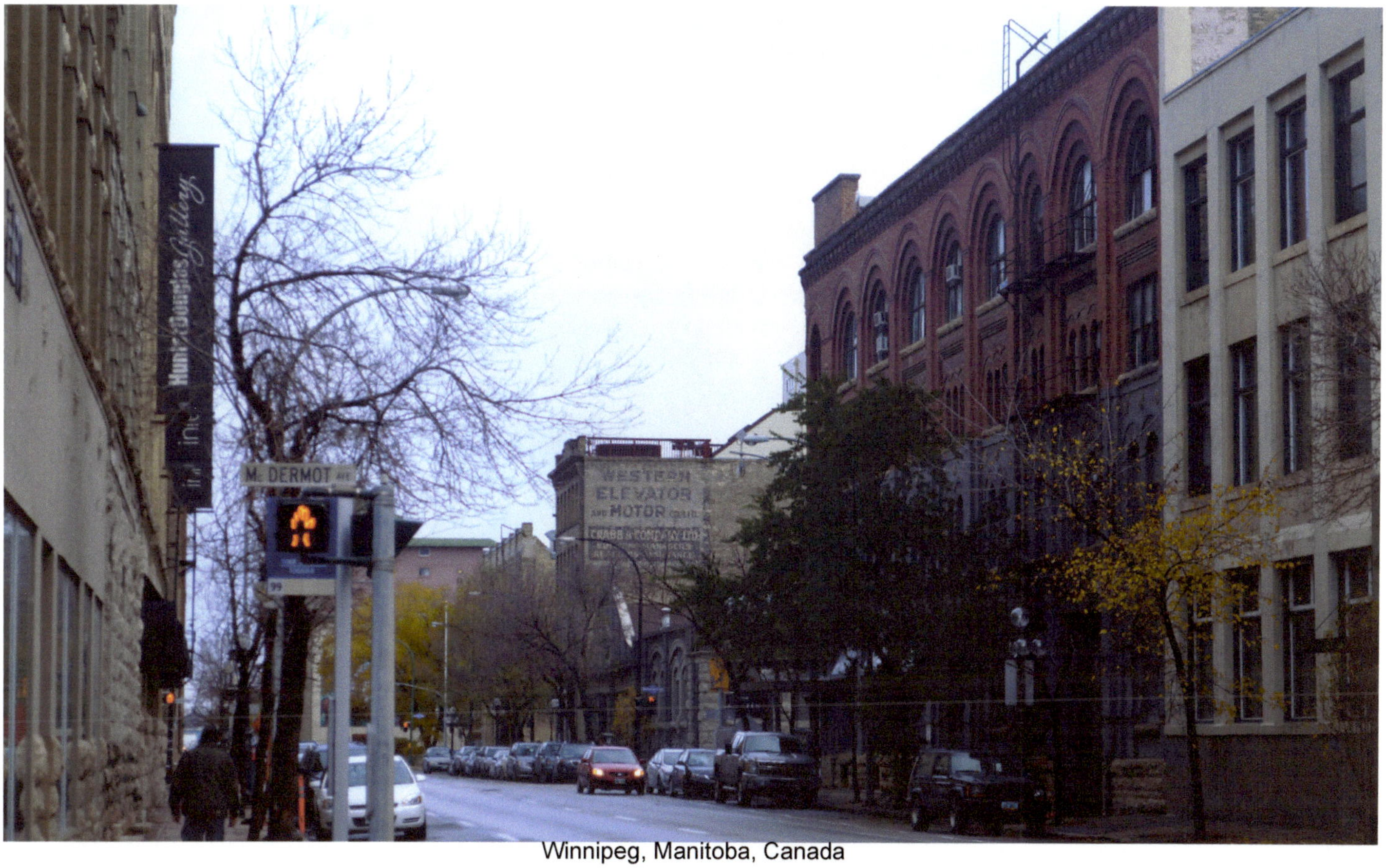

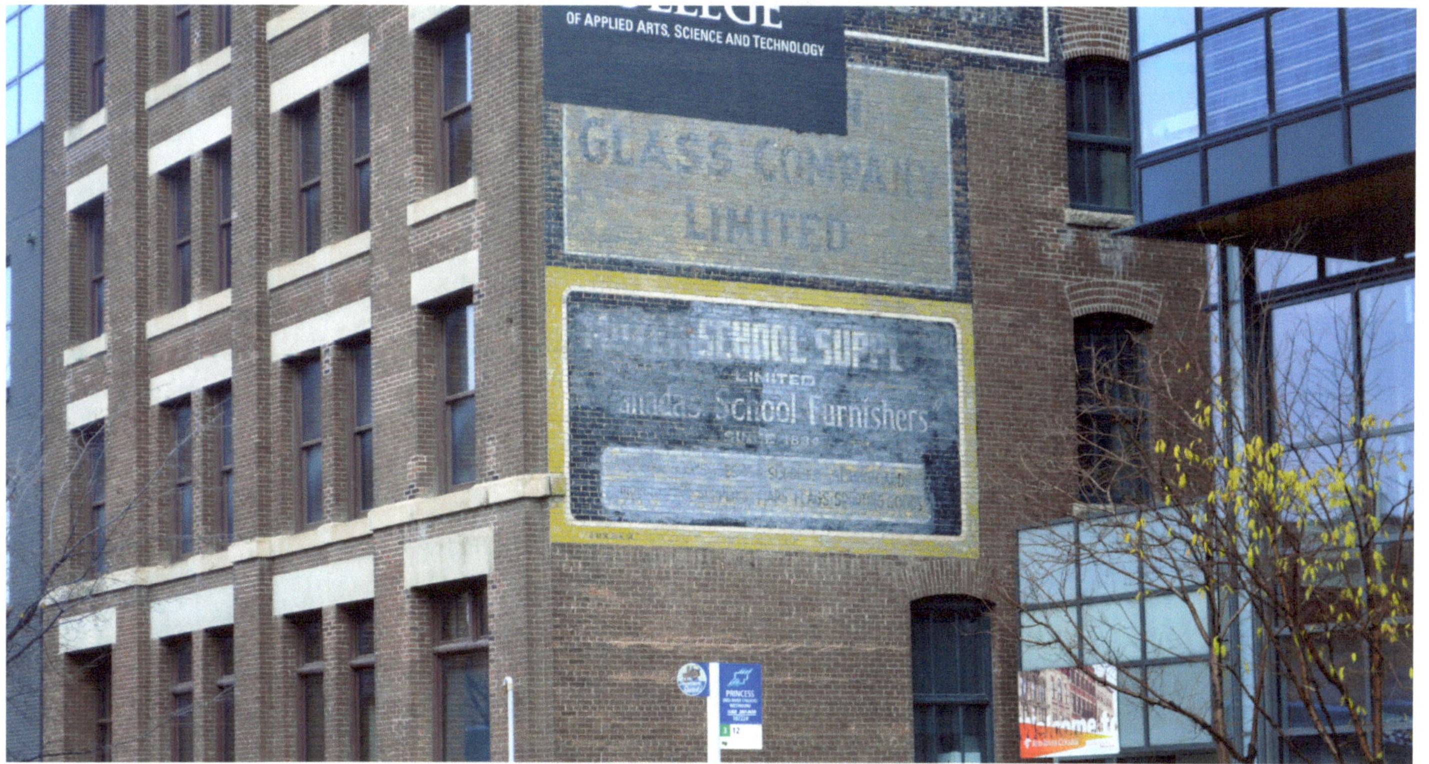

Winnipeg, Manitoba, Canada

Winnipeg, Manitoba, Canada

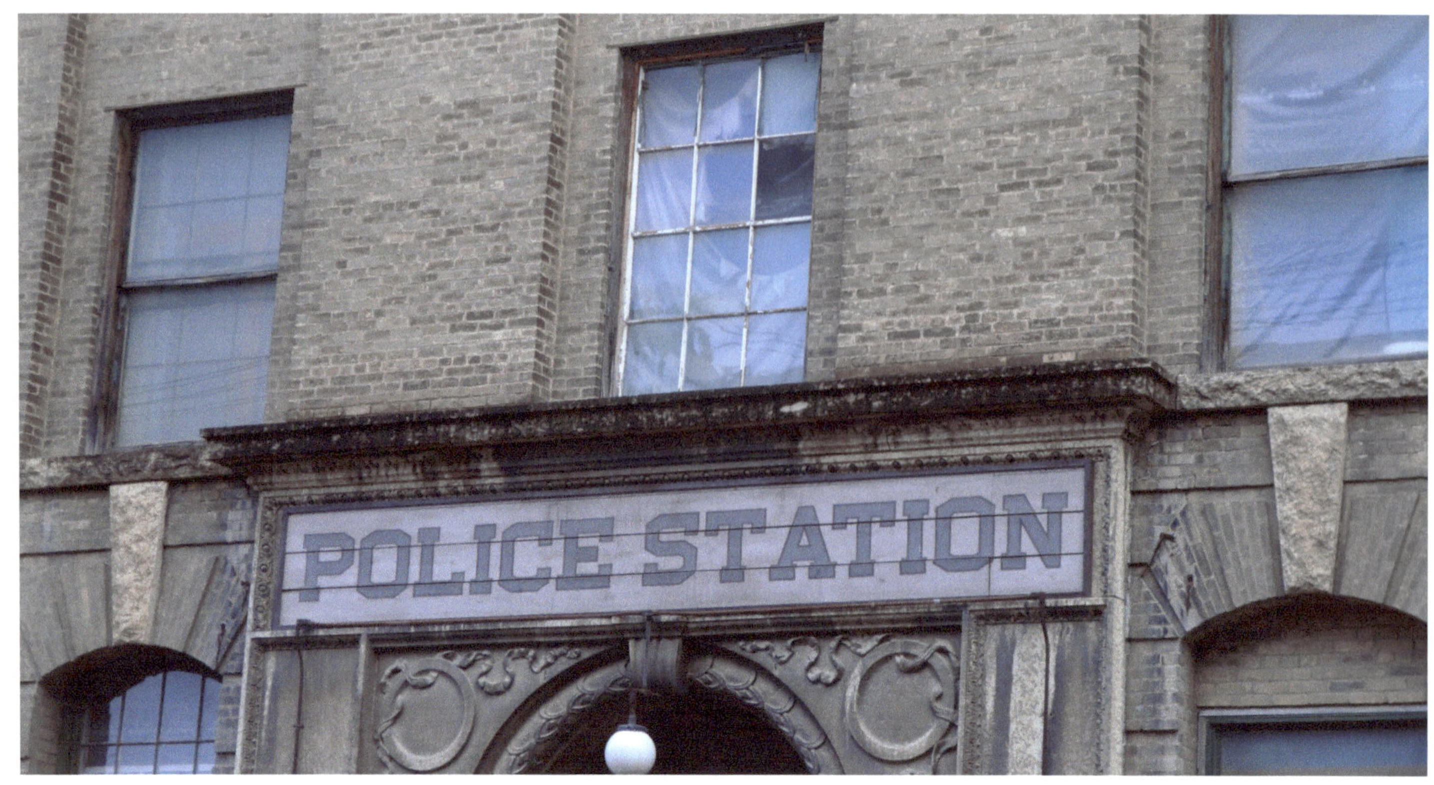

Winnipeg, Manitoba, Canada

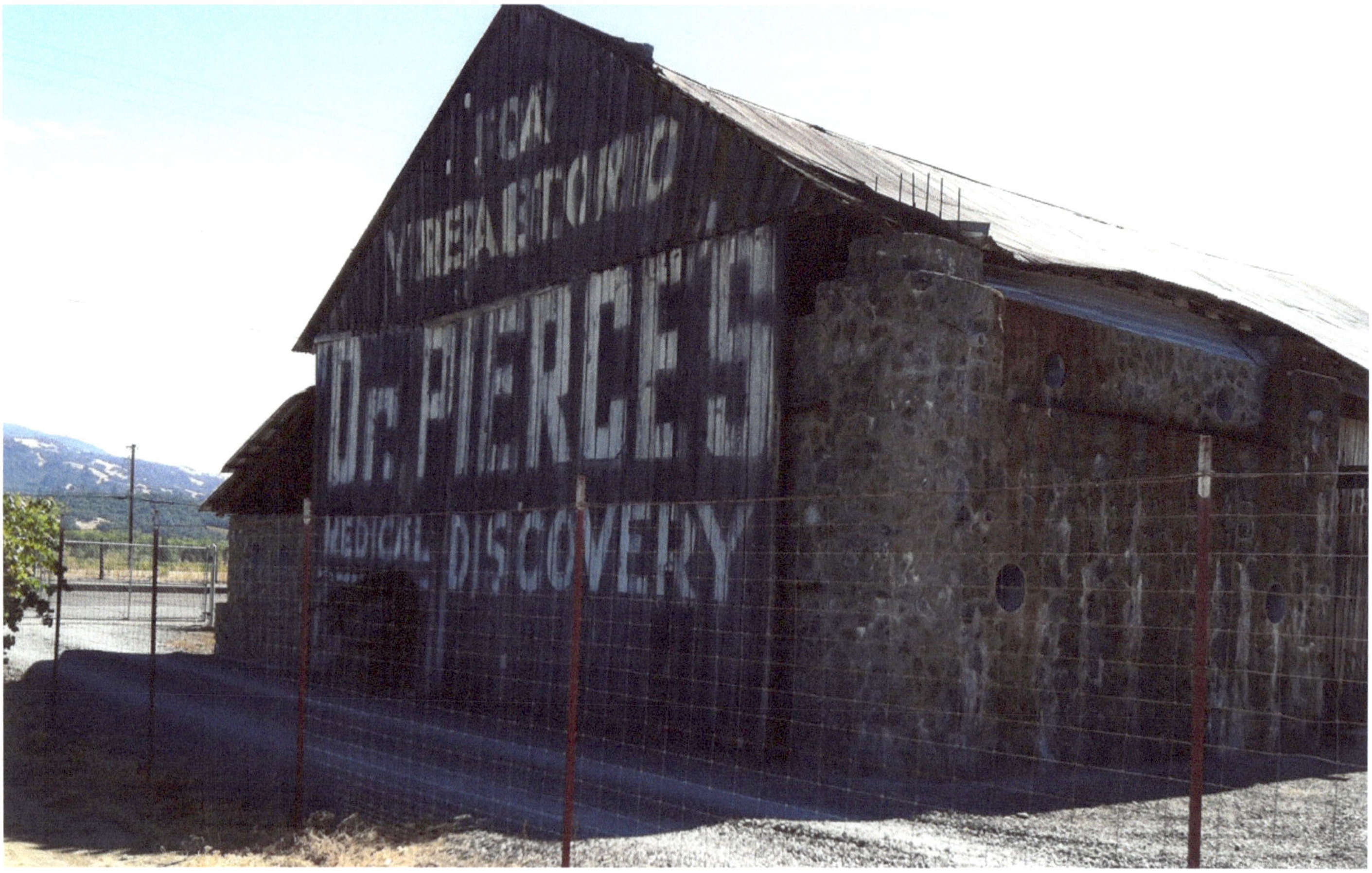

Sonoma County, CA

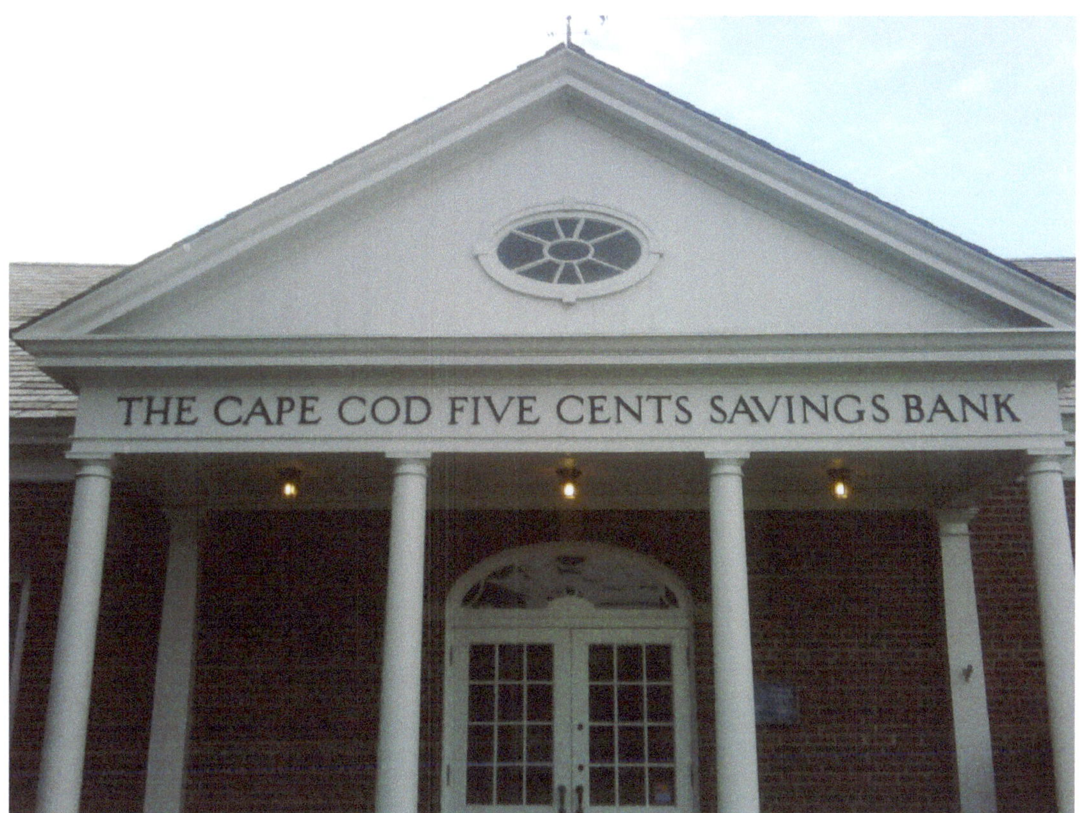

Cape Cod, MA

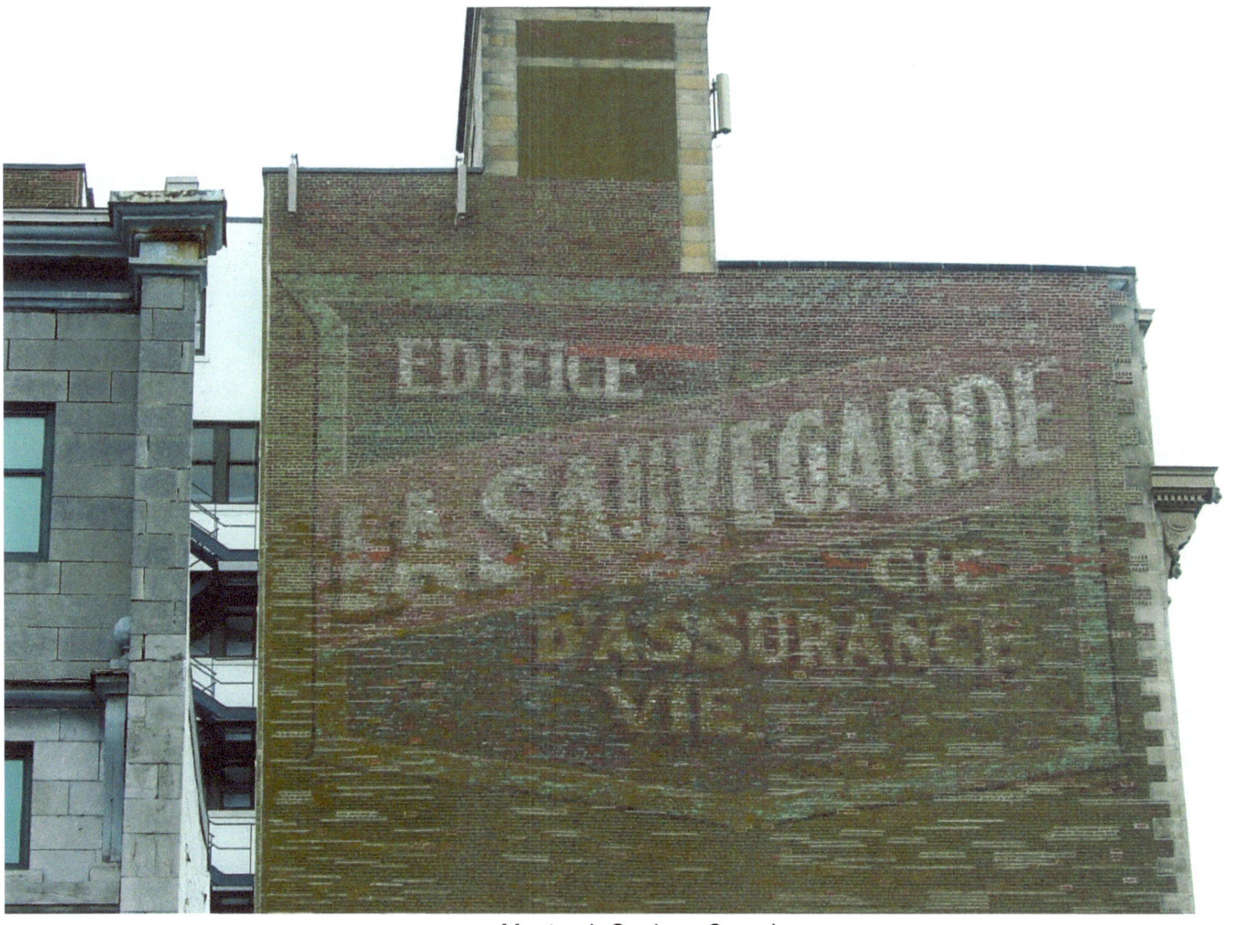

Montreal, Quebec, Canada

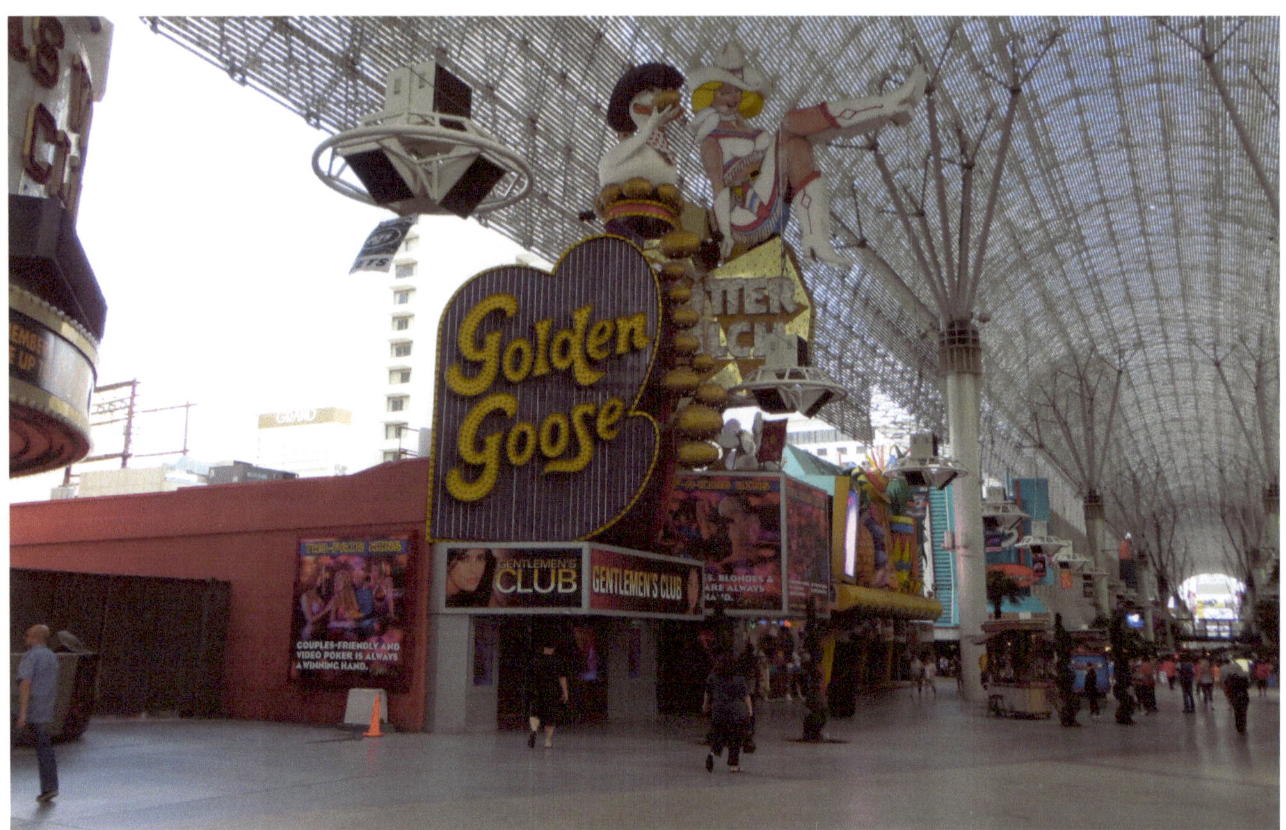

Las Vegas, NV

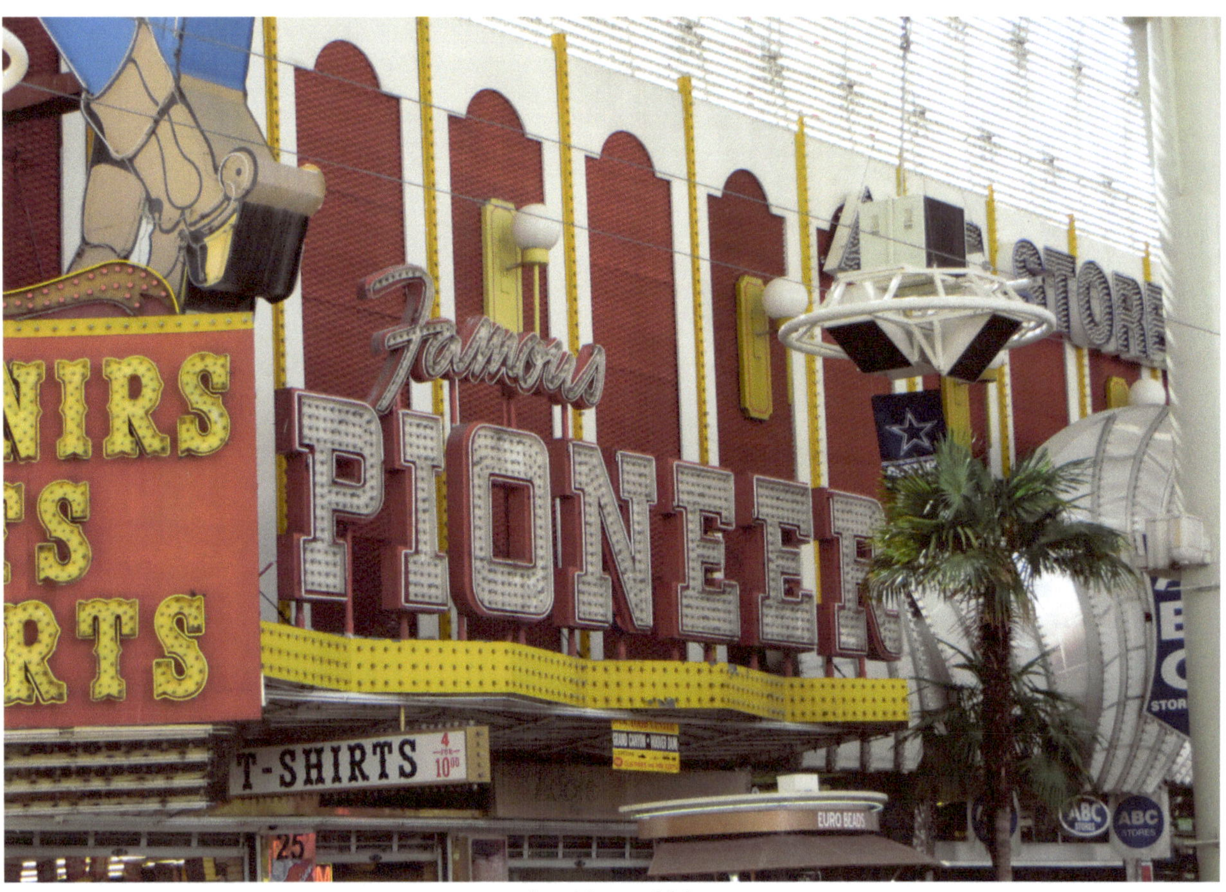

Las Vegas, NV

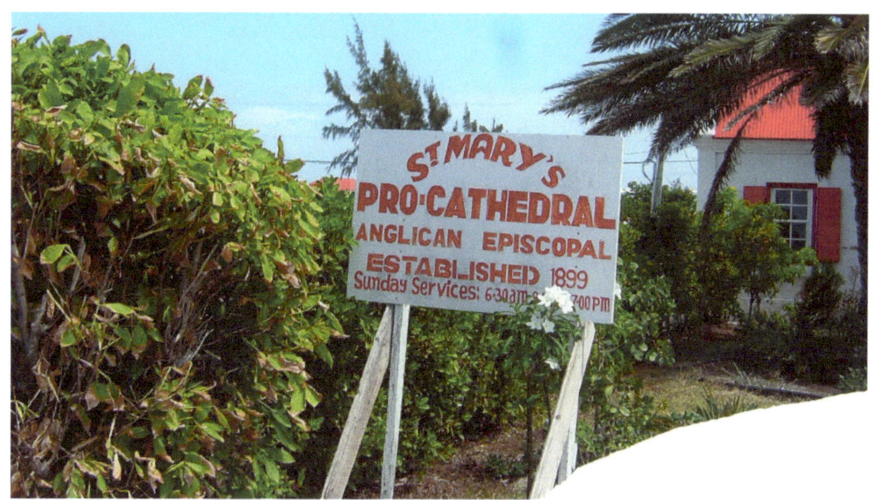

Turks and Caicos Islands

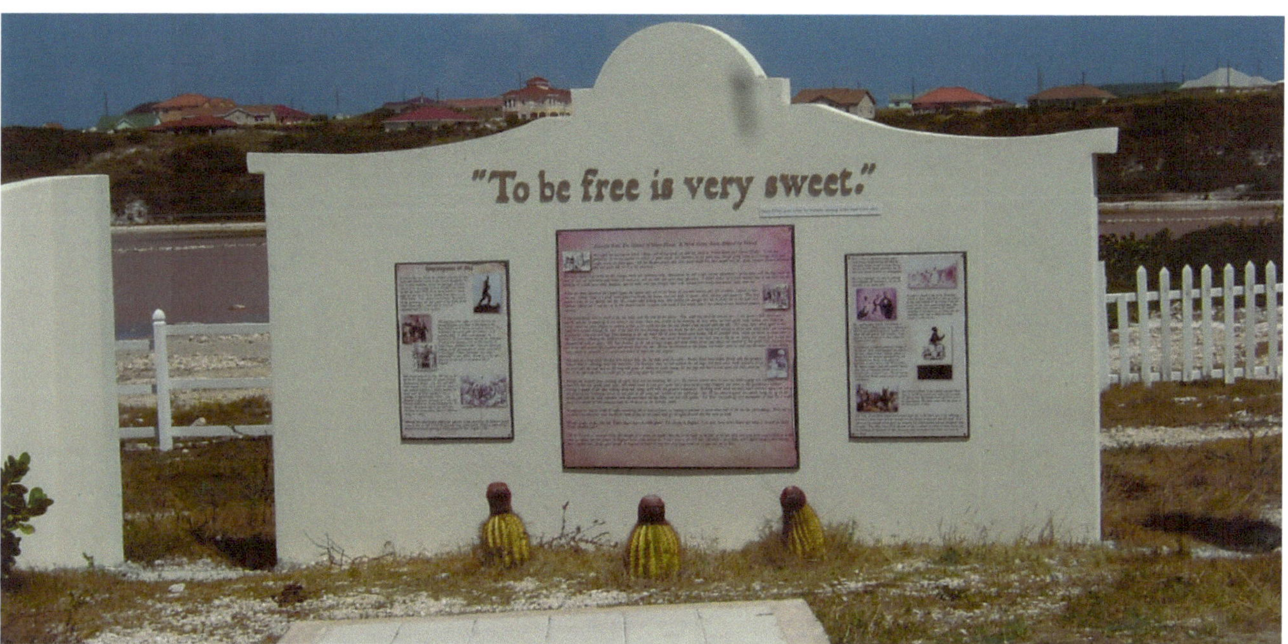

Turks and Caicos Islands

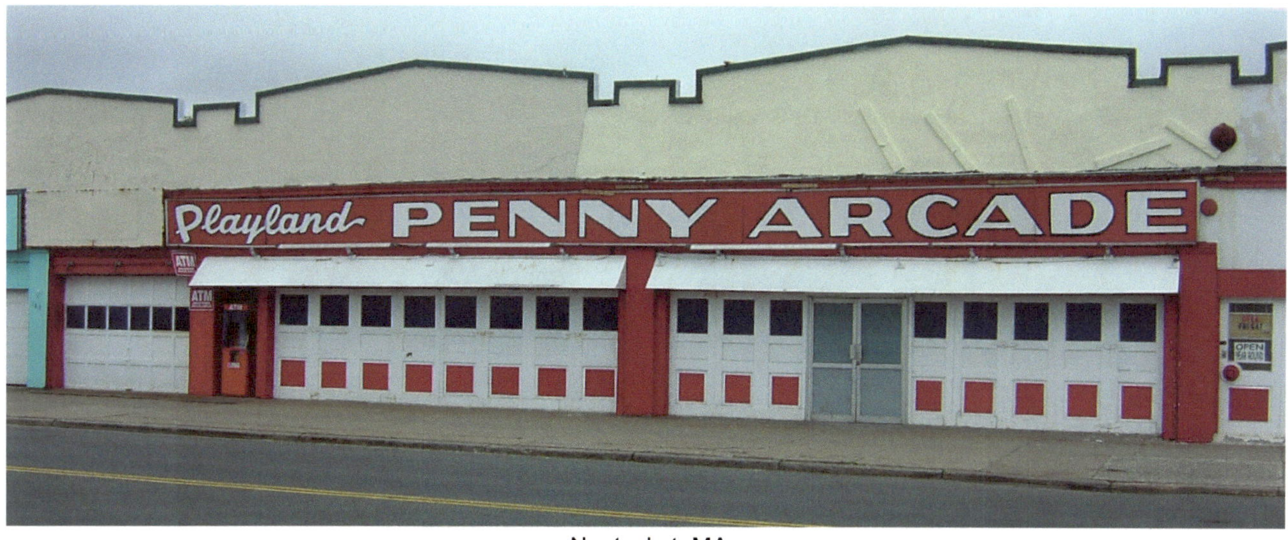

Nantasket, MA

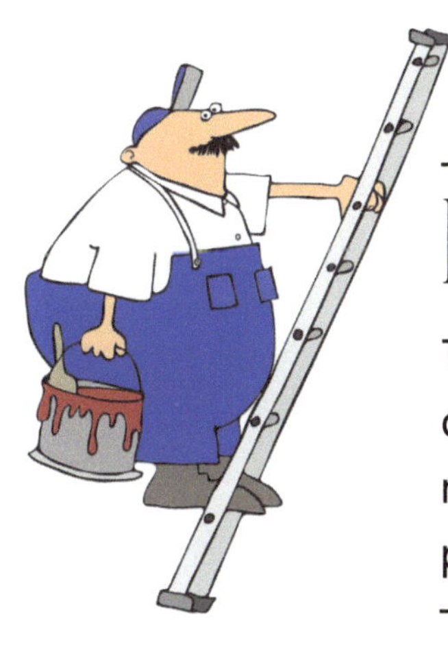

Keeping the Craft Alive

The new (2022) mural in Fair Oaks, California, near our Orangevale home, and Marti Childs' photos of murals in nearby Davis are with us today. Walldog paintings are not a lost art.

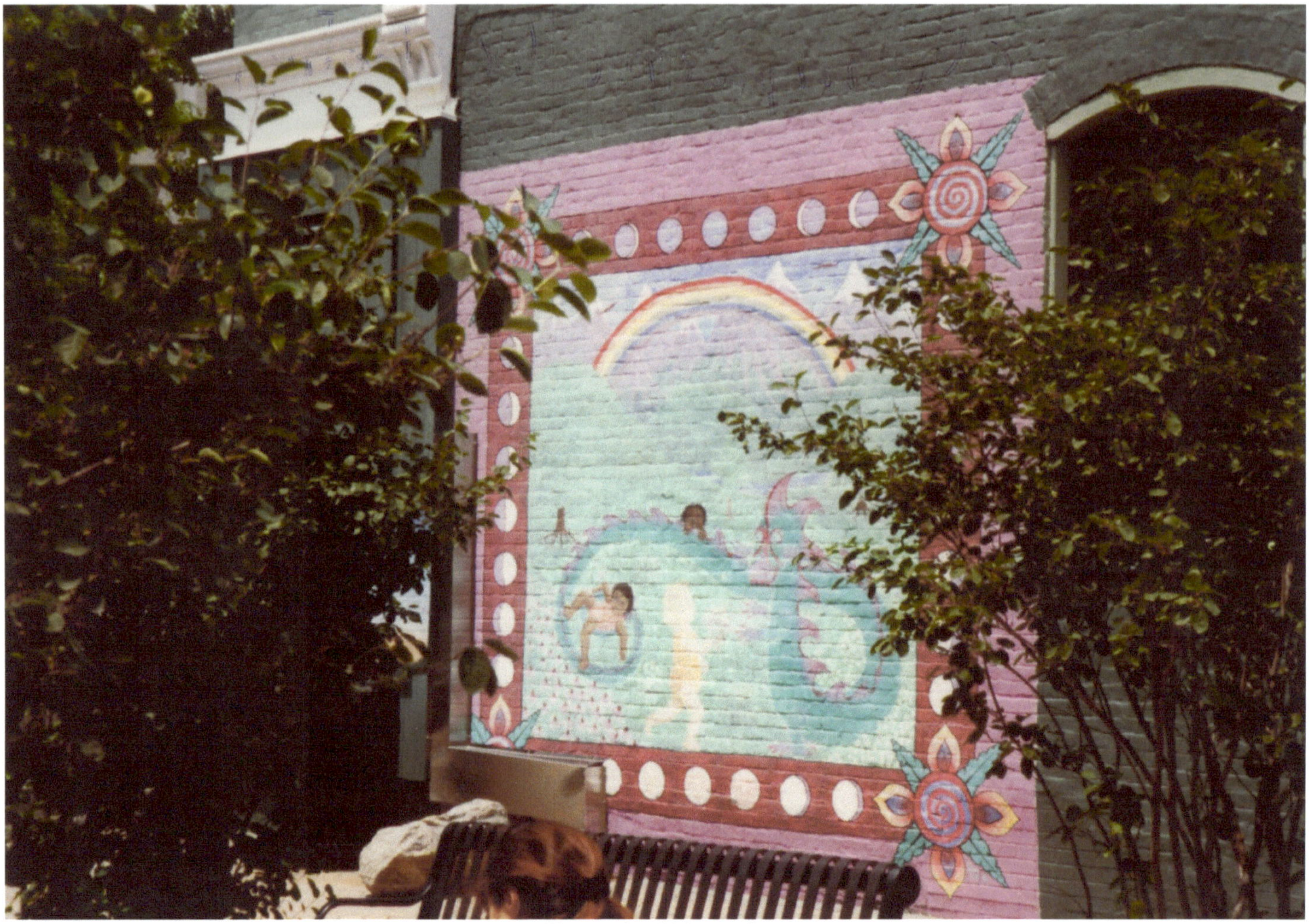

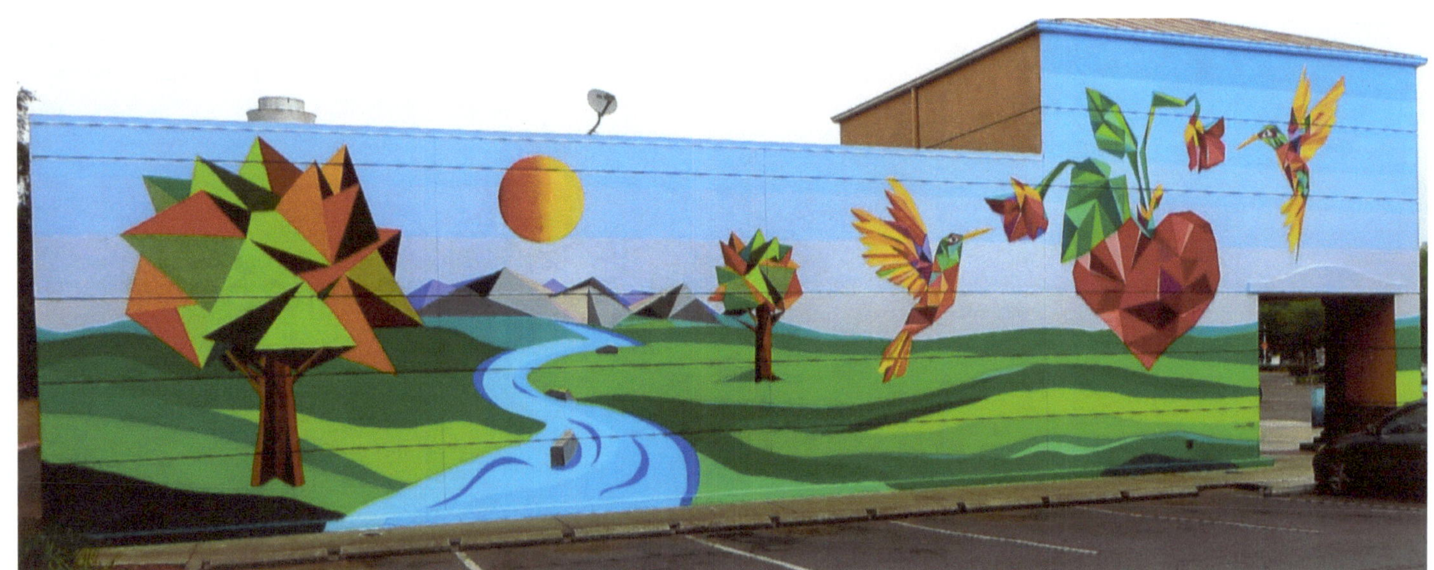

Champaign-Urbana, IL

Fair Oaks, CA

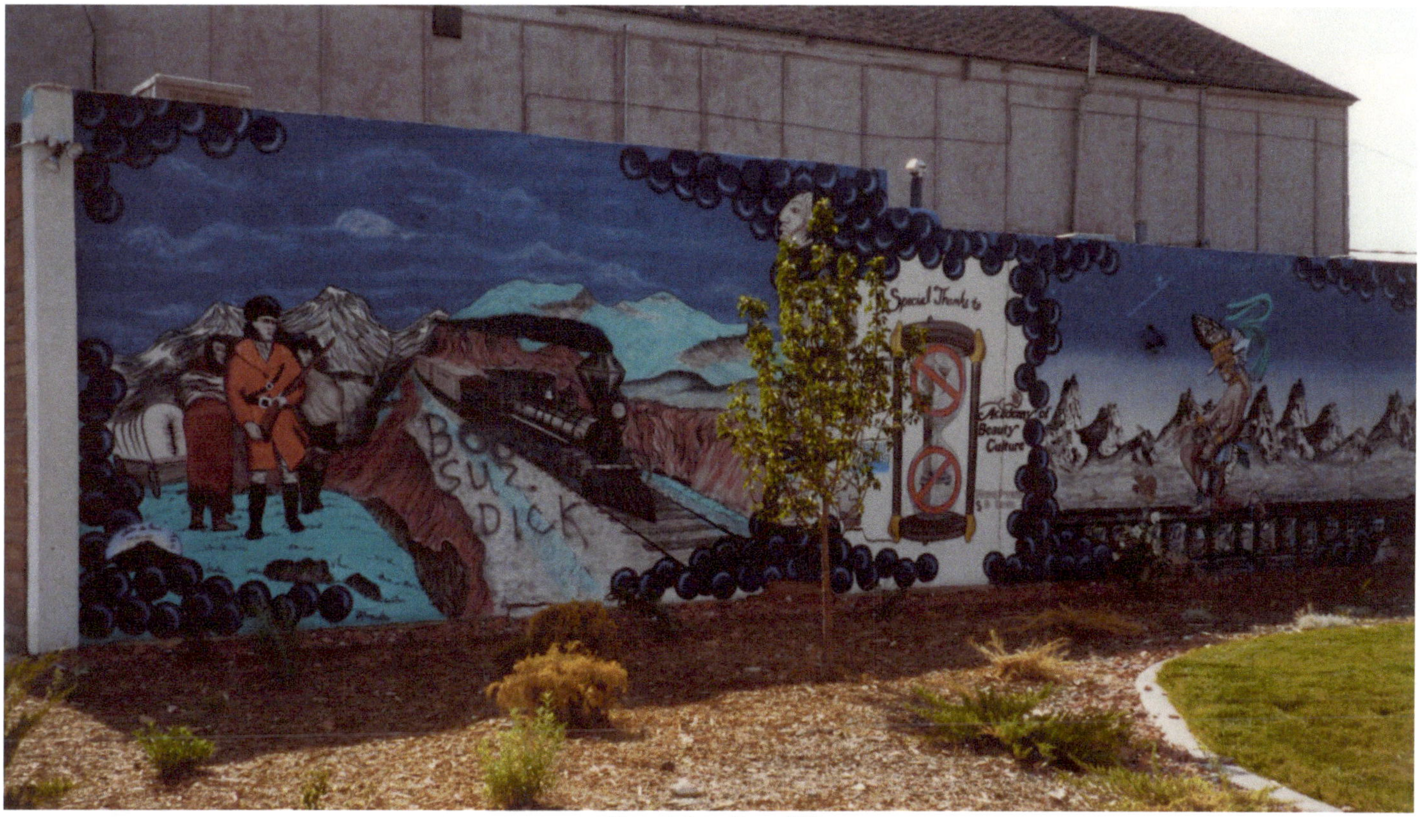

Grand Junction, CO

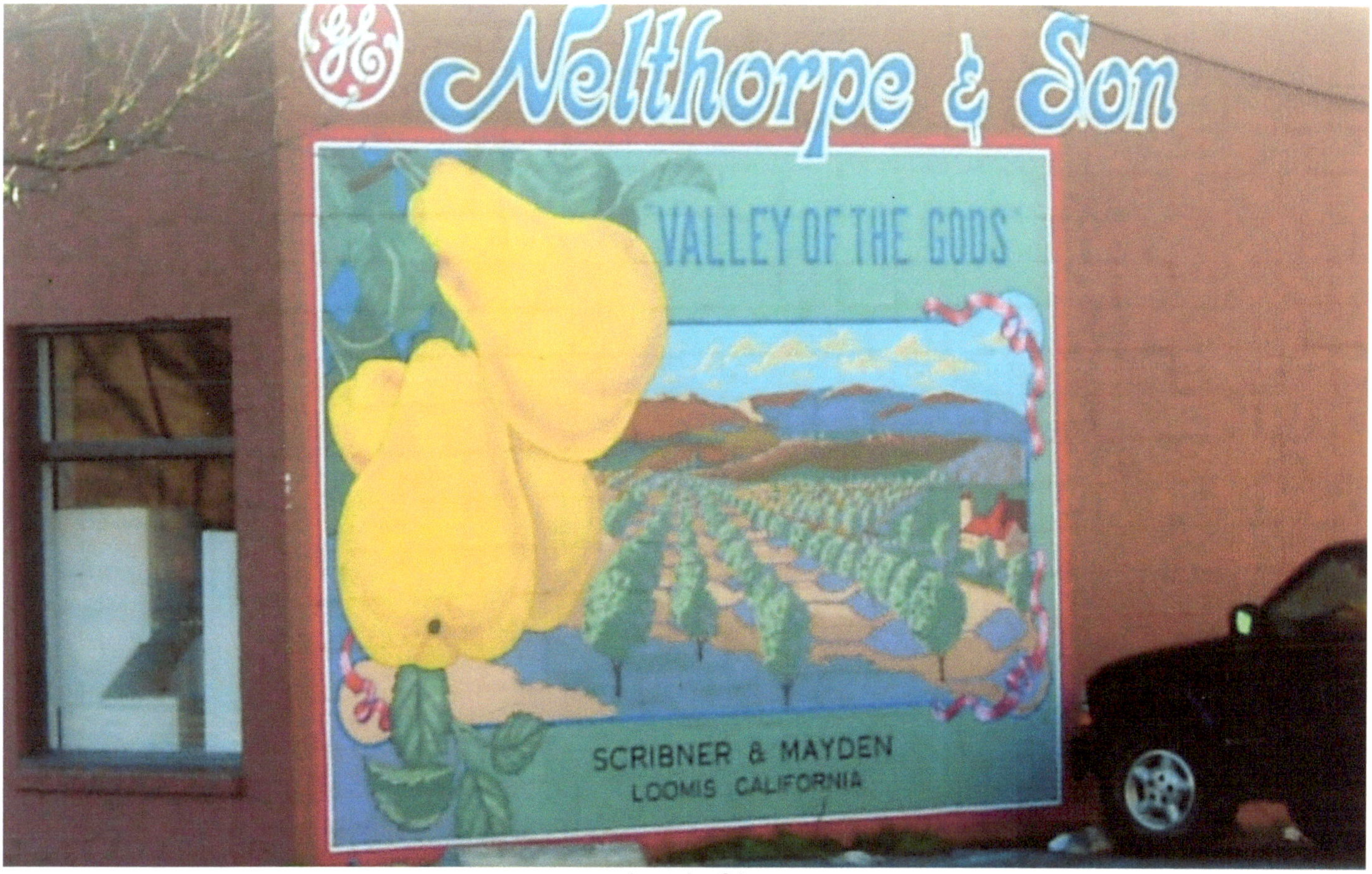

Loomis, CA

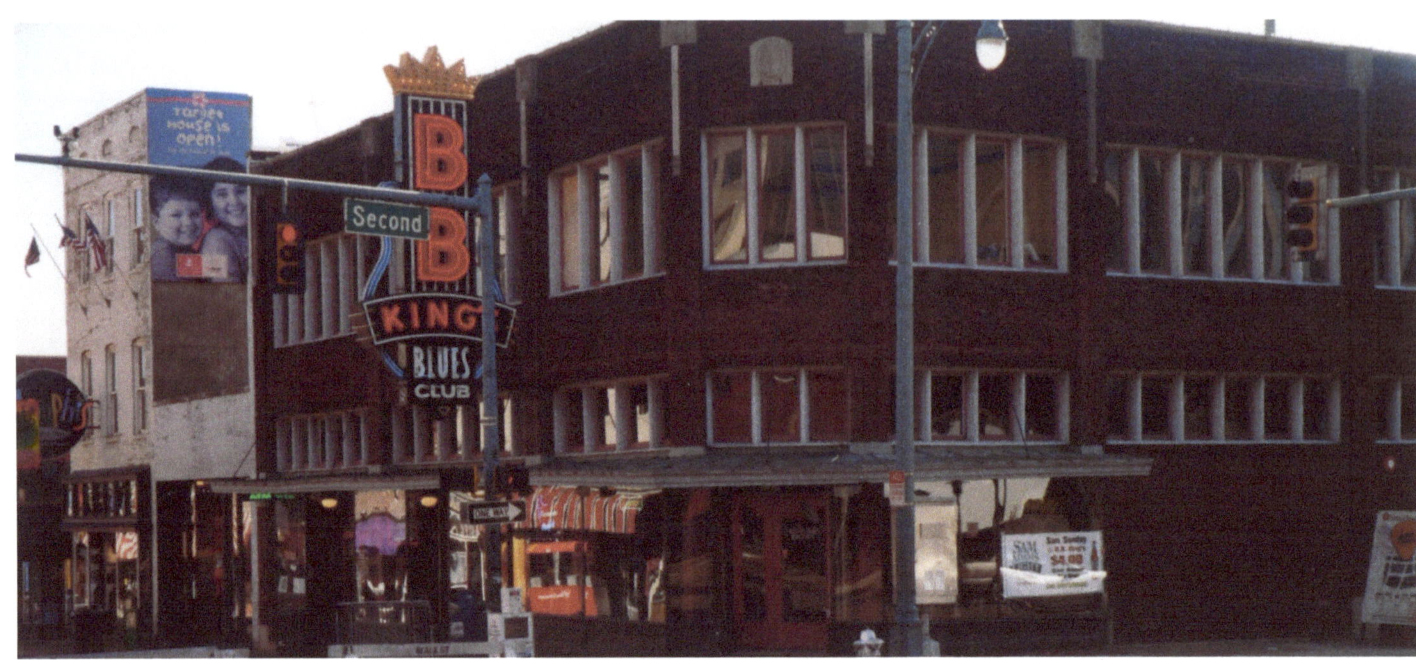

Memphis, TN

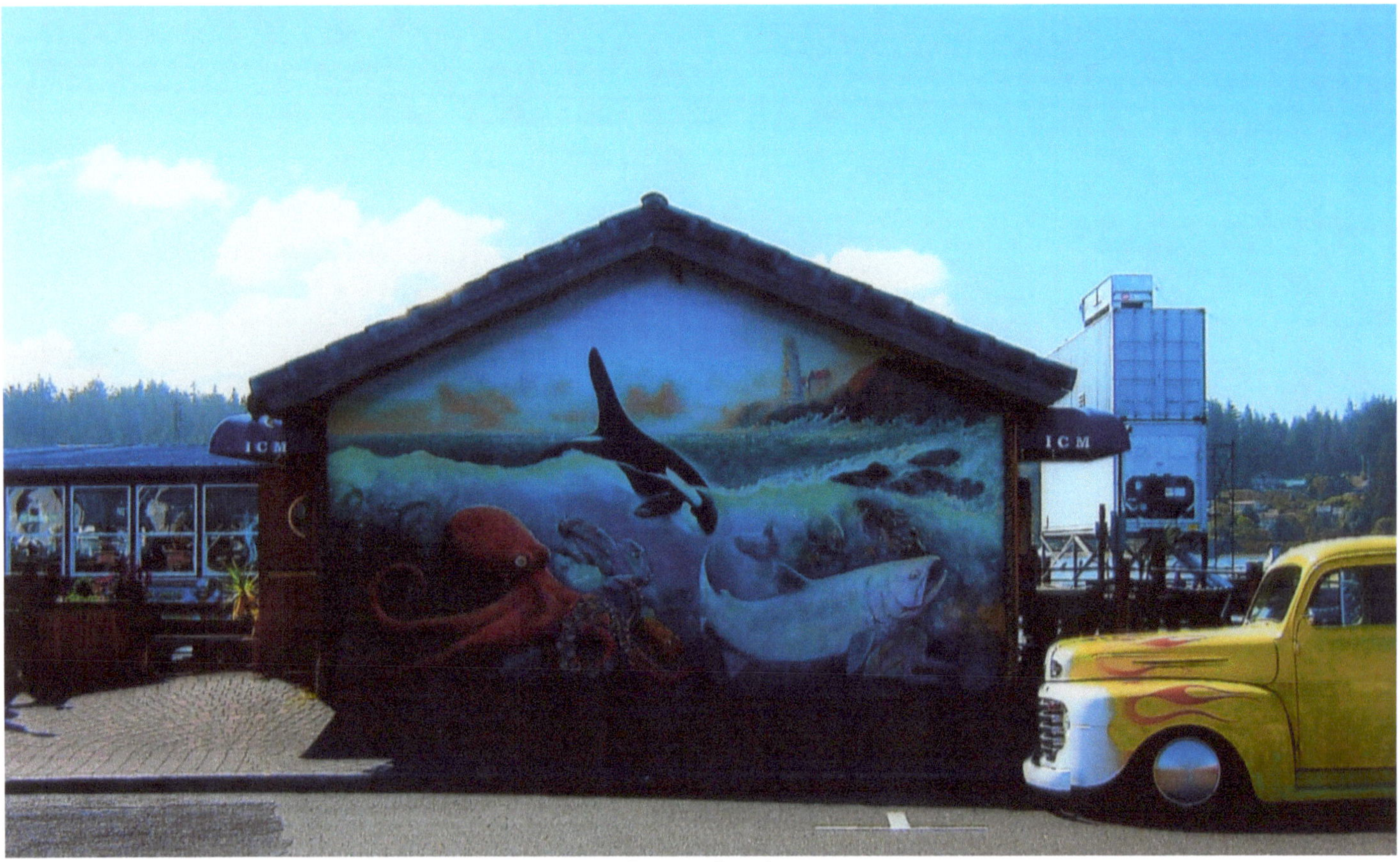

Oregon Coast

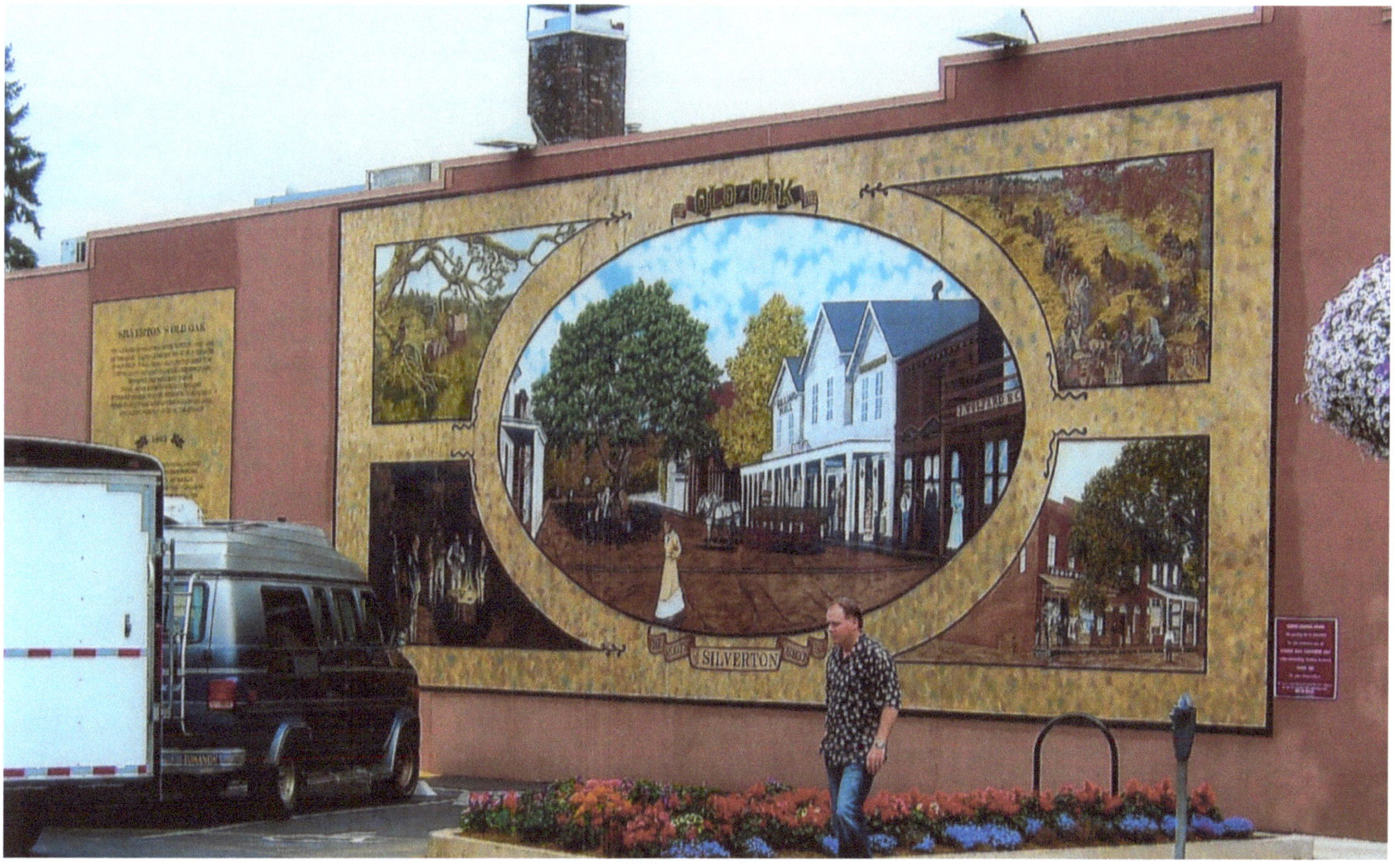

Silverton, OR

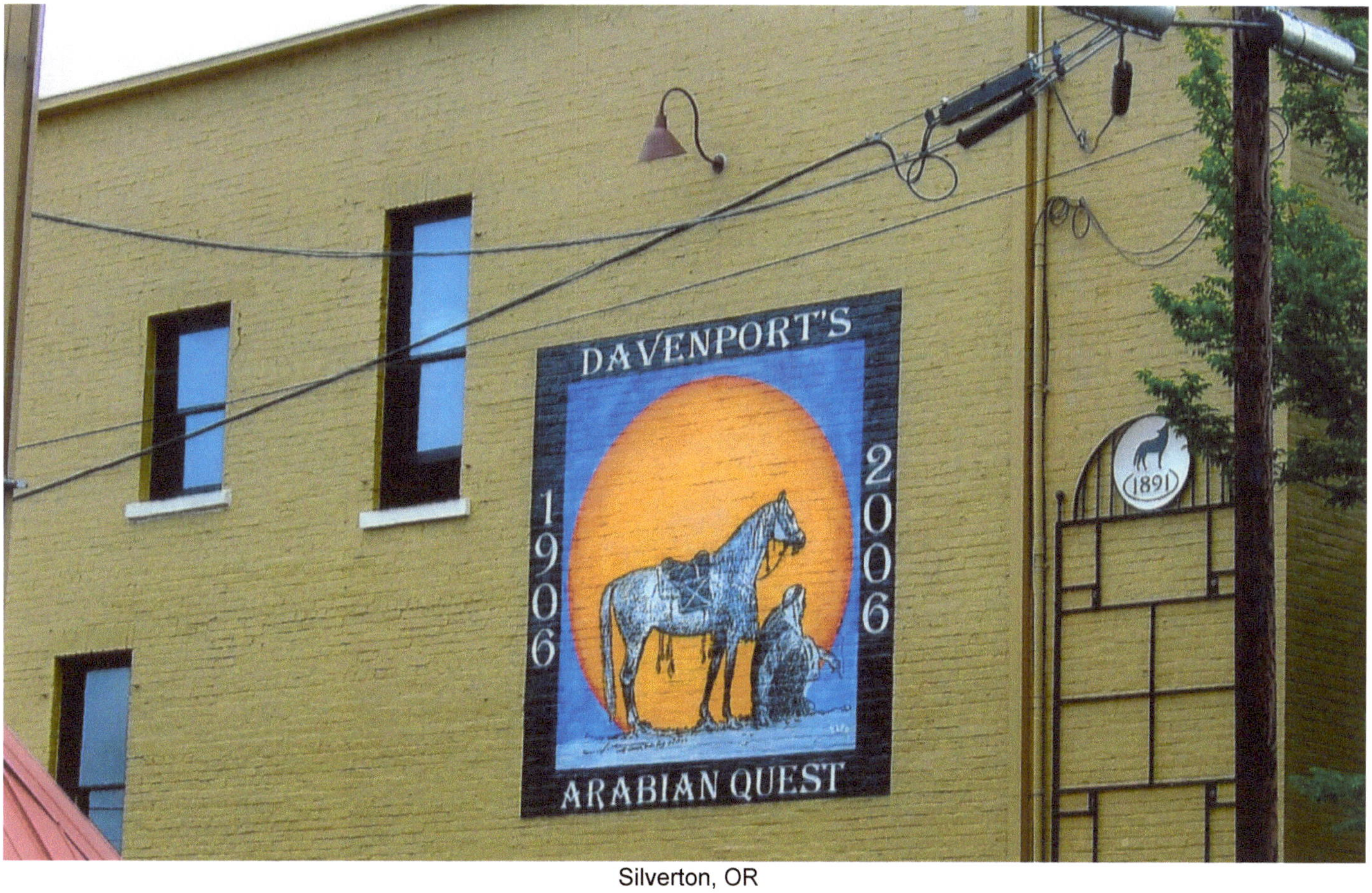

Silverton, OR

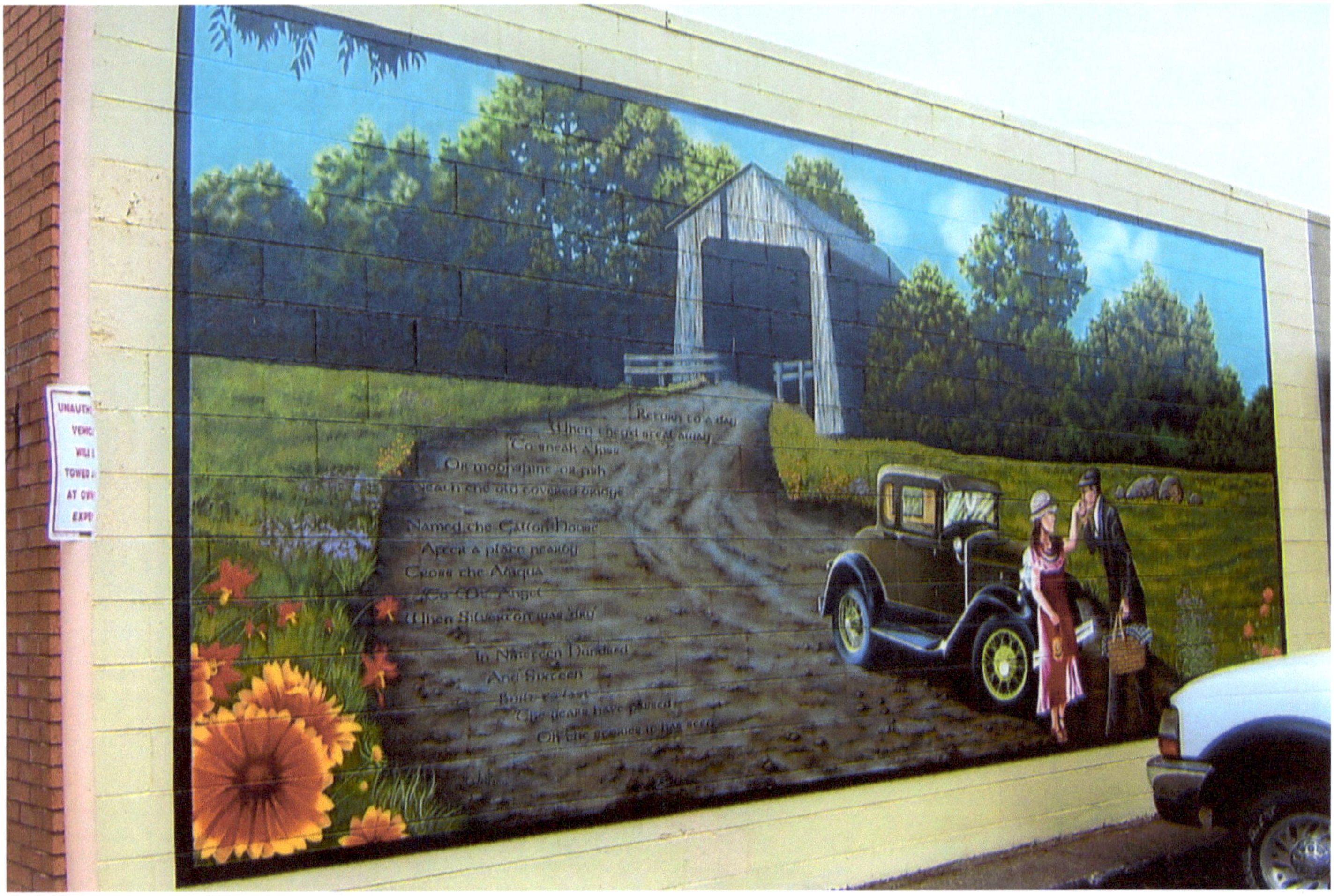

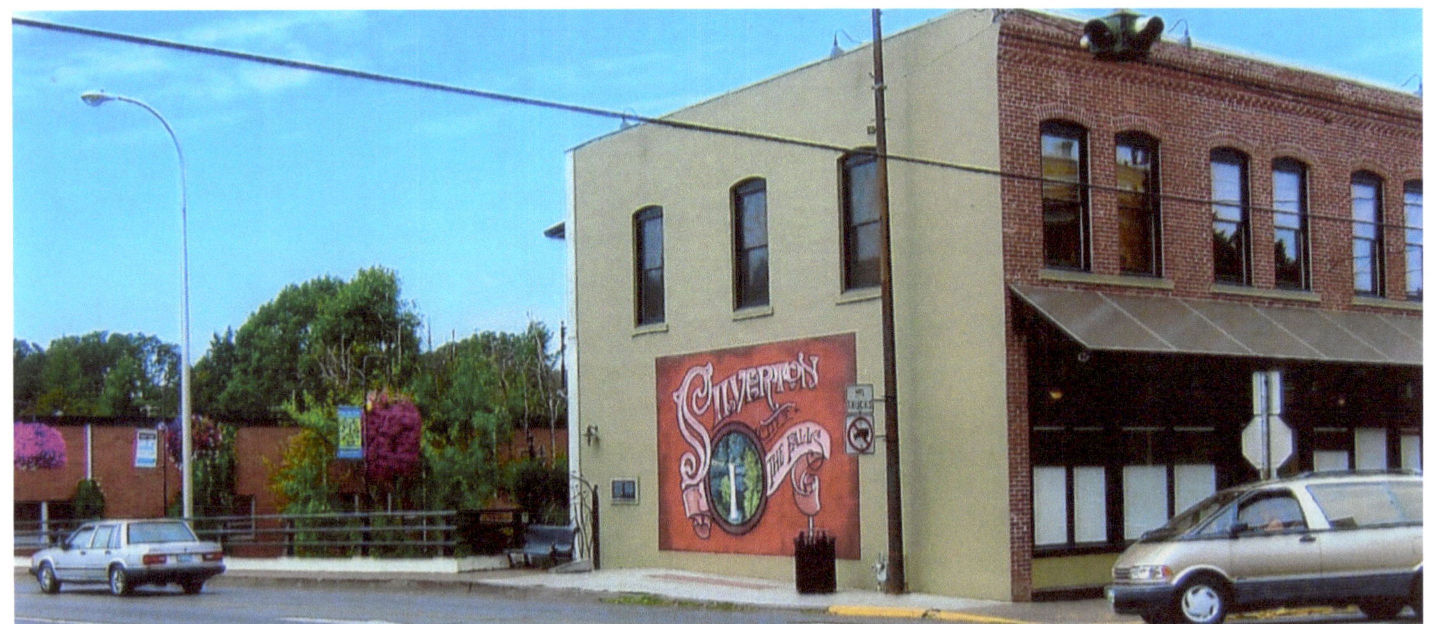

Silverton, OR

Silverton, OR

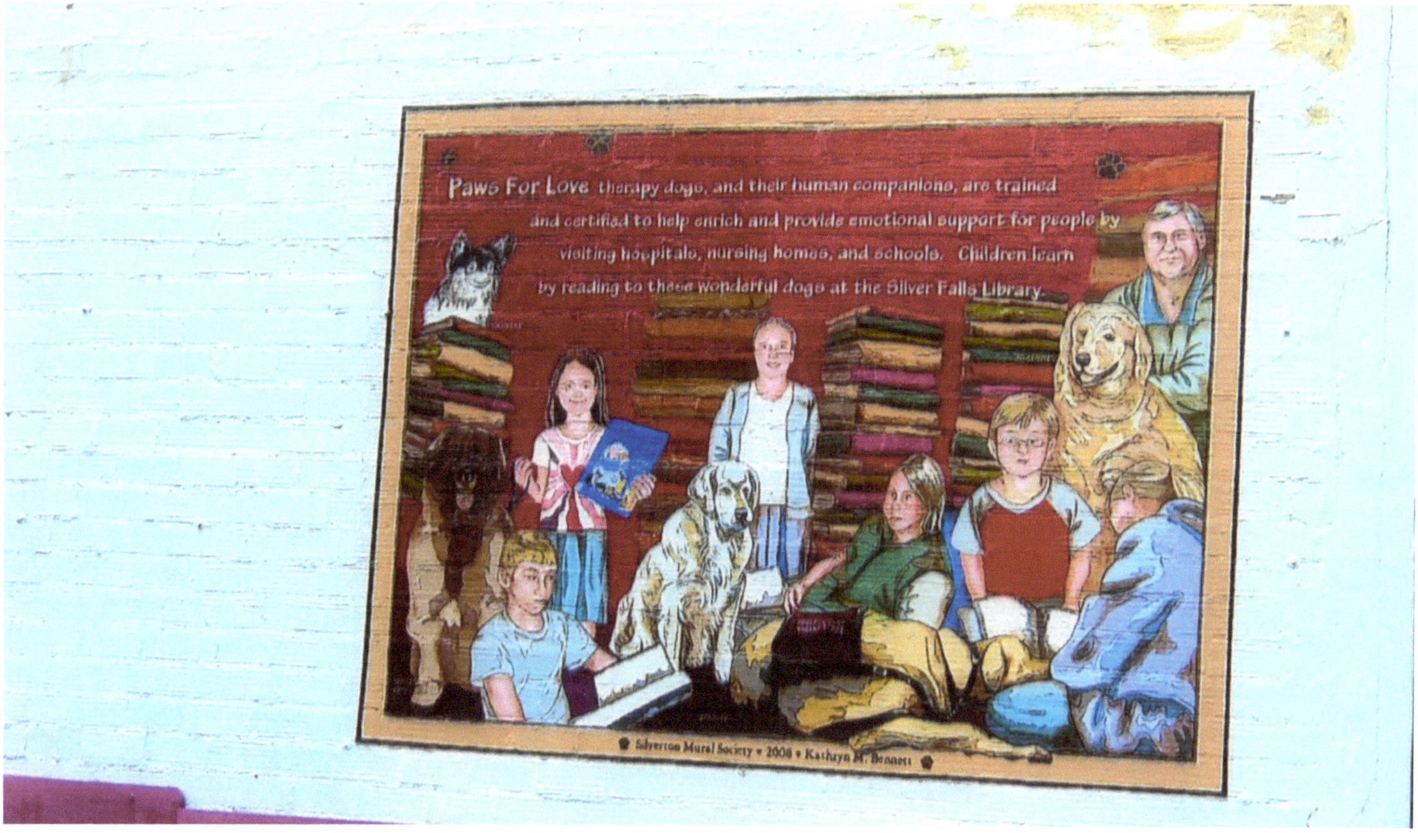

Silverton, OR

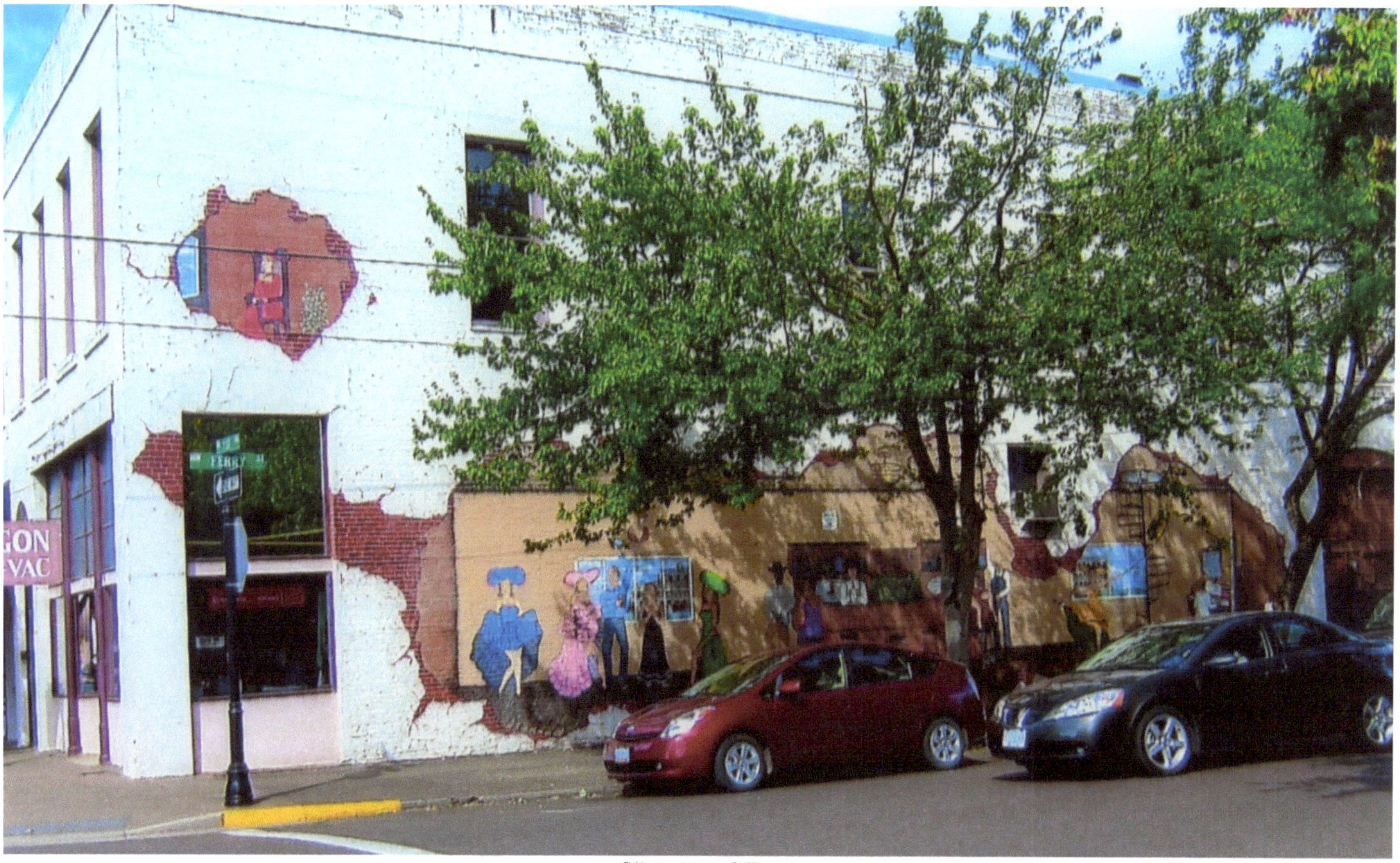

Silverton, OR

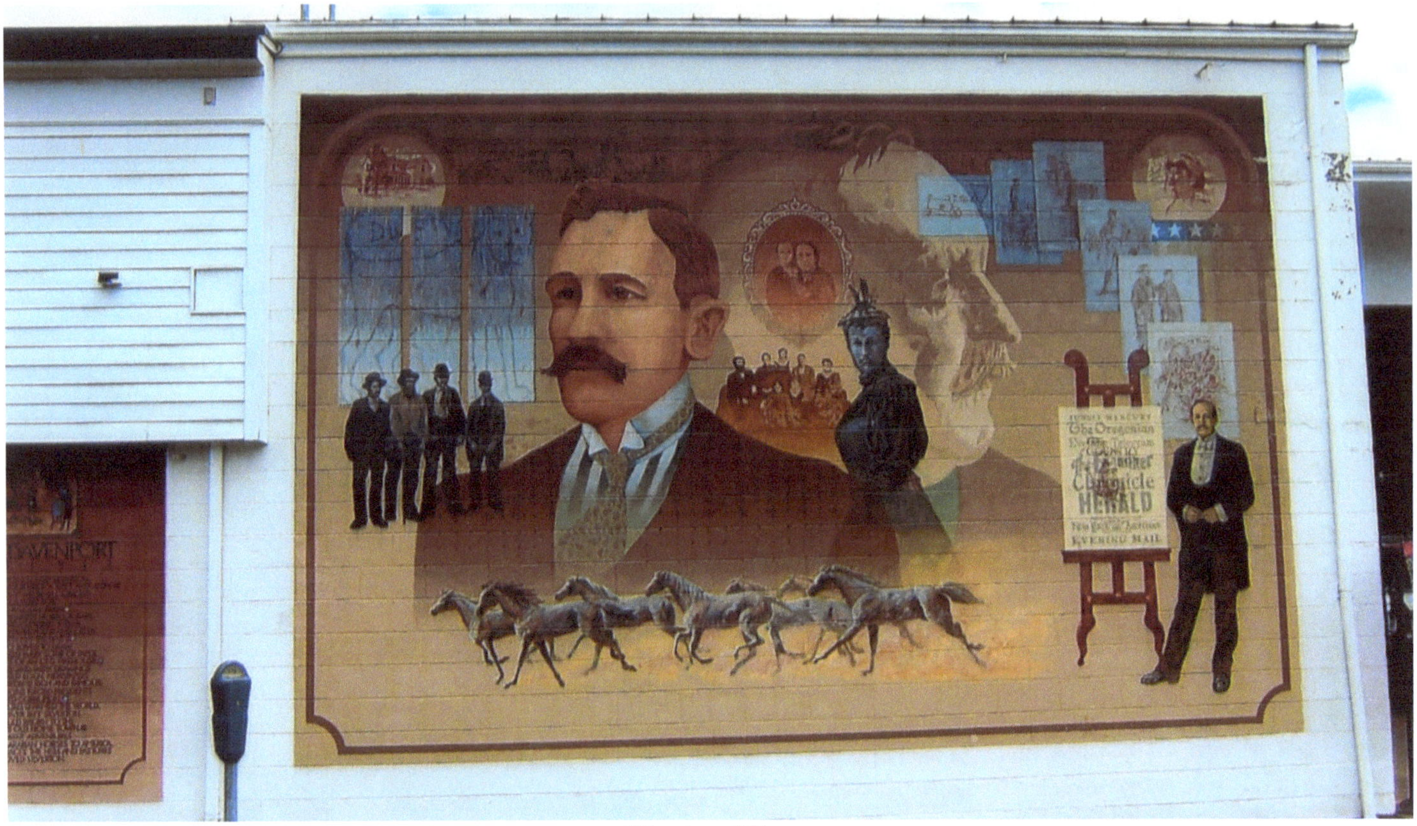

Silverton, OR

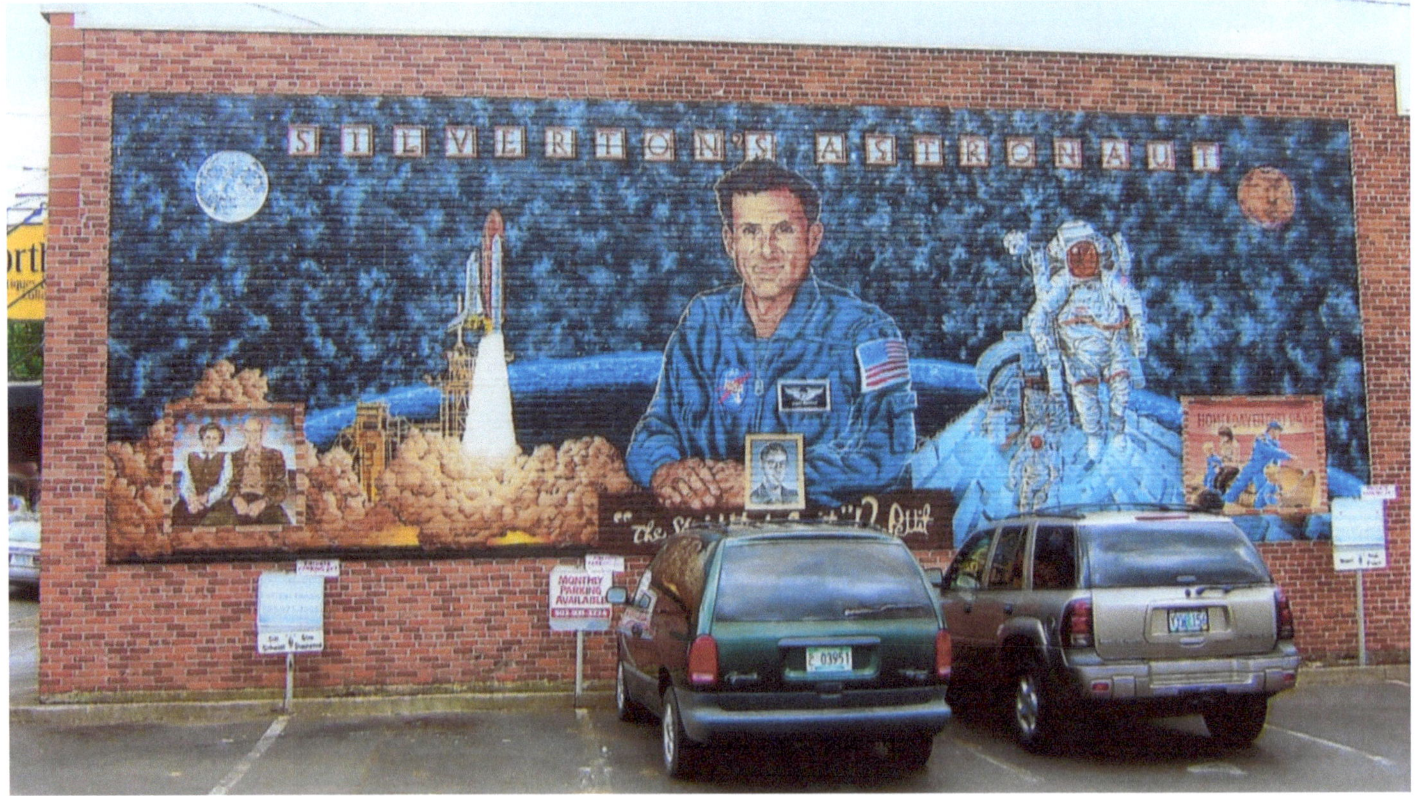

Silverton, OR

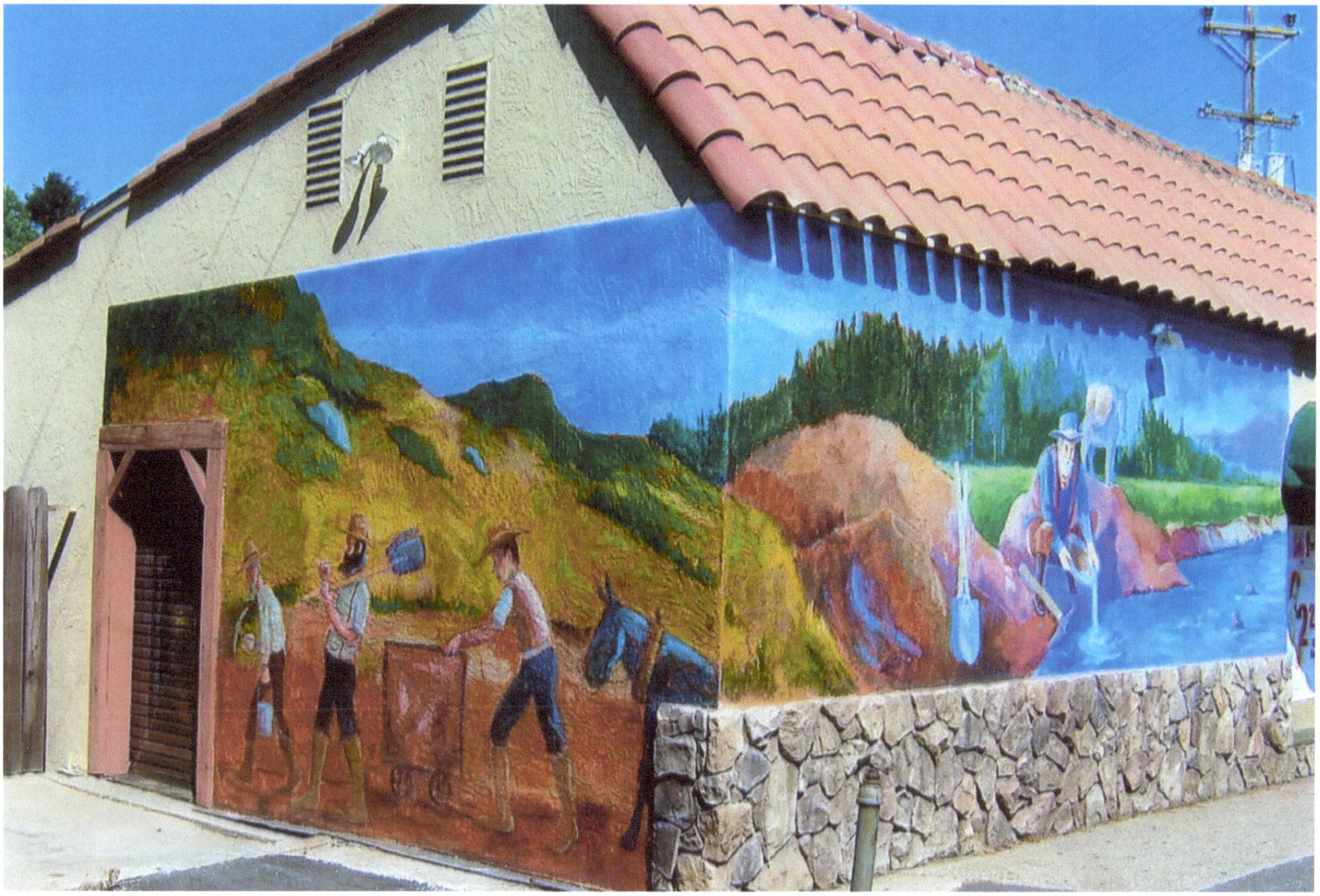

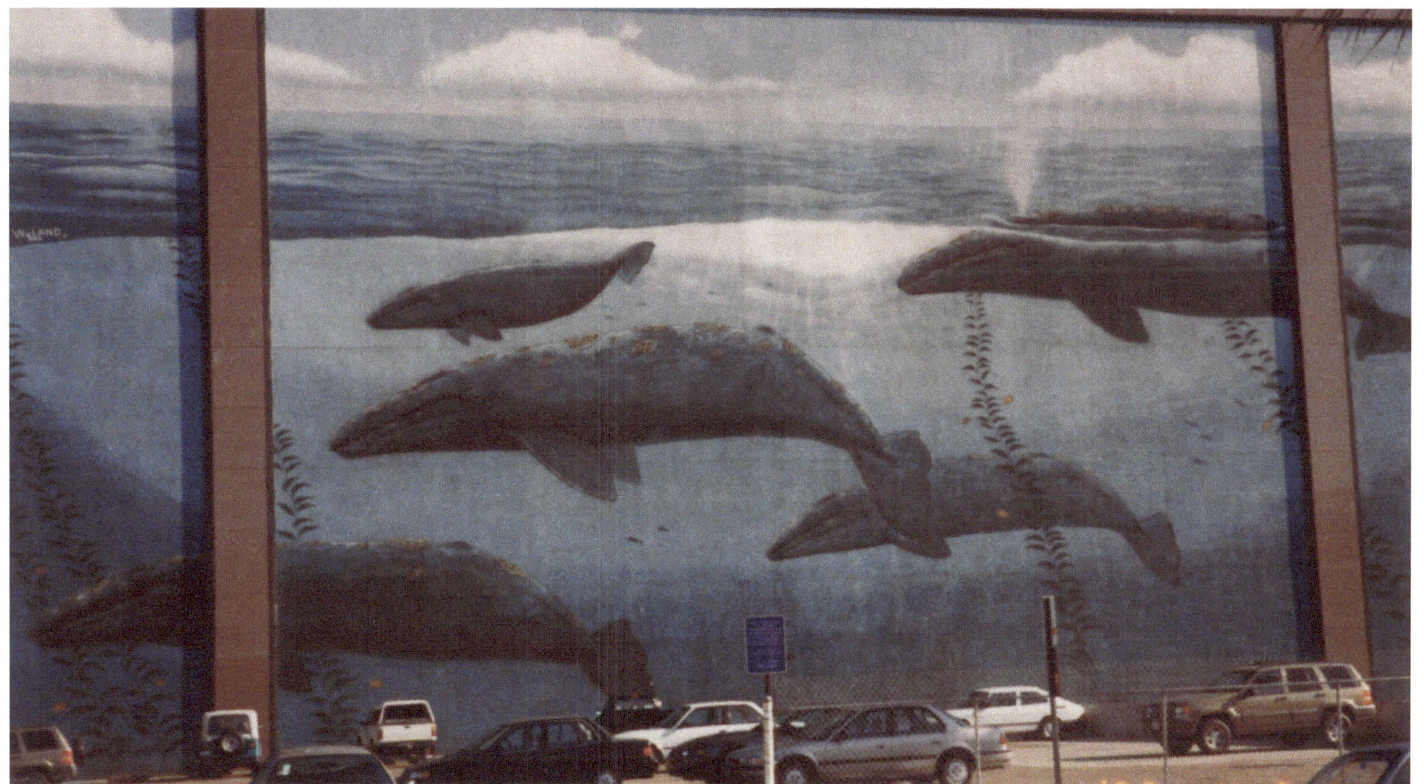

Oregon Coast

San Diego, CA

TRUCKEE, CALIF.
ore Shops
89

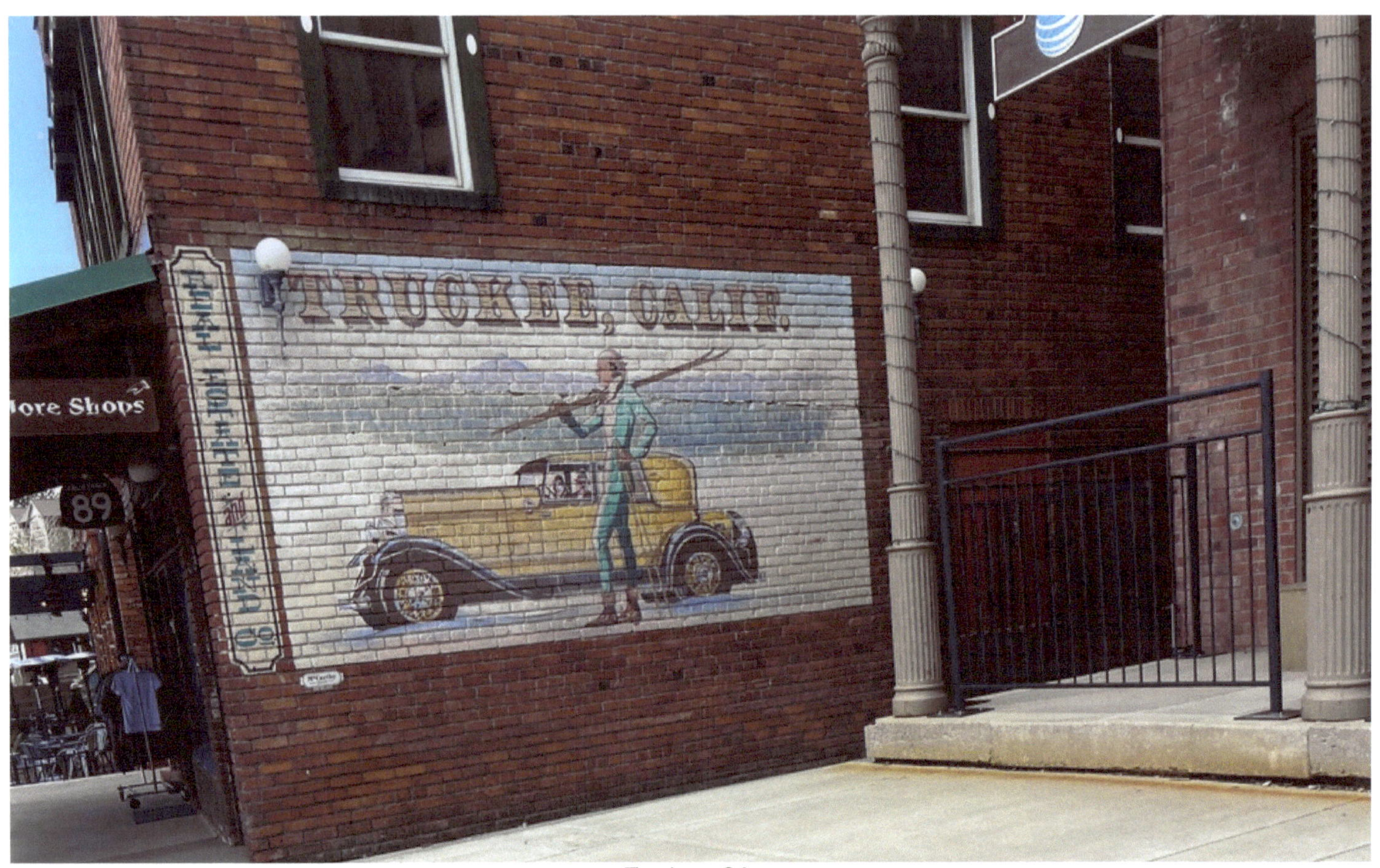

Truckee, CA

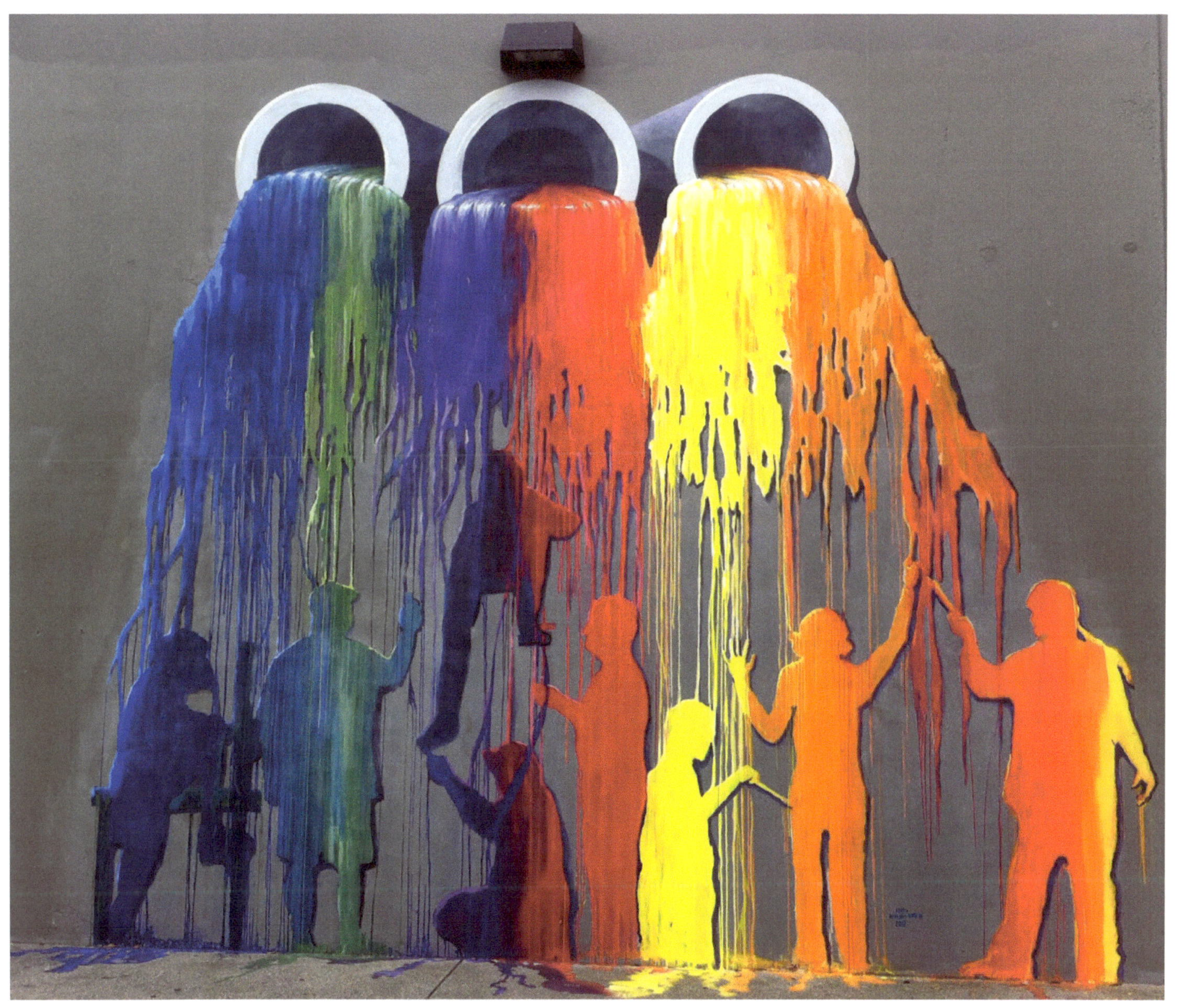

Davis, CA

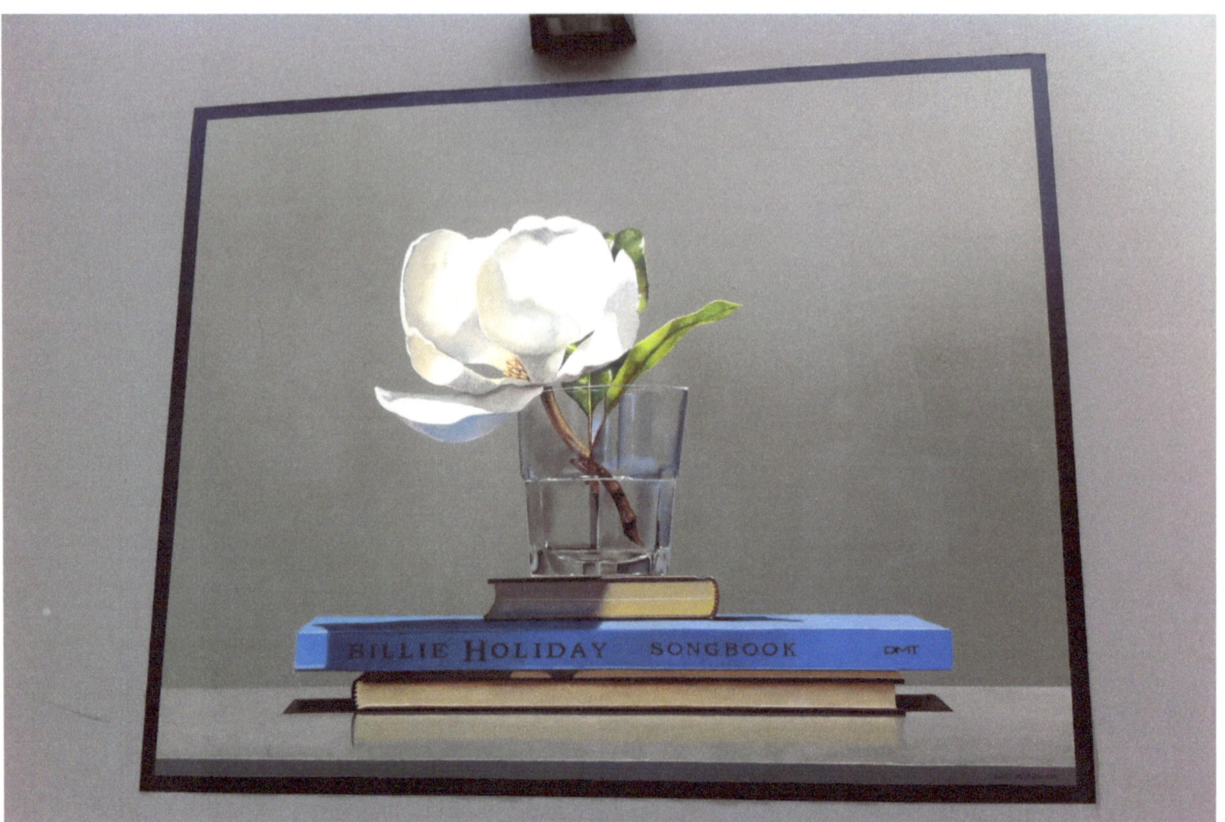

Davis, CA

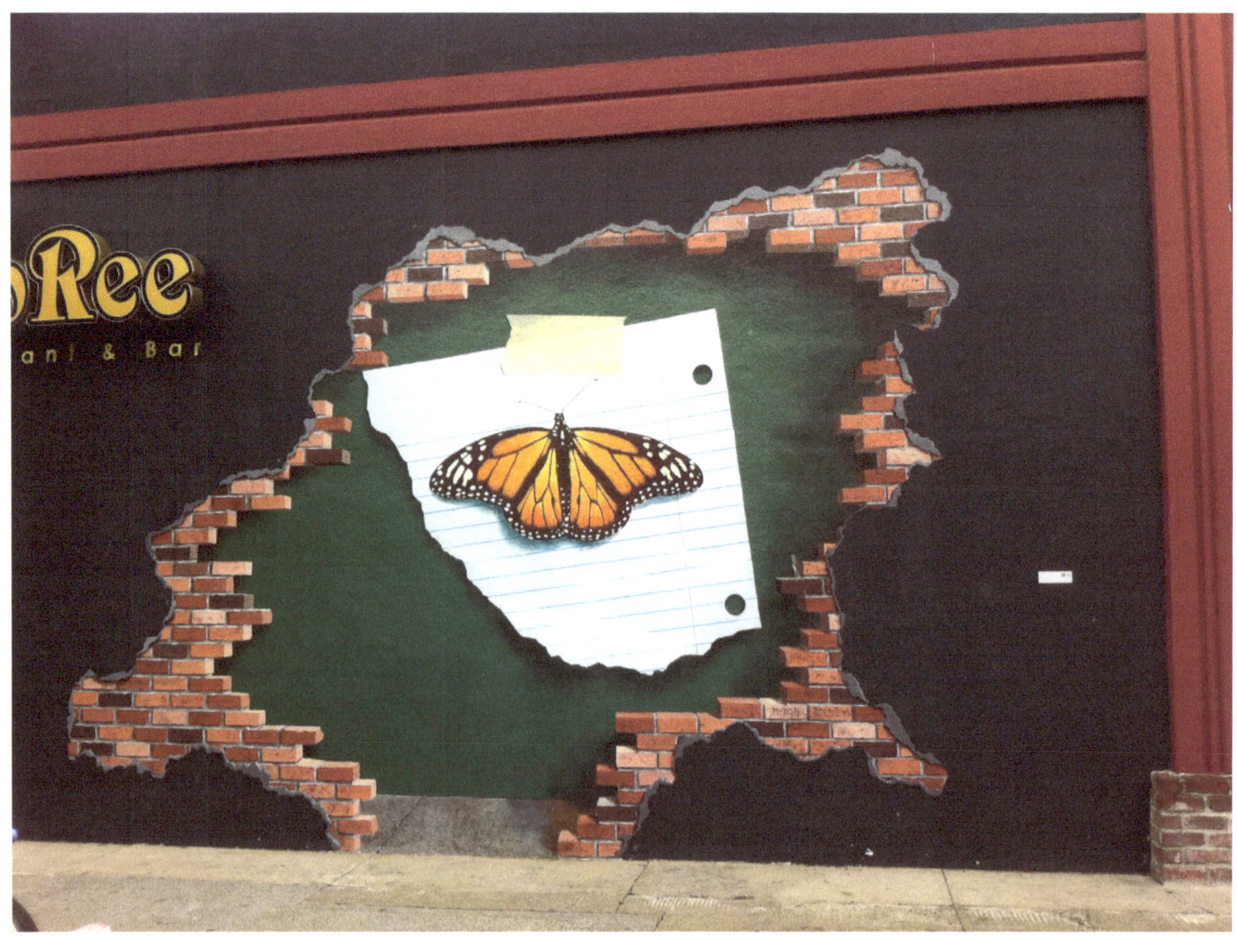

Davis, CA

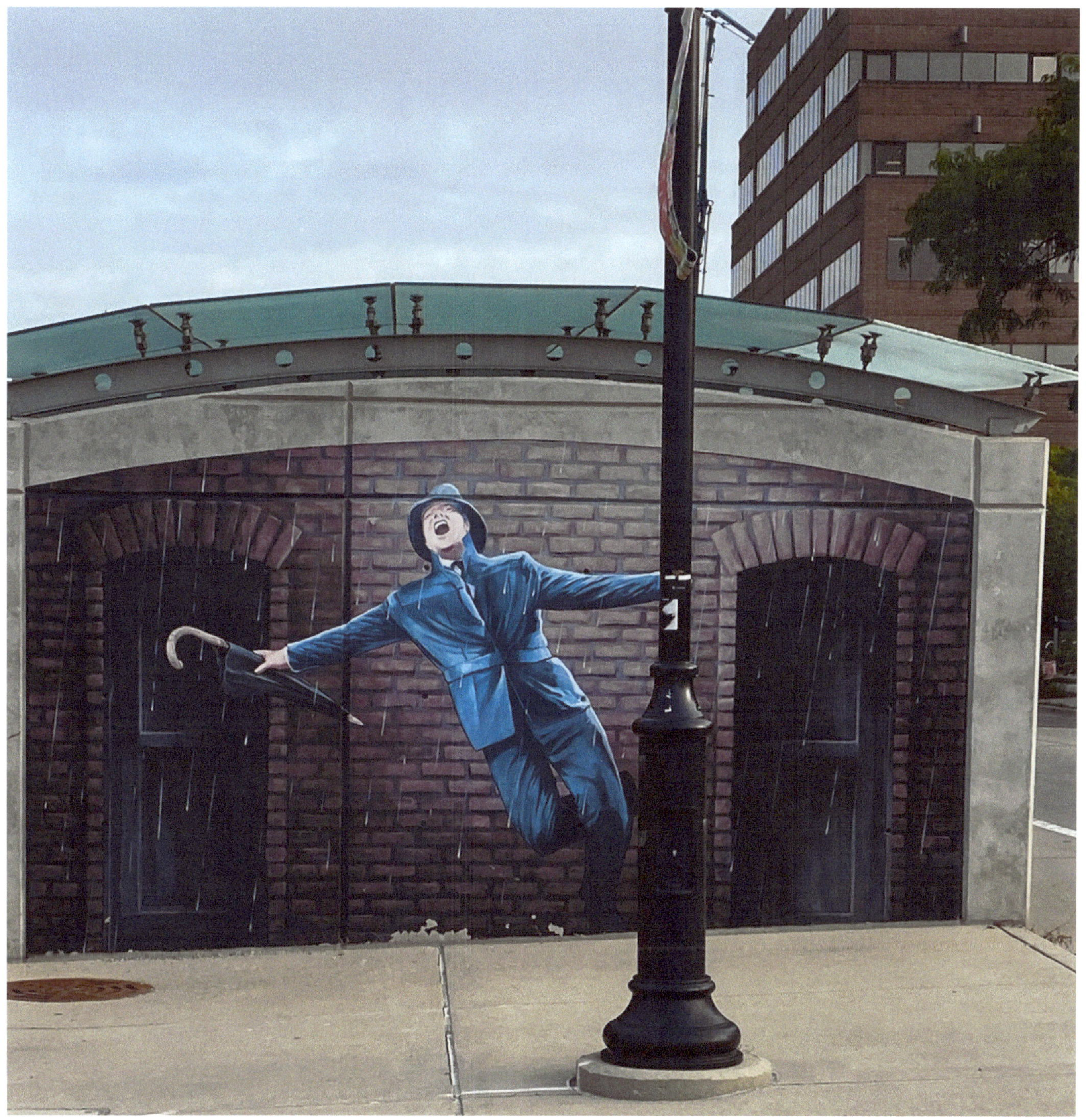

Ann Arbor, MI